THE SHAPES OF TIME

THE
SHAPES
OF
TIME

A New Look at the Philosophy of History

by PETER MUNZ

WESLEYAN UNIVERSITY PRESS

Middletown, Connecticut

The publisher gratefully acknowledges the support of the publication of this book by the Andrew W. Mellon Foundation.

Library of Congress Cataloging in Publication Data

Munz, Peter, 1921-
    The shapes of time.

    Bibliography: p.
    Includes index.
    1. History—Philosophy.   I. Title.
D16.8.M867   901   77-2459
ISBN 0-8195-5017-5

Manufactured in the United States of America
First Edition

For Jacob and Anne

CONTENTS

Es zeigt sich dass hinter dem sogenannten Vorhange, welcher das
Innere verdecken soll, nichts zu sehen ist, wenn *wir* nicht selbst dahintergehen,
ebensosehr damit gesehen werde, als dass etwas dahinter sei, das gesehen
werden kann. [It appears then that there is nothing to be seen behind the
so-called curtain which is supposed to conceal the inner world, unless
we ourselves step behind it. When we step behind it, we do so not only to
see but also to put something there to be seen.]—G. W. F. Hegel

. . . the act of judgment that leads scientists to reject a previously accepted
theory is always based upon more than a comparison of that theory
with the world.—Thomas S. Kuhn

PREFACE

Although the problem of the philosophy of history has been in my mind ever since I was a student, I had no intention of writing about it until I saw how much my own students needed a book to explain to them the methods and purposes of a comprehensive and speculative philosophy of history. I decided to write in order to show that speculative philosophies of history are both important and necessary because they alone can establish the connections between the separate, detailed studies historians specialise in. This book, therefore, was not only written to promote knowledge and understanding but also to protest against the increasing fragmentation of historical researches. Our knowledge of the past has always had to suffer at the hands of mere antiquarians. But their threat was tolerable. Today the threat has become real because it comes from a completely different quarter. It comes, first, from the division of historical studies into such courses as the credit system of any one university requires. And, second, from the intellectual habits of the teachers who cannot get appointments and promotions in these universities unless they devote themselves to the writing of impeccable monographs. In this way, both teachers and students forget that the study of history is the study of a process that started in Sumer and led to World War II and the rise of the Third World. Without a comprehensive philosophy of history, which links the separate fragments historians are forced to concentrate on, one is bound to lose sight of the significance of the whole enterprise. The purpose of this book, therefore, is to show how speculative and comprehensive philosophies of history are not only necessary to make sense of specialised studies, but also feasible — a point that is usually denied in the many papers and books devoted to the subject. Since speculative philosophies of history are out of fashion, I have been obliged to engage in a great deal of controversy. I have felt a sense of urgency to rescue the study of history from the hands of academic specialists and the speculative philosophy of history from the dissecting tools of analytic philosophers. This sense of urgency has made me write *cum ira et studio*. To establish my arguments all the more effectively, I have made no attempt to conceal my broad philosophical standpoints.

The book is addressed to historians, to students of history, and to those people who enjoy reading books about history. For this reason I have not only taken care to avoid philosophical jargon but also to consider many authors who are not professional philosophers, very seriously.

The book presents a coherent argument which begins with a demonstration that, though history is concerned with the passage of time, historians cannot avail themselves of the temporal contiguity of events as a skeleton for their stories. From there the argument advances, step by step, to the consideration that the difference between history and fiction is not as great as most people like to suppose and that historical knowledge is not a mirror image of what happened in the past. It leads to the final conclusion that speculative philosophies of history are both possible and necessary.

The first draft of this book was read to a special seminar arranged with great kindness by Eugene Kamenka, at the Unit of the History of Ideas at the Australian National University in Canberra. Although I was not able to persuade all members of the seminar of all my theories all the time, I wish to take this opportunity to thank especially Eugene Kamenka, Walter Kaufmann, Quentin Boyce Gibson, Francis West, John Passmore, Robert Brown, Henri Arvon, and Hiram Caton for the patience with which they listened and for the vigour with which they attacked my arguments. In a different sense I wish to thank Ewa and Paul Hoffmann in Tübingen for their continued hospitality, which has made it possible for me to cast my net more widely than I could have done in New Zealand and which has made it possible for me to sit on the windowsill where Hegel used to sit when he was a student and from which he stared for hours on end at the pump in the courtyard of the Tübingen *Stift*. I also wish to thank the staff of the Reference Department of the Victoria University Library for their patient and ingenious help and the Internal Research Fund of Victoria University for their generous financial assistance. Last, not least, I thank all those of my students at the Victoria University of Wellington who showed sufficient bewilderment by the specialised and ill-assorted courses they have to attend to make me write a book to dispel their bewilderment. I hope that, when they have read this book, they will take up their Hegel and their

Toynbee, disregard the warnings issued by their orthodox teachers, and discover a new sense of purpose in the study of history. The study of history is, after all, the study of the past, which we cannot alter and since we cannot alter it, we might as well know exactly what it is we have to live with.

INTRODUCTION

The history of historical knowledge is the exact opposite of the history of the natural sciences. The history of our knowledge and awareness of the past began as pragmatic knowledge. From Thucydides to Machiavelli historians were occupied with the teaching of politics by example. History was the *magister vitae*, the teacher of life. During the sixteenth and seventeenth centuries this pragmatic approach declined sharply and was followed by a modern period of purely useless but theoretico-academic knowledge to discover the truth about the past, to find out what actually happened, and to detect the definitive shape of time. This modern phase of historical knowledge is dominated by disinterested curiosity and serves — apart from the futurological element contained in Marxist-inspired historical writing — no practical purpose at all. It even attained a tinge of irony once historians became sufficiently sophisticated to understand that time is not the sort of thing that can have a definitive shape and that history therefore is of necessity being constantly rewritten.

In our knowledge of nature we have gone in the opposite direction. It all started with grand speculations about the elements and the essential nature of matter. People were interested in reading the book of God and in deciphering the hidden messages of planets. It was all done to satisfy contemplative curiosity and to assist meditation. During the sixteenth and seventeenth centuries there came the enormous *volte face*, highlighted by Bacon and Descartes. To know, they said, is to be able to manipulate. Knowledge is power. From that moment onwards, knowledge of nature tended to cease to be contemplative theory and became linked to technological success, which became the final touchstone of truth. Here we have in history, a progression from pragmatism to contemplation and in our knowledge of nature a progression from contemplative theory to pragmatism. The two lines, one ascending and the other descending, intersected somewhere during the late sixteenth century.

The picture of the two lines moving in opposite directions (I am intentionally refraining from identifying the line that moves down and the line that moves up) would not be complete if we did not remind ourselves that during the modern pragmatic phase of scientific inquiry, the contemplative or charismatic[1] purpose of scientific knowledge was never lost sight of. In 1543 Copernicus wrote that he wanted, above all, to understand 'the movements of the world machine, created for our sake by the best and most systematic Artisan of all'. And 400 years later Einstein remarked that 'what I am really interested in is whether God could have made this world in a different way; that is whether the necessity of logical simplicity leaves any freedom at all'. It will be generally admitted that if it had not been for this constant charismatic purpose, scientific inquiry and discovery would have flagged, even though countless minor technological discoveries might have been made. In the history of science this persistent conjunction of charismatic purpose and pragmatic inquiry is of primary importance and proved fruitful.

In the study of the human past, unfortunately, there has been no comparable fruitful conjunction during the modern period. As the study of history entered its nonpragmatic period and was carried on to satisfy curiosity, it came to be dominated by an increasing spirit of specialisation and fragmentation. The study of the sources tended to become an end in itself until most historians nowadays are experts in certain sets of sources and admit quite openly that their interest in the knowledge to be derived from these sources about the past is only secondary. At the same time, the charismatic purpose has continued to assert itself. But it has dominated philosophers rather than historians. The philosophy of history was pursued vigorously from Vico and Herder to Hegel, Spengler, and Toynbee. But it failed to hold the attention of practising historians. Indeed, it not only failed to hold that attention but it became increasingly frowned upon by academic historians who developed an attitude of fastidious contempt for the speculative philosophy of history, a contempt which they had derived from Leopold von Ranke (1795–1886), the grandmaster of source criticism. In the study of the past the charismatic purpose, which remained so strong in the study of nature, was not allowed to exercise a fertilising influence.

In the study of history we are therefore confronted by a peculiar spectacle. Although history is one of the oldest studies, its nature is one of the most misunderstood ones. In modern times, more and more historians began to imagine that they were engaged in a purely empirical enterprise that consisted of transcribing events. We thus get the paradoxical situation in which a science or branch of knowledge became dimmer and less aware of its true nature, the more mature and sophisticated its methods of particular inquiry and research became.

This last observation, however, needs an important qualification. While practising and academic historians advanced from triumph to triumph in their meticulous source criticism, philosophers, though they shared the unease that had come to surround the speculative and charismatic interest in the philosophy of history, subjected various aspects of historical knowledge to very detailed and searching scrutiny. This scrutiny took place in two major phases. There was first, at the beginning of the twentieth century, a prolonged debate, especially in Germany, about such questions as whether history is a science or an art, whether the study of history is nomothetic or idiographic, whether historical knowledge relativises all values, and whether history explains or describes. When all arguments on all sides had been fully examined and debated at great length, interest in these questions began to flag. And then, during the forties and fifties of this century, the arena moved from Germany to Britain and America and a new debate was started. It centred on the questions of whether historians employed universal laws, under what conditions universals provided explanations, whether the employment of explanatory laws impeded or promoted the composition of narratives, and how history was related to the social sciences. The problems were not really new but the terminology was. Like the earlier phase, the new phase produced a large number of books and a veritable mountain of fastidiously argued papers, which were published in journals and, some of them, later collected in book form.

Although in both phases the same problems were discussed, there are fundamental differences between the two phases of critico-analytical reflection on history. One only has to compare the chapters on hermeneutics in a contemporary German introduction to the theory of history[2] with such collections of papers and essays as have appeared frequently in England and the United States[3] to spot the difference. In the first, German phase, the accent was on the importance of understanding the past. The past was seen as a series of incomprehensible conundrums. It was examined to find out how one could make sure to understand what people in the past had thought. Scholars came near to reducing the study of history to a theological problem: they treated the past as consisting of texts that were supposed to be authoritative though obscure and the meaning of which had to be disclosed.[4] They tended to forget that even if the past were disclosed, one would only achieve a very partial insight because, after all, the people who wrote those texts could well have been mistaken and not written the truth. To understand what people in the past meant is to understand, at best, how mistaken or hallucinated or mendacious they were. If one confines oneself to attempts to uncover what they meant, one merely scratches the surface, despite the fact that the immense laboriousness of the hermeneuticists always conveys an impression of unfathomable profundity. In the second, Anglo-Saxon phase, the accent was on the importance of explaining to our modern satisfaction how one thing had led to another regardless of the opinions that people in the past had held. With such attempts, history tended to be made into a social science and the hermeneutic problem was lost sight of. Again scholars overreacted. This time they tended to forget that if we explain what happened by using our own logico-scientific criteria, we may explain the past to our own satisfaction but do scant justice to the people of the past, who more often than not used quite different criteria. If it is a mistake to treat the past as if it were a theological problem, it is also a mistake to treat it as if it were a mere problem in the social science that is relative to our modern logical culture. In the second phase, scholars only dealt with the tip of an iceberg, for what counts as an explanation to modern man is not necessarily an explanation.

It would therefore be quite untrue to say that there has been a lack of interest in the nature of historical knowledge. On the contrary, if anything, there has been a surfeit of it. The real trouble is not lack of interest, but the fact that the interest is focussed on the wrong problem. The real problem is the divorce of academic, unselfconscious history from speculative and philosophical history. The present book is an attempt to concentrate on this real problem.[5] The papers and books mentioned in this text all deal explicitly with the analytical philosophy of history. They examine what it is we know when we have historical knowledge; they scrutinise the methods employed by historians and examine the relationship between historical knowledge and other knowledge. Needless to say, the authors of these books have usually been influenced by one or the other of the prevailing and fashionable schools of philosophy and, for the most part, though not exclusively, they are philosophers rather than practising historians. With the publication of all these books, it has come to be established that one distinguishes analytical philosophy of history from speculative, substantive, or synthetic philosophy of history. The latter kind of philosophy is the sort of philosophy that has been propounded by Hegel and Marx, Spengler, and Toynbee. Professional historians to a large extent have preferred to keep aloof from speculative philosophy of history. They agree with that analytical philosophy of history that has come down almost unanimously against speculative philosophy of history,[6] although they view that analytical philosophy of history, too, with bemused scepticism. Their refusal to take speculative philosophy of history seriously comes mostly from professional pride, whereas their bemused scepticism about analytical philosophy of history is due to a lack of training in the necessary philosophical prerequisites. But the professional historian feels that as long as the general conclusions of the analytical philosophers of history support his professional prejudice against speculative philosophy of history, he need show no further interest in the whole matter.

In one way or another, philosophers and historians have joined in their contempt for the speculative philosophy of history. To the philosopher the consequences of this contempt are peripheral. But to the historian, although he does not realise it, this contempt will be fatal because it will deprive his activity of all meaning. The first signs of the fatal disease are very apparent. The number of good students who enroll in history schools in the modern university is constantly declining. Bright young people are no longer interested in history. They find the subject boring and irrelevant. They can no longer be fobbed off by insistence that the study of history is a good preparation for politics. When the study of history meant the reading of Thucydides and Tacitus and when politics meant the politics of Renaissance Florence or Tudor England, the advice that history is the *magister vitae* was good advice, for it helped students of Athenian or Roman politics to keep their heads above water and, in the environment of a Tudor scene, possibly on their shoulders. But today the study of history means the investigation of the origins of Parliament and debates on the causes of the English Civil War. The politics of the modern national state or the modern supernational state are not clearly affected by either of these questions.[7] The only sensible way in which one can therefore justify and recommend the study of separate pieces of history is by drawing attention to the speculative philosophy of history and by showing how every single problem one studies is relevant to a philosophy of history. If this cannot be done, the study of history must become more and more pointless. There is intrinsic merit in reading Chaucer and Yeats, even if one cannot see the connection between the two poets. But there is no intrinsic merit in the study of Tudor parliaments or modern trade unions, unless one can see how they are linked.

In a very influential book, published just after the end of World War II, Karl Popper attacked the philosophy of history and held it responsible for the war as well as for the inhuman massacres perpetrated by Nazis and Stalinists. Whatever Popper's arguments against the philosophy of history were, a dispassionate reading of *The Poverty of Historicism*[8] shows that the main attack was directed against the scientific pretensions of the prophetic and deterministic aspects of the philosophy of history. Both he and his many readers ceased to ask whether there were other facets of the philosophy of history worth preserving and whether these other aspects are essential to the survival of the study of history. They forgot that the philosophy of history tends only incidentally to make predictions of the future but is in reality concerned with the meaning of the past. In this way Popper underpinned the ordinary historian's contempt for the philosophy of history with a philosophical argument. The historians who saw themselves essentially as craftsmen took comfort in finding their prejudices philosophically confirmed and inconveniently forgot that such philosophical confirmation, if unchallenged, would eventually bring about the demise of their own craft.

In a lower key, philosophers have simply remarked with pride upon the fact that analytical philosophy of history seems to have replaced speculative philosophy of history.[9] They have overlooked the fact that the speculative philosopher of history rendered a service to historians that no analytical philosophy can possibly render. Therefore one cannot congratulate oneself on the replacement unless one is absolutely certain that the analyses that have brought this replacement about are without fault. Genuine philosophy of history is something too important for our knowledge of history to be left in the hands of professional philosophers and logicians. No matter how great their expertise, they lack the necessary concern. Its consequences are too far-reaching for it to be dismissed in the near-contemptuous manner in which professional historians nowadays are invited to dismiss it.

Since I am writing with the concern of the practising historian, I have set out to question the conclusions of the analytical philosophers, which have discredited all speculative philosophies of history,[10] and hope to have discovered that stringent analysis and reexamination, far from discrediting speculative philosophies of history, open several possible as well as necessary ways in which they can be justified. In this sense, the intermission caused by the advent of analysis was salutary, but neither fatal nor final. The general consensus that all speculative philosophy of history is an illegitimate pursuit is based on a variety of false analyses of the nature of historical knowledge, and the self-congratulatory conclusion that speculative philosophy of history is rightly superseded by analytical philosophy of history is unwarranted.

In pursuing the argument, I will therefore take care to avoid oversubtle discussions of problems that are of no concern to the historian. I propose to neglect, for example, the problem that must arise when one considers the possibility that the past is a mirage. One can suppose that God made the world a split second ago in such a way that it embodies all the evidence and all the memories necessary for creating the illusion that it is millions of years old. I believe, and this belief has been confirmed by countless philosophers, that there is no argument to disprove this supposition. People who hold it must severely be left to holding it.

The present book is written to bridge the gap between analytical and speculative philosophy of history. It probes analytically; but not to show that speculative or substantive philosophy of history is redundant or fanciful. It is written to demonstrate that the difference between ordinary history, which is the professional historian's legitimate pursuit, and speculative philosophy of history is merely a matter of degree. If I cannot bring the philosopher and the historian together, I hope at least to reconcile the speculative historian and the professional historian.

For this reason this book is yet another contribution to analytical philosophy of history and makes no attempt to offer a speculative philosophy of history of its own. But it is a contribution with a difference. It aims to vindicate the speculative philosophy of history. Furthermore, it pursues this aim not as a labour of love and not in the mere disinterested conviction that peace is better than strife. It pursues this aim in the belief that unless ordinary history and the philosophy of history are brought closely together, the former will gradually die of inanition. This does not mean that I aim to defend all philosophies of history or any particular philosophy of history. On the contrary, I will establish a clear distinction between historicist and nonhistoricist speculative philosophies of history and examine the weaknesses of the former and the strengths of the latter. But all in all, my defence of speculative philosophy of history is undertaken to solve the crisis of historical scholarship and historical science.

The crisis of historical scholarship or science has arisen of late for a very obvious reason. Today we have run out of easy opportunities for exciting discoveries. Scholarship used to be sustained by this excitement regardless of meaning. During the nineteenth century and the earlier part of the twentieth century a large number of archives that had been closed for centuries were opened up. Historians could therefore plunge into their exploration with vigour and all the acumen for criticism they were capable of. Thus there appeared editions of documents and of chronicles. New histories were written on the basis of these editions or on the basis of mere calendars of these documents. But it is clear that there was to be an end to these halcyon days of historical scholarship. The day on which all the archives had been ransacked and examined was bound to dawn. In some cases, meticulous historians were able to prolong their activities by claiming that a previous editor had been careless and that his work had to be done over again. But there is an end in sight even for such overscrupulousness. Every academic teacher of history will know how increasingly difficult it is becoming to find suitable research topics for his graduate students. We all live at a time when the kind of historical scholarship that depended on unexplored documents and chronicles is coming to an end. When it does, and if it remains established that the study of history is to be confined to minute research into disconnected fragments, fewer and fewer intelligent people will want to devote their time to it. Thus we will be left with the great works of historical erudition and interpretation that were produced during past generations. But we ourselves will lose all living touch with them and gradually we will cease to be interested in them; and Henry Ford Sr. will have proved himself right — not because history *is* bunk but because our lack of involvement in it will make it *appear* to be bunk. True, history continues to happen and documents will therefore continue to be left. But history cannot happen as fast as it can be researched, and if historians rely on the arrival of new documents, their efforts must of necessity outrun the production of documents. We have already reached the point where for every statesman and even for every minor politician there are ten Ph.D. students waiting to pounce on his papers after his death.

This crisis, if it is not to close all the doors that lead to the past, can be resolved only if historical research is related once again to a philosophy of history or, better still, to competing philosophies of history. Only if every piece of research can be judged and discussed in terms of a philosophy of history rather than on its own intrinsic merits of meticulous and accurate detection work, can historical scholarship and historical knowledge remain a living science. It is conventionally assumed by professional historians that speculation kills research. This book is written on the assumption that the opposite is true, that research will soon be killed by the absence of speculation and that continued insistence on nonspeculative research will eventually defeat its own purpose.[11]

This task can best be achieved by a reexamination of a large number of conventional arguments and by an explanation of points that have often been made before. I will therefore deal with all the traditional problems of the theory of history — with causality, objectivity, interpretation, truth, and the relation of history to the social sciences. There will be a discussion on whether history is the history of thought and whether it has to be rewritten all the time. There is a plain acknowledgement that in the past discussion has focussed on all the right subjects. This book will therefore not present new insights and new analyses. It will instead seek to explain, for the most part, old ones to show that, provided they are interpreted correctly, they do indeed add up to the conclusion that ordinary history and speculative philosophy of history are much closer to each other than is commonly believed.

I do not think that one needs to justify the view that there is a crisis in the study and teaching of history. The crisis has often been discussed and nobody would deny that it exists. But people differ in the explanations they give of this crisis. Lionel Trilling thinks that the crisis was brought about because people in modern times are less and less prepared to accept the past as a story 'told by a rational consciousness which perceives in things the processes that are their reason'.[12] He links, and one must agree with him, the distrust of history to the decline of the novel. Our modern age, he says, is 'uneasy with the narrative mode'. I cannot discuss the problem of the modern novel; but I wonder whether Trilling is not putting the cart before the horse. He believes that the declining interest in historical narrative is due to a declining interest in rational explanation, which presents one event as the intelligible succession of a preceding event. I would put it the other way round. It seems to me that the interest in historical narrative has declined because the narrative has become divorced from the general preoccupation with the philosophy of history. There is no point in particular narratives if they cannot be linked to the general search for meaning. I would see the decline in the interest in the narrative mode of the novel as a consequence of the decline

of interest in history, not the other way round. After all, history
is much older than the narrative novel and it is very likely that the
latter is only a by-product of the former. When history declined,
the novel was bound to follow.

G. R. Elton has given a completely different explanation.[13]
He says that history is essentially concerned with the fact of
motion and that 'without a sense of time and change, of life and
death, history ceases altogether to be history'. He explains the
growing contempt for historical narration by the surfeit of evidence that is nowadays available to the student of the past. Confronted with this surfeit, he argues, historians despair of narration
and attempt instead to put the pieces of evidence together like a
jigsaw puzzle, which when properly assembled, will provide a
static picture of a system at any one particular point in time. I do
not doubt that Elton's observation is correct. But again I think
that he is putting it the wrong way round. The narrative mode is
failing to command attention because it has become divorced from
the philosophy of history. For this reason historians try to make
the best of the surfeit of evidence by treating it like a jigsaw
puzzle. After all, the argument from the surfeit of evidence only
concerns modern and early modern history. It is hardly true of
ancient and medieval history where the amount of evidence
available has not significantly increased of late. And yet we find in
these fields exactly the same lack of interest in narrative history
as we find in early modern and modern history, not to speak of
contemporary history.

Yet a different explanation is given by J. H. Plumb.[14] He
argues that modern industrial society, unlike the commercial,
craft, and agrarian societies which it replaces, does not need the
past. He believes that in modern times, the past is being extermi-
nated from the consciousness of man. I doubt whether this argument is true. To begin with, almost all sociologies of modern
industrial society are very aware of the fact that modern industrial
society is a recent phenomenon that developed out of and on the
basis of the destruction or displacement of these earlier societies.
For this reason, these sociological accounts are very interested in
the past. Moreover, we know of hundreds of primitive societies devoted to commerce, crafts, and agriculture in which the interest
in the past is either minimal or nonexistent. One can therefore
hardly agree with the view that our modern industrial society has
an in-built antagonism to the past. I would argue, on the contrary,
that that antagonism results from the demise of the philosophy of
history. Modern man is nothing if not utilitarian. If he cannot be

made to see how the study of any particular history is related to the wider question of the meaning of history, he will consider it useless.

The most sensitive and penetrating diagnosis of the modern antagonism to history is given by Hayden V. White and the passage must be quoted in full:

> The modern writer's hostility towards history is evidenced most clearly in the practice of using the historian to represent the extreme example of repressed sensibility in the novel and theatre. Writers who have used historians in this way include Gide, Ibsen, Malraux, Aldous Huxley, Hermann Broch, Wyndham Lewis, Thomas Mann, Jean-Paul Sartre, Camus, Pirandello, Kingsley Amis, Angus Wilson, Elias Canetti, and Edward Albee — to mention only major or currently fashionable writers. The list could be extended considerably if one included the names of authors who have implicitly condemned the historical consciousness by suggesting the essential contemporaneity of all significant human experience. Virginia Woolf, Proust, Robert Musil, Italo Svevo, Gottfried Benn, Ernst Jünger, Valéry, Yeats, Kafka and D. H. Lawrence, all reflect the currency of the conviction voiced by Joyce's Stephen Dedalus, that history is the 'nightmare' from which Western man must awaken if humanity is to be served and saved.[15]

This analysis not only hits the nail on the head but also proves my contention that the historian figures as the extreme example of repressed sensibility when he is not a philosopher of history in the speculative sense. For, after all, although it is true that Ibsen uses the through and through academic historian Tessman to represent the side of death in *Hedda Gabler*, it is also true that he uses the grand speculator and philosopher of history Lövborg to represent the side of life. And all the writers whom Hayden White quotes are thinking of the Tessmans. Not one of them would have chosen a Lövborg. In all these books the historians are modelled on George Eliot's Mr. Casaubon in *Middlemarch*. There is not a single writer who thought of the great speculators like Vico, Herder, or Hegel as the prototype of 'repressed sensibility'.[16] White's observation also highlights another matter. Western society has always been a 'hot' society in the sense in which Lévi-Strauss uses the term. A hot society is a society in which the historical process (i.e., the passage of time) is internalised and made the moving power of its development. Cold societies, by contrast, are societies that give themselves institutions to annul the possible effects of the passage of time on their equilibrium and continuity in a quasi-automatic manner.[17] Western societies are obviously of the hot variety. They attach much importance to God as the God of history, their Christian theology is, historically oriented, their nationalism is always understood to be a historical phenomenon, and in their science, cosmogony, and evolution, both biological and geological, play a dominant part. It is, therefore, all the more remarkable that White can observe with justice that modern Western man is turning against historical consciousness and is seeking to transform his social image from that of a hot society to that of a cold society. There must be, given the inherently and traditionally founded hot character of Western society, a very special reason for this transformation. I am certain that it is to be sought in the divorce of academic historical study from the speculative philosophy of history. The best service one can render, at the present time, to the knowledge of the past is to show that philosophies of history are viable intellectual enterprises and that we should despise the Tessmans and Casaubons and look with admiration upon the Lövborgs.

    In fairness I must add that I also owe thanks to J. H. Hexter. The publication of *The History Primer*, with its avowed contempt for philosophy, is an extreme provocation.[18] Its contempt for the philosophy of history, whether analytical and substantive or speculative, is bound to promote further the lack of interest in narrative history. Hexter's justification of the divorce is likely to have an effect opposite to the one he intends. The book has to be taken seriously because it is written by a practising historian and since it is written by a scholar who knows what he is talking about, it raises all the important issues. But the high-handed dismissal of the famous, and in some circles notorious, covering law theory, is a sharp warning. Perhaps it is ironical that in my book the covering law theory, propounded both by Popper and Hempel and by Popper somewhat earlier than by Hempel,[19] is the very girder of the bridge that will span the gap between ordinary history and speculative philosophy of history. It is ironical, because neither Popper nor Hempel, neither the inventor nor the propagator of the covering law theory in the form in which it is relevant to historians, is in the least bit interested in any speculative philosophy of history.

    In fact, part of Popper's fame rests on the explicit denunciation of all speculative philosophy of history and Hempel too would probably want to disclaim the use I propose to make of the covering law theory. Nevertheless, I propose to argue that Popper and Hempel have forged a tool that can solve our problem and the students' frustration. Hexter's urbane attempt to bypass the covering law can, therefore, not be allowed to go unchallenged. The covering law theory has been challenged and criticised by many philosophers. But their books are rarely read by historians. Hexter's attack is of a different kind, for he writes for historians and speaks with the authority of a historian who writes very fine narrative. His elegant style and his reputation as a historian are bound to make *The History Primer* an influential book. Hexter thinks that the crisis of history is partly or even largely due to the intrusion of philosophers. It is no matter that he disagrees with Morton White and proudly proclaims that he has never even read Wittgenstein. But it does matter that he is unaware of the ubiquitous and all-pervasive importance of the covering law or, at least, of the need for an appropriate substitute. For this reason the appearance of Hexter's book is the second immediate occasion for my writing.

At the outset I must state that the discussion of the several topics centre upon an argument. This is done not only to give them coherence, but also to stress one particular point. The point is that while it is freely admitted that human nature differs from age to age and from society to society and that people espouse all sorts of ideas, beliefs, thoughts, and values, their minds function in an identical manner. If it were not for that similarity in the functioning of all human minds, there would be no chance of historical understanding and, for that matter, of any kind of understanding other people. It has become fashionable to call this basic similarity of mental functioning 'the structure of the mind' and to label all explanations based on it as 'structuralism'. I am not concerned with labels and I would like to stress that my own version of structuralism is both considerably more simple and more comprehensive than any of the fashionable varieties. It is indeed extremely simple. I take it that the basic structure of the human mind consists in the fact that we can only think by referring particulars to universals, by subsuming particulars under universals, or by recognising particulars as instances of universals. We can distinguish two kinds of universals, concrete universals and abstract universals. Each kind of universal has its own mode of subsumption. But that is all. The content of the universals must differ, but the modes of operation do not.

The strongest argument in favour of this very simple view of the structure of the human mind is that all important contributions to philosophy from Plato to Lévi-Strauss have been entirely concerned with this question of the relation of the universals to the particulars. Plato's theory and Aristotle's criticism of this theory and the resulting distinctions between *ante rem*, *post rem*, and *in re* and the quarrel between nominalists and realists and

their subschools are too familiar to need comment. Hume introduced a new factor into the discussion when he argued that universals cannot be observed to exist and their presence in our
reasoning must therefore be attributed to a sort of animal habit.
Kant countered this explanation by insisting that the ground for
the presence of universals is to be found inside the human mind
itself, and Hegel thought of extending Kant's theory by his
demonstration that these grounds are not statically and genetically
inherent in the human mind but are a sort of self-explication of
mind that took thousands of years to emerge. Next we come to
modern positivists, pragmatists, and linguistic philosophers, who
all react against Kant as well as Hegel by reiterating the arguments
of Hume. They do not appeal to animal habit to justify the universals they recognise to be of central importance in our knowledge
of the world. They prefer to call them provisional hypotheses or
'inference tickets' for the making of particular statements. On the
other side, Freud was fully aware of the central place of universals.
When he summed up his psychiatric theory by the famous maxim
'we all suffer from memories', he clearly took it for granted that
these memories are psychological universals. They can shape later,
particular experiences because of their ability to subsume. A man
who sees in his king or president a father-figure could not do so
and would not do so if his memories of his own father were
nothing but a particular memory. The hold the memory of his
father has over his mind can only be explained by the view that
that memory is a universal of some kind or other. More recently
Lévi-Strauss' effort to explain that the reasoning of very primitive
people is very much like our own reasoning has to start (one could
even argue that it has to end) with the view that the basic mental
operation common to all people in all societies is the ability to
classify things, experiences, and thoughts as either A or not-A.
This ability is an example of the collection of particular instances
in universal classes.

Nobody has ever been able to deny the central importance of
universals in human thought. Positivism and its many offshoots
have fallen victim to the compulsive ubiquity of universals. According to all positivist credos the meaning of a proposition is its
method of verification. Universal propositions by their very nature
cannot be verified and according to positivism are therefore lacking
in meaning. But since we all know that they do not lack meaning,
positivism reduces itself *ad absurdum*. If further proof of the universal importance of universals is needed, one can recall that all
controversies on the methods proper to the social sciences centre

upon the question of the role of universals. All laws, customs, conventions, cultures, and traditions mould and constrain individuals. But how and to what extent? What is the exact nature of that constraint and in what precise sense is the collective prior to the individual? There are many answers ranging from Durkheim at one extreme to methodological individualism at the other. But no answer denies the crucial importance of universals. The question that has been debated and will presumably always be debated is the question as to the precise nature of the relation of the particular to the universal. For the purposes of the present book we can content ourselves with the observation that reasoning by subsumption of particulars under universals is the basic structure of all human minds and eschew the tricky and more metaphysical question as to the exact nature and status of these universals and of the precise relation in which they stand to particulars.

The intrusion of universals into the representation and understanding of the particular is only a special instance of a wider problem: how events are infigured to turn them into icons of the temporal process and how facts are related to the conceptual matrices within which they have to be embedded if they are to count as facts. The flow of time, to say nothing of a Cabinet meeting or a battle or the transformation of a religious brotherhood into a trade union, cannot be represented in a book other than by the employment of artifices. Flesh and blood, cannons and crowds can be evoked or referred to by words in books made of paper. But that is the most we can do. We cannot directly portray or represent them. As far as painting and sculpture are concerned, this has been recognised for a long time now. The media in the shape of canvas and oil paint or marble, rather than the human figure or a landscape, are the primary determinants of what is represented. And these media are by no means infinitely pliable. But historians, almost alone of all researchers and certainly less so than artists and natural scientists, have so far rarely shown sufficient sophistication and self-knowledge to appreciate the magnitude of the problem created by the inevitable intrusion of *their* media. They have always proudly taken their distance from myth, novel, and epic and fondly imagined that they, unlike novelists and poets and myth-makers, merely report what actually happened. When pressed, they defend their claim that they are reporters of what actually happened, by showing that they are merely transcribing sources — completely forgetting the fact that the sources too are largely shaped by the media through which we know them. For the rest, historians prefer to push the whole prob-

lem aside and continue in their dogmatic slumbers, disturbed by
nothing more than the occasional self-effacing dream of self-
congratulation for honesty, rectitude, probity, and critical acumen.

But when all is said and done and when we have scratched the
bottom of the barrel of the sophistication to be achieved by
Quellenkritik ('source criticism') and *Zettelkasten* ('box of notes'),
we are still left to face the hard truth that we are being had and
are having others. For the truth of the matter is that there is no
ascertainable face behind the various masks every story teller, be
he a historian, poet, novelist, or myth-maker, is creating. He is
telling a story and the story is all we have.

Nor can the problem be resolved by treating it as a problem of
translation. For whereas we can translate a photograph into a
painting and a painting, taking its life into our hands, into a verbal
statement and an English text into a Russian text, we cannot translate what actually happened (i.e., the flow of time) into anything.
We can translate what somebody *thought* happened into another
language and seek to establish equivalences between different
media — at least up to a point.[20] But we cannot translate reality;
for to do so we would have to have a picture of or a text about it
in the first place. We can change one medium into another —
although even that is admittedly risky.[21] But we cannot change
reality as it stands into a medium without the medium leaving its
heavy trace. And if we do, we are clearly not doing translation.
Translation is always concerned with substitutions of media, but
never with the substitution of a medium for reality. Whatever the
rules evolved for safeguarding translations from one medium into
another, they cannot help us to find our way from what actually
happened to any representation of it. Or, putting it more generally,
we can translate one form of consciousness into another. But we
cannot translate reality as such into consciousness. Whatever it is
that happens between reality and consciousness, it is not a problem of translation. It is more properly alluded to by the thought
that reality or its several parts activates our consciousness; but
even then we have no reason for thinking that it does so in a
straightforward or causal manner so that our consciousness ever
functions as a photographic plate — not that a photographic plate
is ever simply causally related to the original. Or, whatever the
mode of causality involved is, we have no way of knowing it because we cannot know the nature or the nonnature of the original.
We can translate one consciousness into another; but we cannot
translate something we are not conscious of into something we
are conscious of. That is why we can compare and check differ-

ent consciousnesses but we cannot check any consciousness by looking at something we are not looking at — and this is what, in effect, we would have to do, if we were to test its adequacy or correctness by referring it to what actually happened. These reflections are not new. But most people are reluctant to face their ultimate consequences. Thus, for example, it is often stated with relish that one cannot have a full-scale model of England in one's back garden.[22] 'The ideal limiting case of a reproduction is reduplication, and a duplicate is too true to be useful. Anything that falls short of the ideal limit of reduplication is too useful to be altogether true. And this goes not only for maps, but also for descriptions, pictures, portraits and theories'.[23] But behind this statement there does lurk the untenable assumption that a reduplication, though useless, could be 'true', that is, the assumption that behind the mask there is a face and that we might check the adequacy or truth of the mask by peeping at the face that is hidden by it. But the ineluctable truth is that there is no face behind the mask and that the belief that there is is an unsupportable allegation. For any record we could have of the face would be, precisely, another mask. We cannot have proof that it is a genuine 'record' of the face and every possible glimpse of the face would be, by its nature, yet another mask.

Ever since Plato philosophers have wondered what the matrix is that enables us to convert potential facts or events into actual facts or events. Plato suggested that the matrix is his Forms. Kant suggested that it consists of the categories of the understanding together with the forms of our perception such as time and space. In modern times language itself has been a strong candidate; for language is deceptively close to a system of meaning that is self-contained and prior to experience. And, if not any one particular language, then Chomsky's deep structure of language. Better than Platonic Forms or Kantian categories, it can be seen as a possible matrix that is prior to objects — and anything to qualify as a matrix has to be prior. We understand a language because it is a system of meaning and it is perfectly true that we do not have to watch an object or an event to see whether a certain sentence has meaning. The meaning of linguistic expressions does not depend on verification even though its truth might. This fact, so strenuously argued against all shades of positivism by Wittgenstein in his later years and for completely different reasons by Chomsky, does indeed make language a strong candidate for the matrix. For the matrix literally creates objects and events and does not depend for its meaning on the objects and events to be present in the first

place or prior to the matrix. Like a system of good manners or of
cooking or of conventions in dress or indeed like any system of
rules of any game, language can be meaningfully understood without reference to anything outside itself and can be translated into
another language without regard to the 'truth' of anything it says
and without reference to anything other than itself.[24] But despite
the attractiveness of the candidature of language for the matrix,
the candidature must fail. For, in the last analysis, language is not
a set of rules of a game and is not the same as a system of conventions in dress. A system of fashions in clothes, it is true, signifies
nothing and its essence consists in the process of signification, not
in what the clothes signify.[25] But a language, though it is superficially *like* such a system, is really quite different. The rules of
chess, Wittgenstein observed correctly, signify nothing beyond
themselves. But the rules of language are means that help us to
use language as a pointer. And insofar as language points at things
and helps us to identify them, language signifies something other
than itself and cannot be understood unless we keep looking at the
world. Language is *like* a game or *like* a system of fashions. But it
is not *the same as* a game or a system of fashions. If language's
candidature for the matrix were to be confirmed, we would have
to show that we can use language sensibly *before* we know what
to use it for.

Where then does the matrix come from? It comes from
something much more homely than Plato's Forms or Kant's
categories — though they too play their part. And it comes from
something more ordinary and general than language in any of
its forms. It comes from the human ability to generalise —
leaving aside, for the moment, the question as to the precise
nature of these generalisations.[26]

Starting with the assumption that all human minds have a
basic structure of reason, this book is a somewhat bold attempt to
bring together some very different and even disparate strands of
modern thought. For example, it is a central part of the argument
that there is no irreconcilable conflict between rationalism and intuitionism. It is often held that doctrines that maintain that we
can understand other people, especially the people of the past,
only by empathy, in an artistic or semiartistic manner, are the
direct opposite of the doctrine that states that we can rationally
rethink what other people thought. Contrary to common opinion
I hope to show that, with careful analysis, the conflict between
these two doctrines becomes very slight. Furthermore, I hope to

show that if one pursues a certain analysis, the Popperian criticism of Hegel's and Toynbee's historicism is less formidable than it seemed when *The Poverty of Historicism* was first published in the early forties.[26] What is more, I hope to show that even on a thoroughly Popperian assumption as to what constitutes 'explanation', both Hegel's and Toynbee's philosophies of history can be seen as fruitful, though not necessarily as true, philosophies of history. It is also implied throughout, in opposition to conventional Marxist thought, that Marxist philosophy of history is as fruitful in its place as any non-Marxist philosophy of history. All this amounts to an attempt to reassess the standing of all philosophies of history and stems from a refusal to accept any one at its own valuation. This book is both a reinterpretation of the nature of history and a reinterpretation of the nature of the philosophy of history. I know these are bold claims. But there would be no point in writing a book if one set out with no other aim in mind than to reiterate once again the old stand-points and to justify widely held doctrines. I would be hard put to say whether the book is a critique of historical knowledge or a justification of historical knowledge. Perhaps the best way of putting it is to say that it seeks to criticise what people commonly think they know when they have historical knowledge, and it seeks to justify a kind of historical knowledge very few people believe to be possible.

The general thesis of this book is that time is transformed into history by consciousness and that consciousness is able to bring this transformation about by making use of universals. This transformation is begun by the agents and actors and continued by historians reflecting on the reflections of the agents and actors. The final and natural outcome of such double reflection is the philosophy of history, which is thus seen merely as a culmination of the process by which time is transformed into history. Hence the difference between action, historical narrative of that action, and a philosophical understanding of that narrative is merely a difference in degree. The concept of a philosophy of history is implicit in the process necessary for the transformation of the mere passage of time (the past) into history.

This thesis belongs, one will readily recognise, to the old tradition of philosophical idealism. It is indeed idealism writ small. Philosophical idealism as a general theory is a much wider theory and concerns not only our perception of time and space in general but also the physiological problem of perception and of communication. As a result it is much more difficult to sustain.

I have a great deal of sympathy with it but hope to enlist
support for the narrower theory even from people who have no
sympathy with the wider theory. The narrow view does not depend
on idealism in general. It only concerns one particular aspect of
the problem of time. As time passes, myriads of things happen and
change. Not even the most confirmed realist could claim that it is
possible for the human mind to encompass more than a minute
fraction of these events. Therefore, if the notion of history has any
meaning at all, it must be a meaning dependent on the mind's
capacity to select and to link the selections. That much idealism,
but no more than that, is required for the theory to be advanced
in this book. I simply follow the old strategy, so often employed
by idealists of the most different hues. One begins by pointing out
that the object to be observed, in this case time, is infinitely complex, like a seamless web. Then it follows that such order as can be
made apparent is (1) an appearance of the object and that there
can be many different appearances, (2) is due to the mental operations of the observer, and (3) that truthfulness must be a function
of the relationship between different observers.

Now that I have put both my claims and my summary philosophical standpoint on the table, I wish to conclude by stating
that I consider the present book to be nothing more than a com-
plement to Hayden V. White's superb *Metahistory*.[27] In that book
White has shown that the great representatives of historical consciousness of the nineteenth century arrived at their vision of the
past not from a study of the sources of history, as we are all taught
to imagine, but from the use of certain moulds and matrices best
described in the terms of literary criticism and that even their
obvious ideological commitment was more a function of the categories of story telling than of their sociological location. It is possible that White in his total rejection of positivism and in his studied
disregard for an objective reality, which exists outside the minds
of the creators of historical consciousness, goes too far or possibly
further than is necessary. But all in all, his book does for our
knowledge of history what Auerbach's *Mimesis* and Gombrich's
Art and Illusion have done for literature and painting. It shows
that the medium is more important than the reality of which we
can, at best, have only a dimly intuitive apprehension. After
White's book, there would have been no need for a further demonstration of the same point, were it not for the fact that it contains
only a short theoretical part and is mainly devoted to an analysis
of the historical consciousness of certain major historians of the
nineteenth century. The only justification for my own book is

that I try to generalise and spell out in detail the theory on which his work is based. For good or ill, I have tried to do so by eschewing the terminology of literary criticism, which he so skillfully employs, and have remained close to the conventional philosophical terminology with which I happen to be more familiar.

Chapter Two

THE TIME SEQUENCE

To narrow the field of inquiry, I would like to say at the outset
that I think of history as the science of change. This means that I
understand by history not just any preoccupation with or study
of the past, but a very special study of the past. History is, as the
science of change, concerned with the succession of events — with
the study of how one event is superseded by another. For this
reason, narrative history is history par excellence. No other literary
form is more suited to do justice to the way events supersede one
another and hang together than plain narrative or story telling.
The simple form of narrative reflects change because it consists
of a series of statements that describe events by leading the reader
from one event to the other and so on. This simple form of narrative is an ideal that is often cumbersome and unnecessary. However,
I will centre all discussion on this simple form. The following is a
perfectly good example of narrative; but it is highly abbreviated
and much that must have taken place between the events narrated
is omitted, partly because it is understood and partly because it is
not known. It is a more common type of narrative than the formally more complete kind. It would not be difficult to imagine
how this example could be expanded into a formally more complete narrative of the kind that is the subject of discussion in this
book.

> By 37 B.C. Herod was able to besiege and take Jerusalem. Antigonus was
> beheaded by the Romans and Herod assumed the Jewish Crown, mean-
> while having strengthened his claim by marrying the Hasmonean princess,
> Marianne. When Mark Anthony was defeated and Octavian emerged as
> the sole emperor of the Roman Empire, Herod knew how to continue in
> his favour and even to gain by imperial favour the doubling of his own
> territory.[1]

There are many other ways in which one can look at the past.
One can study, for example, one comparatively short span of time,
say a period of twenty-five years, in a limited region. One can
assume that there was fairly little change during those years and

one can describe the state of affairs during this period. Such activity, though highly interesting, is not like writing a historical narrative, for its chief aim is to describe a static or comparatively static situation. Recently there has been much advocacy of such analytical historical investigation and whole schools have grown up to promote it. There is nothing to be said against it, except that the description of a static state of affairs is not to be confused with history as the science of change. History is the study of how one thing changed into another or how one thing brought about another thing. The analysis of how Parliament worked toward the end of the fifteenth century or how people intermarried in middle class nineteenth-century London, is interesting and can be made to become part of a narrative. But taken by itself such analysis lacks the quality of history. It is not a story. It is the analysis of something that happened to have taken place in the past. The method of such analysis can equally be applied to something that is happening now. In such analysis the past mode is purely incidental and the past is simply treated as a storehouse of examples and materials. Lucien Febvre, the learned and very distinguished French propounder of such 'historical' analysis, carried his advocacy so far as to describe real historians as *historiens historisants.*[2] It is a phrase so choice that it defies translation. It means that in his view it is unfortunate that there still are historians who study history, i.e., historians who tell a story. The very phrase reveals the absurdity of the view it defends. It is like deploring the fact that physicists still attend to physics and doctors to medicine.

However, in view of the enormous prestige that the school enjoys and in view of the extent of its influence,[3] one ought to add that the expression *histoire historisante* was first coined in reaction against a deadly school of French historians who had made the study of documents their chief aim and who 'narrated' the results of their studies in the most boring and laconic style possible. These historians, led by men like Lavisse, Seignobos, and Sorel,[4] moreover, had conceived the peculiar idea that the study of history consists in the study of the history of diplomacy and foreign affairs. They had presumably reached this strange conclusion because by the nature of the case, there are always more documents available for foreign affairs than for any other part of the past. The founders of the school of the *Annales*, understandably, reacted against both the exclusive preoccupation with documents and the confinement of history to the history of international affairs. But they threw out the baby with the bath water. In Britain, R. G. Collingwood, equally bored by similar practices,

came up with a much more philosophical and thoughtful opposition. He denounced this mechanical method of writing history and
proclaimed that all history is the history of thought and ought to
be studied and written in that sense. In France, by contrast, opposition to the mechanical transcription of history practised by
Lavisse, Seignobos, and Sorel led to a less philosophical reaction.
Febvre did not just attack history as the history of international
affairs but attacked the idea that history consists in narration and
branded all narrative history as *histoire événementielle* (the 'story
of events'), when all he really meant was to demand that historians
should not be documentary positivists and should not confine
their attention to international affairs. Marc Bloch, who was
closely associated with Febvre in the launching of this new school,
spelt out his objection to documentary positivism by saying that
if one takes the researches of most medievalists too seriously one
ends up with the impression that in the Middle Ages peasants did
their ploughing with charters. But although Bloch always insisted,
unlike Febvre, that history is the study of change and the study of
man in time, he himself had a very uneasy relationship with the
passage of time. He fondly quoted the Arab proverb that men are
more similar to their times than to their fathers,[5] which indicates
that he too, like Febvre, was really more interested in the syn-
chronicity of events than in chronological succession and narrative.
At any rate it was no accident that *le style annale* turned completely against narration. All in all, then, the massive influence of the
'school of the *Annales*' has led to the view that the past can best
be studied as a series of static systems. In this sense history is
reduced to a sort of social science of the past and can never hope
to compete successfully with the social sciences that study the
present. For the latter have always more material and information
at their disposal and the social science approach to the past remains
handicapped because of the gaps in our information. Despite this,
one can turn the study of static systems of the past into history
by describing two contiguous systems and then show how one
dissolved into the other or how the other destroyed the one, and
so forth.

     The prestige and popularity — it is hard to know which is the
greater — of the school of the *Annales* depends also on a modern
institutional factor. The study of history has become monopolised
by universities. Universities are staffed by people who need promotion and to get promotion they have to prove themselves great
specialists to the satisfaction of their professional colleagues. Now
it is much easier to establish a professionably viable reputation by

showing expertise in a small field consisting of a static system than by writing large-scale narrative. For this reason the philosophy of the school of the *Annales* has found wide support and is used to buttress historiographical practices that are rooted in academic institutional situations rather than in sound reason.

We will return later to a consideration of how one can study how static systems, or systems presumed to be static for the sake of study, supersede one another. For the time being we will confine our attention to history as the science of change and presume that plain narrative is most capable of doing justice to its aim. A plain narrative, which presents events as chains of cause and effect and in which one event is the effect of another and at the same time becomes the cause of the next event, is the basic form of historical knowledge.

This does not necessarily mean that the narrative must at all times be completely unilineal in the sense that it consists of only one such chain of cause and effect events. In any one narrative there can be a great richness of such chains, some long, some short. Some will cut across others so that one event can be located at the crossing of two or more chains. A large-scale narrative will, as a rule, consist of an assembly of lots of smaller scale narratives.

At first glance this narrow definition of what we choose to consider as history might be taken to solve all subsequent problems. Indeed it is often said that insofar as history is plain narrative, the historian is simply a man who traces the succession of events in time. He has to be astute and accurate and very critical in his assessment as to what he accepts as true (i.e., what he thinks really happened). But once this initial detective work is completed, the historian is very much like a recording machine. He keeps one eye on the events as he knows them; and the other eye on his paper and transcribes the events that happened onto his paper without any further thought. Indeed, the less thought the better. In this sense the historian really blots out all those parts of his mind that are not strictly devoted to detective work, and in this case one could presume that a police training college is a much better training ground for a future historian than a university. There he will learn how to cross-examine witnesses, how to distrust eye witnesses, how to dintinguish a forged signature from a genuine one, and so forth. For the rest, the writing of history is believed to be a semimechanical transcription and in that sense, the writing of history is just about the only trade a man can ply without any brains at all. The detective does the work and the 'historian' records the succession of events in time. Many years

ago R. G. Collingwood described this kind of historical activity
as working with scissors and paste. One could perhaps amend his
description by saying that the scissors-and-paste historian must
also be a detective sergeant. There are two very good historians
who have unfortunately lent the not inconsiderable weight of
their authority to this delusion. Fustel de Coulanges, in an im-
passioned moment, leaned across his lectern to be nearer to his
students and thundered, 'It is not I who is speaking, but history
itself', thus subscribing to the belief that he was nothing more
than a mouthpiece or a recording machine. And Sir Frank Stenton
once proclaimed that the acid test of a good historian is the
ability to edit a charter, thus subscribing to the idea that a detective sergeant or perhaps a detective inspector would make the
best historian.

It requires very little critical reflection on the nature of events
to understand that there can be no foundation to this simplistic
view of the historian's activity. In view of the acute ability to sift
documents and to witness accounts displayed by historians, it is
perhaps a little surprising that they should not have been able to
afford the philosophical reflection necessary to discover that the
historian is anything but a recording machine and that the writing
of history is an activity completely different from tracing events
in their succession in time. But historians like to think of themselves as empiricists, as people with a hardheaded and tough-
minded grasp of facts. They are not fond of speculation and
therefore have an in-built resistance to the kind of critical philosophical reflection necessary to detect that their activity is not an
activity that traces the succession of events in time.

Every event is infinitely subdivisible.[6] For this reason one
cannot take it that an event is a hard and fast *datum*, something
given to the historian as a result of critical detective work.[7] I
prefer to use the word 'event' rather than the word 'fact', because
it is easier to grasp how events are infinitely subdivisible. Consider
the event of the outbreak of World War II. There is no doubt that
it took place. But it is an event that covers a fairly long span of
time, starting perhaps with Hitler's order to invade Poland and
ending with Chamberlain's broadcast that we are now 'in a state
of war'. This event can easily be broken up into a very, very large
number of subevents. One of these subevents is the event of the
crossing of the frontier between Poland and Germany by the left
boot of a certain German soldier. Now this subevent admittedly
occupies a very small span of time, but even so it can be further
broken up. The event may cover only three seconds, but it can

be broken up into subevents each of which covers one second. And each of these subevents can be further broken up into events covering less time.

It is important to distinguish 'facts' from 'events'. Any fact that took place covers a span of time. But at the same time we are accustomed to refer to the presence of a table in a room as a 'fact'. Now this fact is infinitely subdivisible only in the sense that once we have split the table into its constituent neutrons and electrons, there may emerge nothing other than a field of energy. The only thing that is infinitely subdivisible in our sense is the presence of the table as an event (i.e., as something that covers a span of time). Insofar as we can imagine that a fact covers no time or practically almost no time (we cannot; but for the sake of argument, we can intuit this difference between a fact and an event) we also admit that there is a limit to its divisibility. An event, however, by its very nature, covers a span of time; and therefore it is infinitely subdivisible. For this reason it might be preferable to abandon the habit of speaking of historical 'facts' and to keep to the habit of speaking of historical 'events'. This is merely a matter of usage and not of great consequence. But it is easier to probe the difficulties of composing a historical narrative when we speak of events rather than of facts.

There is another distinction that has to be spelt out. It does not follow from the observation that events are infinitely sub-divisible that a statement describing or referring to an event is infinitely subdivisible so that every event-statement is *composed* of other event-statements. We are here concerned with events in a substantive sense, not with events as described in propositions. All talk about event-statements rather than about events belongs to a metalanguage and might indeed raise problems with which we are not here concerned.

It follows from these observations that when a historian con-structs a narrative in which one event follows upon another, he is not, whatever else he is doing, tracing the succession of events in time. Every event he records is a construction made up of its sub-events. And every event he fastens his attention on implies the omission of all the subevents. Suppose that a historian makes, before writing a narrative, a chronological list of all the events he means to incorporate. No matter how full this list is for any chosen span of time, say from noon of August 1, 1939, to mid-night of September 3, 1939, an infinite number of events has been left out.[8] And here I am thinking not only of all those myriads of events that are immediately considered irrelevant to the story of

the outbreak of the war, such as the flowering of a daisy in a field
in the Argentine. I am thinking of all those subevents that could
quite easily have been inserted between the points of time on
which the two events listed are to be found. Such a list can, therefore, never be complete. Any attempt to make it more complete
must lead to a further attempt to insert yet another subevent
between any two points, and so forth *ad infinitum*. The conclusion is therefore inevitable. Time by itself does not provide the
connecting link between the events listed by the historian. A large
number of points in time are simply skipped when the historian
goes from one event to another and then to the next and so on. In
other words, the historian is not tracing the succession of events
in time when he turns his list of events into a historical narrative.
He may, on the whole, prefer to narrate the earlier events before
he narrates the later ones. But even such a rough chronological
order is not mandatory. Some cause and effect chains are chains
because of a teleological cause that is in fact later than the effect.
But this is a minor consideration. The main point to be noted is
that whatever it is that makes the events hang together as a narrative, it is not their succession in time. Time is therefore not the
factor that provides the link. Historical time, to sum up, is not
identical with temporal succession. This means that the historian
is not just a recording machine, which, once the initial detective
work as to which events took place and which did not, is done,
transcribes them in their temporal order. It also means that the
historical narrative is a genetic story not because of its basis in,
but because of its divorce from time. In a historical sequence, the
temporal sequence is not identical with the cause and effect chain.
It is tempting to identify the passage of time with causality and to
think of an event that precedes another event as the cause of the
other event. If it is true, however, that events are infinitely subdivisible, this simple identification of time and genetic causality
must break down.

Consider the example of a cell biologist who watches and
describes the growth of cells under a microscope. It looks as if he
traced the changes in the cells and the genesis of an embryo by
merely watching the passing of time and by recording the changes
the cell undergoes as time passes. One could imagine, superficially,
that in his case, at least, the earlier state of the cell is the cause of
the later state and that embryology for one is based upon an identification of the passage of time with a genetic process. Closer
inspection shows that the cell biologist too is highly selective in
his observation and does not identify the genetic process he is

watching with the passage of time. First he singles out a number
of events under the microscope; and then he established links
between these events, which are different from links provided by
the passing of time. The links he uses to establish connections between one event and another are a finite set of general laws culled
from biochemistry and physics. On the basis of these laws he can
watch how one event leads to another, how one cell is transformed
and grows. Since he does not discuss in his capacity as a cell biologist the validity of these laws and since he is not concerned with
the question of whether laws culled from theology or psychology
should be admitted in addition to the laws of physics and biochemistry, he is operating with a definite set of laws. If someone
were to argue with him and suggest that he should assume that one
cell is gifted with conscious intelligence and is planning, for example, its own division as a sort of strategy of growth, he would
rightly be entitled to dismiss the suggestion as not being part of
the 'science' he is pursuing. But we may as well be clear as to the
real nature of that science. The histologist and the embryologist
are very selective and restrictive in the choice of their general laws
and as a result have the events they seek to link in genetic succession selected for them in advance.[9] They operate on the basis
of a definition of what general laws are admissible and in this way
they are able to create the appearance, but an appearance only, of
being self-sufficiently devoted to watching the passage of time.
The identification of the genetic process with the passing of time
is made possible by that appearance. The definition of the admissible laws is taken for granted and, as such, is beyond discussion.
Hence it appears as if the cell biologist is watching the cell's
passage through time when in reality he is establishing links between selected events and other selected events on the basis of
certain laws the choice of which is not open to question.

The historian, on the other hand, is not in such a fortunate
position. He deals with people who are conscious or with people
who could be conscious. He deals with institutions created or
operated by people who are conscious and he has to reckon all the
time with the possibility of false consciousness, with deception,
with illusion. At best, he has to reckon with different consciousnesses, that is, with people having different views or ideas about
one and the same situation or institution. Hence there is no finite
set of laws which he can use and no conceivable way in which the
admissibility of laws can be defined or determined. He has to
reckon with the possibility that any law at all, even a false one,
may have to be invoked. For the cell biologist, the disappearance

of time as the string on which events are strung together presents
no problem. He has a definition of the type of general law he can
use to link events. But to the historian the disappearance of time
presents a real problem because he has no way of defining which
general laws are admissible for stringing single events together.
Every and any law which has ever arisen in the consciousness of a
man at any time and any place is a potential candidate to be taken
into account. Of this, more later. The difference between the cell
biologist and the historian, therefore, consists in the fact that the
former can count upon a criterion for the admissibility of general
laws and the latter cannot. For this reason, the cell biologist, when
he speaks of genesis, gives the valid appearance of speaking of a
series of temporal changes undergone by a cell as it endured
through time and in this sense, the passage of time is identical with
the growth or decay of a cell. Once he understands that time
passes, he also grasps the meaning of causality, or vice versa. Once
he grasps how one state of a cell is the cause of the next state because he can fall back on a set of general laws defined in advance,
he also defines the meaning of the passing of time. But the historian is not a cell biologist and can therefore not depend on this
simple appearance of an identity of causality with time. Historical
narrative in all cases is not an account of biological genesis, though
they may often enough look superficially indistinguishable. When
a historian describes the growth of parliamentary institutions in
Britain or Sweden, he may think that he is doing something very
similar to the cell biologist who is watching the growth of an
embryo, and indeed the historian often borrows terms from the
histologist. We must remember all the time that when he does so,
he is using them metaphorically.

    If one identified the passage of time with causality, one would
have to admit that there are such things as developmental laws,
that is, laws that describe or determine the process of time change
through which any particular entity, be it a biological cell or a
parliamentary institution, has to pass. The very notion of such
developmental laws is untenable as Karl Popper has conclusively
demonstrated in *The Poverty of Historicism*.[10] We shall return to
this problem in the last chapter, where I hope to show that part
of Popper's argument consists in tilting at windmills. But even for
the time being it is important to stress that the theories of evolution, histology, geology, and meteorology do not operate with
developmental laws that describe the course any one set of events
have to take. On the contrary, they all make use of general laws
to show how one condition leads to the next. Take meteorology

as an example. The weather office can predict what the temperature and the cloud position will be like in the afternoon of any day before it observes the temperature of the earth and the wind strength in the morning. The weatherman then uses his knowledge of the behaviour of air in certain temperatures as a general law and deduces with the help of that general law what the weather will be like in the afternoon. His prediction looks like a time sequence. But it can assume that appearance of temporal causality only because he has made use of a number of general laws about air and temperature, about the cooling processes, and about the relative weight of dry and damp air, and so forth. Exactly the same is true, for example, in the theory of evolution. On the very last page of *The Origin of Species*, Darwin outlines the finite set of 'eternal' laws he used in telling the story of the evolution of species. He shows, thus, that he never thought that there is a law of evolution or of development,[11] but that he constructed his narrative of the evolution of species by using ordinary general laws. In this way he was able to produce a genetic story and create the appearance as if the mere passage of time determined the particular course evolution had taken.

There are no hard and fast events. Every single event is a construction. The event called the outbreak of World War II can be broken up into innumerable subevents. That does not mean that it did not take place. It only means that it is not hard and fast. It means, further, that some people (in this case, lots and lots of people) decided to place any subevents together in such a way as to give rise to the view that the large event took place. But it is conceivable that other people might have assembled some of the subevents concerned in a different manner and collected others in a different chain. If this is done one would come up with events that took place at the same time and the same place but which would bear no resemblance to the event 'outbreak of World War II'. The same applies to very small events. Consider the event that John entered my study at a certain moment. One might argue that at least this small incident is a hard and fast event. Either John did, or he did not. If he did not the event did not take place. But analysis shows that the matter is more complicated. The event referred to by the statement that John entered my study at a certain moment in time is really a series of events put together. The first subevent is the opening of the door; the next, John's first step; the next, John's second step across the threshold, and so forth. Let us now suppose that someone accepts the second subevent, but instead of linking it with

the third, links it with an event that undoubtedly took place
but that had no place in the original series. I mean the event that
John's forward movement displaced an amount of air that was
pushed back into the corridor. He could then link that event to a
further event about a volume of air inside the study changing
places and so forth. Here we would get a story about the same
place and the same time, but one hardly similar to the story that
John entered my study. The two series of events have at least one,
possibly more than one, event in common. But the series are quite
different from one another. This shows that we cannot look upon
events, not even upon small-scale events, as something that is given
and the occurrences of which are the hard core of historical truth.
For this reason nothing is so irritating to the thoughtful historian
as the layman's constant request for the hard core of history, the
'facts'. One can distinguish the genuine historian both from the
layman and from the amateur by their views as to what are the
'facts'. The thoughtful professional will know that every event, no
matter how small, is a construction and that for every time and
every place many events can be constructed. The layman, the
amateur and many amateurs masquerading as professionals, will
believe that facts are facts. Ironically, the only hard and fast thing
in our knowledge of events is our knowledge that certain events
did *not* take place. If John did not cross the threshold and did not
jump over it, then the story that he came into my study must be
false. Similarly, if none of the subevents assembled in the big
event 'World War II' took place, the story that World War II
broke out would be a false story. The hard part of the historian's
knowledge is therefore not the events he knows to have taken
place — because they could have been constructed into quite
different events that actually took place — but the events he
knows for certain *not* to have taken place. For example, the statement that Napoleon lost the battle of Waterloo is a description of
a highly composite event of which some of the subevents or
elements could have been assembled together with other events
into a very different composite event. It is therefore not a description of a hard and brute fact. But the statement that Napoleon
won the battle of Waterloo or that the battle took place in 1850
is hard historical material in the sense that it can be falsified, for
at least some of the crucial subevents it consists of can be shown,
beyond shadow of doubt, not to have taken place.

Although this conclusion sounds startling, it requires only a
little reflection to show that it is really quite obvious. Let us
suppose that we have a jumbled up set of subevents numbered as
follows:

$$1 \quad 2 \quad 3 \quad 4$$
$$5 \quad 6 \quad 7 \quad 8$$
$$9 \quad 10 \quad 11 \quad 12$$

It is clearly possible to draw a circle around any set of them to assemble them into an event. Thus we can get an assembly of 9, 6, 3, and 4; or an assembly of 12, 5, and 3; and so forth. And since each of the listed subevents can be presumed to be already the product of a similar kind of assembly, the processes of breaking up and of assembly can be carried on indefinitely. When we stare at the set of subevents listed, *any* assembly is possible and we are therefore not entitled to say which assembly is an accurate one and which assembly is not accurate. Indeed, the only thing we can say with real certainty is that an assembly that includes an unlisted subevent, say 13 or 14 or 15, is not a possible assembly and that the event that includes subevents 13 or 14 or 15 or any one of them is an illicit assembly. The event portrayed by it or referred to in it did *not* take place.

We might usefully reflect on Bishop Berkeley here. Berkeley argued that events that are not perceived did not happen. He has found few people who have followed him literally. But there is nevertheless an oblique truth in his contention. He made the mistake of claiming that the existence of an event depends on its being perceived. I think that almost all people, albeit for different reasons, would reject this claim. Berkeley's mistake was to equate perception with existence. He ought to have claimed that the shape or configuration of existence must be equated with perception. Nobody can sensibly question that any of the subevents in the above list occurred. But one is obviously forced to claim that any one configuration in which they appear is entirely dependent on perception or on whatever mental operation one prefers to think of. The thing that is in question, therefore, is not, as Berkeley thought, the existence of objects, but their configuration. It is configuration, not existence, which depends on perception.

This view of looking at the potential configurations of events and at the multiplicity of potential assemblies, must, of course have an important bearing on the question of historical truth. But we shall postpone a detailed discussion of truth to chapter 8. In the meantime it is sufficient to state that it is possible that the event particles, the occurrence of which can be ascertained for the day and place on which Caesar is alleged to have crossed the Rubicon, can be assembled in a thousand different ways, none of which need include the event Caesar crossed the Rubicon. But the one event into which they cannot be assembled is 'Caesar did

not cross the Rubicon on that day'. If we tried *such* an assembly
we simply would not be able to find all the required particles, although some, no doubt, could be found.

If this account of the method of assembly of subevents into
events — to mention only one discernible stage in this infinitely
complex process — is correct, it must come as a surprise that we
nevertheless have knowledge of something that we can call the
history of Rome or the history of the French Revolution. For if
the method of assembly is as arbitrary as it is claimed, it must
seem strange that two people and often whole cultures come up
with an agreed set of events that form a coherent story. There is
in fact a conventionally accepted series of events that we choose
to call history. That story is so conventionally accepted — always
allowing for minor divergences and disagreements — that it has
the appearance of absoluteness and creates the impression, which
is more than superficial, that it is a recital of what really happened.
For how, one might ask, is it possible to get so many people to
settle for one particular kind of assembly of subevents?

Despite the appearances, however, this accepted series is
arbitrary. The agreement is a simple convention, accepted by
common consensus. One need not be misled by the use of the
word 'convention' and conclude that the consensus is arrived at
lightly. The consensus is in part due to cultural conditioning and
to any one prevailing educational system. But that conditioning
and that system are, in turn, derived from the sources (the contemporary accounts and documents that are extant) of our knowledge of the past. These sources reflect the same interest, the
same preoccupation with the same or similar universals that the
people who give their consensus have. The precise nature of these
universals and their relationship to each other will be examined in
detail in chapter 4. Since we tell our histories on the basis of these
sources and as a continuation of these sources, we are pragmatically *not* free to put the story of the past together in any old way
we like. A discussion of the crucial importance of sources will be
found in chapter 7. Though logically free, we are constrained by
the fact that we have to rely on sources to continue the kind of
yarn that was started several millennia ago. And the compilers of the
sources themselves were, several centuries ago, constrained by their
knowledge of earlier sources and the kind of consensus they gave
rise to. Hence the appearance that the history we know and accept
is not an arbitrary creation. In a sense, of course, it is indeed not
an arbitrary creation. But the reasons for the absence of arbitrariness are cultural and ideological, not logical. The accepted version

of the past does not look arbitrary because it is an ongoing tale, a continuation of earlier tales. If we made an experiment in thought (in Einstein's sense) and started from scratch in every generation, there would be a vast number of completely divergent histories of the past and these histories would then indeed appear as arbitrary. Although even then we would have to rely on sources and thus be forced, up to a point, to abide by the conventional shape and conform to earlier tales. The appearance of absoluteness derives, however, not from the genuine absoluteness of the story we tell of the past but from the fact that no story teller is alone and that no story teller ever starts from scratch.

In the case of an event in the medium size range, the problem is purely theoretical. When we observe John entering a room we would be very hard put, though there is no denying that it would be theoretically possible, to link his crossing the threshold with anything other than his reaching a chair and sitting down. The surprise is only called for at the extreme ends of the scales. When larger constellations are involved, there is occasion for surprise and special explanations are needed. At the far end of the scale of events, it is clear that we are biologically conditioned to link the movement of John's arm with his head rather than with Bill's arm and not to detach his rump from his legs and link the legs with the legs of the chair he is sitting on. Even further down the scale, there is no conditioning at all. If we link Bill's muscular movements with events in his brain cells, we do so because we have been told of laws of neurophysiology that force us to establish such links and here it is our respect for the authority of the experts in neurophysiology that would make all other links absurd. At the other end of the scale, there is cause for genuine surprise and need for a special explanation when we always link the outbreak of World War II with Hitler's personality. Why, for example, do so few people neglect Hitler and link the outbreak with the constellations of the planets? The answer here lies in the field of political experience and ideological conditioning. Whichever way one looks at it, it is only in the middle range of events that no special surprise and no special explanation for the large consensus is needed. When we are dealing with very small and with very large events, there is justifiable surprise and different kinds of explanations for any prevailing consensus are required.

The process of time by itself does not allow us to identify anything as an event, either small or large. The observation of the passing of time can only create an impression of an undifferentiated continuum bound to create giddiness and a blurring of vision

in the observer. If the continuum is to be differentiated we first
have to imagine that we remove such time structure it has — as if
we were fileting a fish. Thus we get something like a mollusc — a
wobbly, still undifferentiated mass, now even deprived of its time
skeleton. To reassemble this mass we have to select and to construct. We can do this only by introducing nonempirical factors,
where 'nonempirical' does not mean metaphysical but something
not derived from the observation of the passing of time.

We can see time in shapes or icons rather than just endure its
flow or watch it as a seamless web or an undifferentiated continuum because we employ special methods to watch it. We use
universals of some kind or other that enable us first to isolate
particle happenings and hypostatise them and, second, to link any
two particle-happenings to make larger happenings, and so forth.
In practise the two steps amount to the same kind of mental
operation and these operations will be examined in chapter 3. But
we must be very clear that we could not isolate the particle-
happenings in the first place without having first, at least in
theory, isolated even smaller particle-happenings and combined
at least two of them to form the particle-happening or subevent
mentioned earlier. This method of giving shape to time or
of isolating identifiable icons is the same for the historian
looking back over and from a long distance and for any one
agent 'making history' or personally involved in the passage
of time at any moment. Without this method, both historian
and agent could only stand by and watch, stupefied, the
liquid stream of time rushing past. In Samuel Becket's play
Waiting for Godot there are two characters on the stage. After the
departure of the visitor with the dog, one of them sighs, 'Well, at
least it helped to pass the time'. The other replies, 'Nonsense, time
would have passed anyway'. Although Becket has no further comment, it is clear that the first character speaks like a historian or an
agent who is making history. To him, time has a shape and appears
as either this or that. The second character merely intuits the
seamless web of time and observes correctly that any particular
appearance of the seamless web can make no difference to its
mysterious character. Whatever he is, he is not a historian.

Where does the impulse for the transformation of the past into
history come from? There may be many reasons for the transformation. One of the most powerful ones is the observation of
change. Change takes place all the time. If change is periodic, it
assumes the appearance of a cycle and in that case the past is
likely to be transformed into a series of cycles that do not differ

from one another so that change is again eliminated from the shape that time assumes. If change is slow it cannot be observed. The ancient Egyptians must have known that the custom of building mastabas gave way to the custom of building pyramids and that eventually pyramid building was abandoned. But the change was spread over so many centuries that people did not become aware of it as change.[12] When change is rapid, it becomes noticeable. The generation that lived through the coming into use of the motorcar must have been very conscious of change. When change is noticed, people become curious about the past, and since the past as such cannot be taken in, they seek to give it shape by transforming it into history.

The experience of change need not be social. It can be both personal and visionary, and we have a famous and striking description of the impulse to write history by Edward Gibbon:

> Yet the historian of the decline and fall must not regret his time or expence, since it was the view of Italy and Rome which determined the choice of the subject. In my Journal the place and moment of conception are recorded; the fifteenth of October 1764, in the close of evening, as I sat musing in the Church of the Zoccolanti or Franciscan fryars, while they were singing Vespers in the Temple of Jupiter on the ruins of the Capitol. But my original plan was circumscribed to the decay of the City, rather than of the Empire: and, though my reading and reflections began to point towards the object, some years elapsed, and several avocations intervened before I was seriously engaged in the execution of that laborious work.[13]

There is another reason for wishing to write history and for wishing to see the past not as a flow of time but as a series of stories. Time and space are, in our common experience, not symmetrical. The experience of time (the passage of time) is demoralising and depressing in a sense in which the experience of spatial extension is not.[14] If one thinks of the passage of time as the accumulation of differences in the same space,[15] it is clear that the passing of time diminishes and deprives us. At any one point or area in space something that was there a moment ago, disappears and whatever takes its place only does so to disappear again and so forth. Our experience of space is quite different. If we think of space as differences that take place at the same moment of time, then the experience of space is enriching. At one moment there is only one thing; and then at the same moment, there is more than one thing and so forth. Through our awareness of space we gain something, we get more. Through our experience of time, we lose things. One of the strongest impulses for the conversion of time into history is based on this asymmetry between time and space. We can combat the depressing experience of deprivation through time by trying to assimilate the passage of time to the extension of space. And this is precisely what we are doing when we are writing history. When we see the past as a story, we give shape to time. And since there is no absolute shape that we could give to time, it might be more appropriate to think of the transformation of time as a process of putting sets of masks over the face of time.

THE COVERING LAW

Now that we have established that the historian — together with a
very large number of other people — cannot depend on temporal
sequence to make events hang together, we have to search for a
principle other than time to make events genetically or causally
relevant to each other. Over two hundred years ago David Hume
showed that we cannot directly observe causality and that we
therefore can never think of any one event by itself as the cause of
another event. In chapter 2 I have done little more than explore
the consequences of this observation for the historical narrative.
Hume pointed out that we can only think of two events as causally
connected because we have watched similar events happening in
succession lots of times. In other words, his analysis showed that
we cannot rely upon the fact that two simple events are temporally successive to conclude that they are causally connected. We
have to have knowledge of a frequent connection between two
types of events and only then can we conclude that there is a
causal relationship between these two events. In the thirties of
the twentieth century, Karl Popper provided a formal description
of this analysis. He said that when we have an event, which he
called the 'initial condition', we can connect it with another event,
which he called the 'prognosis', if and only if we have a general
law to the effect that the event referred to in the initial condition
always produces the event referred to in the prognosis. For example: If John slips on ice (initial condition) and we know a sort
of general law that if people slip on hard ice they will break their
legs, we can infer from the initial condition that John broke his
leg (i.e., the prognosis).[1] Without the general law there could be
no connection between John slipping and John breaking his leg.
The two events are not strictly connected with each other in temporal sequence, but the general law enables us to see that they
hang together. The initial condition can be seen as the cause and
the prognosis, as the effect; and since the general law is the factor
that establishes this particular kind of relationship, it can con-

veniently be called a causal law. Causality, in short, depends on
the presence of a general law — needless to say, on the presence
of a true general law.[2] There is no need to distinguish for the
purpose of this analysis between laws that are *really* true (whatever that might mean) and laws that are *believed* to be true on
evidence that may often be flimsy. At any rate standards of flim-
siness and rigour vary enormously.

It is easy to see that this analysis has a direct application to
our problem. Deprived of temporal succession as the connecting
link, we are left with loose events hanging in the air. But if we
know that we can fall back on general laws, the events will not
remain loose for long. They can be connected with each other with
the help and in terms of general laws. In this sense general laws
provide the skeleton that we lost when we found that time by
itself does not provide one.

The specific application of this model, which explains how
events hang together, to history was worked out by Carl Hampel
and has since been the subject of a long debate.[3] To begin with,
the model has become known as the 'covering law model';[4] and
the initial condition has been rechristened the 'boundary condition' and in most discussions of the application of the model to
specifically historical narrative, the term 'prognosis' has been
dropped altogether. The disappearance of the term 'prognosis' is
quite justified when we talk of historical narratives. The term was
first used because Popper pointed out that when we have an initial
condition and a general law, we can infer by a process of logical
deduction what is bound to happen in the future. In history there is
no need to know in advance what is bound to happen. In science it
was right to call the inferred event a 'prognosis'. It was indeed some
kind of prediction and in the natural sciences the ability to predict is,
of course, of prime importance. But when we are dealing with
history, we presume that the events are known anyway. All we are
concerned with is to know what kind of connections can be established between them. We know that John slipped; and we know
that John broke his leg. All we want is the connection between
these two events or, if we cannot find one, a connection between
John slipping and another event. Hence for the historian, the need
for prediction is negligible, if not superfluous. Since we are dealing
with the past, we know what happened and we do not really need
to predict. Nevertheless the predictive power of the model need
not be passed over completely in discussions of its application to
historical narrative. Very often the historian has an initial event
but is not immediately in possession of the next event. Working

in archives he is confronted with a vast amount of material and it is very timesaving for him to be able to predict with the help of a general law which event or events might be thought to follow upon the initial condition. The general law enables him to know where to look for information. If he finds it, he can proceed. If he does not, he must try another general law. For this reason, the predictive power of the covering law model, though a negligible aspect as far as history is concerned, can become, at times, a great timesaver.[5]

It is obvious from the foregoing account of the covering law model, that, contrary to common belief, it is not absolutely essential to draw a clear distinction between generalisations and general laws. General laws are formally very exacting. When one is facing a general law, one is also aware of the conditions under which it would be falsified. When one is facing a mere generalisation, such as 'when people slip on ice, they will break their leg', one is not facing such a severe condition and, indeed, many generalisations are acceptable even though we know perfectly well that they do not always hold and that many people, for example, slip on ice and do *not* break their leg. What is more, many covering laws are either trivial or truisms. When one concentrates on giving explanations, both truisms and trivial laws stick in one's gills because they obviously provide little or no explanation. But if one is interested, as we are, in the ability of the covering law to bridge the gap between isolated events or to link subevents into events, a trivial law or a truism will do as well as a generalisation or a general law.[5] When one is exclusively concerned with the problem of what constitutes an explanation in the scientific sense, the distinction between general laws and mere generalisations and the avoidance of truisms becomes extremely important. But in my present argument I am interested in showing how general laws or generalisations can be used as covering laws to bridge the gap between one event and another event, or between one subevent and another subevent. Both historians and philosophers have been so exclusively concerned with the problem of explanation that they have completely overlooked the fact that, the problem of explanation apart, the covering law model plays an essential role in the construction of events out of subevents and in the assembly of events into a coherent narrative. For if one can put the slipping on ice and the breaking of the leg together into a coherent story, one obtains a narrative. Whether this narrative contains a scientifically genuine explanation or not is a matter of secondary importance. If one focusses one's attention on the power of the covering law

to construct a narrative, one will see that general laws and generalisations all perform the same function and it does therefore not
matter, for the purpose of the present argument, whether the
covering law is a genuine general law or a rashly accepted generalisation.[7]

Let us next turn to the manner in which the notion of causal
law is used here as synonymous with that of covering law. Generalisations are not causal laws in the sense in which general laws are
— not by any stretch of the imagination. And yet, I wish to say a
word in defence of the present synonymity. The whole concept of
causality has a fascinating and interesting history. Animist doctrines were replaced, over two milennia ago, by Aristotle's four
kinds of causal explanation, and in the seventeenth century
Newton's concept of force provided a new model for causality.
Then came Hume and, after Hume, Kant; and in 1912 Bertrand
Russell proclaimed in his presidential address to the Aristotelian
Society that sophisticated scientists had ceased to look for causes
in Hume's sense and that Kant's solution of Hume's problem had
therefore become unnecessary and that scientists were now only
concerned with the search for functional correlations. As is well
known, Einstein was never happy about such an abandonment of
the simple notion of cause and I believe that in contemporary
physics some explicit concept of causality is used again.[8] In the
present argument, the notion of cause is loosely present when we
speak of generalisations and when we speak of general laws.
Despite the looseness, there is good reason for this proposed usage.
Since we are concerned with the construction of narratives and
since such a construction depends on our ability to bridge the gap
between any two single events not connected by temporal contiguity, the covering law is really a thought in somebody's mind.
Insofar as it establishes, albeit in a loose sense, a connection
between the initial condition as the cause and the prognosis as the
effect (the narrative is a story that leads from cause to effect), it
is the sort of causal law that states that something is the cause of
something else when people think it is. Whether, in fact, people
are right or wrong in thinking so is an entirely different matter.
The point of importance is that in this argument the notion of
cause is somehow assimilated to the human experience of being
able to *cause* something or to *effect* something by an action. If we
speak of something as the cause of something, we mean that there
is a relation between A and B very much like the relation between
a will and an act performed to achieve what the will has in mind.
This kind of mental willing can be considered a cause and could

be considered a paradigm of causality. Since there are so many different ways of looking at causality, from Animism and Aristotle to Russell and Einstein, there is no reason why this particular paradigm should not also find its rightful place. At any rate, it is not an original one. It was first adumbrated by Vico and fully elaborated by that strangely eccentric and now almost forgotten French philosophical genius Maine de Biran, who did make somewhat unjustifiable absolutist and universal claims for it.[9] And, I would like to repeat that in this paradigm, for which no absolute claims are made and which cannot be in any way exclusive, the distinction between general laws proper and mere generalisations becomes fairly unimportant. And at any rate, the paradigm seems specially useful when one is interested, as we are, in showing how narratives are constructed. It may well be correct that it is less useful when one is exclusively interested in problems of explanation.

If mental acts of will and the expectations of the changes they are likely to bring about are the paradigm of the general laws, generalisations, and lawlike statements we use in the construction of the narrative, it is indicated that these causal laws, whatever their shape and form and whatever their explanatory capacity in a scientific sense, are thoughts about the connections between events or subevents and not descriptions of the relationships we are certain to exist in the world. I think that their thought character is the real reason why we cannot say whether they are or are not true. We can only say that they are thought to be true. Their thought character is a much more cogent reason than the obvious impossibility to verify a general law conclusively for suspending and even for disregarding a judgment about their ultimate truth.

To bring out the full range of implications of the covering law and its importance in the writing of narrative, let us consider the following example. Here is a list of eleven events presumed to have taken place at a certain moment in time and space. Any number of other events can be inserted and both the events listed and all events inserted can be infinitely broken up into subevents. Temporal sequence therefore is absent despite the chronological order and temporal sequence does not provide a link between these events or any pair of these events.

1. Napoleon gets up.
2. Napoleon brushes his teeth.
3. Napoleon feels a slight pain in his cheek.
4. Napoleon receives a message that the Austrian army is advancing.
5. Napoleon eats his breakfast.

6. Napoleon signs a marching order for his army.
7. Napoleon sees a doctor about his pain.
8. Napoleon's armies begin to move.
9. Napoleon gets dressed.
10. Napoleon presides at a meeting of his generals.
11. Napoleon rebukes one of his generals.

There is no conceivable general law that would enable us to connect all eleven events with one another in one sweep. Such a
general law would have to assert for example that 'if events 1 and
2 take place, then events 3 through 11 will follow in that order'.
But since our evidence for a general law of this nature is the single
occurrence of this sequence of events, it can hardly be said to be a
general law, whatever the precise meaning of 'general' in this context may be. But we can establish connections between sets of at
least two events by making use of a variety of general laws. If we
take the general law that if a person has a pain, he will be irritable,
we can see a connection between no. 3 and no. 11. No. 3 will be
the initial condition and no. 11 the prognosis inferred from no. 3
with the help of the general law. Since we know of no. 11 independently, there is no point in stressing the *predictive* power of
the general law and hence it is indeed a little misleading to keep
on calling it the prognosis. Nevertheless, in terms of the general
law employed, no. 3 will become the cause and no. 11, its effect.
Here, then, we have a very brief story, something like a mininarrative. The pain leads to irritability. There is change from one
state to another and, an important implication, there is intelligibility. The two events form an intelligible whole, something that
German writers on the subject are wont to call a *Sinngebild*.

A *Sinngebild* is an event plus another event plus a general law
that explains one to be the effect of the other. One event by
itself makes no sense. Two events by themselves make no sense.
But two events plus a thought like a general law do. The general
law connects the two events into a unit we can understand. The
Sinngebild is therefore the simplest intelligible constellation of
events. It consists of two events *linked* by a universal. Since we
can safely presume that Napoleon himself or an eyewitness was
aware of the possibility of this connection between nos. 3 and 11,
we can take it that whatever intelligible whole these two events
present was an intelligible whole even at the time of Napoleon.
Hence the resulting *Sinngebild*, although clearly capable of further
analysis of the kind we have presented, can in a sense be considered
to be part of the historical situation. For every historical fact, as
Maurice Mandelbaum put it, 'is given in some specific context in

which it leads to another fact'.[10] Unfortunately many writers on this subject have been misled into thinking that the *Sinngebild* is hard and fast and not itself amenable to further reduction. For this reason it is worth repeating that although there is no denying that such a *Sinngebild* is always part of the historical material and is thus presented to the historian like a *fait accompli*, there is nothing special or mysterious about it. It results from the operation and employment of general laws and more specifically from the fact that these general laws are, of course, also employed by the people who are the actors in the events in question. Hence the *Sinngebild* appears to be much more built in than it actually is. This appearance is, however, misleading: the *Sinngebild*, the basic unit of intelligibility, is by no means intractable.

Indeed it is very tractable. To see how tractable in fact it is, let us try another general law. 'If a person has a pain, he will see a doctor'. This law will establish a relationship between nos. 3 and 7. Suddenly we find, through the employment of a different law and one that by no means contradicts the first, that no. 3 is no longer linked to no. 11 but to no. 7. Here we get another rudimentary story, another mininarrative. Or try yet another general law. 'If a person wants power and is at war with his enemies, he will seek to counteract the movements of their forces with a movement of his forces'. If we use this general law, we will get a link between nos. 4, 6, 8, and 10 and obtain yet a different narrative.

The *Sinngebild* is therefore not a hard and fast concatenation of single events. It depends, on the contrary, on one's choice of general laws or on the choice of general laws made by the actors concerned. The distinction between the two kinds of choice will be explored in chapter 4. Here we will content ourselves with the discovery that the unit of intelligibility is relative to the general law employed and that the relevance of the single events to one another depends on a general law and can be altered through the employment of different general laws.

Since I have used the example of Napoleon, one can easily gain the impression that this way of explaining the construction of the historical narrative commits me to the view that history is a story that can be written only in terms of individual action and individual will, and that my account of the construction of the historical narrative implies some kind of methodological individualism or the view that processes other than individual wills cannot be taken into account and that social forces or processes and impersonal economic factors cannot be allowed to play a decisive role. The example I have used does indeed consist of events that contain or refer to individuals. But the example was chosen for the sake of simplicity and is not supposed to imply a belief in individualism and an exclusion of nonpersonal or nonindividual forces from the historical process. In reality, everything in the example I have used applies also to inanimate occurrences or to crowds; earthquakes, epidemics, the laws of supply and demand, ballistics, and so forth can all be shown to come into the narrative in exactly the same way as the individual thoughts of Napoleon and the circumstances surrounding his life on that particular day. All inanimate or institutional factors are linked to each other or to individual human beings in exactly the same way, that is, by universal laws. If nobody knows of a universal law that links population decline to epidemics, nobody can see population decline linked to epidemics. And, in that case, it is forever doubtful whether population decline is in reality linked to epidemics. There is no absolute and external or independent proof that it is, for one might just as easily suppose — as indeed has frequently been done — that it is linked to the will of God. If somebody sees victory as a divine favour, then the two events (victory and divine favour) are linked causally in his understanding, even though we today would not believe such a universal law or generalisation to be true. In any case, the ubiquity and necessity of general laws for the construction of any narrative sequence applies equally to individual acts and to impersonal forces, processes, and institutions. As Louis Mink has correctly pointed out, on R. G. Collingwood's behalf, it is much easier, when one is investigating methodological problems, to discuss briefly Caesar's crossing the Rubicon or Napoleon's breakfast than a large event such as the decline of the republic and the rise of monarchical power in ancient Rome.[11] This point is of great importance because the present argument would lose much of its relevance to the study of the past if it committed one to any kind of methodological individualism or, what would be even worse, to the belief that history is made by great or little men and by nothing else. The totality of all the things that happen in time may not be exclusively a process transcending individual actions. But no account of the construction of a historical narrative can be taken seriously if it commits one to the view that it is or that it is not. My concentration on Napoleon's breakfast and, in later chapters, on Caesar's crossing the Rubicon is entirely due to the need for simplicity and should not suggest a belief in the undue importance of either Caesar or Napoleon.

My explanation of the manner in which a historical narrative, large or small, is composed, must recall A. C. Danto's thesis that 'narrative sentences are so peculiarly related to our concept of history that analysis of them must indicate what some of the main features of that concept are'.[12] Since Danto's very similar starting point leads him to a conclusion diametrically opposed to mine,[13] it is important to discuss the different conclusions he and I draw from the observation that our knowledge of the past comes in the form of narratives. It is therefore subject to the exigencies of narrative construction and does not depend on our ability to perceive the totality of the flow of time or, as Danto calls it on page 180, on our ability to compile an 'Ideal Chronicle'.

On page 143 Danto starts, correctly it seems to me, with the observation that 'narrative sentences refer to at least two time-separated events'. This part of the analysis is true and important because it draws our attention to the fact that a narrative reports events that are not chronologically contiguous and it implies that a narrative sequence, unlike the time sequence, is not temporally continuous. But then Danto goes on to say that such sentences only *describe* the earlier event to which they refer and that the second event is something in the nature of an explanatory addition, the occurrence of which cannot be verified at the time the first event occurred. Thus he says for example on page 61 that only when the Renaissance had occurred did it become clear that Petrarch had caused or opened it by the ascent of Mount Ventoux. At the time the ascent was made, it was impossible to know that it would be the cause of the Renaissance. This is perfectly correct. But it is not correct to conclude, as Danto does, that the fact that the ascent is a cause of the Renaissance depends on knowing that the Renaissance has occurred. Of course one has to have such knowledge. But the knowledge that the ascent was a cause depends on a covering law, not on one's mere knowledge that the Renaissance occurred. If one had only such knowledge and no covering law, the occurrence of the Renaissance would still not permit us to designate the ascent as its cause.

Nobody would want to quarrel with Danto about the contention that the two parts of the narrative, the ascent and the Renaissance are time-separated and that the second part could not have been verified at the time of the ascent and that the second part determines the causal significance of the first part. But Danto is wrong in concluding from these observations that narrative sentences describe *only* the first of the two events they must contain. They also describe the second event. But — and here comes the important difference between Danto's analysis and mine — the

first event appears as the reason for or as an explanation of the
second event because somewhere there is a tacit covering law.
Danto seems to make the mistake of believing that the second
event bestows significance on the first and therefore makes the
first event appear to be its explanation without the intervention
of a covering law. The two events are time-separated; but the
reason why they hang nevertheless together is that there is a tacit
or explicit covering law. If one overlooks the operation of the
covering law and the role it plays in making time-separated events
hang together, one will easily come to the strange conclusion, as
Danto does, that the second event does not describe anything at
all at the time the first event took place — or at least that whatever it purports to describe is as yet in the future and therefore
incapable of verification as an event that has occurred. Danto,
correctly, takes out the time skeleton. But instead of replacing it
by the framework provided by covering laws, he leaves the gap
and thinks that narratives consist of at least two parts of which
only the first is a genuine description.

The truth of the matter seems to be quite different. Both parts
are descriptions of events and the reason why they stand in an
intelligible relation to each other is that the gap has been bridged
by a covering law. Danto's omission of covering laws in this context is all the more remarkable as he discusses them sympatheti-
cally and at length in his chapter 10. He appears to be captive to
the widespread belief that covering laws have exclusively something to do with explanations in social science and that they have
nothing to do with the constitution of the narrative itself. In view
of the fact that Danto sees so clearly that the narrative is not a
reproduction of the time sequence, his failure to understand that
covering laws are a substitute for the time sequence is doubly
regrettable. Danto is very much on the right track with his insight
that the significance of every event changes as new events happen
and that at no one movement can one think of an event as definitive. But he is wrong in thinking that the reason for this situation
is to be found in the fact that new events keep happening and that
these new events project a new significance on earlier events. It
is true that the occurrence of new events has something to do with
it. But the real reason why it has is that their occurrence suggests
new covering laws. The new significance of the earlier events derives from the covering laws that place them into relations with
events that were unknown at the time the first events took place.
The new events project a new significance on the earlier events

only because of covering laws. Without covering laws the occurrence of new events would make no difference to the earlier events.

Even if one leaves the question of the role of the covering laws aside, Danto's account has to be amended. He fails to distinguish between long-range narrative sentences ('Petrarch's ascent of Mount Ventoux opened the Renaissance') and short-range narrative sentences ('Caesar's foot got wet because he put it into the waters of the Rubicon'). The distinction is important because in short-range sentences the second event is known, even though it occurs later, to the actor; whereas in long-range sentences, it is not known to the actor. It follows therefore that, covering law or no covering law, in the short-range sentence situation the actor is himself capable of understanding the significance bestowed upon the first event by the second event. But in the long-range sentence situation the actor is obviously unable to do so and one has to wait for a historian. Danto's observation that only the first part of the narrative sentence *describes* an event applies, therefore, only to long-range sentences. In short-range sentences both parts are descriptive as far as the agent himself is concerned and the resulting *Sinngebild* appears to the agent. In the long-range situation any *Sinngebild* is due to a historian. The distinction, though not absolute, is important in view of the distinction to be made in chapter 4 between explanation and interpretation.

Naturally there are a number of difficulties in the covering law model. To begin with we must note that the model makes nonsense of the time-honoured distinction between the natural sciences and the historical sciences. It used to be said that the general sciences are concerned with general laws and the historical sciences with particular events. The natural sciences were therefore called nomothetic and the historical sciences, idiographic.[14] But we now see that the historical narrative depends on the links between particular events; that these links are not provided by mere temporal succession; that we need general laws to establish links; and that the links that can be established are relative to the general laws employed. Thus the old distinction breaks down. Historical knowledge, insofar as it is embodied in narratives, is completely dependent on general laws even though these general laws are used to establish links between known particular events rather than to make predictions about events that have not yet occurred. At most, one can say that there is a difference of emphasis between the natural and the historical sciences. The former use general laws mainly for prediction and the latter use them mainly to link

known events. But the difference in emphasis does not amount to
a difference in form.

There is, however, another aspect to the matter. In the historical sciences, general laws employed are frequently of a very trivial
kind. They are often so trivial that it would be absurd to mention
them explicitly. For instance, the historian often uses a general
law to the effect that if someone raises his hat, he means to greet
somebody. This general law is tacitly understood and we are all so
familiar with it that any explicit mention would make it look
ridiculous. This circumstance, must, however, not make us blind
to the fact that even such a trivial general law plays its formal part
in the establishment of a *Sinngebild*. For that matter, though
trivial to us, the law is far from trivial in societies where people do
not raise their hats. This example leads us to the next point. Not
all people wear hats and not all people who wear hats raise them as
a sign of greeting. The habit is very Western and specifically confined to male persons. If we use the general law that people who
raise hats mean to greet somebody, we are clearly not using a law
that is genuinely general.

In the natural sciences, on the other hand, general laws are
always explicitly mentioned and are never of a purely trivial
nature. They are considered to be genuinely general and are held
to have unlimited universality. Now here is a real difference between the natural and the historical sciences. Both sciences make
use of general laws and they cannot be distinguished from one
another because one does and the other does not. But the natural
sciences use general laws that are considered universal in an unlimited sense;[15] whereas the historical sciences use general laws
that are by no means universal. On the contrary, the historical
sciences not only use general laws that are often trivial, but they
also use general laws that are not genuinely general. The generality
of laws used by the historical sciences is strictly limited to a certain period. In other words, many of the general laws used are of
limited universality.[16]

Next comes the question of truth. Clearly, general laws that
are not true cannot be used to establish links between events. How
do we establish the truth of general laws? Broadly, the procedure
in the natural sciences is similar to the procedure in the historical
sciences. A general law is true if we can find lots and lots of cases
where the initial condition and the prognosis are linked together.
The general law that pain makes people irritable is true if we find
that lots of people who are in pain are irritable. This is, of course, a
very rough way of putting it because it sounds as if we established

the truth of general laws by induction. In strict logic, the truth of
a general law cannot be established by induction because no matter
how many instances of a link between pain and irritability we have
observed, we are not entitled to conclude that the link will hold
good tomorrow. A general law can therefore be said to be, at best,
provisionally true. And, more precisely, it is provisionally true as
long as it has not been falsified. But for the sake of the discussion,
I will bypass this more correct way of stating the case for the
truth of general laws and continue the more colloquial way of
speaking about the matter. We say then that the truth of the law
depends on the frequency with which we have observed the link
between the two events in question. But here we get a circularity
problem. First we know that there is no link between the two
events without a general law. Next we know that the general law
likely to be able to establish such a link has to be true. And finally
we see that the truth of the general law capable of establishing the
link depends on our prior observation of the frequency of the
occurrence of the link.

There is a vast literature devoted to the problem and the
manner in which natural scientists deal with it.[17] I am afraid that
historians must remain content with the knowledge that the problem is incapable of resolution as far as they are concerned. The
circularity is inevitable. The historian's narration links events in
a causal sequence because the historian makes use of certain general
laws, and he is convinced of the truth of these general laws because
he sees that the links between the events in his narration are not
singular but have occurred frequently.[18]

If there is no logical solution to this circularity, there is, for
the historian, a practical one. As the historian examines and sifts
documents and records, he will come across not only evidence that
allows him to establish that certain events took place, but also
evidence of general laws. Every chronicle he peruses and every
charter he examines, either tacitly or explicitly, provides him with
general laws in the truth of which the people he is dealing with
used to believe. They may be laws that are no longer valid, such
as that masturbation causes insanity; or laws in the truth of which
he himself no longer believes, such as that catatonic schizophrenia
is caused by satanic possession or that certain commands are
transmitted by angels. But that does not matter. What matters is
that the historical material he is dealing with is full of general laws
and that he can use these general laws to establish links between
single events. In other words, since the general laws he is using are
not of unlimited universality but of limited universality, there is

no obligation on the historian to confine himself to those general
laws he himself would employ. On the contrary: general laws are
ready made for him and he need therefore not become involved
in the hopeless tangle of the circular problem described above. The
historian as historian is not really concerned with the truth of
these general laws. All he wants to know is whether people believed
them to be true. In this sense there is an important difference
between writing history and the examination of the truth of general
laws.

The natural sciences and the historical narrative differ, moreover, very profoundly in the use they make of general laws. In the
natural sciences, the whole emphasis is on the general law. The
natural scientist is foremost confronted by an effect, that is, the
prognosis. He then tries to formulate a general law, of which the
prognosis is a particular instance, and an initial condition, which is
another particular instance of the general law. With the help of the
general law he can then establish the initial condition as the cause
and the prognosis as the effect. The initial condition is the *ex-
planans* and the prognosis the *explanandum.* Finally, to test the
validity of the general law he deduces, with the help of the general
law, the prognosis from the initial condition and if the prognosis
turns out to be the case, he will take the general law to be a good
hypothesis. If the prognosis turns out to have been false, a further
question arises. How long will he be permitted to search for an
event to make it true and how far afield may he go? It is only in
rare cases that a conclusive falsification can be produced. The more
usual situation is that the events predicted in the prognosis cannot
be found. But if the prognosis is actually falsified the general law
must be taken to be false too.

For the historian the situation is entirely different. The historian does not formulate the general law to explain the prognosis.
Nor is he interested in testing the general law by deducing a prognosis from it with the help of the initial condition. On the contrary,
the historian usually confronts an initial condition and a variety of
events, further down the chronological scale, which could be
linked to the initial condition. The potential prognosis, in other
words, is well known to him long before he concentrates on the
general law. He will turn to the general law to establish a link between the two events in question and thus make use of the general
law as if it were some sort of tool to select the second event. He is
not primarily interested in the discovery of general laws at all. The
logical scheme of his reasoning is identical with that of the natural
scientist. But he puts his emphasis in a different place. The general

law is used as an instrument. It is not, as in the case of the natural sciences, the ultimate purpose of the exercise.

For this reason the historian's use of the general law is very much more limited in scope than the natural scientist's. The latter is really interested only and exclusively in the truth of his general laws. The historian, since he is interested in linking particular events rather than in establishing the truth of general laws, is prepared to make use of general laws whether they are universally valid or not. And indeed he is often prepared to make use of general laws that he knows to be false in the light of his own knowledge but that he has good reason to believe to have been acceptable to the people he is investigating. Of this more in chapter 4. For the time being we must note this fact and understand how it helps to differentiate the historian's use of the general law from the natural scientist's use.

Whatever the difference, the logical model of reasoning is identical and ubiquitous. It is therefore very surprising to find that the ubiquity of the method and particularly of its presence in the composition of the historical narrative has been stubbornly and repeatedly denied. The first detailed criticism of the covering law was put forward by W. Dray in his book entitled *Laws and Explanation in History.*[19] It seems to amount to this. Dray, significantly, chooses an example not from history but from motorcars. He supposes that his engine seized up and that he is looking for an event that hangs together with this event. The covering law theory would suggest that one find a universal law, such as 'when there is a leak in the oil reservoir, the engine will seize up'. If one then discovers that the oil had indeed leaked from the reservoir, this event would then hang together with the seizing up of the engine. But Dray points out, rightly, that the seizure of the engine hangs together with the leak of oil only via a lot of other single events, such as that the pistons will not move when the cylinder walls are dry and so forth. He concludes from this that the covering law that was invoked first is superfluous, because what really makes him understand the seizure of the engine is the series of single events by which it had come about. He thinks (page 66ff.), if I understand him correctly, that the series of single events leading to the seizure is a *substitute* for the covering law. But this does not seem to be true. For what he calls the series of single events leading up to the seizure is known to him only through the functioning of other general laws. Without other general laws, he would never get such a series and I cannot agree with him, therefore, that the series is a substitute for the covering law. If there were no general laws at all, he would be faced by a mollusclike collection of single events and by nothing else. His having a series of steps leading to the seizure of the engine depends on his having a skeleton; and this skeleton must be a covering law or a set of covering laws. Let us consider his series:

1. A leak appears in reservoir.
2. Oil runs out of reservoir.
3. No oil gets into the cylinders.
4. The cylinder walls are dry.
5. The pistons do not move.
6. The engine seizes up.

The first covering law used establishes a connection between nos. 1 and 6. Now Dray observed rightly that this general law is very vague and that one gets a much better series if one takes in nos. 2, 3, 4, and 5. But unfortunately he forgets that nos. 2, 3, 4, and 5 make a series only because we can invoke other laws that establish the connection between them. The series 2, 3, 4, and 5 by itself is therefore no substitute for covering laws in general but presupposes several general laws that, taken together, are an alternative to the first vague general covering law.

In justice to Dray, it seems that what he is saying is this. To account for the breakdown of an engine we need lots of little and special general laws. If we have only one large, all-embracing law it would be too general to be meaningful and would amount indeed to something little more informative than the generalisation, used above, that people who slip on ice tend to break their leg. In this case it would come to something like this: 'Engines break down if they are neglected'. Dray, exclusively interested in the explanatory power of covering laws, is justified in his scepticism of the explanatory power of these wide and vague generalisations. But we have seen that such scepticism is unnecessary when one is interested in the potential for narrative construction rather than in the potential for explanation. On the other hand, he goes on, if we have too many little, special general laws, they cease to be 'general' and, if we have one for every specific transition from event to event, they are not general laws at all and therefore cease to have explanatory power. Dray, one concludes, would like to maintain that the employment of general laws is either redundant (i.e., they are too general) or false (i.e., they are not general enough). But such an objection to the covering law model tries to turn a mere matter of degree into a serious argument. There is force to the objection if one is interested in explanation. But the objection becomes

spurious when one is interested in the potential of the covering
law model for narrative construction.

Dray is a philosopher and his book has not been widely used
by historians. But quite recently J. H. Hexter, a well-known historian, has added the weight of his authority to the contention
that the role of general laws in historical narratives is negligible.
His book *The History Primer*[20] is certain to be widely read by
historians and will become influential. His argument, therefore,
deserves careful study.

In chapter 1, entitled 'The Case of the Muddy Pants', Hexter,
with less excuse than Dray, uses again an example not taken from
history. He points out that when Willie is asked by his father why
he came home with muddy pants, there are three types of answer
open to him. He can, first, explain that one gets covered with mud
when a muddy area is entered at relatively high velocity by a per-
pendicular rigid or semirigid object, long in proportion to its base
at the point of contact. Since mud is a lubricant, the base will
accelerate more rapidly than the entry speed of the object and
consequently the centre of gravity of the object will move in a
downward and backward arc. Hence the fall and the mud on the
pants. There is no need to go into further details. The point is
clear. Willie can give an answer in terms of a general law culled
from physics to link the mud on his pants with his fall. Hexter
rightly offers this sort of explanation as an example of the employment of a general law. He then adds that there are two other
types of explanation open to Willie. Willie can simply say: 'I
slipped and fell in a mud puddle. O.K.?' And, third, he can say
that he was late coming home from school and to make up for
lost time, he took a shortcut through a field where he was chased
by rough boys. To get away from them, he ran and since there
had been recent rain, there were mud puddles in the field. He
skidded, fell, and was covered by mud.

Now Hexter argues that the first explanation in terms of a
general law or laws taken from physics is not an explanation at all
because although undoubtedly a true account of what happened,
it does not provide an answer why Willie on that particular day
should be covered with mud. The second answer, Hexter admits,
is too laconic and leaves out everything one would like to know.
The third answer he finds satisfactory. So far, we have no quarrel
with Hexter. But then comes his peculiar comment. He maintains
that only the first answer is an answer that makes use of a general
law. The second answer, he says, must be amended. The third
answer, he invites us to believe, is a narrative not dependent on

general laws. He finally says that when the second answer is to be amended, it must be amended in the sense of the third answer, not in the sense of the first answer. Obviously he feels, and one must agree with him, that the third answer really provides the sort of story one wants to hear about the muddy pants. Whereas the first answer is neither here nor there. Hexter thus thinks he has shown that the covering law model is by no means essential to the construction of a historical narrative.

It would seem that Hexter has made a simple but unpardonable mistake. He assumes that covering laws are always laws of physics or possibly chemistry. But this is not so. The mistake is intelligible because the laws of physics and chemistry are more obviously universal than those employed by historians; and, moreover, the latter are often so trivial as to remain difficult to detect. It requires a certain amount of logical formality to detect the ubiquity of laws that are not genuinely universal and fairly trivial. One needs a little formal analysis of the narrative of the third answer to find that that narrative depends every inch as much on general laws as the first answer. The laws, in this third case, however, are not laws of physics. They are laws of everyday life and conventional psychology. They are general laws nonetheless; and if they were not tacitly understood, Hexter's narrative about the boy coming late from school, taking a shortcut, being chased by boys, and falling into mud puddles left by heavy rain of the previous day would not make any sense at all.

Take a closer look. The first two events in the narrative concern staying late at school and being in a hurry to get home. Hexter takes it for granted that they are irretrievably 'linked' simply because they do not require us to invoke a law of physics to explain them. Superficially we can indeed explain the hurry by doing no more than to refer to staying late at school. But the fact that they do not require a physical law is beside the point. They still require some kind of general law. On the face of it and considered in isolation, there is no reason why we should link them and say that Willie was in a hurry to get home because he was kept late. On the contrary, there is a general law, perhaps not of unlimited validity but certainly valid in the society of which Willie and his parents are part, that children are expected home within a reasonable time after the end of school. This law may be trivial, it may be tacit, and it may not apply to social situations in which there are working-class parents and in which the child has a key to his home and is accustomed to let himself in because his parents are not likely to be home until much later. But in certain parts of the world and among certain social classes, to wit the American middle classes, this is a general law nonetheless. And it is because of this law that the first two events related in the narrative are understood to make sense and to be relevant to each other. And so it goes on. Take the tacit and often trivial general laws away, and the third answer provided by Willie would be nonsensical. And, for that matter, even in this third answer there are two events, the skidding and the being covered in mud, which, to hang together, require us to invoke a physical law about mud as a lubricant, and acceleration, and the changing centre of gravity, and so on. Without that law, one could not possibly understand why, when Willie skidded, he got covered with mud. Indeed, without that law (as people ignorant of it might genuinely conclude), when Willie skids he simply accelerates his progress and thus makes up for lost time. This law, though clearly a law of physics, is so well known and so generally accepted that it needs no spelling out. Hexter is therefore able to link two events at the very end of his narrative without noticing that he has employed yet another general law. Hexter's whole argument depends therefore on his suppression of the general laws he uses. He is able to suppress them because at first sight the laws in question are so trivial that they are tacitly understood. But once we become aware of them, we see that they are present and that without them, the third narrative would be incomprehensible. Once we have understood this, we see that the sole difference between Muddy Pants I and Muddy Pants III is a difference in the kind of general laws employed. In the first case they are general laws of a physical and scientific nature. In the third case they are mostly trivial, partly social and partly psychological, and only in one or two instances physical. But there is no difference in the logic of the explanation that pervades Muddy Pants I and Muddy Pants III.

Much of the disagreement about the covering law model stems from a problem of terminology. First of all there is the implicit assumption that since the general laws are claimed to be essential to *historical* narratives they must themselves be 'historical' laws. Naturally, it has been difficult to find any general laws that are in a specific sense 'historical'. The second law of thermodynamics, for example, is specifically a physical law and we all know what is meant when we describe it as such. But one could not possibly think what one would mean by claiming that a certain law is historical when the subject of historical study is everything that has happened in the past and how one thing changed into something else. Since history deals with politics and fashions, with food

and economics, with furniture and social classes, everything can be
termed 'historical' — or better, nothing should be termed 'historical'. The word 'historical' refers to a mode of treatment, not to a
quality of substance. It is therefore wrong to reject the covering
law model on the ground that it is impractical because there are no
specially 'historical' laws that can be used to employ it. The laws
employed by the model are ordinary laws. Many are trivial, some
are taken from physics, others from sociology or economics, some
from religion or psychology, and a great many from the vast field
of superstition. But general laws of some sort are essential. Throughout *The History Primer*, Hexter writes on the assumption that as
long as a general law is trivial, it is not necessary. Nothing could
be further from the truth.

      Another terminological habit has encouraged an even more
deep-seated opposition to the covering law model. Many philosophers have got into the habit of referring to it as the 'Covering
Law Model of Historical Explanation'. This is indeed the precise
title by which it has become known. This usage indicates that the
covering law model is specifically concerned with explanations of
a historical kind or with explanations in history. Philosophers
therefore think that the title indicates that the advocates of the
model believe that all explanations ought to be historical.[21] They
therefore often criticise and attack the model because they can
think of other ways of explaining things. The real trouble here is
a terminological one. If one calls the model the Covering Law
Model of *Historical* Explanation, one will be inclined to think
that the explanations referred are explanations in *history*. If one
refers to the model as the Covering Law Model of Historical
Explanation, one will be inclined to think that the model refers
to cases where history is explained rather than narrated or described. In fact, the model is simply a model of explanation and
it does not matter whether the explanations are explanations in
history or explanations of a historical nature or of a nonhistorical
nature. But above all, the model not only shows us what would
count as an explanation. It shows us — and this is much more important for the present purpose than anything else it might show
— how single events can be made to hang together and form a
mininarrative and how mininarratives can be linked into proper
narratives. For that matter, it also shows us what we mean when
we speak of an event. We mean, when we speak of an event, the
assembly of two smaller events or of two particle-events into an
event with the help of a general law. However, there is a good
reason why we should continue to refer to it as the Covering Law

Model of Historical Explanation. In performing the service of constituting events and of enabling us to link events into narratives, general laws or covering laws also provide intelligibility. Since the particle-events and the mininarratives are not linked arbitrarily but are linked by virtue of a general law that is believed to be true, the link becomes meaningful and thus the event and the narrative become intelligible. In this sense, linkages of this kind constitute explanations and for this reason the full title of the model is justified.

The concentration on the alleged explanatory power of the model has led to countless other difficulties and objections and it has to be admitted that these difficulties often derive not only from the terminology but also from the fact that the model was first proposed by Popper with a view to the natural sciences and, therefore, to the model's explanatory potential. Thus there has arisen a long debate as to whether the model is supposed to be prescriptive or descriptive. P. Gardiner,[22] Popper, and Hempel usually take the view that it is prescriptive and that it is a standard of explanation scientists and historians ought to aim at. It is irrelevant here whether natural scientists can or ought to aim at formulating their explanations in terms of the model or not. Historians certainly do not always do so and their 'explanations' are nonetheless satisfying or, if they are not, they fail to satisfy often for different reasons. Both Dray and Donagan[23] have been quick to seize this point and have argued that they do not wish to prescribe to historians how explanations in history ought to be formulated but that they merely wish to describe what historians are actually doing. In their descriptions they include, therefore, explanations used satisfactorily by historians that do not conform to the model at all.

Another problem that has arisen from the concentration on the explanatory potential of the model is the question of whether the covering law model provides necessary or sufficient explanations. One can easily see that the covering law, especially when it is supposed to be a general law in the strict, scientific sense, provides a necessary condition for the event to be explained by the initial condition.[24] But it is well known that when we have a historical narrative we are often very satisfied with a sufficient reason. Now sufficient reasons are precisely the sort of reasons supplied when the covering law is a mere generalisation or even a truism. But if one sticks to the view that the covering law must be a strict general law, one commits oneself to the view that the reasons offered in historical narrative are necessary conditions. In other words, one commits oneself to too much and precisely to something that is not required. Only when one recognises that the main usefulness of the covering law is that it makes the construction of narrative and the assembly of subevents into events possible can one see that the debate whether the covering law demands too much of the historian is superfluous. When one concentrates on the importance of the model for the narrative, the whole question as to whether the covering law provides sufficient or necessary *explanations*, or both or neither, becomes very secondary.

One of the chief criticisms and reasons for the rejection of the covering law model is that it is supposed to make narration impossible. 'Narrative coherence between episodes', Haskell Faine writes, 'depends, at bottom, upon showing how one episode leads to another', and he goes on to state that since narration consists in showing up the genetic connection between the separate events in the narrative, positivists who use the covering law model have failed to do justice to narration.[25] Faine is by no means alone in the view that the employment of the covering law prevents narration.[26] The irony of the situation is that the covering law model is the factor that alone makes narration possible. Without the covering law we would never obtain a mininarrative, let alone a proper narrative. Again, terminology and the propounders of the covering law model themselves are responsible for this misunderstanding. The model was first proposed as a paradigm of explanation. The possibility of narration and the dependence of every mininarrative or particle-narrative on the model was not even mentioned. For this reason many philosophers have thought that, since historians are primarily interested in narration, the covering law model is useless and some have even gone so far as to say that it actually prevents narration. They mean by narration a sequence of events that stand in a genetic or cause and effect relation to one another. They forget that there can be no such genetic relationship without the covering law. The great opposition between philosophers alleged to be positivists because they uphold the covering law model and the philosophers proclaimed to be interested in history and story telling turns out to be a nondebate. There is no conflict between the covering law model and narration. The conflict appeared real as long as the model was believed to provide a paradigm of explanation. It ceases to be real as soon as one understands that the elementary consequence of the employment of the model is the creation of a mininarrative. The model, far from preventing the creation of narrative, makes it possible.

A further difficulty is created by the fact that Popper based his original presentation of the model on his concern with natural science and on the model's potential for scientific explanation.[27] This concern for explanation limited his interest in the descriptive qualities of the model to a demonstration that explanation and a certain kind of description are very similar. But this is where he stopped. He never probed the application of the model, as is done here, to the problem of the historical *narrative*. The argument of this chapter is that whatever the explanatory value of the model, its main importance for the historian consists in its ability to explain the existence of historical narratives in face of the fact that mere temporal sequence does not. The model, that is, the linking of an initial condition to a prognosis, whatever explanatory value it has, makes possible a minimum narrative by connecting two events and this is the sense in which it is of fundamental importance to the historian. For the historian its explanatory potential is secondary, though important; and its predictive power, though pragmatically valuable (as I hope to show in chapter 7), superfluous.

EXPLANATION AND INTERPRETATION

So far we have concentrated on the composition of the historical narrative. We have been interested in the establishment of cause-effect chains and of how events are seen to hang together. The narrative is the most suitable literary form to do justice to one's knowledge of how one event leads to another. Since the narrative consists of interlocking and interweaving cause-effect chains, it contains explanations why things happen and how they happen. The historian's story, provided it is well told, is a story of explanations. Nevertheless, it is necessary now to take a closer look at the explanatory power that is built into every historical narrative.

At the outset we can blandly claim that the explanatory power of the narrative depends on and is due to the general laws that underlie, tacitly or explicitly, the historical series. The general laws create the cause-effect chains and the causes are the explanations of the effects. In this manner every narrative provides explanations by the mere fact that it is a narrative of events that hang together. The explanatory power is derivative and can be taken for granted. But it poses nevertheless a number of problems and invites a number of important distinctions.

For many years historians used to wrestle with a problem that they called the problem of historism. The historians who first woke up to the fact that it is a problem were Germans and they called it the problem of *Historismus*.[1] The word had been carelessly translated into English as both historicism and historism. Since 'historicism' has been given a specific meaning by Karl Popper, who used it to describe the doctrine that there are developmental laws in history and since this doctrine has come under very heavy attack by him,[2] it is better to agree to refer to the problem I have in mind as the problem of historism and reserve the word 'historicism' for the doctrine rejected by Popper. The problem of historism arises when one reflects that any event in an historical narrative is *sui generis*. It is a particular event that stares the historian in the face. It is something that is presented to the historian's attention. Any attempt to reduce it or subsume it under a general law, it is argued, fails to do justice to its uniqueness. *Individuum est ineffabile:* the individual as such cannot be explained. Any explanation must detract from its individuality. The historian can therefore, at best, only describe. He cannot explain. For a long time it seemed as if the problem of historism was insoluble. It forced historians to content themselves with mere description and would not allow the possibility of explanation.

Consider, for example, the case of the bishopric of Osnabrück where after the 1648 Peace of Westphalia and throughout the eighteenth century a Catholic bishop was succeeded by a Lutheran bishop and a Lutheran by a Catholic. The arrangement seemed, in terms of cold reason, nonsensical. Either, so reason dictated, the doctrine of *cuius regio, eius religio* should be maintained or the matter ought to be decided once and for all by the standards of which was the true religion. But in defiance of such cold reasoning, the compromise was a *modus vivendi.* Rationalism, it was argued, could not provide an explanation. One had to understand the arrangement in terms of historism as an organic growth determined by its own inner and uniquely individual law. The historian, therefore, has to employ historism if he wishes to understand.

This recommendation calls for a number of comments. First of all, one could easily suggest that there is a third dictate of reason, even more rational than the preceding two. This third dictate lays down that when people and opinions are divided, it is best to compromise and the arrangement by which there was an alteration of confessions was a rational compromise. This explanation should have appealed even more to the dyed-in-the-wool rationalist than the other two. The conclusion is that it is by no means necessary to fall back on historism to understand the history of the bishopric of Osnabrück in the eighteenth century.

Next we can see how an insistence on the unique individuality of the situation in that bishopric can lead from historism to historicism. One begins by looking at the chain of events as something that cannot be explained rationally. As an alternative, one looks at that chain as an organic development and contrasts such organic development or growth to an arrangement capable of rational explanation. One ends up by looking for the organic law of growth that determines the chain of events allegedly incapable of rational explanation. In this way historism usually leads, sooner or later, to historicism. The connection is not a necessary one; but in practice it is difficult to avoid. We will return to the historicist implications of historism and to the problem of developmental laws later. For the moment, we will confine our attention to historism proper.

Closer examination, however, shows that historism is a non-issue. Let us consider an example. At the Congress of Vienna, Metternich asserted the principle of legitimacy. This is a unique and particular event. There is something absolutely individual at its very core. We can turn and twist and provide definitions of the idea of legitimacy; we can relate it to our own experience of illegitimacy. We can try to understand it negatively by contrasting it to our own belief that legitimacy is neither a sound nor an important principle of political organisation and so forth. But no matter what we do, Metternich's assertion of the principle of legitimacy will always escape us. If *individuum est ineffabile*, historical understanding is concerned with individuals in their historical individuality and uniqueness; and therefore historical understanding is a sort of a nonunderstanding. It is more a resignation in the face of the particular uniqueness of events.[3]

There is, however, one circumstance that renders this approach pointless and that raises our hope in face of historism's intellectual pessimism. Granted that Metternich's assertion was absolutely unique, we must also grant that Metternich was a thoughtful man or a thinking human being. We can therefore assume that he tried to understand what he was doing or asserting. We may not know precisely what he was thinking about his assertion. But we may presume that he was thinking something or that, which is not quite the same thing, he could have thought something if he had tried. In other words, although Metternich's assertion of the principle of legitimacy stands as a unique fact, we also know that he tried or could have tried to understand it and to explain it to himself. This means that somewhere at the back of his mind there must have been a general law, tacit or explicit, in terms of which he connected the principle of legitimacy to another event and that his assertion of the principle together with that general law and the other event made some kind of explanation. Since Metternich was given to thinking, we may safely infer that somewhere there must have been a general law of which he knew and which helped him to understand his assertion of the principle of legitimacy. Historism is, therefore, not the formidable problem it used to be taken to be. At least insofar as the events the historian is dealing with are events that concern human beings, we can assume that no matter how unique these events were, the human beings involved with them tried to understand them even as the modern historian does. And therefore we can assume that some kind of explanation of these events is to be found at the very source of these events. If we can seize the general law or laws used by Metternich, for instance, we can repeat the thought processes that accompanied his assertion of the principle of legitimacy and we can try to understand him just as he tried to understand himself. The historian is therefore not condemned to mere description, and the problem of historism is by no means unsurmountable. The reason why it is surmountable is not that we deny that there was something individually unique at the heart of Metternich's assertion of the principle of legitimacy but that we know that he must have sought to understand his assertion in one way or another. He had to make sense of it. The assertion was a meaningful unit of intelligibility to him, a *Sinngebild*. The historian's task, therefore, is to recapture this *Sinngebild* and to understand Metternich as he understood himself.

R. G. Collingwood, both philosopher and historian, was more aware of this situation than any other writer. Unfortunately he saddled us with a terminology that has proved misleading and unacceptable to many people.[4] Collingwood pointed out that since we must understand Metternich as he tried to understand himself, we have to recapture his own *Sinngebild*. He said that we must 'enter into Metternich's mind' by reenacting Metternich's thoughts in our own minds.[5] No practising historian would deny that there is a strong intuitive element in all historical discovery as there is indeed in all scientific discovery. But if we could not reach beyond this purely intuitive element and if the historian would have to remain confined to acts of empathy, historical understanding would remain allusive and idiosyncratic. I do not even mean to deny that there will always remain something allusive and idiosyncratic in our knowledge of history and of other people's minds in general. But there is, at the same time, a strong element of rational intellection that is capable of being tested and of confirmation and that can be communicated to other historians and to the readers of narratives without an irreducible appeal to empathy and intuition. Collingwood, in other words, did not do full justice to himself. I think that his failure to do justice to himself and the many misconceptions of his term 'reenactment' stem from his neglect of formal analysis. Had he subjected the concept of reenactment to a formal analysis, he would have discovered that our ability to reenact anything that went on in Metternich's mind was due to the fact that both we and Metternich use universals of some kind or other and that our ability to reenact is therefore derived from a mental habit we share with Metternich and takes place *via* the universals he and we employ. Collingwood also did another injustice to himself. He wanted to show that the conventional positivistic or realistic way of looking at history as a record of the succession of events in time was a mistake. To do so he argued that the historian does not simply record but he also reenacts. Through his failure to provide a formal analysis of the meaning of such reenactment, he needlessly weakened his own case.

Collingwood aimed to explain that historism was not the impasse it was proclaimed to be. He wanted to show how we can understand even though the events we want to understand are unique. To avoid our exchanging the impasse of historism for the impasse of empathy or reenactment, we only have to amend Collingwood's terminology and fall back upon the presence of general laws. As long as we keep reminding ourselves that general laws not only are employed by modern historians to make single events hang together but must also have been present in the minds of the people who were concerned in these events, we have a perfectly rational method of explaining historical understanding without making use of empathy. I think that what Collingwood really meant was to say that we can understand Metternich, for example, as long as we can get to the general law or laws that Metternich knew and employed to understand himself. If we put it in this way, we can use the notion of reenactment without fearing that it might be clouded by the notion of empathy or confused with intuition. The effort to find the general laws Metternich knew is a perfectly rational task of historical research. We can find out what books he read, who his teachers were, how he reacted to them, what social background he came from, and so forth. In this way we can form a fairly precise picture of the general laws and ideas he knew and held to be true. Thus we can 'enter into his mind' without an act of empathy. We can reconstruct his thought processes without resorting to intuition. We can concentrate on the general laws he knew and thus understand how, in Metternich's own mind, the assertion of the principle of legitimacy hung together with other events. The only thing that suggests that the historian in the last instance must fall back upon irrational empathy is Collingwood's use of the word 'reenactment' and its associations. Our analysis clearly shows that the process is far more intellectual and rational than Collingwood led us to believe.

Collingwood's insistence on reenactment was naturally taken to be an argument in favour of the view that history is basically an art.[6] I do not think that the debate whether history is an art or a science is of any importance. Above all, I do not wish to suggest that the historian does not need at every moment and every step an artist's sense of judgment and of fitness and even an artistic power of intuition. I do not even think that the pursuit of science is wholly unartistic and I know that there are many forms of art that require a high level of intellectual planning and discrimination. The debate as to whether history is art or science is therefore a purely semantic one. Insofar as history is art it is difficult to think critically and philosophically about it and insofar as we are here thinking critically and philosophically about it, we are really trying to deal with that area and those aspects of history that are capable of rational method. We have already indicated in chapter 3 that there is an important difference in the uses to which natural scientists and historians put the general laws they employ. If that difference makes history an art, well and good. If the likeness between science and history makes the latter a science, also well and good. The only thing that matters is that we should know that there are many forms of both scientific and artistic pursuits. If we here stress the purely intellectual and rational aspects of historical research, this lies more in the nature of our approach and aim than in the substance of historical research. The demonstration that Collingwood's reenactment does not have the irrational associations it conjures up in the minds of many readers should not be interpreted as a demonstration that history is a science rather than an art.

Having cleared the air in regard to both historism and empathy, we are left with the insight that historical understanding consists essentially in the employment of the same general laws that were employed by the people the historian is studying. We can say that we understand Metternich when we understand him as he understood himself. Such understanding is made possible by the fact that we assume that all human beings are capable of reasoning by relating particular events to general laws and that is indeed the most universal way in which human beings understand themselves. The historian merely recapitulates when he uncovers the general laws that were used by Metternich. If the historian wants to find out 'what really happened', he has to find not only that Metternich asserted the principle of legitimacy but also how Metternich understood his assertion and how he explained it to himself. The general laws used by Metternich are therefore part of what actually happened and the description of these general laws provides an explanation of Metternich's actions.[7]

Since we can and must assume that general laws were made use of in the past as much as in the present, we can also assume that there is an operational affinity between the mind of the historian and the mind of the people he is studying. Collingwood, following Croce, always maintained that it is necessary to use empathy and to reenact the experiences people had in the past. Without such reenactment, he said, the historian cannot understand.[8] With this way of putting it there creeps in a subjective and intuitionist factor. But there is a different way of putting it. We can say that we can understand the people of the past because we can gain access to their minds when we use the same general laws that they used or could have used when they explained themselves to themselves. In this formulation of the procedure there is no stress on empathy, reenactment , and intuition. There is a simple recognition of the basic mental structure of all minds. The difference between the modern historian and the person of the past is in the content of the general laws they use, not in the fact that they use general laws. If the historian knows what the general laws used by the person in the past were, he can gain access to his mind *without* falling back upon empathy. Alternately, we might say that such access is precisely what we mean by empathy. Either way, there is nothing irrational, mysterious, or mystical in the procedure. Admittedly, the method does not give us access to every nuance of feeling but only to the more rational ways in which people explained themselves to themselves. Their subtlest subjective feelings escape us even as our own subtlest, purely deep subjective feelings often enough escape us. But we can assess and repeat their own rational assessment of the situation in which they found themselves provided we can gauge the general laws they used. We do not know how they felt themselves to be, but we can reconstruct their thought processes. Given the role that general laws play in all historical understanding, the gap between Popper's rationalism and Collingwood's intuitionism is narrow.[9] For Collingwood, Popper says

> analysis of the situation serves merely as a help — an indispensable help — for this reenactment. My view is diametrically opposed. I regard the psychological process of reenactment as inessential, though I admit that it may sometimes serve as a help for the historian, a kind of intuitive check of the success of his situational analysis. *What I regard as essential is not the reenactment but the situational analysis.* The historian's analysis of the situation is his historical conjecture which in this case is a metatheory about the emperor's reasoning. Being on a level different from the

emperor's reasoning, it does not reenact it, but tries to produce an idealised and reasoned reconstruction of it. . . . Thus the historian's central metaproblem is: what were the decisive elements in the emperor's problem situation? To the extent to which the historian succeeds in solving this metaproblem, he understands the historical situation.[10]

As we shall soon see there is more to the problem of understanding than Popper allows because one must always distinguish between an understanding in terms of the general laws available to the person we wish to understand and understanding in terms of general laws available to the person who wishes to understand. For the time being, however, it is important to note that Popper's formulation reduces the differences between intuition and rational reconstruction to a matter of emphasis.[11] Both Popper and Collingwood agree that history is the history of thought and that the thought is the different general laws thought by the people the historian is studying. Popper's situational analysis is devoid of intuitive elements and eliminates the necessity of psychological identification with the people to be studied. But it is compatible with Collingwood's reenactment and may indeed be very close to what Collingwood really meant. Both Popper and Collingwood agree that such basic detective work as there is is completed only when we have found out what the people in question thought; that is, we must find the general laws they used to explain themselves to themselves.

The question of explanation in the historical narrative has been bedevilled by a misunderstanding. It is no exaggeration to say that the whole recent literature on the subject is exclusively concerned with a problem that I would consider to be the least important problem.[12] It is concerned with the examination of when and under what circumstances explanations explain in the sense in which Einstein's theory of relativity explains the observations made in the Michelson-Morley experiment or in which the law of gravity explains why apples, when detached from the branch on which they grow, fall to the ground. That is, the question is approached as if we were looking for rules of thumb or criteria of what constitutes an explanation of a certain phenomenon — a phenomenon that happens to occur in, among other places, historical narratives. In this sense, the problem is really a problem of the methodology of the social sciences in general and hardly of interest to us in the present context. The real problem of explanation is something quite different. It is concerned with the fact that explanations of some kind or other are part of the structure of the narrative itself and are those parts of its structure that make

it an intelligible narrative. Explanation becomes a problem because
every narrative has an in-built explanatory structure. Without it,
it would not only not be intelligible but it would not even be a
narrative. We have to examine the types of explanation that are
built in and the manner in which they are built in. The problem
of explanation is the problem of why narratives are intelligible —
not the problem, as is so commonly thought, under what conditions
the rise of Parliament in Tudor England, or the growth of Fascism
in modern Europe, or the decline of the birthrate before the Black
Death of the fourteenth century can be explained.

   At first glance, we can introduce a simple and seemingly exhaustive distinction here. When the historian is using the same
general laws as were used by the people he is talking about, he is
giving historical explanations.[13] When the historian is using general
laws that are known to him but that could demonstrably not have
been known to the people he is talking about, he is interpreting.
It must be clear at once that the explanatory power of both kinds
of general laws must be equal. I mean by this observation that
both explanation and interpretation amount to a *Sinngebild*. In
both cases there is a creation of an intelligible unit. As long as a
general law that is believed to be true is used, two single events
can be brought into an intelligible relation to each other. It does
not matter whether the general laws are explanations (i.e., were
not known to the people involved). Formally a general law is a
general law and will operate in an 'explanatory' manner. But there
is a world of difference between explanations proper and interpretation. If we want to find out what really happened — and ever
since Ranke formulated this aim of historical research all historians
have admitted that that is what they are really trying to discover —
we must seek to explain in the narrow sense of 'explanation'. The
historian must try to find out the general laws that were used by
Metternich and must refrain from explaining by using general laws
that were not known to Metternich. For example: let us assume
that Metternich knew a general law that said that most people will
live peacefully under the rule of a legitimate king. We can then
take it that he used this general law to link the avowed aim of the
Congress of Vienna to establish stable peace with his assertion of
the principle of legitimacy. The aim of the congress, with the help
of the general law that most people live peacefully under legitimate
kings, becomes thus the cause of the assertion of the principle of
legitimacy. In this way, the historian can provide a cause-effect
chain that is a narrative that presents Metternich as he presented
himself to himself.

By contrast, we can safely assume that Keynes' general law that state-directed investment creates employment and raises demand was not known to Metternich. Similarly, we know that Freud's general law that many people resolve their Oedipal conflicts by attacking their fathers or father-figures was not known to Metternich. Nor was Metternich aware of Marx's law which says that the state is the instrument by which the exploitation of the lower classes is effected. Keynes, Freud, and Marx lived after Metternich, and any historical narrative that seeks to explain Metternich's assertion of the principle of legitimacy or any event in Metternich's life in terms of these laws is an interpretation.

The distinction between explanations that are proper explanations in the narrow sense and explanations that are really interpretations is fundamental and important. Unfortunately, it is not possible to keep the two kinds of explanation in separate watertight compartments. Indeed, the more we probe, the more blurred the initially clear distinction between explanation and interpretation becomes. We have seen that we were able to give a more rational account of what is involved in reenactment than Collingwood had led us to believe because we can assume that all human beings are capable of rational thought that relates particular events to general laws. Now we find that it is this very assumption that blurs the important distinction between explanations proper and interpretations. Explanations proper are more historical than interpretations and the difference between them helps us to distinguish between what really happened and what later historians think happened. But historians are human beings too and therefore capable of exactly the same kind of rational thought that consists in relating particular events to general laws. Hence when they are making use of the general laws *they* know rather than of the general laws the people involved with the events they are writing about knew, they are not doing anything that is radically different from what the people they are studying were doing. For this reason alone interpretation, though ostensibly different from explanation proper, is an activity that is rational and valid. Furthermore, given the fact that we can only understand if we make use of general laws we know of and hold to be true and that Metternich was subject to this limiting condition as much as the modern historian, we will find that when the historian is dealing with people less learned and educated than Metternich, he will have to make large assumptions as to the general laws they *might* have known and employed and so will have to invoke interpretation much sooner than he would like. All in all, it will become apparent that explanations proper and interpretations can be distinguished at best only in degree and that they are much more interwoven with one another than our first formulation allowed.

To begin with, it is impossible to make an absolute distinction between explanations and interpretations because one and the same general law can be an explanation or an interpretation, depending on the point of time at which it is employed. If we use the example of Petrarch's ascent of Mount Ventoux again, we see that any general law that links the ascent causally with the Renaissance is an explanation of the Renaissance but an interpretation of Petrarch for the modern historian as well as for any post-Petrarch historian. For Petrarch himself could not have thought of such a law and could not have linked his ascent to the Renaissance; but any Renaissance man could have thought of his Renaissance frame of mind as the effect of Petrarch's ascent and therefore the link between the ascent and the Renaissance is an explanation for him. Whether the causal connection between the ascent and the Renaissance is an explanation or whether it is an interpretation depends therefore entirely on the position of the observer.

Next, we must be on our guard with the expression 'the general laws that could have been known to a certain person'. There is no difficulty with the general laws that we know for certain were known to a certain person. But if we limited our understanding to those laws, our range of understanding would soon be pulled up short. It is legitimate to use also those general laws that were not known to a certain person but could have been known. But the expression 'could have been' is ambiguous. In one sense it means 'could have been known in theory'; that is, they were general laws to which the person had access, general laws that were invented before him or bandied about by people whom he could have known but happened not to know. In another sense it implies something about the mental or intellectual equipment of the person in question. An imbecile of the first century B.C., for example, could not possibly have known a general law that Caesar could have known. In his reconstruction of the situation in which a certain person thought by using general laws, the historian has therefore to be extremely cautious. Among other things he has to form a careful assessment of the intellectual capacity of the historical figure he is studying, of his range of reading or listening, and similar factors.

Let us begin with an ideal case. Let us suppose that we have a record of a statement by Julius Caesar why he crossed the Rubicon.[14] The statement says that he crossed the Rubicon because he wanted to secure power in Rome. In Caesar's mind the Rubicon crossing and the desire to secure power in Rome are linked as cause and effect because we know that Caesar was aware of a general law that stated that ambitious men who want to secure power in Rome have to defy the law that prohibited Roman armies from crossing the Rubicon. Caesar knew the general law to be true and we know that he knew. We can therefore invoke it and understand him as he understood himself. We can enter his mind and think as he did. There is no mystery here. We have a good explanation of his defiant and illegal action. Moreover, we know and he knew that the general law employed did not have unlimited validity. Its validity depended on the existence of the Roman republic and it applied to the Rubicon and not to any river in any part of the world. It is not a trivial law and not a natural law. It is a compound of legal enactment and plain commonsense psychology. It makes Casesar's political ambition and the crossing of the Rubicon into an intelligible unit, a *Sinngebild.* Finally it is worth stating that the modern historian has the same confidence in the truth of the law for that time and that place as Caesar had himself. The example we have chosen presents no difficulty of any kind.

But suppose a historian is not satisfied with this explanation. He can hardly reject it because he knows the general law to be true, and he knows that Casesar knew it to be true, and he knows that both initial condition and prognosis actually happened. Nevertheless an historian can keep on searching. He will then also come across the event that Caesar reached the other side of the river. He knows a general law that says that men who wish to reach the other side of a river will cross the river. With the help of this very trivial general law of almost unlimited universality, he will be able to explain why Caesar crossed the river. The intelligible unit that thus emerges differs from the first one and could be considered subsidiary to it. But somehow it does not add up to an explanation in the context of Caesar's political career.

Next, consider the possibility that there was a general law about the fate of men who cross the Rubicon that was enunciated long before Caesar and that could have been known to Caesar but was in fact not known to him. Suppose the law said that men who cross the Rubicon at the head of an army will suffer the nemesis of power and come sooner or later to a violent end. Here we come up against the first real difficulty. Logically, the employment of such a general law to create an intelligible unit of events is legitimate and remains within the sphere of proper explanation. The use of this general law would explain the chain of events that led

from the Rubicon to Caesar's murder and one could even imagine
that since it is likely that Caesar had heard of this law, he was
actually motivated by an unconscious death wish. But since the
general law was in fact *not* employed by Caesar even though it
could have been, we are now really moving beyond mere explanation without actually entering the field of interpretation.

Next, we come to the historian who looks at Caesar and dis-
misses all these explanations. He says to himself that he knows
that aggressive men want to ravish their mothers or a mother-
figure and that Rome was such a mother-figure to Caesar. This is
a general law well known to many modern historians but certainly
not known to Caesar. On the assumption that the law is true for
all men who have grown up in a family situation, we can take it
that it was true for Caesar, though he did not know it to be true.
It is a law of limited universality but its range certainly includes
the situation in which Caesar grew up. Its employment will link
the crossing of the Rubicon to Caesar's dictatorship of the republic
and create an intelligible unit slightly different from the one we
have found above. Here then we are clearly in the realm of interpretation. The law could not possibly have been known to Caesar
but presents a truth that applies to him. After all, we know that
apples fell off trees long before Newton discovered the general
law that explains why. Not even the post-Newtonian apple knows
this law. And people watching apples before Newton did not know
it either. But this does not invalidate the application of Newton's
law to the fall of an apple in the year 500 B.C.

The psychoanalytical law about mothers and mother-figures
would have been quite unintelligible to Caesar.[15] It presupposes
psychological concepts and a power to analyse symbols that were
beyond the reach of even the best-educated ancient Roman. But if
we consider another modern law about the class struggle we may
find that although Caesar did not know it, he might have been
made to understand it if he had had an opportunity to hear of it.
The law says that all political contests reflect the class struggle.
Caesar was not a plebeian and feared that a continuation of the
civil war in Rome would lead to a plebeian revolution and thus
deprive his own class of power. Hence he crossed the Rubicon.
Caesar did not obviously think in these terms. But he could have,
although the 'could' has here a different meaning from the 'could'
in the nemesis of power example. In that example it merely means
that Caesar could have used the general law about power, but did
not. In the present example it means that he could have used the
law of the class struggle had he had the chance of meeting a
modern Marxist.

We can now see that the possible kinds of general laws that can be employed in this situation can be ranged in a scale. At one extreme there is the law that was in fact known to Caesar. Then comes the law that was not known to him but that could have been known to him. Next comes the law that could not have been known to him but that could have been accepted by him had there been an opportunity for explaining it. Finally, at the other end of the scale, there is the law that could not have been known to him and that he could not have understood no matter how much explaining one might have tried. And yet it is undoubtedly true that all these laws create intelligible units that include the crossing of the Rubicon.

What are we to make of this situation? To begin with we find that instead of a simple distinction between explanation proper and interpretation we have come up with at least four distinct possibilities. One is an explanation proper. The next (a law that Caesar could have known but did not know) moves away from strict explanations but remains a sort of explanation. The next (a law that could not have been known to Caesar but that he might have been made to understand) is an interpretation that could at a pinch be turned into an explanation. The last (a law that was not known to him and that by no stretch of the imagination he could have been made to understand or appreciate) finally places us squarely into the field of interpretation.

The next observation is equally important. There can be no definitive history of anything. Once again we must note that Hexter's formulations though correct are so simple that they obscure rather than clarify the issue. On page 80 of *The History Primer*[16] he points out that young Willie is capable of unbiased selection of events both for explanation and judgment. When his mother asks him why he stopped off at Jamie's this afternoon, Willie replies that he walked home from school with Jamie and that Jamie had asked him whether he wanted to see his new electric train, and that he did want to see it. Hexter comments rightly that Willie shows himself capable of selecting from a very considerable number of data the items necessary for a historical explanation. But Willie's undisputed skill as a historian depends, first of all, on his and his mother's knowledge of several general laws. There is the general law that when little boys are asked to inspect new electric trains they usually answer in the affirmative. And secondly, there is a general law that says that when people stop off at friend's places, they will come home later than they would if they did not. These laws are trivial; but if Willie did not know them, and if his mother did not know them, and if Willie did not know that his

mother knew them, they would not enable him to select the relevant events and put them together into a story that made sense to
him and to his mother. The ease with which Willie selects what is
relevant depends on his knowledge of general laws and in his belief
in their truth. The case shows that Willie feels at home in a given
culture and in its universe of discourse. As Hexter says, the matter
is really very simple. And yet, as he also points out correctly, the
matter is also very hard, because Willie has to *know* of general
laws, tacitly so and trivial though the laws may be. Hence there is
a complexity in the situation that only appears less complex because Willie has interiorised the whole problem. Now suppose that
Willie were transplanted into a different environment or that he
were a person with a different background; in that case the general
laws that he had interiorised would be quite different and he
would then come up either equally easily or less easily so with a
very different story. The way Hexter presents the example makes it
look as if there were something definitive about Willie's explanations,
something final. But on inspection, we find that there is nothing
final in these explanations at all. They depend wholly on Willie's
background. Change the background and the stories he is likely
to tell will change.

The same is true for historical narratives in general. As time
passes, new general laws were invented. They may belong to
physics or to economics, to political science or to the realm of
private experience. There are sciences like chemistry, which we
presume to have become a permanent acquisition, and there are
sciences like mental magnetism and mesmerism, which were widely
believed to be true during the eighteenth century but which are
now completely discredited. In the twenties of this century it was
widely believed by Viennese middle-class parents that they ought
not to handle their babies lest they destroy their potential for
independent growth. In the fifties Bowlby made history in the
United States by demonstrating that babies that are not handled
and cuddled have their growth retarded and may actually die. In
the seventies the Women's Liberation Movement insists that above
all mothers must not cuddle their babies too much lest they turn
into possessive mothers. When I was young it was believed that
spinach is essential for physical growth, and now that I am middle
aged it is believed that too much spinach causes cancer of the
kidneys. Or take a look at those hoary sciences of phrenology and
physiognomy. They are completely discredited together with
mesmerism and the belief that magnetism can cure diseases. But
astrology has still its ups and downs and who is to say that as our

knowledge of solar and stellar radiation increases it will not enjoy a new era of credibility. People who believe or disbelieve any of these theories are bound to form very different units of intelligibility. Or consider a topic that has always played a great role in the writing of history, the question of fame. 'All men seek fame'. This general law was almost universally believed to be true in the classical world of Rome and Greece. But long since we have come to understand, first, that achievement and the fame that comes from it do not depend on individual effort but on genetics and that the talent for it is randomly distributed. The ancients thought it depended in part on virtue and will power and in part on *fortuna* and that if *fortuna* smiled too much, the gods might become envious. If one achieved too much fame one might overstep the limits set by fate. But since we have come to recognise the role of genetics, we do not think that achievement is due to merit or effort and therefore find that the fame that goes with achievement is often far from 'deserved' and certainly never an index of virtue. On the other hand, since genetics is so far beyond our control, we are actually more sympathetic to the ancient concepts of fate and *fortuna* than our enlightened manner of thinking would allow us to admit. Moreover, in quite recent times we have also discovered that fame depends largely on the mass media and on one's relations with the gentlemen of the press, television, and radio and that being picked by them has very little to do with merit but a lot to do with fate or *fortuna*. Hence, unlike the ancients, we often find fame ridiculous rather than glorious. For these reasons, the desire for fame is much less of a motive power than it used to be and, therefore, the general law that rendered such excellent services to ancient historians is much less useful today.

How, for instance, are we to understand Alexander the Great? He was given to the search for fame and in ancient days much of the debate about him centred on the question whether such desire was permissible, or whether he overstepped the good measure of human life, or whether he was entitled to do so because he was divine.[17] To the modern historian such considerations are beside the point. He is more likely to ask himself whether Alexander was sane or insane, whether he was a visionary who wanted to unite mankind[18] or a power politician lacking the customary scruples.[19] Obviously, when we deal with Alexander today we do not believe that the general law that all men seek fame offers an explanation that is intelligible to us.[20]

As sciences come and go and as some sciences progress, new laws come into focus and old laws come to be discarded. As a result the possibilities of creating new units of intelligibility (*Sinnge-bilde*) keep changing all the time. And, equally important, the status of these units of intelligibility keeps changing. To an eighteenth-century historian writing about an eighteenth-century person, an explanation in terms of mesmerism might have seemed an explanation proper. To the same historian, writing about a man in the twelfth century, any such explanation would have been an interpretation. To a historian working in the twentieth century, an explanation in terms of mesmerism applied to an eighteenth-century person would be an explanation proper, but one that is barely intelligible. And if a twentieth-century historian wrote about the man whom an eighteenth-century historian had explained in terms of mesmerism, he would, without doubt, not explain him in terms of mesmerism. On the contrary, though he might refer to mesmerism as an explanation offered in the eighteenth century, he would dismiss such an explanation as an instance of false consciousness and seek to replace it by an explanation in terms of the class struggle (i.e., by an interpretation).

This complex situation arises from a simple stark fact. For the most part, the general laws used by the historian looking back and the general laws used by the person he is looking back upon coincide only rarely. The very first example of how Caesar explained the crossing of the Rubicon is in a way exceptional. Here the general law employed by Caesar and the general law employed by the historian coincide. The general law concerns the lust for power and it is held to be true both by Caesar and by the modern historian. But it often happens that the general laws that make a unit of intelligibility to the modern historian are not the general laws that would have created a unit of intelligibility to the person he is thinking about. This was probably the case in the example of the class struggle and quite certainly the case in the example drawn from psychoanalysis.

One might argue that the simplest way out of the difficulty is to stick to explanations proper and that only when we explain Caesar in those terms in which he explained himself to himself do we understand him correctly. But this argument misses an important point. When the terms that Caesar used are the terms used by a modern historian, there is no problem. But when the terms used by Caesar are not intelligible to the modern historian, an explanation proper does not get us very far. The crux of the matter is that the idea of 'explanation proper' is slightly ambiguous. It hides an important element. It hides the fact that when Caesar explains himself to himself he may well understand what he is explaining, but that when a modern historian explains Caesar in the same way, the result may be double Dutch to a modern reader. Suppose we are dealing with a man of the sixteenth century in England to whom theological controversy was very important and who thought almost entirely in religious terms. A modern historian will look upon these controversies and these terms with complete incomprehension.[21] He may, good historian that he is, take note of them and use them to explain Thomas More or the earl of Leicester as these men explained themselves to themselves. But if he does this, he will fail to understand them, for these controversies and religious terms fail to carry conviction to the modern ear. He can take a shortcut and belittle the preoccupation of these men with religion, as A. Rowse has done in his account of Leicester,[22] or allege, as H. Trevor-Roper has, that despite his protestations, Archbishop Laud's real motivation was not religious.[23] But clearly such a shortcut places the description in the field of pure interpretation and thus fails to make the modern reader 'understand', though it helps him to understand. On the other hand, if the modern historian stays with the sixteenth-century terms, he will also fail to make the modern reader understand.

The problem arises for a very simple reason. In many cases, when confronted by a universal law once believed true but no longer accepted, we have no difficulty in understanding it, even though we consider it false. But we often come across generalisations about religious passions, the readiness to kill for nationalistic or communal reasons or for theological dogma that we find hard even to understand, let alone consider true generalisations.[24] It is at this point that we cannot rest content with a simple search for explanations but must seek to substitute interpretations. For a modern interpretation, though it is an interpretation, is more intelligible to the modern reader than an explanation that explains things the way they would have been intelligible to the people in the past. Such substitutions can be arbitrary, as when a historian brushes aside an explanation in terms of a passion for religious dogma and replaces it by an interpretation in terms of the class struggle or communal loyalties. In other cases, such substitutions can be controlled by the consideration that there must be a link between the explanation that has been brushed aside and the interpretation that replaces it. If there is such a link, we call the substitution a translation. Such substitutions are of the greatest importance, for when we substitute a modern interpretation for an old explanation, we are not only achieving a greater degree of intelligibility but we also mean that our explanation, because it is more intelligible, is truer, As we shall see, such a concept of truth cannot stand up to *ultimate* scrutiny; but it is nevertheless correct that as we increase intelligibility we also think that we are approaching a higher degree of truth. There is an important sense, though not an absolute one, in which intelligibility is linked to what we imagine truth to be. It is more intelligible to explain the rise of a dynasty with the help of the term 'charisma' (i.e., to interpret it) than to explain it, as people in the Middle Ages were wont to do, by pointing out that that dynasty possessed a larger number of relics than another dynasty.[25] The transfer of relics from one dynasty to another is to our way of thinking not only an unintelligible way of accounting for the mechanism of change, it is also a crude and false way of accounting for it. The fact that we know that people in the Middle Ages used the transfer of relics to account for the change of power does not help. Their generalisation about relics has to be replaced by one that is acceptable to us. If we passed up the opportunity for replacing an explanation that is unacceptable by an interpretation that is acceptable, we would deny that there is a growth in knowledge and that we moderns do know more than people in the past did (even though we are not sure what the notion 'more' exactly means). At any rate, we do believe we know more about climate than ancient or primitive witch doctors and in that sense, at least, it is legitimate to speak of a growth of knowledge and to argue that the substitution of an interpretation for an explanation is an advance in knowledge and that a refusal to substitute amounts to a refusal to avail ourselves of our knowledge.[26]

Since we are certain that we know more about the workings of society and about psychology as well as about physics, chemistry, and biology, our modern interpretations are not arbitrary substitutions for the explanations offered by the people of the past. They are not only more intelligible to us but are also 'truer'. If we did not constantly substitute interpretations for explanations, we would deprive ourselves of the opportunity offered by our better, modern knowledge to expose many ancient explanations as illusions. Unlike an explanation, an interpretative general law is not part and parcel of what actually happened, for it was not part of the thoughts thought by people we are writing about. Despite this, an interpretative general law is an essential and effective part of the story the historian has to tell.

Here, then, we have a good reason why we cannot stick to explanations proper and why we cannot eschew interpretations. There exists, however, also another reason why substitutions are necessary. As we have seen, the notion 'explanation proper' is slightly ambiguous; but this ambiguity exists in more than one sense. At any one time any individual may have a choice between a number of generalisations to explain himself to himself and to others; or, and this is equally conceivable, he may choose one general law to explain himself to himself and another to explain himself to his friends or to the public. And in addition to the ambiguity arising from this kind of choice, we are often hard put to decide whether to admit as an explanation proper only those general laws that were actually and demonstrably known to the agent to be explained or whether we should also use those that might have been known to him and exclude only those that could, demonstrably, not have been known to him. Even here we have to be on our guard, for we have seen it is actually doubtful how much 'Oedipal consciousness', in the modern psychoanalytical sense of the term, we are entitled to attribute to Caesar. But even on the quite ordinary level we often find competing generalisations that show that we have to make substitutions. Many years ago, to take a concrete example, Charles Beard published a book in which he showed that the men who framed the American Constitution were not prompted by the desire to safeguard freedom but by class interest and the desire to protect their landed property.[27] This book presented an obvious interpretation and substituted general laws about the class struggle and the nature of the state for the generalisations advanced in the eighteenth century by Washington, Jefferson, and Franklin. Recently there has appeared a book by Edmund S. Morgan, *American Slavery, American Freedom*,[28] in which a completely different general law is used to explain, broadly, the same events. Morgan argues that the class struggle in the American colonies abated visibly when black slaves were introduced. Black slavery, he argues, obliterated the class struggle among the whites and so it came about that the whites were able to formulate their belief in freedom and frame the Constitution on the working assumption that the socioeconomic differences among the white inhabitants of the colonies had become negligible when compared to the presence of black slaves. In this way belief in freedom and equality was made acceptable among whites who were not equal. Although this theory does contain obvious interpretative elements ('class struggle' was not a commonly used term in the eighteenth century), it is conceivable that the authors of the Constitution could have looked upon themselves in some such light as Morgan suggests. His theory, therefore, could rank, on the whole, as an explanation. Nevertheless, it does

compete with another, older and more widely accepted explanation that says that the colonists, and this would include the land-
owning classes of Virginia as well as others, derived their attitudes
to freedom and equality from seventeenth-century England.

Or let us compare two books that have recently appeared in
France. They deal, among other things, with changing attitudes to
Christianity and especially death rituals in the eighteenth century.
M. Vovelle[29] suggests that baroque piety weakened during the
eighteenth century and gave way to a progressive de-Christianisation
and that this general law (with very limited universality) can be
used to explain that testators increasingly stopped regulating
funerals and that there was a corresponding decline of death
rituals. Against this Ph. Ariés[30] uses a completely different general
law. He points out that during the eighteenth century the family
became a smaller and more tightly knit community than it had
been in previous centuries, and people were, therefore, able to
trust their immediate relatives to take care of their funeral without
having to make explicit provision for it in their will. On this
general law, the change in the provisions of the last wills are explained, although it would not necessarily follow, as Vovelle maintains, that there was de-Christianisation and a disappearance of
baroque piety. Although the initial conditions are the same in
both books — the absence of special provisions for funerals in
wills — Vovelle, with the help of one general law, links it to the
disappearance of baroque piety and Ariés, with the help of
another, links it to the rise of the family as a closely knit unit.
The question is how the two general laws — both admittedly of
limited universality — are related to each other. They are obviously
competing explanations rather than interpretations, for both are
based upon explicit statements or absence of statements in last
wills and testaments of Frenchmen in the eighteenth century and
can be considered as the sort of general laws people would have
advanced in the eighteenth century had they been interviewed
on the matter. If they compete, they must be substitutable and we
can see, therefore, that substitutions can take place not only when
there is need to replace an explanation by an interpretation but
also when there are competing explanations.

In the face of all these examples it is clear that substitutions
are made all the time. The question is whether there is any real
necessity for them to be made. Substitutions are necessary because
in the last analysis one obtains a *Sinngebild* or a mininarrative, let
alone an intelligible explanation, of one event by another only
when one believes the covering law one employs to be true. In this

sense the question of truth and the question of intelligibility are intimately connected. The possession of relics will count as a cause of the rise of a dynasty only to people who believe the general law that relics cause the rise of dynasties to be true. To those people the event that A possessed a relic and the event that A's house became the ruling dynasty will make an intelligible narrative. If one does not believe the general law to be true, the two events will not appear to be related and the sequence they form will be an arbitrary, not an intelligible, series. With a stretch of the imagination one can always understand that some people in the past or in another society should have believed this law to be true even if one does not believe it to be true oneself. There is nothing *so* weird that one cannot, with an effort, understand why some people should believe it to be true. If one peruses the large German literature on the problem of the difficulties of understanding, one gains the impression that the problem of understanding is well nigh insuperable. But this is far from being the case. The real problem is not how far our imagination and our ability to understand why some people should have believed something implausible, improbable, or too weird to be true can reach. The real problem arises because if *we* do not believe a certain general law to be true we will not accept the sequence of particular events linked by the law, and we must, therefore, see the particular events to be linked to different particular events. Unless we can believe the general law to be true — as distinct from understanding that it should have been held to be true by other people — we cannot believe that the same particular events are linked into a narrative sequence. In short, the potential for explanation of a general law depends on the belief that it is true.

If people believe the general law about relics to be true, they can explain the rise of a dynasty. People who do not believe it to be true can nevertheless understand the rise of that dynasty in terms of that general law because they know that the people at that time believed the law to be true and therefore were inclined to pay homage to the dynasty who had the relics. But this way of understanding the rise of the dynasty is fundamentally different from the way in which the people who believed the law to be true understood the rise. We understand the rise because we are tacitly invoking an additional law, which says that when people believe something strongly (i.e., the dynasty-making power of relics) they will act accordingly, (i.e., accept the dynasty which holds the relics). In this way we can understand how the relics functioned in the past or in a strange society; but we can do so only with the

help of a law which we believe to be true and of which the people
in the past or in the strange society had no knowledge. While we
can therefore understand all that is to be understood about relics,
we do so in a way different from the way in which the people who
believed the law to be true linked the events. They did not need a
law about the connection between belief and action; we do.

Since the explanatory potential of general laws depends on
whether they are believed to be true and since standards of what
is believed true vary, substitutions are necessary and inevitable.
Thus we come to the conclusion that we must distinguish between
what actually happened and what really happened. In the Middle
Ages people believed the law about relics to be true. If we note
this fact and stretch our imagination far enough to understand
why and how they could have persuaded themselves of something
so improbable, we have found out what *actually* happened. Empathy, Collingwood's reenactment, or Popper's situational analysis
by themselves only help us to find out what actually happened.
But if we want to find out what *really* happened, we must seek to
obtain a sequence of events linked by a law that *we* believe to be
true. In the present example this obliges us either to supplement
the law that says that relics cause the rise of dynasties with a law
that says that if people hold a strong belief they will act on it, or
to exchange the original law for one that we believe to be true and
that would connect the rise of the dynasty with an event other
than the possession of relics. This distinction between actuality
and reality is far from specious. It is of fundamental importance
and shows how unsatisfactory Ranke's slogan 'to find out what
really happened' is. The German original is simply ambiguous for
Ranke uses the word *eigentlich*. It has become customary in
English translations to use either 'actually' or 'really' as if the
difference were of no importance. But now we have seen that the
difference is of fundamental importance and that Ranke's famous
statement fails to distinguish between actuality and reality. We
can always find out what actually happened by simply contenting
ourselves with explanations and by accepting the events in such
concatenations, and constellations, and sequences as they appeared
to the people who acted in them, or who first reflected on them,
or who first observed them. Even if we do not accept the general
law they used as true, we can understand readily that *they* did
accept it as true and thus we can understand why they should have
come up with one subevent and with one sequence of events
rather than with another. But if we want to find out what *really*

happened, we must employ general laws that we believe to be true. Hence the need for substitution.

The real problem of hermeneutics, I would suggest, is therefore not how one can tortuously understand why some people should have been persuaded that relics can cause the rise of a dynasty, but which substitutions are licit, desirable, and helpful and which are not. The problem of hermeneutics in this sense arises from the fact that we cannot think of events or of any sequence of events without thinking of a general law. And since people differ in their opinions about the truth of these laws and since only those that are believed to be true can fulfill their function of tying subevents into events and events into narratives, one is forced to make substitutions and to be clear as to which substitutions are helpful and which substitutions are arbitrary and so forth. The need for hermeneutics, therefore, comes from the differences in standards of the truth of general laws, not from difficulties in comprehension.

To preserve the element of understanding that is contained both in explanation proper and in interpretation, there must be a bridge between the general laws the historian believes to be true and the general laws the person he is studying believed to be true. If an explanation proper is given in terms of a general law that the historian knows Caesar believed in but that the historian considers to be nonsensical, there is no bridge. In such a case the historian's very truthfulness will lead to incomprehension. If we are not dealing with an ideal case in which the law the historian believes in and the law Caesar believed in coincide, the historian must act as a mediator. He must translate and build a bridge between what he holds to be a good general law and what he knows the person he is studying held to be a good general law. The same is true for the movement in the opposite direction. If the historian interprets by using a general law he believes to be true but which he knows was not held true by a person he is writing about, he must endeavour to build a bridge. He cannot remain content with his interpretation.

Consider the following examples. Benedictine monasteries were launched in early medieval Europe as alternatives to society. Monks were to assemble behind walls in complete obedience to an elected abbot and regulate their daily lives in such a way that they extricated themselves gradually from the trammels of sin that social, sexual, and economic appetites had forced on man. In this way they would eventually develop toward a pure spiritual

existence and a contemplation of God, possibly even a unification
with God. Such were the original aims proclaimed by the Benedictine *Rule* and implicit in the *Rule's* reference to the writings of
John Cassian.[31] Historians, less acquainted with Cassian than was
the author of the *Rule*, have seen the monasteries as parts of
society in which gardens and animals, scholarship and crafts, were
more assiduously and more rationally tended than was normal in
the Middle Ages. They explained therefore that monasticism made
a civilising contribution to medieval society of which it was as
integral a part as bishops and kings, manors and cities.

There is clearly a great gap between the explanation contained
in the original reference of the *Rule* to Cassian and the later historians' interpretation of monasticism as a civilising contribution
to medieval society. The notion of monasticism as an alternative
society that would enable its members to phase themselves out is
completely lost in that interpretation. But if the modern historian
simply repeats the original explanation that monasticism is based
on transcendental and contemplative goals, he will not mediate
between the early monks and modern man. If he imposes his interpretation that monasticism was a contribution to civilisation, he
will not mediate either for he will then see monasticism in terms
the monks saw themselves in. One should therefore try a different
interpretation, more connected with an explanation proper.

A different interpretation that does mediate can be found in
the following view. Since monks were subject to a strict spiritual
discipline, they needed fewer props to their egos than ordinary
men and as a result they were less likely to be destracted from the
rational pursuit of any goal they may have set themselves. Spiritual
discipline, successfully applied, minimises the need for saving one's
face and for seeking confirmation of one's status, and by removing
such obstacles it maximises the possibility of applying reason to,
say, economics. Hence monks were able to devote themselves more
rationally to economic pursuits than the average medieval man.
Monasteries, therefore, tended to flourish economically and advance their horticulture, their schools, and their farms far beyond
the level of the surrounding countryside. In monasteries, economic
rationalisation could proceed at a fast pace. This view of the role
of monasteries in medieval society is an interpretation because in
its clear assessment of the economic aspects of monasticism it
goes beyond the terms implicit in the *Rule's* reference to Cassian.
But it does not impose an extraneous view on what happened
when the *Rule* enjoined the monks to read Cassian. It extrapolates
from the reference to Cassian and links our understanding of the

economic peculiarities of monasteries in medieval society to the contemplative and spiritual goal that is part of the explanation proper. Unlike the earlier interpretation, it links parts of the explanation proper with the economic terms in which we ourselves can understand the function of monasteries in medieval society.

In *The History Primer*, Hexter has described the historian's mediation in very lucid terms. He explains there how he came to discover that the fundamental structure of More's *Utopia* is a great 'social instrument for the subjugation of pride'. All previous commentators on More had given different explanations of the structure of More's commonwealth. Hexter found however that most modern readers would be very puzzled when told that an ostensibly intelligent and civilised man like More could get all 'wrought up about the sin of pride so alien to them'. (page 141). Hence he found that his argument in support of his understanding of More should be formulated in the shape of a bridge between the theological discourse used by More and the sociological discourse to which modern readers are accustomed. He calls such bridge-building 'translational' discourse and notes that the direction of the translation is 'as important as its effectiveness'. One starts with More and seeks to extrapolate, not the other way round. In this way, Hexter points out, the consciousness of the modern reader is expanded (page 139); Hexter does not shrink from calling this kind of mediation the 'psychedelic' effect of historical understanding.[32]

The description is cogent and to the point. My only quarrel, if one can call it that, is that it seems to lump together two things that ought to be distinguished, if not in practice then in theory. Hexter, significantly, discusses the whole matter under the term 'rhetoric'. He knows that it is important to convince the reader psychologically, to make the argument ring true and sound plausible. He is therefore somewhat overanxious to state the whole argument for translation and for the direction of the translation as if it were really some sort of psychological ruse. But the ruse aspect of the matter, if it were not supported by a formally valid step of reasoning, would do nothing to convince one of its validity. This minor criticism apart, this whole chapter, entitled 'The Sown and the Waste, *or the second record*', deserves to become a classic in the literature of the philosophy of history.

To highlight the import of the relationship between explanation proper and an interpretation that is desirable and 'psychedelic', I would describe that relationship as a typological one. An event can be considered the type of all those things that are different in content but exhibit a similarity in form or structure. Abraham's sacrifice is the type of Jesus's Crucifixion; the growth of corn from a buried seed is the type of the Resurrection; and the crossing of the Red Sea, the type of Baptism. The relationship between these events and their types so different in content, is typological. In the same sense the relationship between an explanation proper and an interpretation ought to be typological. If it is not, the interpretation is something alien, something that is imposed by the historian on the events he seeks to explain and understand. We can use Caesar and the Rubicon again to illustrate this point. Suppose there are five possible explanations why Caesar crossed the Rubicon:

1. He wanted to ravish his mother (i.e., Rome).
2. He wanted to gain power in Rome.
3. He wanted to protect himself against his enemies in Rome.
4. He wanted to assure the ascendancy of his class.
5. He wanted to salvage his honour.

Of these five explanations, no. 1 is psychoanalytical and no. 4, Marxist. It is reasonable to assume that neither would have occurred to Caesar. The whole series falls into two types. Nos. 1 and 2 are of the same type: Caesar wants to dominate a woman or a woman-figure. Nos. 3 and 4 are of a different type: Caesar wants to assert himself over other men. If we now suppose that no. 2 is an explanation he himself could have put forward, then no. 1, an explanation put forward by a modern psychoanalyst, would be typologically related to the explanation given by Caesar, but no. 4 would not be typologically related. If, however, Caesar had put forward nos. 3 or 5, a modern Marxist would be on safe ground in substituting no. 4 because no. 4 is typologically related to nos. 3 and 5.

If the relationship between interpretation and explanation in the case of Julius Caesar were hypothetical, let us pursue the problem with the help of a genuine case study. The bulk of our information about Pope Alexander III (1159–1172) comes from the report that his friend Cardinal Boso included in the *Liber Pontificalis*.[33] There are also many letters attributed to Alexander,[34] but there is as yet no telling which are genuine and which are not. In his attempt to order and understand the complex fortunes and misfortunes of Alexander, Boso made use of a mythical scheme.[35] He was not the first historian to do so nor the last, and we shall examine in chapter 5 the particular problems raised by the employ-

ment of mythical moulds. Boso was very well acquainted with the
Christian story of redemption through suffering and he knew perfectly well how events are likely to hang together in this story.
Having decided that the schism was a struggle between opposing
forces, Boso followed his mythical pattern of redemption through
suffering. He cast the whole story into that mould and presented
the schism as a struggle between a villain and a hero. Frederick
was the single-minded villain and Alexander, the hero. The story
of the schism is the struggle of the forces of darkness against the
forces of light. The latter eventually prevail because they have
become purified through humiliation, and suffering, and deprivation, and persecution. In his account of Alexander's misfortunes,
all the typically mythical ingredients are present, and, what is
more, the ultimate triumph is not depicted as the result of luck or
shrewdness, but as the direct outcome of a long chain of humilia-
tions and sufferings. Boso resisted the temptation to depict
Frederick as a Satan. But he made it very clear that Alexander
was a Jesus figure. In his description of the great cataclysm, when
Rome was sacked by Frederick in 1167, Boso tells us that Alexander disappeared from sight, but was seen three days later (*sic!*)
'dining with his companions [ought we to read "disciples"?] at the
foot of Monte Circello'. In the end, when Alexander's victory is
assured, Boso makes great play of the fact that Alexander took
formal possession of his kingdom, the city of Rome, on Easter
Sunday. Alexander's long night of darkness ended with his trium-
phal return to Rome and his installation in the city was described
as a form of political resurrection. This mould is a powerful mythical drama and so the story begins with an elaborate description of
the confused circumstances surrounding the double election and
then leads on to Alexander's plight as the victim of Frederick and
Frederick's anti-pope, Victor IV. It ends with the elaborate description of the Peace of Venice in 1176 and the ceremonial pomp
with which the reconciliation of Alexander and Frederick was con-
summated. The opening pages describe Alexander's flight from
Rome and the concluding pages, his return to Rome. The events
between the beginning and the end consist of a recital of the villain's stratagems, plots, conspiracies, aggressions, persecutions, and
injustices; and of Alexander's steadfast and determined manoeu-
vres to resist and defeat them. To underline the dramatic structure
of the story, both the disaster at the beginning and the triumph at
the end are supplemented — ought one to say symbolically supplemented? — by two circumstantial accounts of sea voyages. The
first, surrounded by nautical hazards and perils, was undertaken in

flight from Frederick's persecution; the second, though not unac-
companied by storms and adventures, was undertaken as a trium-
phal procession. On both occasions, in adversity as well as in
triumph, the ships were supplied by Alexander's faithful patron
and protector, the king of Sicily. Sea voyages are rich symbols, and
their psychological as well as allegorical meaning as trials, journeys
into the unknown nether world, are worth remarking on. There is
no time to dwell on this matter but I would like to add that to
Boso as to anybody who lived *before* Romanticism, a sea voyage
was a monstrosity.[36] The detailed description of Alexander's two
sea voyages is neatly balanced by equally detailed descriptions of
the villain's military defeats. The first occurred as the result of an
epidemic in Rome in 1166 that reduced Frederick's armed might
to shambles. The second, equally detailed, but not half as truthful,
is the account of Frederick's defeat near Alexandria. According to
Boso, the city of Alexandria, named after his hero, was the great
Lombard stronghold and the direct instrument of Frederick's complete military discomfiture in 1174. Boso's account of the foundation of the city and of Frederick's defeat at the hands of its
citizens is untruthful and owes its remarkable presence to purely
dramatic considerations.

In contrast to Boso, the modern historian sees Alexander's role
in a clear light. But then the modern historian has the advantage
of hindesight. He knows how the story ended and where the path
led to. He can see that in the middle of the twelfth century there
was the end of an epoch, marked by the almost simultaneous
deaths of Saint Bernard and Pope Eugene III. Saint Bernard had
wielded his influence to establish the papacy like a new Moses, to
teach by ordinances, and to lead men toward God. He had used
his own towering personality and mystical fervour to fire the
leadership of one pope after another. With the disappearance of
Saint Bernard, there was a need for a more politically oriented
leadership. Leadership, as Richard Southern has pointed out,
meant lordship.[37] And the popes descended eagerly into the arena
where lordship was to be won. Alexander took up Saint Bernard's
cue of leadership but translated it into those terms that were
practicable during the second half of the century. He threw himself into the task of ordaining and legislation, or litigation and administration, and by the time of his death in 1181, the papacy's
activity and operation was fixed for two centuries to come. All
this is easy enough for us to discern now. We can count the cases
brought to the *curia* for litigation and the papal decretals and
make a graph of their enormous growth from the pontificate of

Alexander onward. But Alexander himself was not to know where
all this would lead and which aspect of his career would be the
most successful and influential for the future. Looking back, the
modern historian sees Alexander as an important step in the formation of the *curia*'s administrative system. The turmoil, which on
several occasions nearly cost Alexander his freedom and possibly
his life, is forgotten. But this, clearly, is not a way in which
Alexander could have seen himself and the significance of his
struggle. His life, by our standard, was one of personal heroism;
it was not the career of a bureaucrat. Today Southern's view of
Alexander will remain unchallenged. But a hundred years ago,
H. Reuter[38] saw a very different picture even though his source
material was not significantly poorer than that available to Southern. Reuter saw in Alexander a steadfast and uncompromising
fighter for the Gregorian Reform Movement. To us, Southern
sounds more plausible than Reuter. But both are equally distant
from Boso.[39]

I remember when I was a student, twenty-five years ago, the
excitement with which I devoured F. Heer's *Aufgang Europas,* [40]
in which an attempt was made to provide a different explanation
of the pontificate of Alexander. Heer saw Alexander as the
representative of the rising bourgeoisie, pitted against the protagonists of the old order and the old style. Alexander's opponents
were trying to erect or defend a monolithic spiritual order in
Europe, supported on the foundations of an economic feudalism,
which was still prevalent in central Europe but which was fast
becoming outmoded in the West and in Italy. In Heer's vivid imagination, the victory of the Western allies against the Third Reich
had already been won many centuries before because it was
essentially a victory of the rational liberal bourgeoisie over rural
feudalism.

One can, of course, see Alexander as a representative of the
bourgeoisie simply because he was in fact supporting the Lombard
communes against Frederick's imperialism. In this sense, Heer's theory was nothing but a reiteration of part of Boso's story. But Heer
meant something else. He identified the struggle of the sixties and
seventies of the twelfth century as a class struggle by interpreting the
relative importance of the bourgeoisie as the spearhead of Western
resistance to Frederick Barbarossa. In this more special sense, unfortunately, Heer's theory cannot stand up to closer examination.
Although Heer quoted Boso copiously, he completely failed to
understand the mould in which Boso's story was cast. Nothing
was further from Boso's mind than to see the pontificate of

Alexander as a fight of the new style against the old style, let alone
to see Alexander as the representative of a rising bourgeoisie
struggling against the dominion of rural, Teutonic feudalism. I do
not know whether the young generation still gets the same sense
of excitement and exploration in reading Heer that I got, and
there would be no point in discussing his interpretation of Boso
were it not for the fact that it is the *only* interpretation I have ever
come across. And I would like to emphasise not only the 'only'
but also 'interpretation'. For it is a genuine interpretation. Heer
seized an essential feature of Boso's work. Boso *does* represent the
schism, as a struggle between a hero and a villain. In that respect,
Heer was quite correct. But then Heer went further and read into
his scheme his own geographically oriented Marxism; to Heer, the
struggle was between a hero who stood for the lucid, calculating
liberal intelligence of the rising bourgeoisie against the sinister
villainy of an archaic feudal aristocracy. Heer started on the right
point but ended up by telling us not what Boso thought about
himself and Alexander but how *we* ought to understand Boso and
Alexander. It is ironical that one of Heer's many hostile reviewers
criticised him for taking Boso too much at his face value.[41] In fact
Heer did nothing of the sort. He *interpreted* Boso to the point of
standing him on his head. In other words, instead of inviting and
helping us to stretch *our* imagination so that we can see Boso as he
saw himself, Heer, like so many modern historians, is really inviting
Boso to stretch *his* imagination so that Boso can understand *us*
and *our* problems.

On the surface, there is something patently perverse in this
kind of exercise. But we should not dismiss it out of hand. We
know only too well that almost all people both in the past and the
present are given to delusions about themselves, that they are apt
to use ideological arguments to support a false consciousness, and
that we can only arrive at the 'truth' if we strip away their protestations and professions and have a look at what lies beneath. There
is no obvious reason why Heer should not strip Boso and show us
what he *really* meant. Such a quest for a truth beneath the appearance is important — except that we can never be sure which is
appearance and which is reality. For just as we can strip Boso of
his professions to see what he *really* meant, so could he, ideally,
strip us of our pretensions to find what we *really* mean. Philosophically speaking, I am convinced that 'surface' and 'core', 'appearance' and 'reality', 'interpretation' and 'truth' are relative terms
and that when some people peel away what they think is a surface
to reach the core, other people may try to peel away that core to

reach the surface. The one hides the other. But there is no absolute way of telling which is truth and which is mask. There is no telling whether Boso's picture of the struggle between Alexander and Frederick is a symbol that stands for and conceals a class struggle; or whether our picture of the class struggle is a symbol that stands for and explains Boso's conception of the struggle.

While this way of looking at it could be taken as a defence of modern interpretations, it is at the same time an invitation to find out what Boso thought of himself and how he explained the tortuous career and achievements of his friend Pope Alexander to himself. For the more seriously we take interpretation and the more we toy with the possibility that it leads to what really happened (as opposed to what people thought happened), the more seriously we must take what people *thought* happened. Just as the interpretation can throw light on Boso, we must admit that Boso can throw light on an interpretation.

This is the reason why, as far as our knowledge of the past is concerned, all positivism and historical realism reduces itself *ad absurdum.* If we find out what really happened, we have to include Caesar's knowledge of himself. But we also know that he may have had wrong knowledge, that he may have lied or deluded himself. Hence, although his thought really happened, it may not tell us what really happened and it may assemble the subevents in a misleading or wrong manner. It only tells us what Caesar thought happened. If we want to know what *really* happened, we may have to substitute a thought of our own (e.g., Caesar wanted to ravish his mother; Alexander III wanted to bring about the victory of the liberal bourgeoisie, and so forth). But we know that *such* thoughts did not happen at the time we are studying and, though we think they tell us more truly what *really* happened, they are obviously not part of what really *happened* at the time.

It does not help to raise the objection that apples, when detached from their branches, fell to the ground long before Newton discovered why they did. When it comes to the study of history, where the objects of study are thinking or potentially thinking subjects, there is no conceivable way in which we can go beyond their thoughts or our thoughts. We presume that apples always fall, regardless whether anybody thinks why and how. Their causality is presumed to be real and independent of our knowledge. But as far as human beings are concerned, there is no real causality over and above what they think; for, as we explained above, causality is, in this case, modelled on the paradigm of the human will and of the expectations that human willing arouses. Caesar's and

Alexander III's thoughts and our thoughts about Caesar's and
Alexander III's thoughts: this is all we have. In human beings there
is no causality other than their thoughts of causal connections.
For this reason we cannot say that one causal thought is truer than
another or catches real causality more correctly than another. If
there are conflicting thoughts and competing causal laws, we can
only choose according to their intelligibility and plausibility. And
this means that such choices have to be made in terms of cultural-
scientific settings or epistemic systems; for these alone make them
intelligible or unintelligible.

    One can test the truth of this argument by examining Erik H.
Erikson's book *Young Man Luther*.[42] Erikson tells us very convincingly that Luther made his great breakthrough in theological
thought because his father had deprived him in his childhood of a
mother, who alone could have become the guarantor of his established identity (end of chapter 4). Luther's own story was very
different and there is no need to tell it again. Erikson, quite justi-
fiably, thinks that Luther was under an illusion and that what
really happened was that his father, Hans, was too domineering
and threatening for Luther to develop a well-established sense of
identity. But it is clear that the general law that Erikson uses did
not happen in the fifteenth century, but in the twentieth century.
It is no good arguing that though the general law was thought of
by Erikson in the twentieth century it was present unconsciously
and therefore operative during Luther's childhood in the fifteenth
century. Even the idea that there can be operative causes of which
the people on whom they operate know nothing is a modern idea.
There is no way of proving that Luther's identity crisis was really
brought about by a domineering father except by showing that
somebody thought so. And, by the nature of the case, we can only
prove that somebody thought so in the twentieth century. While
we may have reason for believing that apples fell because of gravity
before Newton thought so, we can have no conceivable reason
for thinking that identity crises were brought on by domineering
fathers before somebody thought so.[43] If we presume that such
crises did happen in the fifteenth century before people thought
so, then, at least nobody in the fifteenth century could have connected the two events (father domination – identity crisis) to show
that the one led to the other. One can only connect these two
events if one has the knowledge necessary to do so.

    One of the most widely debated questions in the philosophy
of history is the question whether historians can be objective.
There is no doubt, it is conventionally argued, that they ought to

be objective.[44] But there is wide disagreement as to whether they can be objective. In this bland form the problem is banal. We all know that every human being endeavours to be objective and that we all have in-built obstacles to pure objectivity. The mere psychology of perception acquaints us with these obstacles, and the moment we go beyond pure perception, depth-psychology has taught us to appreciate the virulence of a host of further obstacles. On top of deep-seated obstacles, there is vulgar prejudice and bias. The untrustworthiness of eyewitnesses is a commonplace of every detective novel. Historians must wrestle with this psychological problem as best they can, even as detectives and juries do. The problem in this form is moral and psychological and of no particular interest to the philosopher of history.

The problem becomes of interest to the philosophy of history in the medium range. To delimit the medium range, let us first consider the problem of objectivity in narrow and wide range. In the narrow range it presents itself in the form in which it was raised by Ranke and Becker. Ranke maintained that the historian must be objective and tell what actually happened. I do not think that he meant by this categorical demand that the historian should confine himself to explanations proper. Ranke knew perfectly well that, if the historian did, he would often be confined to retelling superstitious tales that would be unintelligible and, therefore, not objective, because things could not actually have happened in the way in which a superstitious explanation ('God struck him down by lightning') would have it. But Ranke did mean that the historian must extrude himself and his own judgments and present a portrait. In this simplistic form, Ranke's demand for objectivity is incapable of fulfillment, as we have argued on several occasions above.

Becker presented the opposite view. Despairing of the possibility of reaching any kind of final objectivity by presenting nothing but explanations proper, he argues that the historian must allow his own understanding free reign.[45] But I do not think he meant by this plea that the historian should confine himself to interpretations. He simply argued that the only history that can be intelligible to everybody is a history that is written with the help of those universals that happen to be acceptable and intelligible to everybody at any time. In a well-known paper, John Passmore has explained the various ways in which the word 'objectivity' can be understood in different senses, each somewhere between the extreme demand of Ranke and the extreme plea of Becker.[46]

In the wide range, on the other hand, the problem of objectivity is very general indeed. Literary texts are produced through the medium of language, which can, at best, point to certain images or events. But language's capacity to describe them or to render a portrait of them is severely limited by its own structure: it does not point very effectively. One often feels indeed that one might as soon use a car or a saucepan as a word or a sentence. If we did, we often would produce no greater descriptive failure. This, among other reasons, is one of the most important reasons why we are so singularly unsuccessful in describing emotions and faces — both things we are perfectly well acquainted with. Since portraits are unobtainable through language, we can never hope to write history objectively. If nothing else, the structure of the language we have to use intrudes and, in part, ends up by controlling the story.[47]

Let us, therefore, look at the problem of objectivity in its middle range, for in this range it is of great importance to the philosophy of history. It is best to start with terminology. We call an explanation objective when and only when it is an explanation proper. By contrast, an explanation that is really an interpretation is subjective. This terminology involves a shift in the meaning of the terms. Normally we speak of objectivity when prejudice and bias and all other distorting influences are absent. In this sense, the word 'objective' could be applied to both explanations proper and to interpretations. But in this application it obscures the all-important distinction between explanation proper and interpretation. The shift in meaning is suggested to align the adjectives 'objective' and 'subjective' with the two terms 'explanation proper' and 'interpretation'. It follows from what we have said that the distinction between objective and subjective understanding is not absolute. If the interpretation is typologically related to the explanation proper, it is obviously less subjective than an interpretation that is not so related. At the same time, an explanation in terms that could have been known to the person involved in the historical events but were actually not known is less objective than an explanation in terms that were actually known to the person concerned. These graduations apart, the new terminology leads to a somewhat startling but important insight.[48]

For some pieces of knowledge possessed by modern man it is claimed that they are universally true and scientifically supported by evidence. Modern man thinks of himself in possession of a body of general laws that help him to understand not only himself but also the past, regardless of whether or not the people of the past knew of these general laws. There is, for instance the insight that political ideas and practices as well as artistic effort reflect the economic interests of the dominant class in every society. Here we have a piece of knowledge that is taken to be universally true. If it is used to explain what happened in the past, in our terminology, the historian would be doing interpretation. An explanation of the past in terms of this Marxist theory would be subjective knowledge. But since the particular knowledge claims to be universally valid, it transcends what we believe to be subjectivity and objectivity. Marxists argue indeed that it is 'objective' knowledge even though the people to whom it is applied and whom we seek to understand in its terms did not know of it.

If we were in possession of a hard and fast set of universal laws and generalisations which we were certain to be universally recognised as true and in relation to which no shadow of doubt could ever arise, then we would be entitled to use them to provide interpretations, brushing aside, every time, all other historical explanations given by the people we are studying. In this case the concept of interpretation would become an absolute concept and assure us of genuine objectivity, opposed to the mere subjectivity contained in the way in which people are wont to understand themselves. The search for such a hard and fast body of universal laws or generalisations is stubborn and deep seated.

It is in fact a tradition in European thought since Plato to contend that there is a reality behind the appearances and that things are not what they seem. Since the eighteenth century our thinking is specially replete with attempts to nail down that elusive reality behind the appearances, and we have, indeed, come to see that we cannot take anything at its face value. There is no need to mention Hegel and Marx. Freud was certain that he had uncovered the real motive springs of human behaviour in the unconscious and spoke quite openly about his Oedipal desire to solve the riddle of the Sphinx (i.e., to unveil Mother Nature and behold her in her nakedness as she really is).[49] In a slightly less grand manner, ever since Comte, we have had one theory about the real meaning of religious beliefs and practises after another. For Frazer they were fumbling attempts to control nature; for Malinowski, charters for the social edifice; for Durkheim, deifications of the body social — to mention only a few. But even in our modern academic world the obsession has not ceased and I would like to quote in full, as an example, E. Leach's very sophisticated solution to the long and thorny debate whether and how Puritanism had something to do with the origins of capitalism:

> The English pattern runs something like this. The families which got
> themselves involved in the industrial revolution from 1750 onwards were
> families which had managed to accumulate capital over the previous cen-

tury but had not allowed it to set frozen in landed assets. The conditions
for such accumulation had been created at the beginning of the 17th
century by scientific, technical and educational innovations. But, as we
know from observations of what has happened recently in Asia and
elsewhere, technical innovation which creates the conditions for capital
accumulation also tends to favour the Malthusian upsurge of population,
which in turn frustrates the generation of industrial 'take-off'. However,
in England, in the relevant social classes of the relevant period, i.e. 1620–
1750, there was no upsurge of population. Standards of living increased
dramatically but the population remained the same. This in turn seems to
be associated with a very late age of marriage for women and an unusually low rate of illegitimacy. In short, it seems that by round about means,
the Puritan sexual ethic functioned as a system of birth control.[50]

Thus, with one stroke of the pen, Leach unveils the reality behind
the appearances. His theory is all the more remarkable in two
respects: it is truly interpretative, for people in the seventeenth
century had not yet heard of Malthus or the concept of take-off
and could not have offered such an explanation; and it departs
completely not only from Weber and Tawney[51] but also from
countless critics and supporters of the initial theory because it
shifts the whole argument from religious calling, predestination,
and the like to the field of sexual ethics. Similarly, in a completely
different area, E. Gellner has worked out a method of contextual
interpretation of strange and weird and, to us, obviously superstitious beliefs that claims to reveal what these weird assertions
'really mean'.[52]

All these attempts, from the claim of the Enlightenment
that the truth behind superstition had been uncovered, down to
Gellner's very sophisticated method of contextual interpretation
of the statements of primitive people about their gods or the
manner in which the universe functions, are very exciting but they
also are, as experience has shown time and again, extremely doubtful. The interest they command is usually in inverse proportion to
their credibility. Philosophically speaking, 'myth' and 'reality' are
interchangeable terms and what is myth to one person is reality
to another. After all, there is no compelling reason why we have to
think of God as a father-figure rather than of our father as a God-
figure.[53] 'We see in things of the senses', Thomas Mann makes the
aged Goethe say, 'a mask for higher concerns'.[54] One might just
as well stand the statement on its head and consider the higher
concerns a mask of the sensible world.[55] When it was recognised
that one cannot take anything at its face value we should have
contented ourselves with the ability to shuffle the various face
values and to substitute one for another. We should not have

embarked on the hopeless quest for the one and only reality behind the appearances. For the real value of our scepticism in regard to superficial appearances is not the discovery of the one reality that lies hidden behind the appearances, but the knowledge that one appearance, since it is no more than an appearance, can be substituted for another. We should, therefore, seek equivalences and interchangeabilities rather than the dark and permanent core. The primary processes of the unconscious are not the reality behind the secondary processes of the conscious.[56] This does not mean that we should once again take the secondary processes at their face value. We should rather, once the finality of the secondary processes have been rightly called into question, understand that any secondary process can be replaced, in the scheme of things, by another secondary process *or* by a primary process. And, similarly, there is no justification for one single such replacement of magic by science, or of myth by a given social relation, or of an idea by an economic relation. Now that these appearances are called into question, we should seek the ways in which one appearance can be substituted for another. An ideology is not a cloak for an economic relation any more than it is the other way round. But an economic relation can be replaced, when it is used as a general law or generalisation to explain or interpret, as the case may be, by an ideology. We know that the former is an appearance. But so is the latter. There is no earthly reason why the economic relation should be considered the hard and ultimately real rock, for there is no reason for believing that it is and, therefore, no reason for believing that there *is* a hard and ultimate rock of reality.[57] We must think of all these general laws as appearances and of all appearances as interchangeable. It does not matter whether we think that a spire conceals a phallus; or a phallus, a spire. But it *does* matter that we should know that whenever people speak of spires, we may substitute phalluses; and that whenever we speak of phalluses, we should be able to substitute spires. The real meaning of the Enlightenment was not, as is commonly supposed, the ability to unveil truth and reality, but the understanding that all generalisations and laws are appearances and that, therefore, certain appearances can be substituted for others. The thinkers of the Enlightenment performed only the unveiling. It was not until Hegel that the Enlightenment was carried to its conclusion and that the true significance of such unveiling was revealed.

Since we cannot tell which appearance is nearer to reality, or which is reality and which appearance, we must conclude that it is legitimate to substitute in any direction. It is obvious that we can replace an explanation by an interpretation. It is not so obvious, but quite legitimate, that we can consider the interpretation as much of 'reality' as the explanation. It is also legitimate that we should substitute an explanation for an interpretation, and so forth *ad infinitum.* If we seek to understand Caesar, Caesar is entitled, ideally, that we should make ourselves intelligible to him.

But let us return to our historical examples. There is a striking controversy whether the French Revolution was due to a class struggle. It is part of the modern search for an objectively true reality, a search that is prepared to brush all contemporary thought on the matter aside as uninformed, as due to false consciousness, as ideologically biased, and so forth, to maintain that there was a class struggle and that all other versions of what went on must be dismissed. The class struggle, it is widely held, was real, whether people at the time knew it or not; and every other view is make-believe.

The historians who have investigated how people in eighteenth-century France saw themselves and how they felt and thought about themselves are agreed that society was seen as an intricate hierarchy of interlocking and overlapping corporations.[58] As if these discoveries were not enough, it is also obvious that the inhabitants of the eighteenth century could not possibly have thought of themselves as members of social classes for the simple reason that they could not yet have read their Marx. If one takes them at their word, the French Revolution cannot have resulted from a contradiction between a rising capitalist bourgeoisie and a feudal nobility.[59] But should one let the matter rest there? Does it follow that since these people were *not aware* of forming social classes that they did not *actually* form such classes that stood in such a conflict to one another? Many historians have given a negative reply. They argue that these people were captive to a false consciousness. They show that if one probes, one finds that these hierarchically ordered corporations fall indeed into sets of classes that were dialectically opposed to each other. Such probing does not take the testimony of the inhabitants of eighteenth-century France as the last word but proceeds on the assumption that there were more 'objective' criteria such as income and modes of production according to which these inhabitants must be classified.[60] The findings of these historians are impressive but for one circumstance. There is no reason why we should take the criteria of classification employed by these historians as more 'objective' than the criteria employed by the other historians. At first sight it may indeed appear as if income and mode of production were more 'objective' criteria than people's thoughts about their status.[61] But on closer examination one finds that this is not so. The appearance is misleading. If one classifies people according to their income one is in reality classifying them according to a thought about their income (i.e., according to the thought that income is relevant). For this reason the material criterion is not more objective than the mental criterion. All we have is the substitution of one criterion of classification (material circumstances) for another (the testimony of the people investigated). The Marxist method is therefore not more objective but shows itself to amount to nothing but the substitution of one kind of thought for another kind of thought.[62]

The critical observer is, of course, strongly tempted to reject the claims of Marxist 'objectivity' or of any other kind of objectivity. He must keep to his determination to respect the sources, to explain them by explanations proper, and to extrapolate and, at most, to offer translational explanations. If he goes beyond translation, he imposes an alien body of knowledge on the sources of his knowledge and distorts and becomes subjective. But the matter is not quite so simple. In the case of the Marxist example cited above, one might find no great difficulty in resisting the temptation to avoid translation and the imposition of an interpretation. But there are other, more modest pieces of knowledge where it is much more difficult to resist.

Take, for instance, the knowledge that people are more likely to take up a saviour religion and abandon their tribal or civic worship if that tribal or civic worship has been dislodged by economic or political circumstances. People who are footloose, in other words, are prone to espouse a saviour religion. People who are not are likely to remain proof against its messages. Armed with this knowledge we can throw a great deal of light on the spread of Christianity both inside the Roman Empire and among the Teutonic peoples that invaded the empire. Similarly, this knowledge will help us to understand something about the spread of Buddhism into China and the appeal of Nazism in Germany during the twenties and thirties of this century. I myself am firmly convinced of the truth of this knowledge in a sense in which I am not convinced of the truth of Marxism in general. It would be intellectually frivolous to reject this knowledge because its application to ancient Roman or Chinese history would be a 'subjective' interpretation. If we refrained from using it we would deprive ourselves of an important contribution to our knowledge. We would then have to accept the ancient Christians at their own valuation, which was that Christianity triumphed because it was a 'truer' religion than all the others and because God promised both the Emperor Constantine and the Frankish King Clovis that He would help their armies to victory if they espoused the Christian religion. The first part of such a seemingly 'objective' explanation is highly doubtful. The second part is downright false and actually inconsistent with much else we know of the Christian God. It can only be made plausible when we take into consideration the likelihood that King Clovis confused the God of Jesus with the Jehovah of the Old Testament. If we confine ourselves to explanations proper and to extrapolations from explanations proper, we would be at the mercy of what people in the past thought of themselves. It is therefore necessary that we should allow interpretations of this kind, even though in our knowledge we have described them as 'subjective'. We should really allow that they are objective interpretations because we have confidence in the validity of the knowledge on which they are based. We need to remind ourselves that there is a difference between such *interpretations* and *explanations proper*, and that these interpretations are subjective because they do not originally go with the object they are imposed upon and that the explanations are objective because they do. But we must distinguish between a certain kind of subjective interpretation and simple subjective interpretation. Perhaps we should reserve the word 'interpretation' to the former and call the latter 'vulgar interpretation'. If we do not, we are at the mercy of every superstition peddled in the past and deprive ourselves of the ability to understand critically and to unmask explanations provided in the past. Pym and Cromwell made all sorts of protestations about their religious conscience and about constitutional liberty. But we would impoverish our understanding of the seventeenth-century Roundheads if we accepted them at their word and refused to probe and unmask them by using our knowledge of economic class interest and class motivation. We must therefore accept the possibility that some interpretations, though subjective, are really more objective than objective explanations. If we did not accept this possibility, we would make nonsense of the notion of delusion. We know very well that many people are deluded about themselves, and it would be a mistake not to allow for the possibility that many people in the past were deluded about themselves. If we confine ourselves to explanations proper and to extrapolations from such explanations, we could never uncover such delusions. Good history is not confined to objective explanations. History also contains subjective interpretations, which lay claim to a 'higher' objectivity, and these subjective interpretations should be distinguished from vulgar interpretations, which are based on an arrogant attitude of 'I know better than you and I do not need to listen'.

The crux of the matter is that in this way of looking at the problem there is nothing we could sensibly describe as 'objectivity'. All we have is a large number of subjectivities. There is the subjective view taken by Caesar; the subjective view that could have been taken by Caesar; the subjective view that could not have been taken by Caesar but that is typologically related to the view he did take or could have taken; and, finally, there is the subjective view that could not have been taken by Caesar and that is not even typologically related to any of the views he took or could have taken. If you will, the only advance toward something that might qualify for the term 'objective' consists in as complete as possible an enumeration of all the possible subjectivities. But since such an enumeration can never be exhaustive, objectivity even in this oblique sense is a chimera. The historian, it is more sensible to conclude, does not really busy himself with a search for objective knowledge but seeks to weigh subjectivities against each other and proceeds cautiously in substituting one subjectivity for another. Perhaps one might say that he is aiming at some kind of objectivity when the method of his substitutions is carefully controlled rather than wildly arbitrary.

At best the substitution of one subjectivity for another is a knotty problem. Marx wanted to cut the Gordian knot by his grand theory that all mental events are determined by material events. Had he or anybody been able to justify this materialist doctrine, he would have come close to establishing a criterion for something one might have called objectivity. For in this case all those explanations that operated with factors other than materially determined ones could have been brushed aside as subjective hallucinations, delusions, mystifications, ideologies, and propaganda; and all those that operated with materially determined factors could be considered genuine explanations to be substituted for the false ones. But we know today that the materialist doctrine that Marx had to use as a premise for his definition of objectivity is yet another subjective view. And without that doctrine, the concept of objectivity derived from it loses its meaning.

There can be no objective knowledge when the object of our knowledge is a subject or a potential subject.[63] For any subject is

ideally, if not actually, capable of saying how he feels, how he
thinks events hang together, and how they ought to be explained.
In all such cases the subject's views on the matter are of the same
weight as the views of the observer. For this reason there can be
nothing but a multiplicity of subjective views. At least one would
have to have a special theory to be able to single out one or two
of these subjectivities and accord them a privileged status. As far
as we know there is no such theory. The subjectivities are therefore all of equal value and weight. This does not mean that one
ought to refrain from substitutions. But it does mean that substitutions ought to be undertaken cautiously and guided at least by
some regard for typology.

I want to conclude with another example. During the twelfth
century there was a widespread belief that the advent of the
Antichrist was near. According to ancient prophecies the reign of
the Antichrist would be a holocaust and be preceded by increasing
social and economic disturbances accompanied by moral turpitude.
During the twelfth century, therefore, people put one and one
together. They were observing rapidly increasing social dislocation
in central Europe and concluded that this dislocation was a sign
that the coming of the Antichrist was near. We can find speculation about his approach in a great many books and even in more
popular literature as well as in plays written at the time. To the
modern reader the explanation seems strange. First, we know that
the Antichrist did in fact not come, not even in 1260 as calculated
by an arithmetically talented Franciscan friar. Secondly we feel
that it is not surprising that he did not come because, at best, the
image of the Antichrist can only be a symbol. Thirdly, we must
conclude that it is wrong to explain the social dislocation as the
effect of the coming of the Antichrist. It is quite implausible to
us today to accept a later event (the Antichrist) as the cause of an
earlier event.

To make headway and to understand we must go beyond what
people in the twelfth century thought. We can, of course, in the
first instance, describe their explanation, which connects their
belief in the approach of the Antichrist with the social dislocation
and moral turpitude they observed around them. In doing this, we
have discovered a *Sinngebild* that made sense to the people of the
twelfth century. But since that *Sinngebild* does not make much
sense to us, we must seek a different explanation.

We begin by breaking up the original *Sinngebild*, which linked
the dislocation to the Antichrist. It did so on the basis of a general
law that said that the coming of the Antichrist will be preceded by

social disturbances. The social disturbances were thus a sign of the approach of the Antichrist. When we drop that general law because it does not sound plausible to us, we break up the intelligible constellation of events. We are still left with the widespread belief that the Antichrist was coming and with the widespread social dislocation. But now these two events are no longer linked. How can *we* explain them?

We explain the dislocation because we know both of a general law about rapid population growth and consequent dislocation and of the fact that there was an unusually rapid population growth during the second half of the twelfth century. The period from 1150 to 1200 ranks with the fifteenth century and the hundred years from 1750 to 1850 as one of the great periods of population explosion in European history. We can now explain the social dislocation with the help of our general law about population growth and social disclocation. In doing so, we are interpreting.[64] The law was not known at the time. Moreover, it was not known at the time that there was population growth. There were no census and no statistics in the twelfth century. We can now link an event well known in the twelfth century, social dislocation, to an event not well known in the twelfth century but uncontestably true. We can do so by making use of a general law not known in the twelfth century.

What about the Antichrist? We are here left with an event (the widespread belief in the approach of the Antichrist) that used to form part of a twelfth-century *Sinngebild* but that is no longer part of the new intelligible constellation of events. In the new constellation the social dislocation is linked with population growth. Fortunately, we know today of another general law also not known in the twelfth century. We know that rapid social dislocation, when families break up and people move away from each other, and so forth, leads to a strong increase in anxiety. If we now assume that the belief in the approach of the Antichrist was an anxiety symbol, we can link, with the help of our general law about anxiety, the social dislocation to the staggering increase in anxiety. Here we have a new intelligible constellation of events. Dislocation is connected to anxiety and anxiety, to the belief in the approach of the Antichrist.

In the twelfth century, the series of events was simple. There were two events, dislocation and belief in the approach of the Antichrist; and one was the sign of the other. To us, the series is much longer. We have now four events:

　　　　　1. Rapid population growth.

2. Noticeable social dislocation.

3. Increased anxiety.

4. Belief in the approach of the Antichrist.

Events nos. 1 and 2 are linked by a modern demographic general law. Events nos. 2 and 3 are linked by a modern psychological general law. Events nos. 3 and 4 are linked by a modern general law concerning the nature of symbolism. In the process of this interpretation of nos. 2 and 4, we had to postulate more events in the twelfth century than were observed by people in the twelfth century. The test of the interpretation must therefore largely depend on our ability to find evidence that the two postulated events actually did occur. There is no difficulty in regard to population growth. There is a general consensus among historians that it did take place and this consensus is based on the examination of separate pieces of evidence that support the conclusion independently. In regard to anxiety, the situation is not so straightforward. Anxiety is a psychological condition and it is not easy to determine what constitutes a sign of anxiety, let alone possible to observe a direct manifestation of it. Least of all is it possible to find direct evidence for a state of mind. Even in our contemporaries, we cannot ascertain directly whether they are anxious or not but have to be content with observing their behaviour and such anxiety symbols as they exhibit. In the twelfth century, one of the strongest pieces of evidence for an increase in anxiety is the widespread Antichrist expectation. Here then, we are running around in circles. We are aware of the Antichrist expectation but cannot accept as proof of the justification of that expectation that there was social dislocation. Therefore we interpret that expectation as an anxiety symbol and then end up by arguing that that expectation is proof of increased anxiety. It would be more comforting if we had independent evidence of increased anxiety, such as evidence of an unusual increase in nail biting. But we must allow for the possibility that Antichrist expectations and nail biting are alternative expressions of anxiety and if one gets the one, the other is likely to be absent. If this is so, we must content ourselves with accepting the Antichrist expectation as evidence of anxiety because its very presence is likely to have inhibited alternative symbols. I do not think that such circularity completely invalidates the chain of reasoning. It should make us cautious and we must always be conscious of it. I want to stress the presence of such inevitable circularity in ordinary historical understanding because we will see in chapter 9 that all philosophy of history contains a large amount of circularity. It is part of the argument of this whole book that the difference between ordinary historical understanding and a philosophical understanding of what happened in the past is a difference in degree only. The present example serves as a preliminary, small-scale illustration of this point.

The breaking up of the original *Sinngebild* and the substitution of the new, more complex *Sinngebild* is a gain in understanding. The gain is made at the expense of an explanation proper — an explanation that we simply brushed aside. But the brushing aside was not undertaken arbitrarily or tyrannically. We did not simply seize on one event, the social dislocation, and link it to an event not known of in the twelfth century. We took care, on the contrary, to link it to other events in such a way as to reach, in the end, an event to which it had originally been linked in the self-understanding of the twelfth century, to the expectation of the Antichrist. We have substituted new general laws and interpreted events unknown or unobserved in the twelfth century. But the final outcome of the rearrangement embodies a constellation of two events (dislocation and Antichrist expectation) that were linked in the original *Sinngebild*. The interpretation is therefore typologically related to the twelfth-century explanation proper. This means that if we encountered today a twelfth-century Rip van Winkle, we could hope to make our interpretation clear to him. If we had proceeded arbitrarily and offered an interpretation not typologically related to the way people in the twelfth century understood the matter, we could not hope to do so. A Rip van Winkle can be taught new general laws and made to see new evidence in their favour. But he would still expect them to help him to understand why he himself believed that the coming of the Antichrist was near before he fell asleep.

By contrast, let us look at something that would be an arbitrary interpretation, not related typologically to the way people in the twelfth century understood the matter.[65] We know and people in the twelfth century knew that during the second half of that century, in Germany, there was a growing, self-conscious attempt by a powerful group of princes to define themselves as an upper caste of society and to exclude a whole lot of wealthy and influential landowners from that caste. Before that time, there had been no such demarcation. It would be an arbitrary interpretation to link the social dislocation at one end with population growth and at the other with the growing suppression of the social and political aspirations of all those wealthy landowners who did not quite belong to the very top group of princes. Such a linking would appear very reasonable to a modern reader trained in sociology and demography, but would not have appeared plausible to a twelfth-century observer because in this interpretation the Antichrist expectation is simply left out. At best, it would be brought in by saying that it was a belief fraudulently and egotistically fostered by the upper layer to frighten all those whom they wished to keep out, a ruse invented to make the brute fact of social suppression palatable. If the Antichrist was believed to be near, the excluded landowners might accept their fate as being due to the moral turpitude expected to be a sign of the Antichrist. No Rip van Winkle who had gone to sleep in the second half of the twelfth century would recognise this interpretation as something he could learn to understand. He would be confronted with the story that there was a class struggle (a notion he could not possibly relate to anything in his twelfth-century experience), with the declaration that the belief in the coming of the Antichrist was a ruse propagated by self-seeking princes to sugar the pill for those whom they sought to exploit economically and to oppress politically. Both story and declaration are so far removed from the world he knew before he fell asleep that he could never hope to make the connection or even to be taught the connection.

I do not mean to argue that this second, arbitrary interpretation must at all costs be rejected. It is arbitrary in the sense that it is not typologically related to the way people in the twelfth century understood the matter. But it is an interpretation all the same and in that sense not really different from the first, typologically related interpretation. Both interpretations tell us something new about the twelfth century — something that was not known to the people who lived in the twelfth century. One interpretation can be related to what people in the twelfth century understood; the other cannot. But since Rip van Winkles do not really exist, the process of understanding is always asymmetrical. We must try to understand the twelfth century. But we are not under an obligation to frame our understanding of the twelfth century in such a way that it could be explained to the people of the twelfth century. We want to understand them; but they do not want to understand us. As long as we are clear that there is a difference between an interpretation that is typologically related to how people understood themselves in the twelfth century and an interpretation that is not so related, we have done all we can do. It would be a foolish act of self-mutilation if we insisted that only typologically related interpretations are acceptable. The asymmetry is a special feature of a situation that arises in the study of history where the people who are to be understood have lived earlier (and are now dead) than the people who seek to understand them.

The historian as a student of the past has a simpler task than the modern anthropologist who studies people and societies that are still in existence. Our understanding of the twelfth century can be quietly asymmetrical. But if we study the Andaman Islanders or the Nuer, we should not rest content with such asymmetrical understanding, which accepts an arbitrary interpretation, as readily as with one which is typologically related to the way the Andaman Islanders and Nuer understand themselves.[66] When the people and the societies we seek to understand are still alive and contemporary with us, we are under a moral obligation to them not to impose arbitrary interpretations on them. There is nothing to stop us from doing so, and in many cases such arbitrary interpretations can add to our understanding of them. But if we interpret them arbitrarily in this sense and understand them asymmetrically, we are treating them as inferiors and as objects.[67] The historian, dealing with people who are dead, need have no qualms about any asymmetry of his understanding. But the anthropologist, dealing with contemporaries who are very much alive, ought to have qualms, for unlike our twelfth-century ancestors, these contemporaries might conceivably wish to understand us.

We can now see with precision why Ranke's demand that the historian ought to describe what actually happened and all other forms of positivism are both untenable and self-defeating. Even if we suppose that the explanations of his own behaviour that Caesar might have offered are part of what actually happened, the demand that we should describe what actually happened cannot be fulfilled simply by an inclusion of Caesar's explanations of his own behaviour. To begin with, there is the question whether the explanations that he might have offered but did not in fact offer are part of what actually happened or not. But let us leave aside this minor, complicating factor. Let us concentrate instead on the real meaning of the phrase 'what actually happened'. If we want to find out what *really* happened, we cannot necessarily be satisfied with the explanations that Caesar would have offered, because we have every right to presume that he was ignorant or capable of delusions or dishonest. If we want to find out what really happened, we might have to brush his own explanations aside and substitute an interpretation. We might, for example, have to substitute the interpretation that he was engaged in a class struggle or the interpretation that he, deep down, wanted to ravish his mother. Such interpretations pull the wool from our eyes and tell us what *really* happened — as contrasted to what Caesar thought or wanted us to think happened. But by no stretch of the imagination can we claim that any of these interpretations we substitute are part of what *actually* happened. They are part of what is happening today in the minds of modern historians. They are not part of what went on during the first century B.C.

Here, then, we come to the crux of the matter. If we want to find out what really happened, as opposed to what people thought, or wanted others to think happened, we must introduce universals that are definitely not part of what went on at the time in question. The explanations that Caesar offered and even those that he might have offered are part of what happened. The positivist, be he a Rankean or any other kind of positivist, would have to end his investigations with the discovery of these explanations, because he is avowedly limiting himself to the discovery of what went on. But since he is limiting himself in this particular way, he is actually forcing himself to remain content with less knowledge than he might have. He has to remain content with the story that Caesar wanted to put across. If he, on the other hand, sets out to discover what *really* happened (as opposed to what Caesar alleged), the historian has to proceed beyond positivism. He has to introduce into his knowledge of the past elements of his knowledge of the present (i.e., interpretations). At best, therefore, we must look upon Ranke's positivism as a sort of paradox. When taken by the letter, it leads us to illusions about Caesar and, if taken in a wider spirit, it leads us to the real truth about Caesar but also to a kind of knowledge that is far removed from positivism, since it freely mixes up what is going on in the modern mind with what happened in the past.[68]

I have shown that there are many different kinds of understanding. There are explanations proper and interpretations. The latter can be either translations, or typologically related interpretations, or arbitrary interpretations. None of them reveal truth; all of them reveal something. There is no such thing as final truth in any of them because there is no final truth. At one extreme there are explanations proper; at the other, arbitrary interpretations. But even an explanation proper is merely one of many possible ways of linking events. It is no nearer a truth than an arbitrary interpretation simply because it reflects the way the man we try to understand himself saw himself. He, like everyone of us, is given to self-deception. *All* kinds of understanding are veils of knowledge drawn over the unfathomable and abysmal face of reality. And reality itself is not the sort of thing that can be simply transcribed or copied into a book or recorded. It is in every case a reality seen by somebody and thus intelligible to somebody. But everybody is, at the same time, given to delusions of one kind or another so that no single vision of reality can claim a privileged status.

This way of looking at the whole question of objectivity in historical knowledge is nowhere better presented than in Hegel. At the beginning of the nineteenth century he made a staggeringly original discovery. He discovered that the human spirit is not just one of the many objects in the world that can be seen, or known, or perceived, but that it is something that first defines itself in its relation to objects. The discovery was first put in length and detail, expressed in cumbersome terms, in *The Phenomenology of the Spirit*[69] in which he explained that the spirit does not have an 'objective' existence but only a phenomenology. It reveals itself differently at different times; its nature is its appearance, and its appearance depends on the circumstances. Hegel's whole philosophy of history is extrapolated from this view. So many non-Hegelian and even anti-Hegelian writers have since appropriated its central idea that it is quite impossible today to gain a just impression of its originality. The central idea is that the 'spirit' — an all-embracing and difficult word in any language — can only manifest itself to itself. An object manifests itself to spirit; but a spirit can only manifest itself to itself. If I see a chair, I am aware of a *chair*. But if I am sad or know that I see a chair, then there is nothing over and above the fact of such knowledge that can tell me whether I am actually sad or whether I know that I see the chair. If I have a feeling of sadness, that feeling is ultimate in the sense that there is no state of affairs other than that feeling. Whereas if I see a chair, there is a state of affairs (namely, the presence of the chair) that can confirm whether I suffer from a hallucination or whether I am perceiving a chair. A state of feeling or of consciousness, therefore, does not refer to something beyond itself. It can, however, be brought into focus when it confronts the feeling or consciousness of another person. If I say I am sad and confront a person who tells me that I am not *really* sad, there must ensue some kind of clash between these two feelings of consciousness — a battle to the death; or at least a battle until either I assert myself over my friend or he asserts himself over me. Since there is no outside state of affairs to which either of us can appeal, the contest is the only arbiter. Every consciousness, Hegel concluded with uncanny psychological insight, demands the death of another consciousness.

This argument ties in directly with the contention, put forward in chapter 3, that our understanding of causal connections is derived from the paradigm of a mental act that wills to effect a change. There is no telling whether we are right in believing that A will cause B and no way of knowing for certain that A is the cause of B. If we knew for certain, our states of mind, which to a large extent consist of beliefs in causal connections, would have an objective ontology. If we knew, we could say with certainty that our state of mind that a certain relationship of causality exists between A and B reflects a true state of affairs and is therefore a correct state of mind that can be contrasted to incorrect states of mind. But since we cannot have such knowledge, we must remain content with the knowledge that we have states of mind that consist in the beliefs that there are causal relations between A and B and between C and D. We must therefore remain satisfied with the appearances of our states of mind and can never compare them to a reality over and above these states to sort out which of these states of mind is a true state and which is not. When two such states of mind clash, it is impossible for one of them to appeal to external arbitration or to subject the dispute to a test. One mind, unable to appeal to an external authority, can only wrestle with another mind. Hegel extravagantly concluded that the battle must be battle to the death of one mind. In a more peaceful spirit, I would like to suggest that we examine the substitutability of one state for another, work out the various types of possible substitutions, and remain content with the never ending interplay of permissible and not so permissible substitutions.

MYTH: AN ALTERNATIVE COVERAGE

When historians carry out their researches and compose their narratives, they are apt to get involved with problems of explanation and interpretation and the problem of how interpretation is related to explanation, though, for the most part, they do not consider the latter problem as consciously and conscientiously as they ought to. For this reason they often tend to lose sight of the wider problem — the problem of the meaningfulness of the story or narrative they compose. At a lower level, the meaningfulness or intelligibility, as we have seen, is necessarily built into the story because there could be no story without general laws or universals that are very much *like* general laws. But a story in which a wild and uncontrolled hodge-podge of universals are employed will not read well and will possess only a very low degree of intelligibility. There must be a unifying factor, something like a principle that encompasses the kind of universals employed. Hayden V. White has explored the role of these unifying factors in great detail and with much precision in his book entitled *Metahistory* and has shown that for the major historians of the nineteenth century these unifying principles consist of four Modes of Emplotment — Romantic, Tragic, Comic, and Satirical; and of four Modes of Argument — Formist, Mechanistic, Organicist, and Contextualist. He further shows that these four modes have ideological implications — Anarchist, for the Romantic and Formist; Radical, for the Tragic and Mechanistic; Conservative, for the Comic and Organicist; Liberal, for the Satirical and Contextualist. The analysis is clinched by the argument that the four tropes (metaphor, metonymy, synecdoche, and irony) 'are paradigms, provided by language itself, of the operations by which consciousness can prefigure areas of experience that are cognitively problematic in order subsequently to submit them to analysis and explanation. That is to say, in linguistic usage itself, thought is provided with possible alternative paradigms of explanation'. He then goes on to show how the representationality of metaphor is linked to Formism,

how the reductiveness of metonymy is linked to Mechanism, and
how synecdoche is integrative in the way in which Organicism is.
'Metaphor', he continues, 'sanctions the prefiguration of the world
of experience in object-object terms, metonymy in part-part
terms, and synecdoche in object-whole terms.' Irony stands apart
because it is metatropological and 'provides a linguistic paradigm
of a mode of thought which is radically self-critical with respect
not only to given characterisation of the world of experience but
also to the very effort to capture adequately the truth of things
in language'. Also, irony is transideological because it can be

> used tactically for defence of either Liberal or Conservative ideological
> positions . . . and it can be used offensively by the Anarchist and the
> Radical. . . . But, as the basis of a world view, irony tends to dissolve all
> belief in the possibility of positive political actions. In its apprehension
> of the essential folly or absurdity of the human condition, it tends to
> engender belief in the 'madness' of civilisation itself and to inspire a
> Mandarin-like disdain for those seeking to grasp the nature of social
> reality in either science or art.[1]

The body of the book is taken up with the demonstration that
this analysis of writing history applies to the great nineteenth-
century historians. But White could show with equal success that
it applies to the historians of all other ages too. These brief quotations can hardly do justice to the subtlety and sensitivity of the
whole book, which, it seems to me, is by far the most important
contribution to the philosophy of history or — more correctly —
to its theory since Collingwood's book *The Idea of History*, and it
is hoped that after Hayden White's book the discussion of that
theory will never be allowed to revert to the level on which it has
been conducted during the last thirty years. It seemed appropriate
to introduce a summary description of White's argument at this
point because his book, like no other, analyses the principles that
are employed in the organisation and control of the universals
used in the composition of the historical narrative.

Obviously, some histories that are written are more meaningful than others and the whole question of the significance of a
narrative is ultimately wound up with the question why historians
write history at all. When one investigates their reasons, one will
usually find rationalisations. They will say that they study the
past for its own sake, or that they wish to learn from the experience of the past, or that they want to explain the present. It seems
that all these three kinds of explanation are tenuous. At any rate,
if one studies the origins and the history of historical writing, one
will find that one of the strongest reasons for writing history is

that historians wish to write narratives that are meaningful in the sense that they are guided or controlled by a mythic shape or by a shape derived from a myth[2] and that, the minor, in-built explanations and interpretations apart, the thrust of the sum total of the universals employed in the better and more readable kind of historical narrative is closely related to a myth. Such mythic moulds have exercised an enormous influence on the writing of history because the meaning of the myth, whatever it happens to be, is transferred to the story. Because of such transfer, some narratives have a more meaningful shape than others and I would venture to suggest that one of the reasons why historians have always been so concerned with the rise and decline of power (be it of classes, or empires, or communities) is because stories of rise and decline are, in the first place, reflections of myth. After all, one does not *have* to perceive the passage of time in that particular shape of rise and decline. One could just as easily see it as 'one damned thing after another' — to use a phrase employed by the film critic of *Time* magazine to describe the vision of time in the film *Breathless* by Jean-Luc Goddard. But there is no getting away from the fact that a story of rise and decline is more meaningful than a chain of one damned event after another.

It is time now to take a closer look at the role of myth in the composition of historical narratives and to examine how the general shape of the narrative is indebted to, or inherited from, myth.

Since the writing of history does not consist in tracing events as they succeed one another in time, we have come to the conclusion that general laws play an essential part in the composition of the historical narrative. The historical narrative is a highly selective story about the past. It is a very special way of seeing the past in the shape of a story. All those events, and there are myriads of them, that do not fit into that story, are simply left out. They belong to the past, but they do not belong to the story. The process of selection is controlled by general laws termed 'covering laws' because they cover the transition from one event to another.

In the course of our examination of these general laws and of the role they play in the construction of the historical narrative, we have found that they are essential not because they embody profound truths or startling scientific discoveries but because they are general. In fact, we have found that statistically speaking, they are, as far as narratives are concerned, far more frequently trivial and tacit than not. We must now add the observation that general laws are not the only way in which the gap between single events can be bridged. It must be bridged by something general;

but it does not have to be a 'law'. It must be bridged by something
general because the only method by which one single event can
be related to another and the only method by which the very
phenomena we have called events can be constructed is by something general. And there is no other method in which a single event
can be linked to another single event than *via* something universal.
But that universal need not be a general law.

Our examination of general laws has also acquainted us with
the phenomenon of circularity. We have seen that people believe
a general law to be true because they watch how the single events
it covers hang together more than once. Hence the observation
that certain events are frequently connected with one another or
follow one another leads to the 'discovery' or the belief in the
truth of a general law that says that they do. One can look upon
the process of reasoning in question, then, either by starting with
the general law and seeing it as the connecting link, or by starting
with certain single events and seeing how they are linked in our
experience more than once. If one starts with single events, one
starts with a story. If one starts with the general law, the story
follows. But in all cases the stories and the general law go hand
in hand. One could not think of the one without thinking of the
other. One story, however, does not present an occasion for a
general law; whereas one general law does represent an occasion for a
story. To obtain a general law, one must observe the same story
many times. There is inevitable circularity because one cannot
even put one story together without the help of a general law and
one cannot obtain a general law without watching one story happen more than once. In either case one could think of the process
ideally as starting with a general law or with a set of stories about
the same sequence of events.

There is however one special kind of story that does not owe
its existence to general laws. It is the kind of story usually described as a myth. Formally a myth is no different from an ordinary story. It narrates a sequence of events. But in substance there
are important differences. A myth is a story that is sensed to be
pregnant with meaning; a story that has references beyond itself
in a sense in which the story that Napoleon was in pain and became irritable has not. When we hear that Hercules cleaned the
Augean stables or that Marduk fought with Tiamat, we are immediately in the presence of a meaning other than the literal
meaning of the story. The several parts of the story hang together
by an inner logic in which the several parts of the story about
Napoleon as examined in our example in chapter 3 do not hang

together. Such causal relationships as exist in the myth do not
depend on general laws but on supernatural power. The myth,
then, though a story like any other story, is not dependent on the
vicious circle. A myth is a story that exists without recourse to
general laws. Moreover, it is a story that has a meaning beyond the
story, a meaning that can be and indeed beckons to be transferred
to other stories. In this sense a myth is a story with universal significance.

If the historian starts with a story that is a myth rather than
with general laws, he can avoid the vicious circle in which he becomes involved when he starts with general laws. As we shall see,
there are other pitfalls when one starts with a myth. Of this, more
later. With the help of that kind of story one can assemble single
events into a coherent and intelligible story, for the meaning of
the original story is intrinsic: it does not depend on recourse to
general laws, and it extends beyond the original story so that the
original story can be used as a paradigm.

The question of the truth of a myth does not arise because it
carries no time index and only very rarely a space index. When
one wants to check the truth of a story, the time index is much
more important than the space index. If the time at which something is supposed to have happened is given, one can, ideally,
check the story even though there may be no indication of the
place where it is supposed to have happened. As long as the time
is given, one could in theory start by covering every square inch
of the earth to look for confirmation. (This does not apply, of
course, to stories that are said to have happened in places other
than the earth.) But if there is an indication of the place in which
a story is supposed to have happened without an indication of
the time, there is no point in even looking. For whatever space
we look in, if we find no confirmation, we must conclude that
it could have happened in the same space at a different time. And
if we then look in the same place by digging it up and again find
nothing, we must presume that it may have happened earlier still.
The conclusion then is that any story without a clear time index
is not a story that depends for its meaning on its truth. A story
with a time index *and* a space index or even a story without a
space index but with a time index can have no meaning other than
the events it describes. But a story without these indices or a story
without a time index and with a space index *must* have a meaning
beyond itself because it can have no meaning for itself since it
does obviously not refer to identifiable events. Hence a story that
is loosened from a location in time (and possibly, though not

necessarily, also from a location in space) must have a universal meaning or, at least, must mean something *more* universal than itself.

A myth is a story of a series of events and as such is not formally distinguishable from a historical narrative. On the surface the myth of the labours of Hercules does not read significantly differently from a story of World War II. This is not really surprising. The absence of the time index in the myth makes it impossible to check whether one Hercules ever did clean the Augean Stables and whether the latter actually existed. But the events in the myth are particular and concrete, and are a story, and purport to relate what actually happened (whether 'actually' or not is wisely not mentioned, though the 'once upon a time . . .' opening formula constitutes an admission that the 'actually', in this case, is of little importance). Nevertheless, no myth is an arbitrary invention. It is telescoped experience and we can often follow the process of telescoping in great detail.

Where, in fact, do we get the sense of a meaningful story from? We get it from the basic experiences of nature and life. There we know how things hang together in an important way without being dependent for that knowledge on chronological contiguity. The most basic kinds of experience are:

1. The cycle of the seasons.
2. The polarity of male and female.
3. The presence of conflict and combat.

It is possible to introduce variations into the three types. Thus, for example, no. 1 can be seen as a set of combats between summer and winter; or it can be seen as an ascent toward summer; or as a decline into winter. No. 2 can be seen as a conflict between the two poles or as a coming together of two opposites into Oneness. No. 3 can be seen as a series of trials before the achievement of a triumph; or as a quest for an ultimate triumph. On top of these basic variations, further *meaning* can be injected into the stories relating these basic experiences both by reshuffling of the single phases and by formalisation and repetition. But all variations and the further injections are derived from basic experiences, so that the meaning remains inherent in the variations and when it is eventually transferred to a historical tale that is constructed in the image of a myth, the meaning goes with it and is, in all cases, *derived* from the myth.

We can therefore distinguish between abstract and concrete universals. Universals are always necessary. Without universals, the

human mind cannot link events. But universals can be of two
kinds. If they are general laws, they are abstract universals. A
general law will say that all heavy bodies fall and then every single
body that falls is an instance of the general law. This is why we
call the general law an abstract universal. It is 'abstracted' from a
limited number of particular instances and sums them up, so to
speak. There is, however, a second kind of universal, the concrete
universal. The concrete universal is a story of particular events
told in such a way as to give rise to the impression that it is a type
rather than a unique concatenation of events. If one tells the story
that a certain car at a certain day crashed into a certain tree, one
is simply relating a particular story. But if one tells a story how
Hercules laboured to clean the Augean Stables, one is telling a
particular story in a manner in which it is a paradigm or type of
other stories. It is a concrete story; but, though concrete, capable
of reflecting other stories and of explaining them as replicas of
the original story. For this reason we call such a story a universal,
and more precisely, a concrete universal.[3] It is, though concrete,
a story that has a significance beyond itself. It is, if you will, a
paradigm that allows us to use it as a sort of ostensive general
principle.

The most striking instance of concrete universals is myth.
Myths are concrete stories told of particular people, relating
specific events. They are nothing if not concrete. Yet, they always
lack specific time and place indices and this facet alone gives them
a universal air. They obviously do not just report a simple set of
events but they report a set of events in such a way that other
people in other places can identify with them and mirror themselves in them. Insofar as historical narratives depend on universals
that are not abstract, they owe a great deal to myth. A concrete
universal is a story that can be used as an instruction on how to
put together events so that they make an intelligible story.[4]

At first sight, this contention seems a contradiction in terms.
We are accustomed to think of myth and history as antithetical
because we take the former to be an untrue story and the latter
to be a true story. History, we say, begins where myth ends. Historical knowledge, we believe, replaces myth. We destroy mythical
belief to gain genuine historical knowledge of what really happened. And indeed this commonsense view that myth and history
are opposites is deeply enshrined in the very origins of historical
study. The first Greek historian who ever applied himself to the
study of the past as history was Hecataeus, a direct forerunner of
Herodotus. Hecataeus came across the story about Io and Zeus.

The myth told that the first Egyptian kings were the descendants of Io. Zeus had loved Io and Zeus' jealous wife Hera had changed the poor girl into a cow and made the cow drift from country to country until it reached Egypt. There the spell had been solved and this is how Io got to Egypt. Hecataeus did not believe in spells and jealous wives of Zeus. He therefore explained that Io must have reached Egypt because she had been abducted by Phoenician merchants who sold her in Egypt as a slave. Here we find a stark example of the opposition of myth to history. Hecataeus destroyed a mythical story to recover its factual core.[5]

There is no denying that much history was and still is written to destroy incredible stories referred to as myths. But it would be superficial to let the matter rest here. In another important sense, there is no downright opposition between myth and history, the one a story that is false and the other a story that is true.

Intellectually unsophisticated people find it hard to think in terms of abstract universals. Abstract universals, though easy to recognise, are not easy to conceive. Concrete universals, though very ubiquitous, are not easily identifiable as such. Concrete universals, for this reason, are not easily used to construct history, and abstract universals, though easily recognised, are not always at hand. For this reason we find that less sophisticated people for the most part do not see the past as history. They know that there is a past and that in the past the seasons, and the days, and possibly the years succeeded one another. But they can think of the past merely as a succession of cycles. They can say that such and such an event happened in a spring and that that spring preceded a summer. But they cannot say whether that certain spring was before or after another certain spring. In fact, they cannot really identify a certain spring as distinct in time from any other spring, even though they can identify it as being after a winter and before a summer. Although they can see how summer leads to winter, they cannot see how the events of one particular summer led to the events in the following winter. Basically, then, one can distinguish between societies in which people can see the past as history and societies in which people cannot see the past as history. It would be a mistake to think of the former as more advanced and of the latter as backward. For there is no obvious sense in which the past *is* historical and it is therefore wrong to maintain that those who cannot see it as historical are lacking in intellectual understanding. To describe the people who see the past as an endless series of cycles as primitive or backward, one would have to prove independently that the past *is* a historical progression.

Then, and only then, could one conclude that the people who cannot see it as such are lacking in intellectual clarity. But the historicity of the past cannot be established. Historicity is simply one of the many possible ways of being aware of the past.

The first distinction then is between people who can see the past historically (i.e., as a story) and those who do not. Admittedly the ability to see the past as a story depends to a large degree on the employment of abstract universals. But we have just shown that abstract universals are not the only universals. Concrete universals too can be employed to construct an historical narrative. In societies in which a certain type of mythology is present, the past can, but need not, be seen as history, even though abstract universals are absent.

The concrete universal functions differently from the abstract universal. The abstract universal provides a covering law that bridges the gap between one event and another. The concrete universal provides a paradigm, a sort of expectation of what a story might be like. It arouses an expectation of what kind of event might be linked to another event and how one thing might have led to another. The story told of the past in terms of a concrete universal myth will not be a slavish replica of the myth. But it will follow its main outlines and present the same shape and direction. When people are used to the myth that God created the world for a certain purpose, they will expect that most stories they are told will reflect creativity and purpose. History and myth are therefore not just opposites. In an important sense they are also complementary. Myth can give rise to history.

If one wants to distinguish between myth and history, one must not rely, as so many historians have done, on the criterion of credibility. If one scrutinises every story in regard to its inherent credibility, one might be able to dismiss some as myth. It is, for example, more credible that Alexander the Great had 5,000 warriors than 50 million warriors. But since standards of credibility change often quite rapidly and certainly at least slowly, this method is not very useful, for in the long run only logical contradictions are certain not to have happened. Everything else is, in some way or other, 'credible'. The only sensible way of drawing a line between myth and nonmyth is the method of dating. If we can assign a date to an event, we can check, in some roundabout way, whether it happened or not. Even here, as we have seen in chapter 3 and will see again in chapter 7, the problem does not admit of a simple solution. But at least, when there is a time index, we are farther removed from the incredible than we are when

there is no time index. If we see the difference between myth and
nonmyth in this light, we can recognise that the origins of historical thinking, supposed to have taken place in the early fifth
century B.C. in Greece and, probably at the same time among the
ancient Jews, cannot be identified as the rejection of myth by
some supposed rationalism. The origins consist, on the contrary,
in the gradual emergence of narratives that contain a larger and
larger proportion of events with a time index. The assignation of
a time index to events was a difficult problem, for the early historians had no fixed point from which to count the years and no
way of relating an event supposed to have happened at one time
in one place to an event supposed to have happened at the same
time in another place.[6] Indeed, the problem of the simultaneity
of events was as intractable as the problem of the chronological
succession of events. At any rate, the emergence of history from
myth was gradual and consisted in the eventual solution of the
problem of time indexing and had very little, if anything, to do
with the imposition of new, allegedly rational standards of credibility. For Herodotus, a story was a story and he had to relate
it.[7] He knew that some stories were more credible than others.
But his main purpose was not to work out standards of credibility.
His main purpose was to try as much as possible to construct a
chronological framework and to work back into the past by relating ancient stories chronologically to contemporary events.[8] The
gradual transformation of mythical tales of the past into historical
tales of the past is therefore essentially linked to the invention of
chronological schemes. The crux of the whole matter lies in the
ability to index time, not in the ability to distinguish tall stories
from true stories and to adhere to rigid standards of credibility.

The mere presence and currency of concrete universals in the
shape of myths is no guarantee that historical narratives will be
written and that the past will be seen as a story, as a sequence of
events. For that matter, the mere presence and currency of abstract universals in the shape of general laws is no guarantee that
the past will be seen as history. Modern Western man is highly
addicted to general laws, but his interest in the past as history is
very much on the wane. And similarly, there are many societies
in which there is an abundance of mythology but very little attempt to see the past as a story. In this context it is no concern
of ours to investigate why this should be so. Our purpose is to
investigate the nature of historical knowledge, and we can content
ourselves with the understanding that the coverage of the gap

between single events can be provided by concrete universals as well as by abstract universals.

It has been an essential part of my argument that historical narratives are not copies of something called 'history' but that they are abstract and selective compositions. The historian can compose such narratives only when he knows what sort of thing a story is. He cannot learn it by looking at something that has happened and copying it. The historian's situation in regard to his story is very similar to the painter's situation in regard to nature and landscape. Both André Malraux in the *Voices of Silence*[9] and Ernst Gombrich in *Art and Illusion*[10] have shown that artists do not 'copy' from nature but from each other. The important thing about an artist is his adaptation of the style of another artist. That style functions as a sort of concrete universal. Without prior knowledge of a style, an artist could not begin to paint. He makes use of somebody else's style and changes it or even revolutionises it, but he does not begin by staring at a landscape. It is, of course, interesting to speculate how the first painter ever began to paint when he had no predecessors to look at. The most likely explanation is that the first painters ever did not paint animals, men, or landscapes, but made abstract patterns and developed their style from these patterns, gradually adapting them to suggest the outlines of a face, a body, or a mountain.[11] Similarly the historian cannot copy from history, from what happened. He copies his style from somebody else and adapts it to tell his own special story. For the historian as much as for the artist, reality is not the sort of thing that can be transcribed. Neither artist nor historian can copy because there is nothing to be copied. The alleged 'model' is a figment of the imagination. The historian, like the artist, must know, to begin with, what sort of a thing a story (viz., a picture) is. Where does he get his sense of story from?

One can get a sense of story from the employment of abstract universals (i.e., general laws). But in actual fact, the beginning of historical writing relied very little on abstract universals and very heavily on concrete universals in the shape of myths. Myths were very widely known and provided historians with their first sense of what sort of thing a story is in contrast to a hodge-podge assembly of events. It is no surprise to find that the earliest forms of historical narrative emerged out of myth or as a continuation of myth, and we must not simply think of myth as something opposed to history, as stories that were destroyed by the writing of truthful history and superseded by historical narratives.

If one reads Mircea Eliade's book entitled *The Myth of the Eternal Return*,[12] one will precisely get this impression. Eliade contrasts myths with profane history. By myth he means stories that are told to explain cyclical ritual. In ancient Babylon, at the beginning of every year, the ritual of Marduk slaying the dragon was enacted. To explain the reason for the celebration of the ritual, a story was told and it said that in time out of mind Marduk had slain the primeval dragon, and so on. The ritual enactment of this event was a repetition. It repeated something that had taken place a very long time ago and both the ritual enactment and the myth were meant, Eliade explains, to convey the idea that time had not really passed but that the same sort of thing kept on recurring. By contrast, there is profane history. It consists of the notion that events succeed one another, that they do not recur, and that time passes, irretrievably and irremediably, never to come back. Eliade concludes his argument by saying that the notion that time passes irretrievably is hard to accept. People therefore prefer to think that what has happened in the past will happen again. In the past Marduk slew the dragon. To deny the reality of profane history, they repeat the slaying of the dragon at the beginning of each year. By reenacting the past, they can abolish the notion of time.[13]

All in all, Mircea Eliade is distorting the relationship between profane history and mythic-cyclic time. He really reserves the word 'myth' for cases where time is seen as cyclic and calls all other visions of time 'profane history'. At most, as I have tried to show, the transition from some myths to profane time is a very gradual transition.

> The relation of tradition to history is complicated. Consider the Passover tradition of Exod. 12:21 ff. as an example. This tradition takes up a ritual practiced by seminomads, who each spring move out of the steppes into the cultivated land where they and their herds can find food during the dry months of the year. In order to prevent the envious demons of the wilderness from hindering them, each family sacrifices an animal and sprinkles its blood on the tent posts. In Israel this custom was taken over to serve as a reminder of the departure from Egypt. The ritual specified the spring season, the sacrificial liturgy, and the family as the locus of the observance. But the function of apotropaic magic, which was of great importance to the nomads moving from the steppes, was dropped. The task instead was one of representing a historically unique event of fundamental significance, Yahweh's saving action during the exodus from Egypt. The historical nucleus is then the deliverance at the Sea of Reeds, but the foundation of the tradition rests on a ritual connected with the spring migrations of seminomads. The tradition is preserved in the Israelite Passover festival.[14]

Here we can follow in detail how a myth that was seasonal, and therefore cyclic in Eliade's sense, was used to bestow meaning on a linear series of events that we would describe as profane history. But the history in question is far from purely 'profane', for we can detect the mythic mould even in its linear version when we hear of the single event, the departure from Egypt. We should therefore never make a simple dichotomy between profane history (meaning 'linear history') and mythic-cyclic history. Even so-called profane history is a way of seeing time under the influence of a mythic mould.[15]

In Eliade's view, the mythological past and the passage of time (history) are opposed to each other. People either accept the passing of time or they do not. I have no quarrel with Eliade's argument. But I have to qualify it. What he says of ancient Babylon and countless other societies is doubtlessly true. But there are societies in which myths other than myths of repetition are cultivated and handed down. These other kinds of myths may co-exist with myths of eternal return or they may not. They are myths that tell stories about what happened in the past. They are therefore similar to Eliade's profane history. They are not quite the same sort of thing as profane history because they contain tall stories, events that are hardly credible, and they play fast and loose with chronological time. In these tales, events separated by centuries are telescoped into one event. Giants fight with human warriors and kings are assisted by magic. In this respect such tales remind one of the myths of eternal return. But there is one important difference. These myths are historical in the sense that they do not present the past as consisting of events that keep recurring at least once every year. They tell a continuous story. In this sense, they are much more like profane history even though they contain much that is pure fable. At any rate, there is no complete opposition between *these* myths and profane history. Profane history accepts the notion that time passes irretrievably and so do these myths. The people who listened to Homer and his predecessors narrating the tales of Troy were completely vague as to when these events were supposed to have taken place. But they did not listen to them because they knew they would take place again. Nor did they listen to fight their uneasy sense of the passing of time. The tale was told in a way that made every listener realise that it had happened once and once only and that it had happened in the past. The internal chronology of the tale was weak and the total chronology was absent. Given this tenuous relationship to chronol-

ogy, it was impossible ever to check any of the events related by
Homer and his bardic predecessors and for this reason people were
readily lulled into accepting fact and fable as if there were no
distinction. We know today that the story of Achilles' heel is not
true and that his divine ancestry did not exist, and we can see
the difference between these fables and the truth of the Trojan
War. But such distinctions are intellectual refinements. The thing
that really matters is that there were myths other than myths of
eternal return. The latter are the opposite of profane history and
are cultivated to fight the depressing sense that time passes all the
time. But the other myths are historical myths — not in the sense
that they are true stories, but in the sense that they present the
past as consisting of events that have happened, and that have
passed, and that will not occur again. In those places where historical myths exist, profane history will not arise in opposition
to myths of eternal return and will not bring people down to
earth and teach them that the past is different from what they had
thought. In such places, profane history will be a mere extension
of the sense of the past. It will make people more critical and
encourage them to sift fact from fable. But it will not introduce
as something new the notion that time passes irretrievably.

Historical myths, as distinct from myths of eternal return,
are therefore the most fertile soil for the development of ordinary
history. These myths will have made people acquainted with historical story telling. Where people are used to historical myths,
they know what sort of thing a narrative is.

It cannot be a surprise that the two places in which ordinary
historical narrative emerged are the two places in which bards had
accustomed people to historical myths. Historical narratives were
first written in ancient Greece by Herodotus in the middle of the
fifth century B.C. and in ancient Israel probably a few decades
earlier. In both places there was a long tradition of historical
mythology, and the writing of profane history was simply a critical
extension of the knowledge that things happen, that once they
happen they pass, and that once they have passed, other
things happen. In other words profane history was not first
written to combat the notion that time does not really exist
or, at least, does not really pass but is repeated or renewed at
least once every year. It was written to confirm an already
established notion of the passing of time. This aspect of the
emergence of profane history is much more significant than
the amount of critical scepticism that went with it. The amount
of criticism that went with it differed from place to place

and time to time. Herodotus was a great deal less sceptical than his immediate Ionian predecessor Hecataeus. But the real difference between the two lay, so far as we can tell, in the fact that Hecataeus busied himself with the rational criticism of myth and Herodotus narrated the succession of events.[16] There are important and interesting reasons for these differences in the degree of scepticism these early historians brought to bear on the matter. But these reasons do not concern us here. What concerns us here is the finding that history emerged gradually and as a matter of course from historical myth. Historical myth had taught people to see the past as a series of stories that do not repeat themselves and this kind of historical myth was used as the prior ingredient in the composition of historical narratives. Historical myth provided the sense of storyhood. People who were acquainted with Homer and with the tales of Jacob and Joseph, regardless of whether every single feature of these tales is true or not, knew the sort of thing a good and intelligible story consisted of. Historical myth provided the style from which later historians copied. In a sense we can say that Herodotus stood to Homer as Titian to Giorgione.

Strictly speaking the word 'copying' is not entirely appropriate. The process should be described as the distention of myth into history. It occupies such an important place in my argument and looms so large in the writing of history that a few examples are called for. In Virgil's *Aeneid*, which we may take for the sake of the present argument, at least in parts, as historical narrative, we can find a secular parallel to the sacred history of man's Fall, Redemption, and Sanctification.

> Out of the flames of Troy there comes forth a remnant destined to restore the defeated people to a height beyond all previous imagining — to nothing less than world Empire. This remnant is battered and tossed hither and thither, the leader is exposed to overwhelming tests and temptations, the people suffer every kind of misfortune; but they persist, and in the end the new city is built which will bring peace and justice to all the world. All this is an example of historical development which men may create if they collaborate with the will of God to fulfill their destiny. Nowhere, not even in the Old Testament, is it possible to find so poignant an account of the divinely assisted ascent of a people.

Compare the myth used by Virgil with the myth that is obviously operative in Sallust's story of the Catiline Conspiracy. Here we find a myth of how 'a whole society degenerates from its primitive vigour and moral purity as a result of the growth of wealth and luxury until men of the highest talents seek to rehabilitate their dissipated fortunes at the cost of the general over-

throw of the state'. Both examples are taken from Richard
Southern,[17] who comments that Sallust's dependence on the
myth of degeneration is all the more remarkable since both Polybius and Thucydides could have provided him with a more 'serious'
view of historical causation. I am not so certain how much more
'serious' these views exactly are; but it is certainly true that
Sallust eschewed them and clung to the myth of degeneration.
Still following Southern, we can explain the difference between
medieval annals and histories by reminding ourselves that it was
possible to write histories as opposed to annals because if

> at one level of experience events seemed discontinuous and chaotic,
> there was another level at which they could be regarded as typical of
> an order that was beyond change. This ambiguity in history which made
> it at once wholly irrational and wholly rational, at once wholly coherent
> and wholly incoherent, was one of the most carefully cultivated experi-
> ences of the Middle Ages. The Old Testament, with its various layers of
> historical truth, was the basis of this experience of order in the midst of
> apparent chaos.

Here, Southern shows, the myth of the Old Testament provided
the formula that enabled some medieval historians to transcend the
annalistic style and to write proper history.[18]
     For simplicity's sake I have equated concrete universals with
myths. I should, however, add that concrete universals are simply
stories of universal significance, that is, stories with a pattern that
can be applied to or read into other similar stories. In this way one
concrete story can supply a meaning not only to itself but also
to other stories, provided that the other stories exhibit a similar
pattern. Almost any concrete and particular story can be used for
such a universal purpose. Indeed, W. Gallie, on page 44 of his book
entitled *Philosophy and the Historical Understanding*[19] contrasts
two kinds of intelligence. One kind of intelligence, he says, can
assemble and discard suggestions, follow leads and evidences,
without being able to fit these into standard *cadres.* Such an intelligence can be of very high quality, but it is not the sort of intelligence that can appreciate stories and histories of some measure
of complexity. The other kind of intelligence can achieve historical
understanding and worthwhile understanding of our fellows because it can fit any story into a standard *cadre* (that is what we
have called a concrete universal) and understand it as an instance
of that standard *cadre.* Gallie, in other words, draws attention to
the importance of one's knowledge of a concrete universal. A
concrete universal lends meaning to another particular story
through a similarity in pattern, a similarity that is very different

from being a replica. An abstract universal can help to explain a
particular because the particular event can be recognised as a particular instance of the abstract universal. But a concrete story
lends meaning in a completely different way. There is no subsumption, and the story it lends meaning to is not a replica of
anything in the concrete universal story. This is why Gallie insists
that only a special kind of intelligent sensitivity can see the
relation between a particular story and a concrete universal story
and understand that the latter is more than just a story and is
indeed 'universal' in the sense that it projects a meaning beyond itself.

But let us come back to the question whether stories other
than myths can be concrete universals in this sense. F. P. Pickering
in two unfortunately insufficiently known books has explained
this matter carefully and eruditely. The first book exists only in
German and is entitled *Augustinus oder Boethius*,[20] and the
second is called *Literature and Art in the Middle Ages.*[21] Pickering
distinguishes two kinds of historical narrative current in the Middle Ages. The distinction is based on the knowledge of two different concrete universals. One concrete universal story relates how
events take place because of *fortuna*, and many medieval historians
wrote their stories by taking their general pattern of how events
succeed one another from Boethius' *De Consolatione Philosophiae*
in which *fortuna* appears as the power that presides over events.
The other concrete universal is Saint Augustine's story of the
struggle between the city of God and the city of man, and many
medieval historians took that story as their pattern and showed
how events hang together because this struggle goes on all the
time. Pickering therefore distinguishes between two main currents
of medieval historical literature. The one current is history à la
Boethius; and the other à la Saint Augustine. Neither Boethius nor
Saint Augustine provided an abstract universal but a concrete
universal — one single patterned story of what is happening in
the world. Both stories were used and, as Pickering observes,
they were used for different purposes. To write history à la
Boethius was suitable for tracing the rise of a dynasty or the
fall of a family or a single man's career. Saint Augustine's
concrete universal was more suitable for writing of the relations
between church and state. I might add that a twelfth-century
historian, Bishop Otto of Freising, used both universals. He
wrote à la Saint Augustine when he wrote his chronicle of
world history and then changed to Boethius when he wrote his
history of the rise of the Hohenstaufen and the early career of

Frederick Barbarossa.[22] All these examples show that a concrete universal does not necessarily have to be a myth, or, at least, not necessarily a myth in the conventional sense of the term.

To understand better how the concrete universal bestows meaning on stories other than itself, I would like to quote B. Snell. In his book entitled *The Discovery of the Mind* he describes what we have called the concrete universal as a 'mythical paradigm'.[23] The mythical paradigm, he says, is offered so that when, for instance, the aged Phoenix tells Achilles the story of Meleager (*Iliad* 9. 527–99) he hopes that Achilles will recognise himself in the figure of Meleager. The story that the Phoenix tells is a particular story. But it becomes a concrete universal or a mythical paradigm because it bestows meaning on Achilles' wrath. The paradigm, Snell goes on, is used because it helps one to establish one's place by means of comparisons. We might add that the comparison is not an exact replica. The Phoenix does not say to Achilles, 'Watch out, all men who are full of ire will suffer misfortune'. If he said this, he would be stating an abstract universal and then Achilles could subsume his wrath under the wrath of Meleager. The mythical paradigm operates in a more subtle, elliptical, and allusive manner. It invites the listener to reflect upon himself, to see possible similarities rather than exact likenesses. It is a model of self-recognition very different from that offered by the abstract universal. The concrete universal does not use absolute identity as does the abstract universal.

The distinction of the two models offered by the two universals is not just a matter of antiquarian or historical interest. In modern times we are all given to thinking in terms of abstract universals rather than in terms of concrete universals. Hence the changing role of fiction in our lives and the ever-increasing importance of the social sciences. One of the significant differences between a novel by Dostoievski and a book of social science like David Riesman's *The Lonely Crowd*[24] is precisely that the latter makes use of abstract universals (e.g., 'at a certain point in time men are prone to other-direction rather than to inner-direction'), whereas the story of *The Idiot* is a long drawn-out concrete story of universal significance because it helps us to reflect on ourselves and to detect similarities between ourselves and the hero. It is a mirror image that is applicable and enlightening even though none of its actual features coincide with those of the person who mirrors himself.[25]

The writing of history in modern times is profoundly affected by this change. There is a preference for abstract universals, and it has found its reflection in historical writing by a growing demand for historical narratives that are based on the social sciences (i.e., on abstract universals). I entirely agree with J. H. Hexter that it is wrong to make this question a matter of principle. He says in chapter 4 of *The History Primer* that sometimes the abstract laws provided by the social sciences are useful and sometimes they are not and that one should not evaluate a piece of historical writing by the amount of use it makes of the abstract universals provided by a social science. We will return to this question in chapter 6.

Lest it be thought that the switch from concrete universals to abstract universals as models for self-understanding is a major achievement of the modern scientific spirit, I would like to mention in passing that the contrast between the two models of understanding played a great role in ancient Greek philosophy. In his *Preface to Plato*,[26] E. A. Havelock explains that Plato's main philosophical purpose was to destroy people's immemorial habit of identifying themselves with the oral tradition. He wanted people to think of themselves as persons who think and know; and who think and know about a body of knowledge that is thought about and known. In other words, he wanted people to stop using the mythical paradigm and to start subsuming themselves under abstract universals. In the wake of his campaign, he hoped, people would stop identifying with Achilles (in the manner of the above mentioned mythical paradigm) and begin to realise that they were persons who thought about Achilles, persons who took Achilles and his antics to be a body of information. Here we have a plea for the replacement of concrete universals by abstract universals two thousand years before the advent of the social sciences. The reaction against using the concrete universal as a model of self-understanding, and the inevitable counterreaction, should therefore not be mistaken as an advance in knowledge or, respectively, as a retrograde step in knowledge. It should be seen as something that happens from time to time. It is true that at the present time the plea for abstract universals and against concrete universals in historical narratives is made in the name of the social sciences. But this particular plea is only a particular instance of a more general and wider movement in human thought and might well have taken place without the social sciences. Better, one should look upon the remarkable advent of the social sciences as an instance of the desire for abstract universals rather than hail the social sciences as a new step forward in human knowledge. If one can look upon them in this way, one will be able to see the present importance attached to the social sciences and their abstract universals for the writing of history in proper perspective. The problem of abstract universals in the writing of history is discussed in chapter 6.

How can myths or concrete universals be converted into history? It would be wrong to think of this conversion as a simple or mechanical process by which a historical date is assigned to a mythical event. It is true that we know of cases where this has been done, where myths have been converted by inserting time and space indices into a narrative as if it were not fable but fact. Whenever myth is historicised in this way, the critical historian is supposed to study the case and to sort fable from fiction and remove the myth from the historical narrative. Historicised myth calls for simple detective work. For further discussion of historicised myth, see chapter 8.

The conversion of myth into history is something quite different from the historicisation of myth. To understand its full importance one has to recall that a historical narrative is something that has to be constructed. It is not a series of events presented to the historical observer by nature or time. Let us presume that somebody, preferably an historian, has noted an event that he considers important or interesting and that he wants to make the subject of a history. In the absence of abstract universals, he might find it difficult to determine which other events to connect with it. But if he knows a myth, he knows a story. He knows what sort of series is a meaningful series of events. He can therefore take his guidance from that myth and shape his historical narrative in the image of that myth. In this way two or more events that really happened are selected from a myriad of events that also happened and made into the sort of story the knowledge of the myth would lead one to expect to have happened. In this way the myth shapes the form of what one thinks took place. In this process of conversion, fact is assimilated to fiction. It might even be a bit falsified and distorted. But whatever is lost in factual truth is made up for by the enormous gain in intelligible storyhood. A myth has a beginning and an end. It impresses this pattern of storyhood on the events and helps the historian to select and shape the selected events into a meaningful chain.[27]

We can see therefore that the conversion does not consist in mistaking something that has not actually happened (myth) for something that has happened (a historical event). Conversion takes place when single events that have actually happened are linked together to make a story by following the outline of story telling known from mythology. The sense of story comes from myth and

our knowledge of a mythical story *precedes* the linking of actual
events. This, in outline, is the alternative to using abstract
universals to link events. Consider an example. When critical historians first looked at the Old Testament and at the *Iliad*, they
immediately jumped to the conclusion that we had nothing but
myths in these works. Eventually it began to dawn on them that
this conclusion was unjustified. They discovered step by step that
in an important sense almost everything reported in these books
was actually true or had a significant relationship to events that
had actually taken place. And today we know for certain that
both the Old Testament and the *Iliad* are real history, but with a
difference.

The difference consists in the fact that we have history composed with the help of concrete universals. The concrete universals
are myths. The ancient authors of these works had a whole lot of
events they wanted to make into a history, a narrative series of
events. They knew what sort of thing a story was from their
knowledge of Hebrew and Graeco-Mycenean mythology. They
used this knowledge to assemble the events they had in mind and
following the pattern of the myths found other events to link
them with. In following the pattern and outlines of these myths,
a certain amount of distortion crept in. Some of the characters
they dealt with, perhaps all of the characters they dealt with,
were assimilated strongly to mythical characters so that much
of the actual truth was lost. Both Jacob and Agamemnon
emerged as figures more akin to mythical heroes than to historical persons. Similarly a certain amount of pure fable crept
into the narrative. And finally, and this may be the most important
distorting result, the compilers of these historical narratives played
fast and loose with chronology. To begin with, since a myth has
no date but begins usually with some such formula as 'once upon
a time . . .', these early historians paid no attention to locating
the events they linked in time. Since it seemed not to matter in
the mythical story, a precise date did not matter in the historical
story either. These historians were not used to the importance of
locating events in time. Their knowledge of mythology had not
taught them to do so and as long as they received their sense of
sequence from the myth they did not think it important to assign
dates to the sequence. Moreover, they telescoped. Since dating
events in time was not important, it was easy to shorten the time
span covered by a number of events and make several events into
one event. In this way a series of wars might emerge as one single
war; or a series of patriarchal figures might emerge as one single

patriarch. Such compression heightens the dramatic effect and thus
gives to the historical narrative a greater appearance of meaning.
It makes it look more like the original myth. And finally, this
absence of time location lulls the critical sense of the historian and
tempts him to allow all sorts of fables and unlikely features to
creep into the narrative. People can be made to look older than
they are likely to have been. They can have direct conversations
with God or with gods and be capable of performing superhuman
feats, not to speak of miracles.

Mythical stories and the assimilation of true stories to myth
play a very important part in the transformation of time into history and enable people to see the past as history. But if the mythical elements gain the upper hand and when miracles and supernatural powers remain to dominate the story, the story will have
a surfeit of meaning at the expense of credible truth. In histories
of this kind, meaning will prevail over truth. To bring about a
proper balance between meaning and truth, the historian must
treat myth more flexibly and more cautiously. When he succeeds
in retaining a kernel of truth in the story and merely uses the
myth as a paradigm to give shape to the story and a model from
which the story derives its meaning, he is not just converting myth
into history or historicising myth. He is then merely assimilating
events to myth so that they make sense. Consider, for example,
the story of William Tell in which there is a kernel of truth.
Toward the end of the thirteenth century somebody murdered
the imperial commissioner in the vicinity of the southern end of
the Vierwaldstatter See. Within less than a century the murderer
was identified as William Tell, citizen of Altdorf; his motive was
established as the liberation of his fellow peasants from the
tyrannous imperial yoke, and his victim was painted in the most
lurid colours. The story was being shaped by mythical traditions
current in the most northern parts of Europe about a wild hunts-
man who had such a remarkable aim that he was able to shoot
an apple or a nut resting on the head of another person. The figure
of Tell was assimilated to this arquebus virtuoso and a tale was
spun that connected his virtuosity with the oath that laid the
foundation for the independence of the four original Swiss cantons
as a result of the murder of the imperial commissioner.[28] Or consider another example. In ancient times there were many assassinations of tyrants. It was alleged that the actual impetus to the
assassinations came from the fact that at least one of the assassins
had a sister, or a wife, or a daughter who had been seduced or
raped by the tyrant. It is very unlikely that all those political

murders should have followed exactly the same pattern and one must indeed conclude that these stories all follow the same pattern because they were assimilated to the same myth. The woman in the story

> owes her existence to the mythical type which normally appears in legend when tyrants have to be slain. The two brothers, or lovers, and the injured sister or wife — the relationships vary — are the standing *dramatis personae* on such occasions. . . . The purely mythical type which shapes such legends is seen in the Dioscuri and Helen.[29]

We may look at Toynbee's descriptions of the role of creative personalities as another example. Toynbee is quite explicit in his use of a mythical paradigm according to which special creativity is preceded by a withdrawal from the commonplace field of activity and his accounts of Gregory the Great and Dante, Saint Paul and Machiavelli, are all modelled on this paradigm.[30]

When meaning, as a result of the mythic paradigm, prevails over truth, we get a vision of the past as purely mythical history. In such cases myth is converted into history. But when there is a fine balance between real events and people on one side and the mythic paradigm on the other, when a kernel of truth is preserved, the process has been described as a process of infiguration of real events by myth. Through infiguration we get a fine mixture of truth and meaning.[31]

In his book on Thucydides,[32] F. M. Cornford has made a very detailed study of the way in which a myth functions as a concrete universal in the composition of an historical narrative. When abstract universals are not available or not considered suitable, an historical narrative can be constructed by what Cornford describes as the infiguration of fact by myth. The word 'infiguration' was coined by Cornford to describe the process by which separate facts are selected, linked, and made relevant to each other so that a whole series of them can be understood as a story and turned into an intelligible sequence with the help of a myth or, to use our terminology, any concrete universal. The concrete universals that Cornford considers to have been used both by Herodotus and Thucydides are the plots of Aeschylus' drama. In these plots there is a theological pattern in which sinful pride is punished by a jealous deity and the action is shaped by the dramatic principle of climax-reversal-catastrophe. Aeschylus had dramatized the events of Xerxes' invasion and worked them into a mythical scheme in which pride is punished by the gods. This scheme was preconceived; it was not observed. If Aeschylus had simply recalled what he had witnessed, the sequence pride-punishment would not have been among the things he recalled. It was something he knew from myth. Cornford shows that Herodotus followed the Aeschylean pattern (page 134). Thucydides criticised Herodotus for inventing embellishments but never discovered the strong mythical ingredient in Herodotus's work. For he himself was captive to the mythical and turned to drama even as Herodotus had done (page 138) to provide a narrative. The story unravelled by Cornford shows that historians can make use of myth. A myth is a story that teaches, for example, that pride is punished by the gods. With the knowledge of this sequence in mind one can select facts and string them together in a meaningful and intelligible narrative. The mythical story is the paradigm on the basis of which other stories are put together. Separate events are figured into myth.

Cornford is also able to show in detail how the infiguration of the story of the Peloponnesian War by the myth affected Thucydides' narrative. Thucydides proved obdurate in his neglect of the economic aspects of Athenian imperialism and insofar as he left out a consideration of the economic factors he provided a narrative that is notoriously strange for the modern Marxist reader to whom these economic factors in imperialism loom large. Since Thucydides is practically our only source of knowledge for the Peloponnesian War, this noneconomic orientation of his narrative has posed many problems to our modern understanding of both Thucydides and the Peloponnesian War. There exist, therefore, strong reasons for seeking an interpretation to replace some of Thucydides' explanations. But there is no reason why Cornford's discovery of the method of infiguration practised by Thucydides should make us particularly sceptical about the story he tells.[33]

In this connection we should also look at Robert Tucker's analysis of Karl Marx. In his book entitled *Philosophy and Myth in Karl Marx*,[34] Tucker comes to conclusions that are markedly similar to those of Cornford. He shows how Marx had absorbed from Hegel the drama of the inner life of man and how he then projected this drama — a drama in which man fights himself and becomes alienated from himself — upon the external world and formed his special vision of an ongoing titanic battle between labour and capital. 'I have suggested', writes Tucker, 'that what he [Marx] actually *saw* in society was alienated man writ large' (page 220). Although Tucker does not use the term 'infiguration', it is clear that he sees Marx's method to be identical to Thucydides' method as explained by Cornford. And, like Cornford, Tucker is very critical of Marx for 'superimposing upon the facts of outer social reality' (page 239) his mythic drama of the inner life of man. In Cornford's terminology, we should say that Marx figured his personal knowledge of men in society into a myth and thus rendered it meaningful and intelligible. Tucker is very critical of Marx's method because it forces him to remain ignorant of what *really* went on. Marx, Tucker says, did not even know proletarians and his whole picture of the proletarians and their class struggle is therefore not of 'empirical origin' (pages 218 and 113). I am certain that Tucker is right. But he is wrong in thinking that one can have knowledge of reality (e.g., of proletarians and their role in history) by an empirical method — as if the proletarians and their behaviour were clearly outlined in front of us, waiting for the historian to come along with his sketchbook to make a record of what was there. If it had not been for Marx's infiguration of his several unconnected experiences into a myth (i.e., the drama of the conflict between inner man and his alienated inner self), Marx would never have been able to see the wood for the trees. If he had simply stared at his social environment he might never have seen alienated men, let alone proletarians. But with the help of the myth of the battle between man and his own self that takes place in the inner mind of man, he was able to string ill-assorted and disjointed impressions together into a meaningful whole.

In the course of such infiguration it is the easiest thing in the world to invent events. The mythical pattern often requires actions that did not take place and characters who did not actually exist. Cornford provides many examples of the way in which infiguration compels modification and sometimes downright invention (page 132). A modern sober historian may find it shocking that infiguration can lead to modification as well as to invention and he may find, at first sight, that he has little sympathy with the employment of concrete universals that lead to such and similar offences.

Critical reflection, however, shows quite clearly that modification and invention of this type is no prerogative of the employment of concrete universals. The same sort of modification and invention creeps into the historical narrative that is composed with the help of abstract universals. If a historian uses, for example, the abstract universal that all holders of power will economically exploit the people in their power, and if he does not find plain evidence that Oliver Cromwell did economically exploit his tenants, he will nevertheless supply the missing events of exploitation. When one confronts him with the fact that there is no evidence that Cromwell exploited anybody, he will reply that the evidence is missing and that Cromwell *must* have exploited the

people in his power because the general law he (the historian) is
employing says so. Indeed, there is no history book in which the
phrase that something *must* have happened or that so and so *must*
have planned to go to war does not occur a thousand times. It
occurs so frequently for precisely the same reason for which the
historian who employs concrete universals modifies and invents.
When an abstract universal is employed, the general law tells the
historian what to expect, and if there is no direct evidence that
what is to be expected did actually happen, the historian feels
more or less justified in postulating that for one reason or another
that evidence is missing and that things *must* have happened as he
expects them to. When a concrete universal is employed, the same
reasoning prevails. The mythical story arouses certain expectations
about the sequence of events and when there is no direct evidence
for some of these events, they are supplied by the imagination.

There are two possible reactions to the discovery that both
abstract and concrete universals lead the historian to modification
and invention. If there is nothing to choose between abstract and
concrete universals one may want to condemn all narrative written
with the help of either. Or, since they exhibit the same faults,
one may accept both. As things are, the first alternative is not
open to the practising historian. If neither kind of universal is
employed, no historical narrative can be composed. There remains,
then, only the second alternative. The universals, whether abstract
or concrete, are supposed to have a heuristic value. Given a certain
myth or a certain general law, one expects certain things to have
happened and the phrase 'this must have happened' is entirely
justified. It becomes doubly justified when one reflects that the
historian is not the only person to employ universals. The people
he is writing about also employed either concrete or abstract
universals. In putting forward certain expectations the historian
is merely following the thought processes of the people he is
studying because he is safe in his presumption that they too had
certain expectations and that these expectations could have been
aroused precisely only by universals. The historian's task is to
find the universals these people employed so that he can see for
himself what kind of expectations were aroused and what these
people were expecting to happen or accepted as having happened.

I have tried to show that there is no basic difference in the
kind of expectation aroused by concrete universals and the kind
of expectation aroused by abstract universals. When we employ
a general psychological law that makes us presume that Caesar had

a mother-fixation we feel that we are on fairly safe ground. Caesar would not have thought so. If we employ a concrete universal that arouses the expectation that a certain king had to slay a dragon before he could take possession of his kingdom and rule it effectively, we feel uneasy because we know that there are no dragons. But we feel no more uneasy than Caesar would have felt on hearing that he had a mother-fixation. All that has happened is that now the boot is on the other foot. Even so, the historian will seek to diminish the amount of purely mythical material that is retained in his story. There is no need to retain the dragon in full. The process of infiguration ought to be more subtle and more complex.

If a narrative is formed under the guidance of the myth that a hero slays a monster before gaining a kingdom, the historian, in composing his narrative, will look for evidence that his king performed a superhuman task before gaining his kingdom and such evidence of struggle as he will find will be presented as an essential prerequisite to the king's triumph. The story about the monster is thus extruded; but the pattern that triumph is preceded by a test of strength is preserved and is used to determine the actual sequence of events and the significance that they have for one another. The method of historical workmanship is here significantly different from the method followed when an abstract universal is used. An abstract universal would state that all kings slay dragons before taking possession of their kingdoms. There is no flexibility here, and the slaying stands in a causal relationship to the possession. In any case, as an abstract universal, the law is false. The myth that a certain hero slew a certain dragon before taking possession of his kingdom is different. It is a concrete universal. There is no assertion of a causal relationship but a statement of a sequence of events that is meaningful and that can serve as a paradigm for a story. The story may substitute a constitutional struggle for the battle with the monster and that constitutional struggle need not be the cause of the triumph. But the triumph is made intelligible if represented as the consequence of the struggle and the story will become intelligible because it echoes a well-known, meaningful myth.

Or, to mention another example, consider the enormous role played by the myth of the loss of innocence. It comes in many variations, but the basic pattern always is that at one time men lived in a state of innocence and then, through a fault or through cosmic design, a process of degeneration set in. On a very broad canvas, the myth lends meaning to the philosophy of his-

tory enshrined in the conception of Ferdinand Tönnies that the
development of human groups in history goes from community
(*Gemeinschaft*) to society (*Gesellschaft*), with the clear indication
that a community is something valuable and meaningful in which
there is a common life and a sense of belonging and that a society
is a mere conglomerate of individuals in which there is not only
a division of labour but also a division of value, opinions, and of
leisure time activities.[35] A similar process of degeneration informs
the theory of Sir Henry Maine that societies develop from status
to contract. Status spells security; contract, freedom and aliena-
tion. If these philosophies of history are narratives conceived on
a very large scale, one can also think of examples of ordinary historical narratives the composition of which is guided by the same
myth. If one reads, for example, the story of the end of the
Roman Republic by R. E. Smith,[36] a work of impeccable scholarship and erudition, one cannot escape the force of the underlying
myth. Until the effects of the final destruction of Carthage were
felt, Smith tells us, the Roman Republic was in some state of
innocence. There was cooperation and patriotism, a willingness
to agree on certain standards of behaviour, and a determination to
preserve the city's religion. After the effects of the destruction of
Carthage and the growth of empire were felt, degeneration set in
right across the board. One inhibition after another was destroyed
and before long there was a struggle of all against all in which the
victory was bound to be for the most unscrupulous and self-seeking
politician. It is hard to say whether the scheme came to Smith
directly from the myth of the loss of innocence or whether it came
to him *via* Sallust. But whichever way it came, the myth is clearly
discernible in the story Smith tells. This brings to mind another
good book, a history of the reign of the unfortunate Richard II
of England by A. Steele.[37] Until the murder of Richard, the
English monarchy, so the story goes, was in a state of innocence.
There was stability and respect fo the law of orderly succession.
When Richard was murdered in the castle of Pontefract, the state
of innocence was lost. 'From now', the author writes, 'the battle
would be to the strong and the race to the swift' (page 288). The
book, again, is a work of great scholarship and cannot be faulted.
But the influence of the myth is clearly discernible. It lends
meaning to the tragedy of Richard II and it does not really matter
whether it came to Steele *via* Shakespeare or whether it was taken
directly from the myth. But the influence of the myth is remarkable because it is of course equally plausible to detect the instabil-
ity of monarchical succession in England long before the reign of

Richard II. Without the myth the murder at Pontefract castle would appear in a very different light. Or consider Marvin B. Becker. In his book entitled *Florence in Transition*[38] he is under the spell of the same myth. Florence, he tells us, was a genuine community until something terrible happened in the forties of the fourteenth century. At that time the halcyon years of communal life and 'gentle paideia' came to an end and made way for the 'stern paideia' of subsequent Florentine history. Here the powerful role of the myth, though not even alluded to by Becker, is all the more remarkable as we have another famous history of Florence in which we are told that the crucial change came much later, at the very end of the fourteenth century; was due to external factors such as the threat of Milanese imperialism; and produced a development that went in the opposite direction. According to this version by Hans Baron,[39] the threat of Milanese imperialism produced in Florence a spirit of republican self-consciousness and of patriotic virtue, which was to prove the seminal influence for the Florentine Renaissance in the fifteenth century. Becker is also remarkable for his attempt to date the loss of innocence with precision. We may again speculate whether the general scheme of his conception is taken directly from the myth or whether it is inspired by Burckhardt. For Burckhardt himself saw the history of Florence in particular and of Italy in general as a decline of the medieval communal spirit and the rise of unbridled individualism. He equated the medieval commune with virtue and morality; and the rise of the Renaissance, with immorality and lack of virtue and made us see that artistic and intellectual excellence is more likely to be accompanied by a decline in communal virtue. Man, he implies, cannot be morally good and excellent in the arts and the sciences at the same time. There is nothing in the 'evidence' that would compel Burckhardt to reach such a conclusion. The conclusion, on the contrary, is heavily indebted to Rousseau, who had preached in the eighteenth century that the arts and sciences are inimical to the moral development of man. It may be a moot point whether Burckhardt took his cue about the incompatibility of civilisation and morality from Rousseau or not.[40] But it is clear that either Burckhardt himself or Burckhardt and Rousseau together were ordering their historical material in the light of the myth of the loss of innocence.

The most striking examples of historical narratives composed by infiguration into myth are epics. Epical traditions exist in many parts of the world. In some places they have been given superb literary shape by poets who are sometimes identifiable. As

a result they have been mainly studied by literary historians and
by literary critics who see these epics as a product of a certain
type of society. Such societies are called by literary historians
'Heroic Ages'. The Heroic Age is an age of transition from tribal
structure to civic consciousness. Such transition and change is
the strongest possible incentive to seeing the past as history (i.e.,
as a chain of events that followed one another and that stand in
causal relationships to one another).[41] In an important sense all
epics are a form of history. Admittedly, the influence of rational
criticism is only slight and often completely absent. But if one dis-
regards the premise that epics are those narratives that originate in
a certain type of society halfway betweeen tribal primitivism and
urban civilisation, one can see that the dividing line between epic
and history is very fine and that the shift from the one to the other
is usually only a matter of emphasis. Looked at in this light,
there are important similarities between the *Iliad* and the historical
books of the Old Testament, between the *Song of Roland* and the
Mahabaratha, between the *Nibelungenlied* and the traditional
history of early Rome. All these narratives contain events that
are clearly mythical in the sense that they cannot possibly have
happened. All these narratives, moreover, show a very cavalier
disregard for chronology. They not only lack an indication of
when the story took place but also telescope generations and fuse
single events that archaeological investigation has shown to be
separated often by centuries. But all this is due to lack of rational
criticism and an exclusive concern for meaning. There is, in this
kind of history, too much dependence on the mythical paradigm.
The infiguration of history into myth is too complete. But these
stories are nevertheless historical stories because they give an
identifiable shape to time. There is not a single myth in which the
actual events and a certain number of persons are not clearly
identifiable. We know today that Abraham was an historical
figure.[42] We know that he did not live as long as the authors of
the Pentateuch allege and we may surmise that he may not actually
have been called Abraham. But the core of the story is nevertheless
true. The same goes for the *Song of Roland* and for the *Nibelungenlied*. The raw material for the *Song of Roland* comes from
Carolingian history and later feudal customs. The raw material
of the *Nibelungenlied* can be found in the history of the Mero-
vingian family of the sixth and seventh centuries A.D.;[43] the raw
material of the *Iliad*, in the history of Mycenae and the destruction
of Troy — whether Troy VI or VIIa does not really matter. In all
these cases, in the absence of abstract universals the raw material

could only become a story through infiguration into myth. The
evidence for the mythical paradigm in all cases is overwhelming.
Agamemnon and Achilles were heroes or semidivinities worshipped
in many places.[44] Siegfried's battle with the dragon is modelled on
the archetype of the myth in which a god wrestles with chaos.
Siegfried himself is a mythical character of light fighting darkness.[45] The character of Brunhilde is modelled on an Amazonlike
mother goddess, and so forth. The childhood of every single hero
we hear of was threatened. The child had to be given away or
hidden because malevolent forces threaten his life. It would be
absurd to deny the historicity of Moses, Jesus, or King Sargon of
Agade because we know that the story that they were threatened
in childhood and had to be hidden from their persecutors is
plainly derived from myth and that they share this mythical
element with Oedipus and Romulus.

We owe one of the most systematic surveys of the mythical
element in epic literature to G. Dumézil.[46] He shows in great detail how in every epic the basic story pattern and the characters
are derived from myths. Unfortunately Dumézil tends to pour
out the baby with the bath water. He not only lays bare the
mythic element in each story but also proceeds to argue that
whenever there are clear traces of myth in a story, it has no
historical content.

It is difficult to argue with a scholar who has so much erudition as Dumézil. But the argument here does not concern his
erudition but the interpretation of this erudition. Dumézil holds
that the traditional story of early Rome, for instance, has no
historical content because he can demonstrate that it has been
moulded by myth.[47] The story of Romulus and Numa, the first
kings of Rome, according to Dumézil, is not historically true,
because we can detect in these kings all the elements of the Indo-
European myth of the two great deities, Varuna Mitra, the first
embodying the power of magic and the second, the force of law.
The early history of Rome is shrouded in so much darkness that
it is not easy to provide clear refutation of Dumézil's argument.[48]
Nevertheless, his arguments and his analysis of his own discoveries
are open to serious doubt; and, if one cannot refute them decisively, his own findings are capable of a different interpretation
that would hold fast to the historical kernel inside the myth.
J. Forsdyke has well described how a historical kernel can act like
a magnet and attract other material until an epic is formed.[49] And
by the time the whole body of material is narrated in epic form,
the concrete universals as well as some possible abstract universals

must have intruded for otherwise one could not obtain a complete epic narrative. Dumézil, throughout his work, has unfortunately chosen to disregard this complicated process of story formation. In his book entitled *From Myth to Fiction*[50] he has reiterated his contention that wherever and whenever we can detect a mythic pattern that shaped the story, we must dismiss the possibility of a historical kernel. Thus he upholds the absolute dichotomy between myth and history and maintains that it is impossible for our knowledge of history to be indebted to our knowledge of myth. In this book he examines Saxo Garmmaticus' chronicle *Gesta Danorum* and finds that the history of King Hadingus contained in the first nine books is heavily dependent on myth. He can be quite certain about this because he can show that this story of King Hadingus is cast in exactly the same mould as the undeniably mythic *Haddinjar*, which we know from Snorri and which we know was available, in one form or another, to Saxo Grammaticus when he wrote his first nine books of the *Gesta Danorum*. Dumézil's case study is of the greatest interest because it is not often that we possess both a historical and a mythic version of one and the same story. Dumézil's demonstration of the dependence of Saxo Grammaticus on the myth we know from Snorri and the anatomical comparison between the saga and the myth is masterly and cannot be questioned. But it does not necessarily follow, as he claims, that this dependence proves that everything Saxo Grammaticus tells us of Hadingus is fiction (page 122). It is open to us to change Dumézil's title and call his book, not *From Myth to Fiction*, but *From Myth to History*, or at least to describe Saxo Grammaticus' saga of King Hadingus as history heavily cast in a mythic mould. Saxo Grammaticus may be a little at fault as an historian. But then, what exactly would we describe as a pure historian? The universal must have come from somewhere; and, without it, Saxo Grammaticus would not have been able to string together the various pieces of historical information he obviously had. Like Geoffrey of Monmouth, whom we shall consider presently, Saxo Grammaticus may have drawn too heavily upon his mythopoeic informant. But without him, there would have been no first nine books to the *Gesta Danorum*.

But let us turn to an example in medieval history to examine the question. It is conventionally assumed that Geoffrey of Monmouth's *History of the Kings of Britain* belongs to the realm of epic or myth rather than to historical literature. Nevertheless scholars have been forced to ask themselves why Geoffrey, when he was writing epic or myth or romance or possibly all of these,

bothered to introduce so much purely historical material into his
book. It seems that the question is wrongly put. We should rather
look upon his work as a species of history in which the mythical
element is very strong. His method of work then becomes clear.
Geoffrey wanted to write a history of Britain and had collected
much historical material for his story. But to shape it and give it
meaning and to select and link all the occurrences into a coherent
narrative in which events were relevant to each other, he made
use of a number of clearly identifiable myths. The myths were the
concrete universals. If he could figure the historical material into
myth, he could make all those people who understood the myths
understand the story of Britain. He used the myth of Oedipus
and made his Brutus kill his father. He used the myth of Moses
and made Brutus engineer the exodus of his Trojans from Sicily.
He used the myth of the Resurrection in describing Arthur's
death and the way in which he was spirited away to Avalon to
await the time for his return. He used the myth of the Holy Ghost
in describing how Arthur was conceived by his mother through a
magic impersonation. He used the myth of *felix culpa*[51] to describe Arthur's death and the decline of the Britons and the rise
of the Anglo-Saxons. In Bede the decline of the Britons is due to
their sin. In Geoffrey the Anglo-Saxon ascendancy is not represented as a punishment for these sins but as a *felix culpa*. The
Anglo-Saxons brought about the death of Arthur, a death from
which some kind of redemption will follow. Geoffrey was a good
story teller and not overanxious to apply rational criticism to the
narratives that resulted from these infigurations. Hence his work
is full of myth and derives its meaning from the presence of
myth. Had he been more subtle, he would have disguised the
mythical elements. 'The presence of a mythical structure . . .',
Northrop Frye wrote, 'poses certain technical problems for making
it plausible, and the devices used for solving these problems may
be given the general name of *displacement*'.[52] Geoffrey made use
of none of these devices, and his failure to do so has astonished
and even angered his critical readers ever since.[53] But this failure
should not blind us to his actual method of work and to the effective possibility of using myth to construct a meaningful and intelligible narrative. Through his potent use of myth Geoffrey com-
bines a maximum of meaning with a minimum of truth. He did
not manage to keep the balance necessary for successful infiguration. One admits readily that Geoffrey was not as good an historian
as Thucydides or Livy. But in the last analysis all one can say is
that Thucydides and Livy managed to maintain a better balance

between their historical kernels and the myth into which they figured them. In all probability some kind of balance between kernel and myth was kept in the traditional history of ancient Rome. We can have no quarrel with Dumézil's detection of the strong mythical element in that story. But it does not follow, as Dumézil concludes, that there can be no historical element in that tradition. On the contrary, there is evidence that the traditional story contains a strong element of historical truth and that the balance between truth and meaning was kept; kept better, at any rate, than by Geoffrey of Monmouth. The traditional history of the origin of Rome has much meaning derived from myth, but not a surfeit of meaning at the expense of truth.[54]

Wherever we look we find that the persistence and the exigencies of form resist a complete portrayal of reality. It would be a mistake to fasten upon this insight as an occasion for resignation. Resignation would be in order if we could form an independent conception of reality and accept that, owing to the exigencies of the form of the medium, it cannot be portrayed or held. But since all conceptions of reality, as Kant long ago pointed out, are subject to the same exigencies, the fact that we are unable to form a conception of reality can therefore be no occasion for resignation, let alone lament. We must, at this stage in the argument, recall a famous theory about Michelangelo and his unfinished sculptures. Many people have believed, and there is some reason for this belief on the evidence of Michelangelo's own letters, that many of his sculptures were left unfinished because he was short of time or money or both and because many of his patrons let him down or because he often quarelled with them. As against this, it has been suggested — and the support for this suggestion comes from the fact that so many of his statues were left unfinished so that one is tempted to think that there must be something more than accidents to the failure to finish — that to Michelangelo these statues were not really unfinished at all. Michelangelo, it would seem, was aware of the tension between his medium (marble) and the person he wanted to sculpt. He knew that the marble had a structure of its own which eventually resisted the person it was to portray. Unless he did violence to the marble, the portrait could not be completed. The so-called unfinished sculptures, therefore, are really compromises between the person to be represented in marble and the structure of the marble. He knew, given the marble, that he could go only so far and no further. A block of marble, he understood, could not be turned into a person. When he left the portrait unfinished, he

nevertheless produced a work of art. For the so-called unfinished
sculpture was really an amalgam of the person to be represented
and the structure of the marble. Michelangelo felt that the fin-
ished product, if it was to be a complete copy of nature, would
have to be completely prized loose from the stone. The stone had
its own laws and form. To shell out the figure and detach it would
be to remove it from the form inherent in the medium and thus
deprive it of its meaning.[55] Michelangelo's attempt to keep a
balance between reality and form could therefore be compared
to Geoffrey of Monmouth's *History of the Kings of Britain.*[56]

We must conclude that there is neither complete fiction nor
complete reality in any narrative. When we say that a narrative
tends closer toward what we conventionally call fiction, we mean
that there is an increase in the concrete or abstract actuality of
the story, according to the universals that are used. When a narrative moves closer toward what critics please themselves to
describe as realism, they mean that it contains a higher proportion
of particular actuality. A narrative can be shifted in either of these
directions. But total fiction is as inconceivable as total realism.
Universals, either concrete or abstract, are genuine thoughts and
not free inventions. If a narrative contains a large number of
blatant universals and if the particular events it relates cannot be
located in time and space, it is nevertheless a true narrative because the universals with the help of which it is constructed portray something that is actual. If, on the other side, a narrative
makes little of the universals with the help of which it is composed and sets great store upon one's ability to locate the particular events it contains in time and space with precision, it is a
narrative that has a high level of particular actuality. All narratives
have actuality; the difference between them is a difference in the
kind of actuality they have and that difference, as we have seen,
is only a matter of degree.

Compare, for example, Tolkien's novel *The Hobbit* with a
good conventionally academic history of World War II. The two
narratives differ completely in their particular actuality. *The
Hobbit* has none. The two narratives will nevertheless have much
in common in their universal actuality. They share the structure
of the adventurous quest, the drama of fear and triumph and of
courage and cunning and anxiety pitted against evil obstacles. It
is therefore meaningless to call one story 'fiction' and the other,
'true report'. And what is more, if the conventional tale is badly
put together and too fragmentarily chronological as if one damned
thing had happened after another, the tales will actually be less

true than the more organised story of *The Hobbit*, even though the latter contains less particular actuality than the former. For the universal actuality is as important a part of the story of World War II as for *The Hobbit*; for the participants in World War II experienced the universal drama as much as any of the special particular events.

One might argue that concrete universals are not the best way to compose historical narratives. But if one is to compare the value of abstract universals and concrete universals for the writing of history, it is not immediately obvious that abstract universals make a better starting point. Abstract universals too, have their pitfalls. People change all the time and as they change, their beliefs in general laws change. If the historian wants to provide explanations proper and see how events were linked in the eyes of the people he is studying, he will find the most extraordinary concatenations and constellations of events, constellations that he often cannot consider to be plausible. As to concrete universals, there are admitted disadvantages, as we have indicated. But these shortcomings have to be weighed against some very practical advantages. The concrete universals that prompted the composition of the *Iliad* and of many parts of the Old Testament produced stories of both dramatic and transcendental impact and therefore made them 'memorable'. In ages when people had to rely on oral tradition, none of these stories would have been preserved and handed down had it not been for this impact. From a purely practical point of view, therefore, while we may regret the lack of proper dates and the telescoping of events, we have to be grateful for the mere fact of preservation. Without myth and its influence on the shaping of these stories, they would never have been remembered. Without the influence of myth, these historical narratives could not have arisen at all. By comparison it seems to be a small matter that they have come down to us in a form that clearly betrays their origin in mythology. History remembered or written through infiguration by myth gives shape to time even though the shape may err on the side of meaning rather than on the side of truth. At least it is time *shaped*.

In his book entitled *The Death of the Past*,[57] J. H. Plumb has paid too little attention to the way in which historical narrative emerges from myth. He equates 'history' with the ability to look upon the past critically and to distinguish fable from truth. He therefore contrasts 'past' with 'history'. The 'past' is an uncritical acceptance of stories that happened in the past. This is far too large a category. There are many societies in which the past is indeed a mere heap of myths and traditions that are accepted uncritically and the only purpose of which is to serve as a norm for behaviour and a validation of institutions and laws. But as we have seen, we know of other cases where myth gradually shapes itself into history and where the main emphasis of historical writing is placed on the historicisation of myth (i.e., the infiguration of history by myth) rather than on the mere sifting of fable from truth. Plumb's simple distinction between 'past' and 'history' is insufficient. It is good for extreme cases but obscures the large area that lies in between.

C. Lévi-Strauss distinguishes between hot and cold societies.[58] Cold societies are societies that seek to annul the effect of historical factors on their equilibrium and continuity. They do not historicise myths (i.e., they do not allow myth to infigure history). Hot societies are societies in which myth is historicised and in which the past is seen as a historical progression. One of the hallmarks, we may add, of such societies is that they seize on an important mythical event and use it as a date from which to count the passage of the years.[59] This date may be the creation of the world or the foundation of the city of Rome or the first Olympic games. Time itself does not provide a fixed counting point. Once such an absolutely fixed point is provided, it becomes possible to order the sequence of events in a way that is significant in respect to that date, so that the whole of the historical consciousness that emerges will reflect the importance of that date. Here again we may distinguish. Some people chose a date like the creation of the world, from which it is possibly only to count forward. Others chose the birth of Christ as a fixed point to make sure one can count both forward and backward because there is a special significance in the fact that there was history *before* the Incarnation.

But in another sense Lévi-Strauss' distinction between hot and cold societies tends to obscure the issue. He argues, especially in *The Savage Mind*,[60] that awareness of history is common to both primitive people and sophisticated people. He believes that everybody knows that the past is a sort of historical progression but that people differ in the manner in which they assimilate that knowledge. In primitive societies the relics of the past, like objects or proper names, are incorporated into the present, and historical events are incorporated into myth. In sophisticated societies, history is cultivated as consciousness of a particular historical narrative. The former mythicise historical events by depriving them of their location in time. The latter historicise myth by shaping their narratives in accordance with the general pattern provided by myth. Although this distinction looks superficially right, analysis shows that it hides the most important point. Lévi-Strauss' description insists that everybody must be aware of the past. But there is all the difference in the world between people who play it down by thinking of it as an endless and chronologically un-datable series of seasonal cycles and people who play it up by seeing it as a linear sequence of events, in which one event leads to another and which can be described by continuous narrative. There is a world of difference between the mythicisation of historical events — a process that destroys sequential narrative and that makes it impossible for anybody to relate himself caus-ally to what has gone before — and a historicisation of myth — a process that gives rise to narrative and that makes it possible for anybody to locate himself in a causal relation to many parts of the past and to transform time past into history.

Chapter Six

THE TAXONOMY OF UNIVERSALS

In chapter 4 we have distinguished between two different ways in which universals can be employed — between using them for explanation and using them for interpretation. In chapter 5 we have distinguished between two types of universals. One could carry on the search for other possible distinctions among universals. To begin with, one could initiate a more searching examination of the differences among general laws, generalisations, lawlike statements, and general laws with limited universality. If we were interested in the explanatory potential of universals such an examination would now be imperative. But since we are interested in the ability of universals to cover the gap between events created by the absence of temporal succession, there is little advantage to be gained by too fine a distinction of this kind.

We could introduce a different taxonomy. We could set up a tabulation of universals that are trivial and therefore tacit and less interesting than any one mininarrative they create; of universals that are as interesting by themselves as the events they assemble from subevents; and of universals that are more interesting than the events they create.

Alternatively, we could classify universals according to subject matter and distinguish those that are derived from chemistry from those that are derived from psychology, and so forth. Again, we could distinguish between universals according to their truth and falsity. But here we would be in difficult waters very soon. For, although we have seen that universals that have to do with mesmerism would not, today, be called true, there are many other universals where it would be impossible to make such a decision with certainty. Some people may doubt whether the transfer of relics from one dynasty to another causes a growth in political power; others may not. If we were to attempt such a distinction, we would simply have to go over the ground we examined in relation to the problem of the necessity of replacing explanations by interpretations. For interpretations become desirable and necessary when belief in the truth of an explanation decreases.

In all these taxonomies it is assumed that the historian is free
to choose his universals, or, at least, that his choice is not dictated
by his subject matter. We must now turn to an examination of the
reasons that may dictate a choice and that limit the historian's
autonomy. We have seen that in some cases the choice is narrowed
by the preference for typologically related universals. But such
narrowing of choice still depends on the historian's power of
understanding and is not derived from or inherent in the subject
matter. On the other hand, there is a limitation of choice inherent
in the subject matter when one finds that one is dealing with
people and societies that show a marked preference for concrete
universals or for generalisations about supernatural powers. If we
recognise such possible limitations of the freedom of choice, we
face a problem. Since the limitations are dictated by the subject
matter, we must form a notion of the nature of the subject matter.
But we cannot form a notion of that subject matter unless we
know the methods we have used to spot and depict that subject
matter. Again we are up against some kind of circularity. If the
historian wants to write a narrative of change, he is supposed to
know the subject matter of change and the mode of change so that
he can choose his universals. Even if he wishes to interpret, he has
to know the subject matter and the explanations it contains so
that his own interpretations can be typologically related to the
explanations. But he cannot know the subject matter until he has
composed a narrative.

The problem we have to examine, therefore, is the relation
between history and other studies. If other studies can provide a
knowledge of the subject matter, the historian can start from that
knowledge. The other studies are the social sciences. What then is
the relation between history and the social sciences? To determine
this relationship, we must subject the social sciences to a methodological scrutiny. We will then see that the knowledge provided by
the social sciences may determine the historian's choice of universals; but that in many cases the decision as to which social science
is to be employed to obtain that knowledge must rest with the
historian. We will see that the historian's lack of autonomy is of a
peculiar kind. In one sense he is not free to choose his universals;
but in another sense, only a historian can determine which choice
is appropriate for any one society or any one age. In this sense
there exists an inevitable interdependence between historian and
social scientist.

Ernest Gellner has sketched a possible classification of the
different ways in which history and the kind of society the

historian is writing about are interrelated. Since his classification is a mere sketch, it does not lend itself to a summary and I will quote it in full:

> We can develop a typology by using the currently fashionable method of binary oppositions and seeing the types which are generated in this manner. The differences in attitude to history which one should expect to be relevant are these:
>
> 1. Naturalistic/discontinuous. A society is naturalistic if it assumes that the events on the horizon are and must be similar in kind to the ordinary events of daily life. Modern societies are naturalistic in this sense. They do not take seriously either an Age of the Gods or an Age of the Heroes, in Vico's terms. But most societies are not naturalistic in this way.
>
> 2. Within the class of societies which have non-naturalistic horizons, it is possible to distinguish between simple and ramified background stories. A ramified one will recognise two or more successive stages, basically dissimilar, within the general framework of the horizon story — such as, indeed, Vico's distinction between the Age of Gods and of Heroes. There is then a double skyline on the horizon — something that, after all, also happens in the physical world.
>
> 3. Cutting across these distinctions, there is the difference between historical and a-historical societies. A rough criterion would be whether a society accumulates more and more generations with the passage of time, whether the ordinary world within the horizons *grows* in size with time, or whether on the contrary the size of the plain within the horizons remains constant, as happens when systematic omission ensures that the number of generations separating the present from the Founding Father remains constant. There will of course be borderline cases between historical and a-historical societies.
>
> 4. The presence or absence of a sense of social structure. By this is meant whether or not a society recognises a radical difference in type of event, or of sequence, of story, *within* the daily, ordinary, non-horizon part of the world — in other words, whether it has a sense of different epochs, or radically different patterns of social life, where the difference is natural rather than super-natural. A simple society which takes for granted the institutional and conceptual framework within which its members act, has of course no such sense of social structure. Its own structure is invisible to it, and others are barely conceivable. Naively, it absolutises one particular set of conventions. But even quite sophisticated societies or historians are capable of this simplicity. It is arguable that Gibbon's vision was of this kind, and I have heard this claim argued. So clearly, holding such a view does not disqualify a man from the highest ranks of creative intelligence.[1]

Gellner then continues to outline his own conception of the relationships between anthropology and sociology and history on the basis of these distinctions. But since his outline is determined by his interest in anthropology and sociology, rather than by an interest in history, there is no point in pursuing his suggestions.

But we must take up his final question as to the relationship between social structure and historical narrative. His question is well put because he starts with the assumption that no historical narrative can stand on its own feet and that history is not an autonomous enterprise.

If we want to answer this question with a special eye on the nature of the historian's narrative, we can see at once that he is subject to some kind of constraint by the exigencies of explanation. When he is writing narrative by using explanations, he is of necessity compelled to use those universals that were used by the people he is writing about. If he is doing interpretation, he seems, at first sight, free to choose. Or better, his freedom of choice is only limited by the fact that he ought to prefer interpretations that are typologically related to the universals used by the people he is dealing with.

For a long time, history was thought to be an autonomous enterprise and the question I am proposing to turn to did not even arise. When history was the *magister vitae*, it was taken for granted that the historian simply related the experiences of the past so that people could learn from them. Since people were then interested in learning from other people's experiences, they assumed that all people were always alike and always had the same experiences. Historians were therefore not very self-conscious and the question whether their enterprise was autonomous or not was simply not asked. During the nineteenth century, when nationalism moved into the foreground of political preoccupations, historians became less interested in teaching by telling people about the experiences of the past. They became, on the contrary, the social scientists *par excellence* in a completely different way. Since the doctrine of nationalism required people to believe that every nation had existed for many centuries even when its existence was not socially and politically noticeable, the proof for its existence depended on the continuity of its linguistic and cultural coherence. Since not even that coherence was obvious to the naked eye, historians had to be called upon to provide the evidence for it in their narrative. Thus historians became scholars who provided the evidence for the political program of nationalism. One of their chief methods was to demonstrate that the ruins and documents of the past, which abounded in every region of the Old World, were not just ill-assorted ruins but were part of the cultural heritage of each nation, monuments to the existence of the cultural continuity of nations that had been politically inarticulate. But as the importance of nationalism declined, so did this particular function of the historian. We must, therefore, take a new look at the particular way in which history is dependent on the different social sciences and examine how the social sciences provide images of societies that compel the historian to choose his universals.

History and the social sciences deal with the same subject matter. They deal with men and women, with institutions and laws, with governments and economics. History is a very old way of describing these matters; the social sciences as distinct enterprises are newcomers. It is natural that many people should have started wondering whether history and the social sciences are really the same sort of intellectual enterprise or not, and if they are different, whether they can or cannot benefit from mutual acquaintance. Historians deal with the subjects indicated *sub specie mutationis.* They are primarily interested in how things change, how one thing led to another, how one thing brought another about. Social scientists often shy away from history because they feel that any changes other than minute ones are not quantifiable. If a social scientist tells us that a fall in the bank rate leads to unemployment, he is telling of change. But the span of time involved in the manner in which one event brought about another is very small. Historians are accustomed to considering not only changes over a longer period but also events exclusively from the point of view of how they bring about changes. By contrast, social scientists feel less concerned with change as such and, in one very important sense, have endeavoured to make the static interrelationship of events their criterion of intelligibility. One can see that on the face of it, the social scientist does not think that a historical narrative is very intelligible and, for that matter, the historian is inclined to attribute little importance to any intelligence derived from the observation of a systematic and functional interplay of events. He knows that events bring about changes and is therefore professionally suspicious when he is told that they can best be uncerstood in the manner in which they are functionally interdependent, that is, in the manner in which they do not change.

The majority of writers on the subject try to sit on a fence and give their conciliatory blessings to both sides and express the hope that a *rapprochement* will benefit historians as well as social scientists. By contrast, G. R. Elton in *The Practice of History*[2] has poured a great deal of thoughtless ridicule on the social sciences to vindicate what he calls the 'autonomy of history'. My criticism of Elton is concerned not so much with his ridicule as with his thoughtlessness. There is much in the social sciences that is indeed deserving of ridicule and I have great sympathy with S. Andreski's *The Social Sciences as Sorcery*,[3] a spirited book in which he shows with much shrewdness that the social science emperor is indeed very naked. Many of the great discoveries of the social sciences are indeed purely tautological. When G. Homans tells us in *The Human Group*[4] that people who interact frequently are likely to like each other, one does not know whether to laugh or cry. Andreski comments rightly that those people who have hailed Homans as the Euclid of social science only demonstrate that they have no understanding of Euclid. Other examples are easy to find. Joan Thirsk has told us that the privacy of the nuclear family unit was swamped as long as village communal life flourished.[5] D. Lerner informs us, and it took him years of research to come up with this discovery, that Anatolian peasants are less advanced toward modernity than the intelligentsia of Damascus and Cairo.[6]

Two serious writers have posed the problem in a different way. In *The History Primer*,[7] J. H. Hexter admits the occasional relevance of social science but points out very sensibly that the historian is by no means deeply dependent on its findings. In an interesting and revealing chart he shows that he himself has made use of very good explanations in history that would get a fairly low social science rating; and that in other cases he has used explanations that would have the full support of empirically based social science. Hexter, in other words, recognises the relevance of social science to history but is not deeply concerned about it. By contrast, R. A. Nisbet, in his book entitled *Social Change and History*,[8] comes up with a diametrically opposite view. He claims that the form of knowledge presented in the social sciences is the only tenable form of knowledge of man and society. He argues that history is concerned with change and that change cannot be observed. He goes further and claims that change is a metaphor and that metaphors cannot have a real place in rational knowledge.

There is nothing to quarrel with in Hexter's measured tolerance. But Nisbet's argument is peculiar. One can grant that since nobody can watch a kettle boil, change is not observable. In other words, Nisbet's argument is wrong not in its claim that change is a metaphor but in its claim that it is the only metaphor employed in rational knowledge. Nobody has *seen* the Roman Empire fall. This is true. It is true not only because nobody can see *change* but also because nobody can see the *Roman Empire*. Granted that change is a metaphor, I would add that change is not the only thing that is a metaphor. It might be debatable whether the 'Roman Empire' is another metaphor or an abstraction. But it cannot be in doubt that the entity referred to by the phrase 'Roman Empire' is as elusive and unobservable — unempirical if you like — as the phenomenon referred to by the word 'change'. Nisbet, I think, is wrong in his analysis. In fairness to him, it must be added that by history he means not micro-history or what we have called the ordinary historical narrative, but more something that is like a full-blown philosophy of history. But since we have argued that the difference between the one and the other is not a difference in kind but only a difference of degree, his aspersions on the philosophy of history at the expense of the social sciences that deal with static systems must sooner or later also apply to ordinary history. Hexter, on the other hand, is not wrong; but he is too cavalier. He is too much a self-confessed practical man who likes to think that he can do without a theoretical inquiry into the relationship between the social sciences and history. Or, at least, he poses as such a man.

Anybody who has the slightest experience of working with historical documents or sources knows that these so-called raw materials cannot be understood unless the historian has some prior knowledge of the kind of society and its economic, intellectual, religious, and technical conditions to which they belong. The historian is therefore not a scholar who starts with raw material but a scholar who has some knowledge prior to the raw material. A charter, a chronicle, an election return, a piece of private correspondence, or a manifesto or treaty is quite unintelligible without a vague preconception of the situation that gave rise to it. The study of the document will, in turn, add to one's knowledge of that situation; but, paradoxically, it also presupposes such knowledge. Historians who are not aware of the need for such prior knowledge often enough end up with such simple dogmas as that the 'state' or the 'class struggle' are historical constants and then proceed to approach their documents in the light of such constants. They take the historical constant for granted because its very constancy seems to obviate the need for scrutiny. But not even such dogmatism denies the need for prior knowledge. It merely minimises the occasion for examining it. Quite recently, G. R. Elton has tried, in a valiant attempt at Anglo-Saxon commonsense, to uphold the autonomy of the historian's craft. He rejects the idea of such prior knowledge out of hand and argues that the historian has simply to acquaint himself so thoroughly with the sources that he becomes eventually able to predict what happened.[9] The thought is charming; but the perspicacity of the observation depends precisely on the truth it seeks to deny. No historian, no matter how learned, could ever foretell anything if he knows nothing but the documents. The fact that many historians can, in fact, foretell what happened proves that they know more than the documents and were able to interpret them in terms of the correct social setting, that is, in an approximately correct appreciation of the social relations that gave rise to them. Many other historians, and their number is constantly growing, have tacitly admitted the need for such prior knowledge but, in a strained effort to maintain their autonomy, have therefore resigned themselves to equating historical knowledge with documentary positivism; to obviate the need for precarious presuppositions, they have put back historical research to the editing of sources.

The historian's thinking is, however, undeniably not only concerned with the study of the sources but also with the presuppositions about social relations in terms of which he interprets them. In every historical work there has always been much implicit jurisprudence, psychology, and economics. And it is therefore hardly surprising that with the modern full development of the science of sociology, historians should have started to look toward that general science of society in the hope that it might at long last provide them with the definitive set of presuppositions that they need for the interpretation of their sources and for placing them into their *Sitz im Leben.*

To define the scope of the following discussion, I would like to say at the outset that I will not concern myself with two fairly innocuous aspects of the *rapprochement* between historians and sociologists. The first aspect consists in the modern growth of interest in social history.[10] This deflection of interest from political history to social history is not a matter of principle but is dictated by contemporary political experiences. The emancipation of the masses has made historians more sensitive to the ancestors of the masses. Hence the dash for parish registers, prison files, and certain types of private diaries or notebooks as source material. But this deflection of interest does not raise any great problems of theory. The second aspect consists in the growing interest in historical generalisations. With the accumulation of more and more material from an ever-increasing number of ages and societies and continents, both historians and sociologists have endeavoured to arrive at certain generalisations about the conditions that favour revolutions or make for the stability of legitimate monarchies, and

so forth.[11] The comparisons necessary for such generalisations
raise certain questions of method, for no two situations are ever
really quite alike, and if one wants to compare in order to gener-
alize, one has to be very careful as to what exactly one is comparing. But here again, no question of principle is involved. Although
there is a large literature on the subject, the problems involved are
always ordinary problems of scholarly care and conscientiousness.

Instead, I propose to confine the discussion to the problem
raised by the *rapprochement* in its strongest form, that is, to the
problem raised by the suggestion that historians must start to learn
from sociologists.

The suggestion is based on the idea that since sociology is the
general science of societies and of social relationships, a historian
ought to study sociology because it contains *par excellence* the
presuppositions he stands in need of. Conversely, the sociologists
admit that they have much to learn from historians because historical knowledge can add much to the general theory of society.
As a historian I am naturally more interested in what historians
can learn from sociologists than in what historians can teach
sociologists. And the following critical examination will therefore
be confined to the first suggestion.

On the face of it, the suggestion is entirely plausible. If
sociology is indeed the general science of how people are bonded
to each other, of how social relationships are constructed and
maintained, then it would follow that sociology is the historian's
presupposition *par excellence,* and in that case the suggestion
deserves a much more sensitive and detailed critical discussion than
it has received from many well-meaning historians so far.[12]

The real and initial difficulty in any such discussion is, however, the problem of what we understand by sociology. There is a
large school of thought that claims that sociology is a newly discovered science, like chemistry, and that its findings, like those of
chemistry, are universally valid and applicable to all social groups
and relationships.[13] As against this wide claim, there is the much
more narrow statement of Alexis de Tocqueville, widely considered one of the founders of modern sociology, that the science
of sociology is not a universal science, but the science of a new
type of society.[14] I think that one can demonstrate broadly that
Tocqueville's narrower claim is justified and that the wider claim
must be rejected.

If one consults methodological instructions for sociologists,
one will usually be told that the sociologist gathers evidence and
data with the help of social surveys and questionnaires.[15] This is

to say, he is a scientist who proceeds by asking large samples of people what they do and think, feel and wish. He classifies the answers under certain headings and thus categorises people according to the answers they give. His findings always must result in groupings and classings and in statements that people with bald heads do this and that orphans do that, and so forth. There is often much discussion among sociologists as to whether under certain conditions it is better to conduct interviews or to ask for written answers to questionnaires and also as to what kind of sampling is adequate. But these are minor refinements and should not obscure the core of the sociological method.

This definition of sociology as the science of the social survey is by no means an arbitrary one. There are many different concepts of sociological method. But it is not too difficult to show that they all bear the stamp of this kind of social empiricism. A few random examples must suffice. E. Durkheim argued that the category of the social is a primary category and that the individual is 'constrained' by the social.[16] By this he meant that a large number of individual instances can be classified according to certain criteria and that once people are grouped by this method, the individual members of the group can be seen to be 'constrained' or determined in their behaviour by the 'social'. It is not easy to say whether this famous statement of method is more than a tautology. But it is easy to detect the fundamental empiricism of the social survey in it. M. Weber formulated a similar thought in a different way. The basic category, he argued, is the 'ideal type'. An ideal type construct is a 'one-sided accentuation . . . by the synthesis of a great many diffuse, discrete, more or less present and occasionally absent concrete individual phenomena, which are arranged . . . into a unified analytical construct. In its intellectual purity, this mental construct cannot be found anywhere in reality'.[17] Weber, in other words, proposed that sociologists ought not to proceed mechanically and not sum up people under certain headings but that the classes or types should be arranged 'ideally' and regarded as standard norms to which people's behaviour merely approximates rather than as constraining factors or as determinants. During recent years, further refinements have been introduced, but not even they can hide the core of the method. If, for instance, one considers a society as a system of legitimate role expectations and holds that interacting individuals must possess some guidance for mutual predictability for the system to be a social order, one implies tacitly that the individuals concerned must classify themselves as well as one another according to

certain criteria. For only when one can identify someone as a
member of a certain class or a collective, can one anticipate what
he is likely to do, that is, what one can legitimately expect.[18] Or
consider a completely different school of sociology. That school
distinguishes between simple societies, in which relations are
multiplex because almost all members participate jointly in a
variety of institutional contexts, and modern mass societies, which
are called complex. In the latter, all relationships are highly
specific because the people with whom one interacts in one
institutional sphere are likely to be quite different from the people
with whom one interacts in another sphere. However, the very
distinction between simple and complex in this sense betrays its
Durkheimian premise. In a complex society, every one of the
institutional spheres in which a member finds himself is a different
collective. One has to watch what people are thinking and doing
and classify them accordingly, to determine which specific role
they happen to be playing. One could not form the notion of
specificity of the many roles played by any one member unless
one assumed that it is possible to classify every member of the
complex society according to different criteria in many different
ways.[19]

No matter which of these many varieties of sociology one
practices or approves of, they all exhibit as a common core the
doctrine of the primacy of the social.[20] It is of great importance
that there is an essential connection between the empirical observation of what people are actually doing or thinking and the conclusion that the social is the primary datum. For if one observes
what people are doing and thinking, one can soon learn to sort
people into groups and classes according to one's findings and then
claim that the social, or the collective, or the legitimate role
expectation, or the ideal type is the primary social datum that
'constrains' the behaviour of its members, or, at least, enables
one to assert what the behaviour of the members is likely to be.
In this sense, the empiricism and collectivism of sociology go hand
in hand and there is indeed a striking resemblance between this
methodological situation and the classical debate as to whether
the universal is *ante rem*, *post rem*, or *in re*.

However this may be, we can now formulate clearly the claim
of sociology and gain an impression of the kind of contribution
it is supposed to make to history. If sociology is the doctrine of
the primacy of the social and if it is claimed that sociology is of
help to history because it provides the necessary presupposition,
then it follows that the importance of sociology to history lies in

the fact that it provides a clue as to the relationship between the individual and the social order. It could help the historian of any society in any age by outlining precisely, prior to an investigation of the specific facts and events, what sort of phenomenon society is. The real difficulty, as will become apparent presently, is that there is no one phenomenon of society but that the term 'society' covers a wide variety of forms of social bonding and association and grouping, whereas sociology uncovers only one special type.

After these analytical reflections, let us take a look at the actual historical situation. Whatever the precise reasons for the development of chemistry, there can be little doubt as to the precise reasons for the development of sociology in the course of the nineteenth and twentieth centuries. At the time of the French Revolution, when monarchy and church, landed property and privileges were swept aside, many people prophesied the end of all social order. When new social relationships emerged and when, in the course of the nineteenth century, the institution of society proved much more resilient than people had believed, thoughtful observers began to ask themselves why the prophets of doom had been so mistaken.[21] It was then gradually discovered that social bonding is much less exclusively dependent on obedience to specific kings, churches, and on certain property rights than people had thought and that alternative bonds are possible. To discover the reasons for this resilience, scholars could not fall back upon ancient traditions and laws and institutions. They could not demonstrate the survival of social order by deducing it from old laws enjoined by God and bound up with traditional rituals. Eventually they had to fall back upon empiricism. They had to start watching how people behaved. It so happened, and this is, of course, no accident, that the people they were watching were equally deprived of the authoritative norms of ancient institutions, ritual, myth, and tradition. To survive socially and to cement the social bond, they could not appeal to authority but had to resort to the one and only method of social bonding that was left. They had to imitate their neighbours or their peer groups or those whom they judged to be their peers or neighbours. In other words, when people reordered their social relationships in terms of peer grouping rather than by tradition and authority, they could only do so by watching and imitating one another and by elevating the principle of mutual watching into the social bond. They proclaimed that the nature of social obligation derives from proletarians behaving like proletarians, Germans like Germans, children like children, and so forth.

In this way, the science of sociology and the subject matter of

sociological study came to coincide. Sociologists, to explain why
social order persisted, had to watch people. And, watching people,
they came up with the discovery that people were watching one
another and imitating one another. Under these circumstances, the
science of sociology and the subject matter of sociology grew up
together, and the growth of the subject matter provided the validation of sociological method. Thus sociological method was able
to explain why the prophets of doom had been wrong and why
societies were surviving the absence of ancient traditional and
ancient authority.

If one looks at the growth of sociology in this perspective, one
must come to the conclusion that it is very far from a universal
science of society in general but is rather very properly the science
of modern industrial urban mass society — whatever term one
wishes to employ. In modern secularised mass society, there are no
sanctions and authorities other than those derived from mutual
imitation and from peer grouping. All standards of right and wrong
are defined in terms of what people in certain groups are actually
doing.[22] And the problem that faces most people is that they have
to decide which group they belong to and how they can reconcile
the often different standards that obtain in the different groups of
which they are members. Faced with these problems, the science
of sociology has become the ideology of modernity.[23] It reflects
the manner in which people are conscious of themselves and of
the bonds that tie them together. For this reason, sociological
books are extremely popular reading because they help people
to decide where they belong and which group they ought to
imitate. The sociologist is therefore the *ideologue* of modern man.
This is far from being a coincidence. Sociology, as I have argued,
was born of the necessity of explaining empirically why societies
survived the disappearance of religion and tradition and authority.
And modern man's social bonds, because of the absence of religion
and tradition and authority, are forged by the only method of
social bonding that remains: the imitation of one's peers.

Let us now take a closer look at the core of historical method.
There is no need to delve into the technical aspects of historical
methods and discuss heraldry and diplomatics, paleography and
sphragistics. For the purposes of the present argument, it suffices
to examine the philosophical, nontechnical core of historical
method. This core is determined, obviously, by the fact that
history is concerned with the past. The historian's description of
the past depends, therefore, on records and sources and documents, which are the clues to what happened.

The primary consideration concerns the sources, the alleged

raw material. The sources, of whatever kind they are, yield the
so-called events. They enable the historian to know that at such
and such a moment war broke out, or that at such and such a time
workers were paid barely enough to buy the daily bread. But
these factual events are not ultimate data. They are subdivisible.
The fact that war broke out can be subdivided into innumerable
further 'facts' such as: the prime minister signed a formal declaration of war; hundreds of soldiers were mobilised, someone fired
a shot, and so forth. And again, each one of these facts can be
subdivided, such as: the soldier who fired the shot first raised his
arm and reached for the rifle, then pulled the trigger, and so forth
ad infinitum. When one considers then the nature of facts and the
nature of the sources that yield these facts carefully, one comes to
the conclusion that there is no such thing as raw material at all.
One comes, on the contrary, to the conclusion that every source,
be it a treaty or the minutes of a conference, an archeological find
or a chronicle, is really not a record of a fact but something like a
mininarrative, that is, a small composition of subfacts into a larger
fact. World War I occurred from 1914 to 1918. This is a fact. But it is
equally obvious that in another sense it is a narrative, composed of
hundreds and thousands of facts, each one of which is again subdivisible and, therefore, also more like a mininarrative.[24]

We are therefore forced to the conclusion that for the historian
there is no raw material at all, but that the raw material he is
confronted with consists of mininarratives; some are very *mini*
indeed, but narrative nevertheless. Behind his alleged raw material,
there is, therefore, always a human mind that has fabricated or
composed these mininarratives. It follows therefore that the
historian's ultimate concern is to grasp the human mind or the
thought that lies behind what purports to be the raw material. In
other words, the raw material is not at all raw. Behind it there lies
thought, and, if one wishes, this thought is the rawest material the
historian ever deals with. To describe or reconstruct what 'really
happened', the historian has to include the thought that lies behind the mininarratives. And no historical narrative that does not
incorporate the thoughts behind the sources is either complete,
or acceptable, or truthful.[25] This leads directly to the chief requirement of historical method to understand and explain every
period of process in exactly those terms in which it understood
itself.[26]

Given the above description of sociological and historical
method, the conclusion is apparent. Insofar as sociology is the
ideology of modernity, of modern industrial mass society, it is of

enormous help to the historian and is, in fact, quite indispensable
to him. Insofar as the historian must understand modern men as
they understand themselves, sociology is invaluable, and it would
be contrary to argue that history ought to be an autonomous
science and ignore the findings of sociology. Sociology has discovered how modern men understand themselves. They understand themselves sociologically. The empirical survey of what
people are doing is the thought that lies behind modern man.
It can express itself in a totally banal and quasi-derisory fashion as
keeping up with the Joneses. Or it can express itself in a more
exalted and truly ideological manner as conforming to the majority
as expressed on voting day in an orderly democratic society. There
are hundreds of stations in between the derisory desire to keep up
with the neighbours and the ideological proclamation that the
will of the majority must prevail. But in all cases, the empirical
observation of sociology and the actual method of social bonding
and of accepting social obligations coincide. The historian must
therefore understand modern man has *homo sociologicus.*[27]

At the same time, this conclusion also reveals the limitations
of sociology for the historian. There were societies before the
advent of mass society in which people did not understand
themselves sociologically.[28] In these societies, social behaviour
and obligation were understood in terms of authoritative myth,
of traditional law and divinely appointed institutions. In such
societies men would not derive their obligations to observe social
bonds and their duties and rights from a majority decree or an
automatically distilled consensus of a peer group, but from the
authority of tradition and myth and ritual. A member of such a
society for instance would conform to the requirements of his
status; but he would not do this because he watched everybody
else whom he judged to be his peers doing it. He would do it
because tradition or authority required him to. In such a society
people would conform to social custom. But custom was autonomous and independent. Whereas in modern mass society custom
is what people conform to. In modern society conformism has
tended to become an end in itself; and modern societies differ
merely in the degree of pluralism they tolerate. In some there is
a plurality of peer groups and in others there is only the totality
of one single group. But these modern societies, whether pluralis-
tic or totalitarian, are a world apart from the premass societies
in which conformism was not an end in itself, but merely a means
toward the maintenance of authoritative custom.

One can make the same point from a different angle. The

modern sociologist goes into a society with his questionnaire or
his interview and establishes the nature of custom by questioning
all members of a significant sample. By contrast, the social anthropologist goes into a society and questions one or two authoritative
informants as to the nature of the custom. He does not proceed
'democratically' as it were, but consults 'those who know'. The
difference in method between the sociologist and the social
anthropologist reflects the differences in the types of society they
investigate. The one investigates modern mass society in which
people establish what the nature of custom is by imitating one
another or by some other method of common consensus. In such
societies, the investigator cannot do anything other than follow
their example and make a social survey to find out what it is that
people are doing. The other investigator studies older, premass
societies in which people consider themselves bound by divinely
ordained norms or by mythically validated authorities such as
kings or elders. His most effective method of discovering the
norms that prevail is to question the men 'who know'. There is a
world of difference between the types of answers the two investi-
gators expect to obtain. The sociologist can only discover the
prevailing norm by watching what people of certain groups are
actually doing; for the people themselves, before they could
answer a question as to the prevailing norm, would have to watch
what their neighbours or their peers are actually doing. The social
anthropologist can discover what the prevailing norm is in the
society he is studying by consulting an authoritative elder. He
would be told that the prevailing norm is prevailing because the
wind god laid down that it should or because the divine ancestor
of the tribe behaved in this particular way in time out of mind.
Given the particular kind of society he is studying, it would be
superfluous for the social anthropologist to take a social survey
of what everybody is actually doing. Whereas for the sociologist,
given the kind of society *he* is studying, such a survey would not
only not be superfluous but would actually be the only method of
ascertaining the norm; for it is precisely the method by which the
people he is studying are wont to ascertain the norm.

One can also look at the distinction in the light of logic
rather than in the light of method. All societies are collectives,
which stand in some kind of normative relation to their individual
members. In virtue of this normative relationship, the collective
enables its members to identify themselves, and it was in virtue
of this relationship that Durkheim spoke of the constraint exercised by the collective. But the constraint can take many forms,

and these forms can be logically distinguished according to two kinds of universals. There is one type of society in which the collective is like a concrete universal and another type of society in which the collective is like an abstract universal. In the case of the society that is like a concrete universal, the individual member will be obliged to conform to a certain norm because of an authoritative myth. That myth is a concrete story ('once upon a time the wind god did this or that'), but it assumes the role of a universal in that it becomes an authoritative instruction for a large number of people. These people will feel that they are constrained by the concrete universal story.

In the case of societies that are like abstract universals, the situation is quite different. The abstract universal is a proposition that takes the form 'all builders do this or that'. Every individual member of such a society will feel that he is constrained to behave in a certain way because all people in his position behave in that way. The abstract universal operates as a norm in a completely different way from the concrete universal. The concrete universal is established by an authoritative tradition. The abstract universal is established by the counting of heads and the classification of particular details. The abstract universal, in other words, is the product of sociological method. It is the result of empirical summing up of interviews and answers to questionnaires. It cannot be applied to traditional and small groups, tightly organised according to lineages and societies, descent groups or clans. In such tightly, traditionally organised societies people are not in the habit of interpreting their identity and their behaviour in terms of their membership by an abstract universal, empirically defined as the sum total of certain characteristics. They interpret their identity in terms of certain authoritative pronouncements of myth. They will say that they occupy a certain status and perform certain actions not because they are 'constrained' by an empirically defined social norm (expressed as a popularity poll, a Gallup survey, or an academically conducted survey), but because they belong to the wind god clan and are doing what they are doing because it was ordered by the wind god in time before mind.[29] The concrete universal exercises constraint because it is a mythical paradigm. The individual recognises himself in the figure of, say, Achilles or Saint Francis, but such a recognition is not based upon absolute identity. The abstract universal, on the other hand, exercises constraint because there is an absolute identity between every member of the class or association and the individual who seeks to understand himself or know himself. In the one case, the individual recognises himself in, without actually identifying himself with, the concrete universal. In the other case, the individual understands himself as yet another instance of all the other instances summed up in the abstract universal.[30] The distinction between societies in which the collective is prevalently concrete and societies in which the collective is prevalently abstract is, of course, not always absolute. Although there seem to be no tradition-bound societies that contain subgroups organised by abstract universals, there are many mass societies organised by one single abstract universal or by a plurality of abstract universals in which smallish groups of concrete universals survive.

For the historian the lesson of these observations is simple and obvious. He must use sociology when he is studying modern mass society because sociology will help him to understand the members of these societies as they understand themselves. But whenever he is studying older societies and prenineteenth-century history, sociology can be of no use to him and must in fact lead to colossal distortions. For any attempt to divide people of these older societies into classes, let alone to ascribe class consciousness to them, is not to understand them as they understood themselves. And the same goes, *mutatis mutandis*, for the employment of other methods of sorting and categorising men into groups according to social survey criteria. The members of the older societies must be understood as they understood themselves, that is, in terms of their myths and their traditions and their supernaturally ordained institutions. To fill the gaps left by the sources and to understand the sources correctly, the historian will be much better served, in his study of prenineteenth-century history, by the methods and the findings of social anthropology.[31]

The present argument about the use and abuse of sociology in the study of history is based on the recognition that history is not an autonomous science.[32] Lest I, as a historian, be charged with letting the side down by such an admission, I would like to conclude with the following considerations. First of all, there seems nothing startling or new in the admission that history is not an autonomous science. This is proved by the fact that ever since the Father of History, ever since Herodotus, the overwhelming majority of historians wrote contemporary history and have only very cautiously and hesitantly worked backwards into the past. They confined themselves at first to the present because there they were sure of all the auxiliary knowledge required for story telling. They clung to the present because they knew that if they ventured into the past, the necessary auxiliary knowledge would be less readily available. The *exclusive* preoccupation of historians with the critical sorting out of the past and the rise of history as the disinterested study of the past dates in reality from the accidental confluence in Europe of a number of incompatible mythical traditions;[33] that is, it was due to an almost accidental and extraneous factor. When historians started to deal with the past, they became doubly dependent on other knowledge. We have it, to quote a random example, from no less an authority than Gibbon that he had to rely on his knowledge of the Hampshire Grenadiers when he wanted to describe the Roman legions.[34]

   If the first consideration merely gives cold comfort to historians, a second will restore their full self-respect. It was an essential part of the preceding argument that there is a great difference between the methods of sociology and the methods of social anthropology and that each method is effectively applicable to a certain type of society. If this is correct, then neither sociology nor social anthropology is an autonomous science either. For to make sure that the correct method of study is applied to the type of society in which it is applicable, these sciences need the advice of the historian. Only the historian can tell whether a certain society ought to be studied sociologically or social-anthropologically, for only he can form an opinion as to whether the people in this society or that understand themselves by making a social survey and validating their custom by social survey; or whether they are wont to consult an authority, be it an oracle, an elder, or a mythical tradition. In this sense, knowledge of history is required before the sociologist and social anthropologist can get to work and therefore stands confirmed as a sort of metasocial science.[35] For the historian studies change and he is therefore *ex officio* competent to say whether a society has changed sufficiently to make sociology applicable or not. The crucial period for the examination of history as a sort of metasocial science is the age of the French Revolution, of the Industrial Revolution, and the period of the Westernisation of Asian and African societies. For it is in these areas that the historian has to investigate very carefully whether a process is to be understood sociologically as a class or group phenomenon in which the individual sees himself or interprets himself as 'constrained' by his membership of a certain collective; or whether it ought to be understood social-anthropologically as a tradition-, or myth-, or authority-directed phenomenon.

   This view cuts across a principle that is becoming increasingly popular among both historians and social scientists. 'History',

writes C. Lévi-Strauss, 'organises its data in relation to conscious
expression of social life, while anthropology proceeds by examining its unconscious foundation'.[36] Even if we leave the whole
question of the historian's primary concern with change aside,
and even if we admit that Lévi-Strauss' passionate search for what
really happened, as distinct from the surface appearances, is more
sophisticated than the old positivist formula announced by Ranke,
this principle remains untenable. As we have seen in earlier chapters, there is no way in which one can distinguish absolutely
between the surface appearances and the unconscious and un-
thought of reality that is supposed to lie behind them. The only
things one can substitute are universals (i.e., thoughts). One can
replace the thoughts of the people one is studying by the thoughts
of historians and other social scientists. Since every image of a
society and of its method of bonding its members is a thought in
the mind of somebody, it is impossible to determine who has the
right thought and who has the wrong thought as to how it is done.
Whatever the differences between social scientists in general and
historians are, they cannot run parallel to the distinction between
the man who studies surface appearances and the man who finds
out the unconscious foundations. If Lévi-Strauss thinks that his
classificatory structure has uncovered the way in which members
of an Australian aborigine totemic clan think of their clan,[37] he
may have entered into their minds and reenacted their thoughts
in Collingwood's sense; and such reenactment is a great step forward when compared with the theories about these clans put forward by Durkheim.[38] But it is impossible to maintain that such
reenactment reveals the unconscious foundations of totemic
clanship since we must at all times suppose that the members of
that clan can be as mistaken about themselves as the modern observer can be. When Lévi-Strauss laid bare the classificatory system
on which the system of bonding and the rule for exogamy are
based, he replaced Durkheim's contention that rules of exogamy
and the taboo of the clan's totem are derived from the fact that
the clan worships its own social cohesion in the form of the taboo
on the totemic animal. Durkheim may indeed have failed to
reenact what went on in the mind of the clansmen. But one cannot accept Lévi-Strauss' claim that just because he seems to have
been able to reenact what went on in the mind of the clansmen,
he has run to earth the unconscious foundations and the reality
of totemic clanship. On the contrary, it is conceivable that Durkheim was the one who laid bare the unconscious foundations of
totemism and that Lévi-Strauss merely discovered what the clans-

men thought or, better, how they counted. However this may be, Lévi-Strauss' distinction between historians who study conscious expressions and social scientists who reveal the unconscious foundations cannot be justified.[39]

If the historian were really an investigator who remains satisfied with conscious expressions and surface appearances of social life, he would have to make way for the social scientist. In this case, the historian could not even claim the province of change as his own. For whatever change is to be narrated, it is done equally well and often better with the help of universals that lay bare the unconscious foundations. In rejecting the principle enunciated by Lévi-Strauss, the historian can stake out his claim with complete self-confidence. If we have shown that he is dependent on the social sciences, we have also shown that the social sciences, in turn, are dependent on him. Only the historian, preoccupied as he is with change, can be an arbiter as to which of the social sciences is to be employed in any one case and whether abstract or concrete universals are relevant for the investigation of any particular period. The social sciences by themselves cannot do this. For the nature of the material is such that it does not carry any labels on the surface. When one is looking at a society, one may well find that it employs concrete universals to explain itself to itself. But since we have seen that there is no reason why explanations in the technical sense of chapter 4 are final and since we have seen that there are many reasons why they must be replaced by interpretations, we cannot accept a society's self-image in terms of abstract or concrete universals, as the case may be, as final. For this reason, the historian with his substitutions, has to be at hand to tell the social scientist whether to employ concrete universals or abstract universals. And, again, it is the historian who must decide whether interpretations or explanations are called for. Durkheim's theory about the totemic clans of Australia were clearly interpretations. He wanted to make the totemic clans intelligible to modern man. Had he retold all the myths about the totems, modern readers would have remained puzzled. By interpreting the taboo on the totemic animal as a symbol of society and by stressing that every society, to survive and keep going, must worship itself, he made the Australian customs intelligible. Lévi-Strauss criticised him because he showed that when we reenact the thoughts of the aborigines of Australia, we will see their customs and institutions in a very different light. He rejected Durkheim's interpretation and substituted an explanation. The debate between Durkheim and Lévi-Strauss has to be assessed.

Only a historian who has studied change can be aware that change has taken place and that modern men are different from Australian aborigines. He is therefore the only man in a position to assess the merits of the two conflicting theories. But historical knowledge, as we have seen, is not really possible unless the source material is studied in the light of either sociology or social anthropology. The relationship between the various sciences discussed is therefore not linear but circular. One cannot embark successfully on the one without having embarked on the other. In one sense, the historian must be the ultimate arbiter as to whether the sociologist or the social anthropologist ought to set to work; in another sense, the historian cannot tell his story, unless he places his material into a social setting provided either by the type of society that emerges from sociology or by the type of society that emerges from social anthropology.

Chapter Seven

SOURCES AND RAW MATERIAL

So far we have blithely assumed that historical work is first like detection and second like understanding. We have proceeded in our discussion as if the historian first had to go to some kind of police training college to learn all about the rules of evidence so that he can distinguish fiction from fact. Once he has achieved skill in this activity, he can proceed to the composition of historical narratives and use his judgment to put together subevents into big events, split events into subevents, and worry about the differences between explanations proper and interpretations. This ready distinction of the two parts of the historian's activity is reflected in a time-honoured distinction between primary and secondary sources. Primary sources, we are told, are the documents on which the historian bases his knowledge. They consist of archeological remains, letters and treaties, charters and proclamations, and chronicles and annals. They are said to be the raw material of historical knowledge. The primary sources are those sources that the historian supposes to find ready-made. They are the material he finds before he goes to work. Secondary sources are the narratives of other historians, encyclopaedias, and dictionaries. They are works written by other historians and contain the attempts of other historians to digest the raw material.

On the face of it, the distinction sounds useful and plausible. The inclusion of annals and chronicles, provided they are contemporary to the events studied, in the primary sources, however, makes one suspicious. Neither annals nor chronicles, no matter how contemporary, are wholly 'raw'. They are written down by somebody for a purpose and therefore always present a first attempt at digestion. But even the other pieces listed under the heading 'primary' turn out on examination to be less primary and less raw than one might suppose.

Let us examine, for instance, an eighteenth-century British election return. This is a document made of paper that says that such and such a person was returned to Parliament after an election

duly held on a certain day by a certain sheriff. Such a document
may be considered to be very primary. It embodies no attempt at
digesting any events, no attempt to explain or to interpret. Without the historian's work on the document, it is a seemingly worth-
less piece of information. But closer examination will show that
this is not so. The document is primary information of one fact
and one fact only. It tells us that a certain man wrote it on a certain day. All the other information supposedly contained in it
about elections and sheriffs and Parliaments, not to mention
electoral customs and constitutional law and the social composition of the shire, is teased out of the document. It is not only
that the document may, though not a forgery, have been written
by the sheriff to hide the fact that on that appointed day he
neglected his duty to hold an election. The possibility that it may
yield information other than the information ostensibly contained
in it is the least reason why we should not consider the document
as primary information. The real reason why we cannot take the
document as primary source material is that we know that it is
an artefact. It was written by somebody for a certain purpose. Its
author knew a great deal about constitutional law and society and
the interrelation of the two. The election return, then, is not really
primary information but something like a mininarrative of an
election or of part of an election. It is a composition. As it stands
it portrays an event. But that event, we recall, can be subdivided.
Without Parliament and the society of the shire in mind, the
sheriff could have assembled the events of the electoral congress
of that day in a different manner and connected them with the
prevailing good weather and told us of something more resembling
a party than an election. The fact that he did not reflects the fact
that a mind was at work and that that mind worked to compose
the subevents into an event, thus providing a miniature story.
Analysed in this way, the difference between an election return
and a contemporary chronicle is only a difference in degree. Furthermore, the difference between a contemporary chronicle and
a full-blown history written by a historian hundreds of years later
is again only one of degree. In short, the concept 'primary source'
evaporates under closer inspection. All sources, we might say, are
secondary.

   If this is so, we must conclude that our assumption that the
work of the historian can be divided into two parts, into a detective part and into a digestive part, becomes unrealistic.[1] On the
contrary. It now turns out that the very examination of the so-
called primary material is not really different from the examina-

tion of the narratives of later historians. In all cases we are dealing with material and accounts that have been composed by somebody and that link events in a certain way rather than in another way. In all cases we must ask ourselves how the events are linked, what methods were used, what the coverage of the gaps between the events actually is.

Oblivious of the precariousness of the distinction between primary and secondary sources, many historians anxious to pre-serve complete objectivity have abandoned the composition of narratives. They argue that as soon as a primary source is digested, the historian's subjective understanding enters into the raw material. They believe that it ought to be kept out and that therefore the careful editing of the source material is the historian's most demanding and chief preoccupation. These historians present us with beautifully edited volumes of charters and chronicles and when all the extant charters have been edited and all the extant inscriptions transcribed, the following generation of historians usually start to reedit them because of inaccuracies alleged to have been made by their predecessors. In this way the work of historical investigation never ends. The editions of a previous generation of scholars are thus added to the primary source material as the errors in transcription made by them are listed in the footnotes of the revised editions. In this way historians come to be occupied not with history but with what they think is the source material of history. Their labours can never end; not because history is constantly and continuously being made and ought to be written up, but because historians keep editing documents and because these editions contain minor errors that ought to be corrected. First we had Migne's editions of the writings of the Fathers. Now much of Migne's material has been reedited and one can foresee the time when we can expect a third round of editions. Similarly, many of the volumes of the *Monumenta Germaniae Historica* are now being edited for the second time. The belief that careful editing is historical work should be described as documentary positivism. The documentary positivist believes that there are data and that the data of history are the main target of his attention and that he should be a positivist by confining his attention to the so-called facts.

It is easy to ridicule and belittle documentary positivism. To begin with, it is a humiliating activity. It is perhaps a little absurd to find a modern highly educated scholar spending his whole life to detect what the author of the document in question knew with-out ado. The historian is, in this respect, really imitating a detective

who spends much effort to find out what the criminal who committed the crime knew anyway. But there is more to be said for
documentary positivism than that. First, it goes without saying
that a critical edition of any source is important. We must know
what it really looked like when it originated, who wrote it, how
it was spelt, and who the people and institutions mentioned in it
really were. Moreover, we must be able to distinguish between the
forged documents and the genuine ones. Insofar as an editor tells
us these things, he is invaluable and is really treating the primary
source like a composition. He tells us who composed it, what went
on in the mind of the composer, and so forth. Documentary
positivism becomes stultifying only when it is treated as an end in
itself and when an historian who has spent years in editing documents refuses to use them for writing a narrative because he claims
that to do so would force him to intrude his own subjective judgment into the raw material of history. Documentary positivism
also becomes superfluous when its finesse of detection proceeds
beyond a certain point, and it becomes downright redundant when
it provides nothing but facsimile prints of the original document.
The only thing to be said for this last activity is that, though ex-
pensive, it is still cheaper to buy a volume of facsimile prints than
for a genuine historian to travel from America to the Vatican to
inspect the original.

One of the great commonplaces in the teaching of historical
method is the demand for accurate reporting so that the historian
can find out accurately what happened. It is believed, for example,
that the greater the expertness of the author of an observation
in the matter he is observing, the greater the trustworthiness of
his report or that we must always accord little accuracy to a report
in which the author is assigned a high place in the world or an
important role in the events he is reporting.[2] But as soon as one
examines these pieces of advice and pushes the examination
beyond the level of commonsense psychology, they will appear
insufficient and misleading. The concept of accuracy is not a
simple concept. Since every story can be broken up into substories
and every substory into subevents and so forth, we can never use
the word 'accuracy' in the simple sense in which it applies to a
story as a story of what really happened. We can never say that a
report is 'accurate' because it *really* describes what happened. A
report can be accurate only in the sense that it repeats accurately
what somebody else has seen or heard. In that sense of 'accurate',
the concept is irretrievably linked to the concept of meaning because the story one compares it with (the complete correspon-

dence of which one accepts as a criterion of accuracy) must have
been an intelligible unit (*Sinngebild*) to its author, whoever he
was.

Alternatively, one could think of 'accuracy' in a different way.
One could consider a substory accurate if one is logically forced
to presume that it must report something that must have happened, even though any known record is of a much larger event.
Thus if we are told of a war, we are obliged to infer that somebody
must have been killed in it. Therefore we may suppose that any
report we have of such killing must be an accurate report, even
though we have no direct way of checking it by looking at the
event in question. But in such a case, the large event (the story of
a war) must make sense to us, that is, to the people who do the
deducing. Whichever way one takes it, one can see that every
demand for accuracy involves a demand to know the meaning of
the story. In some cases one has to know what the story meant to
the author of the report, and in some cases one has to know what
the story means to the modern reader. In either case no mindless
determination of accuracy is possible. Equally, it is not possible
to compile a mindlessly accurate list of events that have happened,
so that one may later invite a historian gifted with the necessary
literary talent to put a narrative together.

We must conclude that there is no genuinely raw material at
all. Everything that has come down to us is cooked by somebody
for some purpose; and I do not mean 'cooked' in the colloquial
sense of 'forged' or 'doctored'. It is simply cooked in the sense
that it is an artefact. It is made up by somebody. It is a mininarrative and when we go to work on it critically we must seek first
and foremost to find out how it was composed. The standards of
discovery and investigation do not in principle differ from the
critical standards we apply to any secondary sources and to such
highly accomplished historical narratives as Gibbon's story of the
decline of Rome. The distinction between primary and secondary
sources, in other words, must be abandoned and we must stop
thinking of the historian's labours as divided into two parts: detection and composition, establishment of the true facts and story
telling.

If it is true that even primary sources are not really primary,
where then is the raw material of history? The real raw material
is present; but it is not 'material' in the sense in which documents
are material. The real raw material of history is thought. Precisely,
it is the thought that goes into the composition of the mininarratives. The events that actually happened and that cannot be

broken down further are the thoughts of the people we are studying. In this sense Croce and Collingwood were right to insist that
all history is the history of thought. The general laws and, in some
cases, the concrete universals are the genuine raw material of history. If we want to find out what actually happened, we must find
out what people thought, what went on in their minds. This is
true in a double sense. We must find out what they thought in
order to understand them as they understood themselves and in
order to understand their actions and plans. But we must also find
out their thoughts in order to understand the documents and
charters, letters and annals, that they wrote down. These documents are their own first attempts at writing history.

An older school of German historians described the smallest
raw unit as the *Sinngebild*. The *Sinngebild* is the most basic unit
of intelligibility provided by the people the historian is studying.
All along we go on the assumption that these people were not
dumb but that they themselves thought about what they were
doing, explained themselves to themselves, and left documents
that reflect these thoughts. Hence the *Sinngebild* rather than the
document itself is the most elementary material of history. But
though it is not possible to break down the *Sinngebild*, it is hardly
very raw. It is a unit that owes its existence to the thought bestowed on events and it does not necessarily matter, as we have
seen in chapter 3, whose thought it is. All we know is that we
cannot, under any circumstances, go back to anything beyond
such thought.

Before proceeding, it is well to admit that despite the preceding argument, a certain amount of information can be culled
from breaking up even the *Sinngebild*. Suppose we have a sixteenth-century menu. As a document it is a basic unit of intelligibility because it is a short narrative of the culinary taste and the
appropriate food for a certain occasion. This meaning is enshrined
in the document and can be understood by the modern historian.
But it is possible to break up the menu and shear it of the thought
that went into its composition. We can disregard the occasion, and
the culinary taste, and the view of what food was appropriate for
the occasion and simply use the mention of pork as evidence that
pork was available, that certain people were able to afford that
much pork whenever a similar occasion arose, and that we can
learn something about the class structure from the fact that they
referred to that kind of meat with a name derived from French
rather than by a name of good Anglo-Saxon origin like pig. When
we cull this sort of information from the intelligible unit, we must

be clear as to what we are doing. We are manifestly not interested in what the people who wrote the document thought but merely in the extraneous information the document is evidence for. For that matter a chemical analysis of the paper or parchment itself will tell us something about the state of technology. We are not going beyond the thought enshrined in it; but we are simply disregarding it. By disregarding it, we are not really understanding what actually happened and we are certainly not understanding what actually happened as the people to whom it happened understood it. We are culling extraneous information from it and we can use this information to build a narrative of events in the sixteenth century by interpretation. We are gaining knowledge of some things that actually happened, but since those things were obviously not part of the things observed at the time, such knowledge is, in a very real sense, not real because it was demonstrably not part of the way the people we are studying were conscious of it. It belongs, on the contrary, to the myriad of pieces of knowledge beyond the horizon of the people we are studying.

When the original *Sinngebild* enshrined in the sources is broken up in this way, we land ourselves with the same sort of evidence that is available to the archeologist when he digs up pieces of pottery and the foundations of buildings. If one looks at such raw material, which contains no evidence of thought, one will readily understand the crucial importance of the thought contained in the evidence the historian is dealing with. The archeologist, left with nothing more than silent raw material, tries very hard but he comes up with nothing better than a bizarre account of what happened. He will speak, for instance, about the 'beaker-folk' or the 'Hallstatt Culture' as if they were genuine societies. All he means in fact is that at certain times and places there were people who used beakers and whose cultural implements were identical with the ones found at Hallstatt. We know perfectly well that the peoples concerned must have had a sense of identity but that it is totally inconceivable that all the peoples who used beakers should have referred to themselves as the beaker-folk. They knew who belonged to their societies and who did not and they must have given some thought to the why and how of their behaviour. Yet the archeologists' picture reflects none of this. It shows us a rigidly mechanical system of classification that bears only the most tenuous and accidental relationship to what we know must actually have happened. The picture is not only poor. If it were just poor it would not essentially differ from many an historical account. It is bizarre because we know that there was no

such thing as a beaker-folk. To speak of a beaker-folk is all the
archeologist can do. But the present argument is not meant as a
criticism of archeology. It is merely meant to show that when
the raw material does not contain traces of thought, the doors to
the past remain closed and such pictures that can be gained of the
past stand in a bizarre relationship to what actually happened.

Archeologists have always been very conscious of this problem and accept the fact that the discovery of archeological remains
without written records cannot lead to more than a description
and a dating of these remains. This sort of limited archeology is
known as 'text-free archeology'[3] . To supplement the meagre
knowledge that is to be derived from text-free archeology, archeologists have often supplemented the purely material discoveries
they make by general laws of their own. These laws are purely
interpretative as they cannot be linked, by the nature of the case,
to anything that belongs to the age to which the material finds
belong. For a long time, especially in Germany, archeologists used
Kossinna's law that any distinct cultural province, no matter how
limited, bears witness to the presence of a distinct race.[4] If Kossinna's law is now discredited, we are witnessing the introduction
of a completely different one. There has arisen in Britain a school
of archeology that is referred to as the 'New Archeology'. This
school uses the postulate that all societies are functioning functionally and that that postulate must be applicable to the societies of the very ancient past as much as to modern societies. If
the postulate is accepted, it follows that one dead artefact can be
used to construct others of which no traces have been found but
that are supposed to be functionally related to it. In this way one
can obtain, on the basis of a few pieces of pottery, a picture of a
complete social organism. This still leaves one very much in the
air as to the nature of change, the origins and the decline of that
social organism. But it is better than nothing and Colin Renfrew
has used the postulate in a very fruitful way in his book entitled
*The Emergence of Civilisation: The Cyclades and the Aegean in
the Third Millennium B.C.*[5] Like Kossinna's law, this postulate
enables the archeologist to convert dead matter (text-free findings)
into something resembling history. But the concept 'text-free'
and the frank admission that something like a postulate or law is
needed to interpret the discoveries made by archeologists proves
my contention that unless there is raw material that is a record
made by somebody and that carries the thoughts that went into
the making of that record on its face it is impossible to construct
a historical narrative and to form a conception of a series of events
and of change.

In chapter 4 of *The History Primer*,[6] J. H. Hexter discusses
the difficulties the historian encounters when he stumbles across
an event that is not obviously and manifestly anchored in a contemporary (i.e., contemporary with the people involved in the
event) *Sinngebild*. The historian knows that it is and that he must
search. But to begin with he does not even know where to look.
Hexter calls the experience the historian can draw upon for knowing where to look the 'second record'. He chooses an example from
his own historical work. Thomas More, although he had made
explicit reservations in *Utopia* about entering royal service, nevertheless entered royal service. Hexter states that it was his (Hexter's)
knowledge of Holdsworth's *History of English Law* and of Pollard's *Wolsey* and his general extensive reading in the reign of
Henry VIII that made him find an answer. The answer was that
More was observing 'changes in royal policy that brought it nearer
to More's views of what was desirable and possible within the
bounds of the existing social order' (page 118). In this example
the second record is actually a study of the history surrounding
More's decision. Hexter did not have to go far afield and, for that
matter, the event he came up with is an event that, it seems, was
not actually in the first record; but it could easily have been. The
solution to the question is so very nearly what More himself could
easily have said in a letter that the second record does not amend
the first record much. But let us look at another example. More
was very enthusiastic in *Utopia* 'for measures to ensure security
for families in case of the premature death or disability of the
breadwinner' (page 119). Where are the other events and the
thought to connect them with this event? Here Hexter, in his
search for the second record, had to go farther afield. He knew
of his own anxieties and family situation in 1950 when he first
encountered this question. His own knowledge of his own anxiety
in this respect made him sensitive to More's problem. With this
sensitivity, which is clearly not part of the first record, he started
to look and found encouragement that he was looking in the right
direction when he found that More's family situation was not
so different from his own. Thus the discovery of the other event:
in 1515 More had a large young family for whose future security
he had 'to engage in work he intensely disliked' (page 119).

We should keep Hexter's terminology and slightly amend it.
The first record is not usually as barren as Hexter's tabulated
examples lead one to expect. If what we said above about primary
sources and raw material is true, then the first record is neither
as primary nor as raw as Hexter's model makes it appear. The
sources themselves contain thoughts about the events they pro-

vide and, indeed we found that at least in the first example, it is
quite conceivable that the first record could have contained
information very similar to the second record. We conclude therefore that there is no rigid distinction between first and second
records and that the first record already contains or could conceivably contain the information provided by the second record.
Hexter's model makes the first record look too barren. He presents
it as if More had not been an intellectual given to a lot of thinking
about himself. Especially when we are dealing with intellectuals,
the chances are that a first record embodies a second record. If a
Sinngebild is an event plus another event plus a thought that
connects the two, we have much reason for expecting More to
provide quite a lot of the thought that connects the two.

Thomas More, of course, is an extreme example. Most people the historian deals with are not intellectuals. There are, for
instance, simple soldiers, rank and file as well as generals. Gibbon
was acutely aware that when investigating Roman legions and their
centurions he could not hope to find much more than a barren
first record. Hence the great importance of the second record. He
tells us in his autobiography that his experience of service in the
Hampshire Grenadiers was of great value for his understanding of
the Roman legionnaries.[7] Since the first record was barren, the
second record's importance increased.

We can generalise. No historian can write good history unless
he has a great deal of experience of the things he is writing about.
If his own second record is barren, he will not make much headway
with the first record. Even when dealing with intellectuals the
importance of the second record should not be underrated. My
own first historical work was about Richard Hooker, an intellectual
if there ever was one. The first record showed that *The Laws of
Ecclesiastical Polity*, originally planned in eight books, was left
unfinished when Hooker died in 1599. There is no clear evidence
in the first record why Hooker stopped writing. My second record
helped me. I know from my own experience as an intellectual that
I easily conceive large plans and draw up skeletons for writing
them down. But as the work proceeds, I usually discover that ideas
have a logic of their own and that I cannot make them do what I,
in a first flash, thought they might do. In this way, many projects
are left unfinished because the ideas I am dealing with or have
espoused are too stubborn. Bearing this experience in mind I concluded that Hooker too must have got stuck. I knew now what to
look for but unfortunately could find nothing in the first record
to bear me out. But I did at least find clear evidence that Hooker
was not interrupted by sudden death. On the contrary, the evi-

dence shows that he did no writing during the last six years of his life, and this means that if he had known how to finish his work, he could have. Thus the second record provided a fairly plausible explanation.[8]

It is well known that much great history is written by men of affairs and that university professors, as a rule, with their very limited experience, do not often make good historians. On the whole, Sir Steven Runciman and Cicely Veronica Wedgewood are better than most academic historians, though there are exceptions. Sir Maurice Powicke is superb and so are David Knowles and Sir Ronald Syme. But especially Knowles, a Benedictine monk before he became Regius Professor at Cambridge, knew from his second record what he was writing about in his history of monks and friars.[9] University professors of course have the advantage of the intimate knowledge of their own university administration to guide them through the mazes of politics and power struggles. But this second record is limited and it can be no accident that so many university professors, conscious of their lack of experience, confine themselves to documentary positivism.[10] The study of what the documents themselves say and the attempt to bring out such a second record, if any, as is actually contained in these documents is more commensurate with their own limited experience. It is therefore a pity that they have set themselves up as the guardians of our knowledge of history. We must be very critical of that guardianship and recognise that it is a guardianship of a very limited area of historical knowledge, and above all we must not make the mistake of identifying historical knowledge with what is taught and approved of in academic institutions.

There is a real advantage in calling the primary sources the 'first record'. They are thus distinguished from the second record, which consists of the experiences and knowledge the historian brings to bear on them. But they are thus also characterised as a *record*. If we call a document a 'primary source', it takes a lot of explaining that it is not very primary. But if we call it a 'record', we implicitly acknowledge that it contains someone's thought because a record is what somebody has recorded. In this way we can draw immediate attention to the fact that every source embodies a thought. It may do so explicitly or only ideally; but in either case, when we fall back upon the second record, we are really only substituting one record for another.

It is an old truism among historians to say that where there is no record, there is no knowledge of the event and, therefore, no history. But I am saying more than this. I am saying that when there is no record, there *was* no event because the event that

Caesar crossed the Rubicon is known to us not only because somebody happened to record it, but also and even primarily because
somebody recorded the several subevents in such a way that they
amounted to the event that Caesar crossed the Rubicon. As I have
argued in several places above, all the subevents in question could
have been absorbed into different events without any subevent
being left over. If this had been done we would not only not have
had a record of Caesar crossing the Rubicon, but there would
actually, strange as this may sound, have been no crossing of the
Rubicon by Caesar. There would have been other events. But the
failure to put the subevents together in this particular way so
that they appeared as Caesar crossing the Rubicon together with
the appearance of other events instead would not only have left
us without a record, it would also have spirited the crossing of
the Rubicon by Caesar away. Better, it would have failed to spirit
it up. In a very real sense, therefore, it is not just our knowledge
of the event that depends on the record. The existence of the
event itself depends on somebody's record of it. As I argued in an
earlier chapter, this position comes close to that of Bishop
Berkeley, except for the fact that perception (recording) is a
necessary precondition for the *configuration* of existence and not,
as Berkeley supposed, for existence as such. With this qualification
I am prepared to take my stand with Berkeley and am not in the
least bit intimidated by Dr. Johnson's famous joke on the matter.
The reminder of the closeness of my position to that of Berkeley
is particularly appropriate in this context, for it draws our attention to the fact that the sources and the raw material with which
the historian deals and which he cannot do without, are more than
sources of information. They contain *in nuce* part of the narrative
with which he finally comes up. Unless one is mindful of Bishop
Berkeley, it is all too easy to misread the nature of evidence.

    Under what conditions can we call a report accurate? We can
never consider its accuracy, let alone judge it, by 'looking' at the
event reported, even if we had a time telescope, because the event
does not exist apart from its configuration. This means that it
does not exist apart from what somebody has reported to have
taken place. Therefore we can consider the accuracy of a report
only by comparing it to a report given by somebody else: first, by
comparing it to a report by a more or less contemporary person
to whom certain subevents appeared connected with each other
in such a way as to have assumed the shape of the event in question; then, by comparing it with reports by people other than
contemporaries, and so forth. In every case, our judgment of the

accuracy of the report depends not on the correspondence of any of the reports with the event, but on the correspondence of any report with any other report. Whether we call this a correspondence or a coherence theory of truth, accuracy and truth become functions of the relationships between different reports. In no way can they be considered dependent on a comparison between report and event. The search for eyewitnesses may have a certain kind of importance. But it has little or nothing to do with the search for accuracy. An eyewitness's report may have a better change than a noneyewitness' report to correspond with what Caesar said. But since no report can correspond with the event, and since Caesar's report itself does not occupy a privileged position among all possible reports, an eyewitness report does not have an inherent guarantee of truth, not even if one could discount something that we all know one cannot discount, the human capacity for wrong observation. Whatever that capacity and whatever steps one can take to diminish and correct it, eyewitnesship by itself is not even ideally a warrant of accuracy. The whole question of accuracy is therefore not connected with the question as to the human potential for accurate observation. Instead, it has something to do with our chances of linking one report with another report and of continuing a certain line of reporting by building it into a narrative.

The view taken here of the nature of the historian's raw material collides head on with the view held by both laymen and many professional historians. Either Caesar crossed the Rubicon, they say, or he did not. This question, they maintain, should be capable of a simple and complete answer. The question why he did, and the question whether it was a good thing he did, and the question what the consequences were, they say, are another matter and can be safely disregarded when one expects an answer to the question whether he did cross the Rubicon. This is certainly the point on which the layman as well as professional historians like Sir Frank Stenton ('The acid test of a good historian is whether he can edit a charter') and Sir George Clark (there is a 'hard core of fact surrounding the pulp of disputable interpretation') display the same robust, but misplaced, commonsense. Another look at the figure on page 33 will show that every one of the subfacts into which the event that Caesar crossed the Rubicon can be broken up can be absorbed in assemblies other than the event that Caesar crossed the Rubicon. If this were done, the event that Caesar crossed the Rubicon would simply disappear or might never have appeared in the first place in the records. Therefore we cannot expect a simple answer to the question whether Caesar crossed the Rubicon. There is not only no simple answer, but whatever answer is given depends on the universals employed in the assembly of the subevents. We see again that the simple search for the facts, for what *actually* happened, is misguided unless it is, in the first instance, a search for the universals that were employed at the time, that is, unless it is a search for the thoughts. Such search will lead us, at first to the universals used by the people who compiled the records. But since these universals are today frequently believed not to be true, they do not necessarily make an intelligible narrative for the modern reader. Therefore there must be translation and interpretation. With translation and interpretation, however, we leave the realm of the things that *actually* happened and as we do so, we leave, when composing a narrative, a straight description of what actually took place. Universals that did not take place at the time enter, of necessity, into our historical knowledge and the whole simple quest of the layman and of so many professional historians shows itself to be misguided. We will do well to recall one of those epigrams Lévi-Strauss tosses off: 'Besides, historical fact has no objective reality. It only exists as a result of a retrospective construction undertaken by people who have lived the events they speak of in a purely arbitrative sense'.[11]

If we wish to understand what the first record says we must gauge the thought it contains or could contain. Unfortunately, the way the human mind is constructed, there is no absolute criterion of what constitutes understanding. We say we understand when the events in question seem connected plausibly. By this we may mean that the thought the first record enshrines is sufficiently general or sufficiently close to our own experience to appear plausible. If it is, well and good and the matter can rest there. We can then say that we understand the past as the past understood itself. But if we are separated from the past we wish to understand by too many centuries or if we have ceased to share its religious preoccupations and the like, such understanding will not necessarily appear plausible to us. We must then seek to translate in the sense described in chapter 4. And if no translation is possible, we must resort to interpretation. But no matter what we do, we never reach an absolute standard of intelligibility. As soon as the observer's standpoint and experience change, an interpretation or even a translation, let alone an explanation proper, ceases to be plausible. Hexter was rightly anxious about the security of his young family in 1950 in the United States, which was then a highly competitive society still practising all the rigours of extreme economic individualism. Had he started investigating Thomas More twenty years later in the bosom of the New Zealand welfare state, in which even illegitimate children are entitled to a full share in the father's estate, his second record would have been very different and he might have found a much greater difficulty in understanding More's anxiety, if he would have understood it at all. Hexter, so he tells us, understood More because he, Hexter, used to be insecure himself. Does it follow, as a general rule, that one has to be insecure to understand insecurity? The answer depends on a strict application of the terminology suggested in chapter 3. If one seeks understanding, one should be able to accept the explanations given by the people one is studying. If these explanations appear to the modern historian false or implausible, it becomes very difficult to write a narrative in which the covering laws consist of such explanations. If these explanations have ceased to be considered true or plausible, the modern historian must interpret. He can, indeed ought, to interpret where he cannot understand. Lack of understanding in this sense means that one finds the explanation given by the agents concerned implausible or even false. Historians have notorious difficulty, for example, with the sources that deal with the lives of ancient and medieval saints.[12] These sources contain all sorts of references to levitation and to a man's ability to tolerate heat and so forth. Such generalisations or lawlike statements are completely implausible to us and we must therefore seek to interpret because we cannot possibly accept that people are weightless, or fly through the air, or tolerate heat of 200 degrees centigrade. As they appear in our sources the stylites or pillar-saints appear bizarre. Peter Brown has attempted to explain why the holy man, nevertheless, came to play such an important part in the society of the fifth and sixth centuries. An explanatory narrative would simply confine itself to the explanations given at the time, that is, levitation was not implausible. But Brown goes further and provides an interpretation so that we today can understand. He shows that the holy man was a product of his society and reflected needs no longer adequately met by other persons or institutions, the need for patronage, for mediation, for the power to allay anxiety. Now this sort of interpretation of the role of the holy man and his levitations is something we *can* understand, for we have experience of the need to allay anxiety and we also know that if one institution fails, another will take its place.[13] But we must be clear as to what Brown is doing. He invites us not to take levitation at its face

value. He tells us that these saints were really incapable of levitation and commanded respect not because they could levitate —
as people at the time believed — but because they could allay
anxieties — a power of which people at the time were not aware
of.

The absence of an absolute standard of what constitutes
understanding makes us very aware of the importance of proper
explanation. As long as we can manage to understand a part of
the past as it understood itself we are still not having absolute
understanding. But at least such understanding is less arbitrary
than a translation, let alone an interpretation, because both translation and interpretation are related in a comparatively arbitrary
manner to what the historian is seeking to understand. Every part
of the past remains what it is. But every translation and interpretation changes as the years go by, as the historian's own experience
changes and as he moves from place to place. Ancient Rome looks
different when viewed from the United States and from New
Zealand. For this reason we are not in a position to disregard the
explanations proper that are part of the past we are studying. At
least here we have something that does not change. Moreover, as
if this were not enough, there is the all-important fact that the
primary sources or the first records embody a great deal of thought
that is hard raw material and hard fact and that we must study
when we want to find out what actually happened. The very
first record is already shaped by these thoughts.

The respect for sources is therefore something essential. We
must treat sources with a holy respect. It is easy to misunderstand
the nature and the reason for this respect. Mostly historians adopt
a devout attitude to their sources because the sources, they say,
embody the facts. These sources tell us whether Caesar crossed
the Rubicon and when and how. It would be foolish to deny that
respect for sources is important for this reason. But if there were
no other reason, one would call such respect mere commonsense
and there would be no occasion for describing it as something
sacred. The real reason for the respect is that the sources are not
really primary but enshrine thought. And since we have no absolute standard as to what would be the 'correct' thought about
any event, the thought that was thought by the person involved
in that event is second best to an absolute standard.

For many centuries historians were not aware of the differences in thought between various parts of the past. They generally
assumed that what is plausible to one person is plausible to another, that human nature never changes, and that whether one is

writing about the ancient Persian Empire or modern London, people explain what is happening to them in the same terms. The peculiar problem of understanding and the problem created by the absence of an absolute criterion of understanding never arose. During the eighteenth century there came a profound change. The German historian F. Meinecke, has described it in detail.[14] He points out that from Thucydides to Gibbon it was believed that human beings of all ages had always spoken the 'same language'. It was only in the wake of the Romantic Revolution that it began to dawn on historians that human nature varies from time to time and place to place and that thoughts that are plausible to one man are not necessarily plausible to another. This change was not due to a mere growth of scepticism. Gibbon knew perfectly well that he was less credulous than Livy. But he thought he spoke the same language and assumed that he could have, given a chance, taught Livy to be as sceptical as an educated eighteenth-century Englishman. The real change was caused by the insight that changes in language, and social order, and religion affect changes in standards of plausibility. Meinecke considered this insight to be one of the great revolutionary changes in the human mind and did not hesitate to compare its importance to that of the Reformation.

To do justice to Meinecke's claim, we ought to qualify and amend it. Meinecke considered Herder and Goethe to have been the heroes of this revolution in the history of thought, with Burke, Moser, and Winckelmann as forerunners. He showed that these thinkers had discovered that all human beings are so individual that they can only be 'understood' in their individuality. As I have argued in chapter 4, page 64, individuality cannot be understood without making nonsense of the concept of understanding. Meinecke's revolutionaries did in fact not wish to make nonsense of all understanding; they wanted rather to show that human beings vary according to the things they consider plausible. In other words, whereas it had been believed prior to that revolution that what was plausible to one person was plausible to another person, it now came to be seen that people differed widely and continuously in the universals they were prepared to employ. It is the great shortcoming of Meinecke's important book that he did not bring this out. In one respect human nature is constant. Understanding can only be achieved through the employment of universals. But contrary to the assumptions made by historians prior to Meinecke's revolution, people differ greatly in the universals they are prepared to employ. Meinecke's revolutionaries challenged the view that people always employ the *same* universals,

but they did not contest the view — and if they did, they were
wrong — that people have to employ *universals*. Meinecke's heroes
were right in insisting that historians have to translate all the time
and that they have to establish connections between the universals
employed by an ancient Roman and a modern European because
these universals differed from one another, and Meinecke was right
in claiming that that insistence amounted to a revolution in historical thought. But insofar as these men claimed that no universals
were employed, they overstated their case to the point of absurdity. For it is precisely the ubiquity of the employment of universals that makes historical narration and historical understanding
possible.

Eugenio Garin, probably influenced by Meinecke and by
Meinecke's revolutionaries, has attributed the discovery of the
need for translation to his own heroes, the Florentine humanists
of the fifteenth century.[15] Whereas the historians of the Middle
Ages had gone on the assumption that the Roman Empire was still
in existence and that any piece of knowledge that had been current in ancient times could still be used, as it stood, in their own
age, the humanists had woken up to the fact that the social and
cultural environment of the Italian communes of the fourteenth
and fifteenth centuries was so vastly different from the climate
that had prevailed in ancient times that all pieces of knowledge
had to be translated to be understood. Needless to say, they did
not only mean by 'translation' that they ought to be translated
from ancient Greek into Renaissance Latin or Italian. The humanists became aware that the meaning of the thoughts of ancient
writers had to be *recovered*. It could not be assumed that the
thoughts of the ancients were the same as the thoughts of the
fifteenth-century Florentines. When Aristotle discussed the city-
state he could not be taken to mean what a fifteenth-century
political philosopher meant when he talked about the government
of Florence. Unlike Meinecke's Romantic revolutionaries, Garin's
humanists never went so far as to claim that the ancients could not
be understood at all but only described in their individuality.

Although both Meinecke and Garin are well aware of Vico,
they manage to account for the revolution in historical thinking
without seeing him in the centre of it. And yet, when all is said
and done, there is no philosopher of history who has expressed
and described more clearly and more cogently the view that universals change and that people cannot be presumed to be all
alike. What is more, he made this important insight the basis of
his philosophy of history and provided specific examples. We may

be able nowadays to improve on some of the examples. Other examples he gave have failed to stand up to scrutiny. But the principle is nowhere stated more succinctly and explicitly than in Vico. Above all, Vico pointed out that the universals used by different people at different times differ not only in content but also in form. For some people mesmerism is true; for others, it is not. This is a difference in content. But when some people use myths and metaphors as concrete universals and when other people prefer to use abstract universals, we have a difference in form. Vico's great importance lies in his discovery that there are not only changes in the content of the universals but also changes in the form of the universals. Early men, he believed, thought in metaphors and myths. Their way of explaining thunder was not just a different scientific theory, but a different kind of perception. In this way, Vico showed not only that human nature changes, but also that it changes in a particular way, that is, from thought in metaphor and myth to thought in general laws. Human beings always think with the help of universals. But there is a noticeable change in the kind of universal they employ. The nineteenth-century evolutionists and positivists from Comte to Sir James Frazer would have done well to study Vico and to take note of his argument that primitive thought is not a mistaken form of scientific thinking, but that it is based on a completely different form of perception. Concrete universals, Vico might have said, are not debased abstract universals. They are simply different kinds of universals. It does not really matter whether one shares the special kind of evolutionism that is implicit in Vico's argument or not. Most of us today would probably reject it. But we must hold fast to Vico's distinction and accept his important amendment to the argument that people are not always alike. In its simple version, the rejection of uniformitarianism[16] merely states that universals change. In Vico's version it states that universals change both in form and in content.

Although it may remain a moot point whether modern historical method owes more to the German romantics or to the Italian humanists,[17] and how much it owes to Vico, it is certain that our own modern maxim that above all we must understand the past as it understood itself and that that criterion of understanding, though not absolute, is the only absolute form of knowledge there is is the direct heir of the Renaissance humanists, of Vico, and of the German romantics described by Meinecke. With this maxim, the modern historian is unique. Herodotus went to a great deal of trouble to find out about ancient Egypt and Babylon.

But he never thought that there was a barrier to understanding
other than the mere absence of factual information. It never occurred to him or to any of his successors that people in different
ages and societies differ above all in their standards of plausibility
and that these differences more than any differences in substance
and customs make it so difficult to understand others as *they
understood themselves.* Today we not only know that there is a
barrier but we have devised elaborate methods to overcome it.
In the past people never tried to understand other people as these
other people understood themselves because unaware of any difference between people and societies other than a formal one, understanding was not a problem. The historians of the past were not
guilty of hybris when they thought that there was no special
effort required to enter into the minds of ancient Egyptians. They
simply took it that the minds of ancient Egyptians were like their
own. Today we know that this is not so. Hence our preoccupation
with understanding others as they understood themselves. Interpretation, though inevitable and necessary, is a secondary activity
for the historian. It is forced on him by the insight that the plausibility of universals of all kinds change. But in the first instance the
historian must always respect the sources and explain the past as
it explained itself to itself. Such explanation, though never final,
constitutes something like a rock bottom in historical knowledge
and even though it is not an absolute, as we have seen, it is the
nearest criterion of absoluteness we can have in historical knowledge. If universals did not change, there would be no need to distinguish between explanation and interpretation.

The perception that universals change has also wrought another kind of revolution in the study of history. As long as people thought that universals did not change and that one explanation
or type of explanation would do for all people at all times, the
study of history was used as a great training in politics. People
thought, if universals do not change, that one can learn from the
experiences of others. If all men are the same, the study of history
is the great teacher of everything one needs to know about politics.
When it came to be realised that experiences differ and that people
employ different universals at different times and that explanations have to make way for interpretations, history ceased to be
the teacher of life.[18] Other reasons for the study of history were
eventually found. But they never quite possessed the same pragmatic force.

To write history is to write the history of thought. The historical narrative is a story of changes, of how one event was fol-

lowed by another. If we want to find out what really happened we must study how people thought these events were linked to one another and how the thoughts of how events are linked change. At this point a misunderstanding is likely to creep in. When we say that history is the history of thought we do not mean that it is the history of intellectual, metaphysical and religious, and scientific systems of thought. It is all too easy, since most historians are intellectuals of sorts, to perpetrate the fallacy that what really mattered in the past were the disciplined and well worked out systems of scientific or metaphysical understanding and that when people in the past reflected on what they were doing, they were understanding themselves in the terms of any one such intellectual system. Nothing could be further from the truth. Highly disciplined intellectual systems are usually difficult to grasp at the best of times. At the time of their propagation they are usually unpopular and controversial. When they do filter through to the more or less common man, whoever he is, they leave a precipitate but one that is often a vulgarisation of the original system or even a distortion. If they do influence history, they do so in a shape that bears little resemblance to their original conception and they do so often much later than the lifetime of their authors or even of the disciples of these authors. There is no denying that they always have a certain uncertain relationship to general thought and that sooner or later some of them have some effect on somebody. But the study of the nature of that effect is a very exacting task and one that is different from the study of the intellectual system or of the doctrine itself. Above all, it is a capital error to describe a certain period in history or a society by naming it after a prominent scientist or thinker. If historians cannot get out of this habit, the least they might do is to heed Nietzsche's advice to entitle their books *Goethe Against His Times* rather than *The Life and Times of Goethe*.

The statement that history is the history of thought means something much more general.[19] It means that all people must think about events or can be assumed to think about events. Insofar as people are human and insofar as we are dealing with human history, we presume that the actors and agents and victims think about what is happening. They think by relating any two events in terms of a general law, or by relating an event to a concrete universal. But think they must and in so doing they put forward a view of how events hang together. Thus they produce mininarratives, which may or may not be blown up into narratives proper. This kind of thinking is not necessarily linked to any special doctrine in any sense other than the sense that a general law must assert something and a concrete universal must be a specific story. History is the history of thought because it studies the content of these universals, abstract or concrete. Nor is it claimed that thoughts motivate people and determine actions so that one can infer what happened by watching what people think. It is merely claimed that thoughts make people link at least any two events in their minds and that such linkages are the raw material of history. There is indeed a great difference between actual motivation and subsequent reflection. The present discussion is concerned exclusively with the latter, but insists that such reflection belongs as much to the actor (and may be different from his actual motivation) as to any subsequent historian.[20]

There is one all-important and irresistible reason why history is the history of thought. The step from one event to the next is not provided by temporal contiguity but depends on a thought. There is no other conceivable connection. The same is true for the link between any subevent and another subevent and between any sub-subevent and another sub-subevent, and so forth. Moreover, thoughts are similarly built into the sources and documents. Whether we proceed downwards toward the raw material or upwards toward the highly structured narrative, it is always the same. It is sometimes believed that the view that history is the history of thought is a doctrine about the nature of the past, a doctrine about the substance of history. I think that the doctrine that the substance or nature of the past is the history of thought is highly debatable. At any rate, it has nothing to do with the view that by its form, historical knowledge is knowledge of thoughts. Quite apart from the problem whether in substance history is or is not the history of thought, the view that history is the history of thought is a doctrine about the constitution of our consciousness of the past. It is a doctrine about method. This follows directly from the argument that universals are an inevitable and necessary ingredient in the constitution of all historical knowledge. A general law, or a generalisation, or a lawlike statement, provided it is modelled on the paradigm that a causal law is a mental act of the will with certain expectations of the changes that that act must bring about (see chapter 3, page 43) is a thought. Similarly a concrete universal is a thought for it relates the occurrence of events, many of which did not take and indeed could not have taken place. A concrete universal is a myth and a myth, since it is not true in the sense that it is not a copy of reality, must be a thought (see chapter 5, page 116). It is a story that exists primarily and exclusively in the minds of men. Insofar as historical narrative depends on universals, be they abstract or concrete, it is the history of thoughts.[21]

We owe the idea that history is above all the history of thought to R. G. Collingwood.[22] But Collingwood arrived at it from explicitly idealistic premises and in many of his books the idea was used not only to explain the nature of historical knowledge but to explain the nature of knowledge in general as well as the fact that human knowledge has a history.[23] Proceeding from the premises of philosophical idealism, Collingwood never devoted much time to comparisons of thoughts other than comparisons of thoughts that succeeded one another in time and replaced one another. In this way he avoided facing the major issue involved in the idea that history is the history of thought. He seems to have imagined or assumed that in each age or for each person the thoughts entertained were the appropriate thoughts. In the present argument, however, we have insisted that one thought is as subjective as any other and that no privileged position can be accorded to any thought. Thus it is not legitimate to consider Caesar's thoughts about himself as less subjective than a modern historian's thoughts about Caesar. Nor is it legitimate to assume that a modern historian's thoughts about Caesar, because of hindesight, are less subjective than those of Caesar. If one accords a privileged status to any thought and takes it to be less subjective than any other, one is an *objectivist*, that is, a person who arbitrarily believes that some thoughts are more objective than others. Collingwood was an objectivist in this sense, for he held that the thoughts entertained by the people of a certain epoch or a certain society are in some sense so appropriate to these people or that society that they must be accorded privileged status. He knew that these thoughts eventually lost their appropriateness. But, according to Collingwood, they did so in an orderly manner. When one age or society ceased, it was replaced by another and the thoughts that had been appropriate to it were correspondingly replaced. Such dislodgement of thoughts was the only kind of criticism or unmasking of their subjectivity he ever envisaged.[24] In this way he avoided the real issue, which arises from the fact that Caesar's thoughts about himself can be presumed to be as erroneous, or hallucinatory, or ideological, or propagandistic, or mendacious as those of any later or of any contemporary observer. If that issue is faced squarely, one will see that the idea that history is the history of thought involves not only the necessity to understand others as they understood themselves, but also the necessity to translate one thought into another. Ideally one must not only translate Caesar's thoughts into thoughts intelligible by and acceptable to a modern observer; but one must also be able to translate backwards, that is, to make the modern observer intelligible to Caesar.

The view that all history is the history of thought has received its greatest challenge from the writings of Sir Lewis Namier and his disciples. Reacting against many generations of historians who had assumed that politicians and statesmen, generals and revolutionaries, are always animated by high sounding ideological principles, Namier points out that we should 'not overrate the conscious will and purpose of an individual' and that we should 'ascertain and recognise the deeper irrelevancies and incoherence of human actions, which are not so much directed by reason, as invested by it *ex post facto* with the appearances of logic and rationality'. He insists that when 'we watch at close quarters, the actions of men are in no way correlated in weight and value to the results they produce'.[25]

When taken as a criticism of ideologically oriented historians who think that the actions of men are prompted by class consciousness or the desire for personal liberty, Namier's point is salutary. But the above quotation contains more than such a salutary reaction. It states, first, that men act and behave without thinking[26] and, second, that the course of events is not determined by thought and therefore not planned. The outcome of actions, it implies, it not planned but determined by factors other than thoughts. Namier's own investigations of the early reign of King George III have done much to establish this view of history. But as H. Butterfield remarked, the same method can be applied to any period in any country,[27] and ought, therefore, be taken as a serious challenge not only to the conventional pre-Namier understanding of English eighteenth-century history but to our understanding of history in general.[28]

The argument consists of two parts that are obliquely related. There is first the argument that men are not prompted by ideas but by the desire to get into and stay in power. When the Labour party opposed the Suez adventure in 1956, it is alleged they did not do so because they thought of world peace and the ideals of the United Nations but because they were the Opposition and it was their business to defeat the Conservatives, who had originated the Suez adventure. When Brutus murdered Caesar, he did it because he wanted to obtain power, not because he hated tyrants. Namier admits that, at best, the thought behind an action is pro-

vided *ex post facto*. But this is precisely where the rub lies. The
ex post facto, as we have argued all along, does not only apply to
the historian but also to the person involved in the action under
discussion. Whether he acts first and thinks afterwards or the other
way round is beside the point. The crucial matter is that he is a
human being who thinks either before or after acting and who
does not act without thinking about something. He may be dishonest and insincere or captive to hallucinations or illusions. As
we have argued, there is no telling whether his thoughts about
his actions are more true than someone else's thoughts about
these actions. But there are thoughts; and if the person involved
is so half-witted, or dumb, or benighted, or inarticulate that he
cannot think or express his thoughts, then he is at least a human
being who could have thought something and who could have
expressed his thoughts. Namier simply jumped to the conclusion
that since many of the thoughts that we have argued are the
rawest raw material of history are interpretations, that is, thoughts
imputed by later historians to the people engaged in certain actions, they do not form part of the raw material at all. There may
indeed have been many Labour Members of Parliament who
joined in the attack on Prime Minister Eden in 1956 because they
were institutionally members of the Opposition. But in looking
back they themselves, not only a later historian, must have or
could have produced a reason — even though the reason may not
have been a greater thought than the thought that the Labour
party ought to seize this opportunity for getting into power. No
matter how we turn, we cannot get away from the fact that there
were thoughts and that these thoughts are not *ex post facto* in the
sense that they are imputed by historians looking back, but *ex
post facto* in the sense that they were or could have been imputed
by the protagonists to themselves by themselves. While we can
therefore readily admit that only on very rare occasions are people actually motivated by explicit ideas, it does not follow as
Namier thought, that history can be drained of its thought content. The naïve critic could suggest that whether George III and
his associates had thoughts about the constitution or not can be
settled once and for all by an appeal to the sources. But such an
appeal will remain fruitless. Namier and his followers will brush
aside any source that contains such a thought as irrelevant or as
proof that George's mind was 'chaotic'.[29] There are enough
sources to build up a picture of voting habits that gives an appearance of completeness; and once the assumption that all thought
is *ex post facto* and therefore not part of the original story is

firmly fixed in the historian's mind, such sources as are to the
contrary can be safely omitted or explained away, as are indeed
millions of other sources and many more millions of events for
which there are no sources. Relevance does not depend on the
sources but on the knowledge one brings to bear on the sources,[30]
and for this reason an appeal to the sources cannot help to settle
any question that arises in regard to the knowledge one brings
to bear on the sources.

The second part of the Namier argument follows obliquely
and insidiously. Having argued from the double meaning of *ex
post facto* that thoughts are not the raw material of history,
Namier proceeds to the conclusion that history is not planned by
thought. It requires very little knowledge of the intricate processes
of history to see that Namier is indeed right. Lenin arrived at the
Finland Station to start a revolution that would make the state
wither away but that, in fact, produced Stalin and the most colossal state we have ever known. There is no need for examples.
Namier assumed that the fact that history cannot be planned and
that the outcome is different from the alleged reason for the
initiative points to the conclusion that when people act they do
not think. But the conclusion does not follow. On the contrary.
The reason why history cannot be planned and why the outcome
is different from the conception is not that people have no plans
but that, since everybody has a plan, these plans cross one another
and cancel one another out in a totally unpredictable manner. It
is sometimes said that Namier came close to thinking that since
history is not the outcome of a plan, it is 'a tale told by an idiot'.[31]
This is probably truer for his disciples than for Namier himself.
Namier's own essays on nineteenth-century history show clearly
that he understood that history, though not the outcome of an
intelligent plan, is nothing if not ineptly planned, with a whole lot
of inept planners frustrating one another and ending up to produce
a surfeit of ineptitude.[32]

Indeed, Namier's essays on the nineteenth century show that
his own historical thinking, when it was not preoccupied with
eighteenth-century British Parliaments, was thoroughly Hegelian,
at least up to the point where Hegel shows that history is the result
of the 'cunning of reason'. It was one of Hegel's major contributions to the philosophy of history to have understood that history
is not planned in the sense that it can be understood, as other
things that are planned, by an examination of what people intend
to achieve. To grasp correctly the relation between intention and
result, Hegel formulated his doctrine of the 'cunning of reason'.

With this doctrine he could go beyond an explanation why plans do not work out. The first explanation is simple. Plans do not work out because the plans of different people tend to cancel one another out or, at least, deflect one another. Hegel went beyond this. He argued that reason (The Idea) is cunning in that it achieves a certain line of development that is overtly contrary to the single plans put forward by the agents. If one wishes to know how cunning reason exactly is, one has to have knowledge of a very general philosophy of history and be in possession of a very large-scale narrative. We will deal with such narratives in chapter 9. Here it suffices to say that if one has such a large-scale narrative, a philosophy of history, one can establish that though any given thought or plan was not realised, it was obliquely responsible, by being deflected or crossed by another plan, for the course narrated or mapped out by the philosophy of history. But it must be admitted that one can establish such cunning of reason only when one has a large-scale narrative. Without a philosophy of history one can see that thoughts do not work out; but one cannot establish that reason was cunning.

It does not really matter for the purposes of the argument at this stage, whether one can or cannot establish that reason was cunning. It matters, however, that we should learn from Hegel that, on the face of it, history does not appear to be planned even though the narrative as well as the sources are full of thoughts and plans.

One might have thought that the strongest challenge to the view that history is the history of thought must have come from Marxist materialism, which says that consciousness is determined by material circumstances. But this is in fact not so. Marxism merely objects to the view that thoughts are the rawest raw material there is. It does not object to the view that thoughts shaped by material circumstances guide human actions and are used to understand human actions. For that matter, the thought that thoughts are shaped by material circumstances and that those thoughts that are not so shaped are false thoughts is not a thought to establish that thoughts play no part in history. It is merely a thought that states that most people's way of understanding themselves must be brushed aside and replaced by the interpretation that they are suffering from illusions. (Thus, the Marxist would argue that when Shaftesbury protested that he was genuinely concerned for the welfare of children he was really concerned with preserving capitalism by removing those practices that might discredit it.) This particular Marxist thought is an attempt to

show that one *particular* kind of interpretation is not just one
more interpretation but an objective truth. In this sense, Marxism
is not an attack on the view that history is the history of thought
but an attempt to establish that it is the history of one particular
thought. The real challenge to the view that history is the history
of thought does, therefore, not come from Marx's inverted idealism but from the generalisation of Namier's peculiar belief that
once an institution is given, one can describe and account for the
actions of people in that institutional framework without thinking
about their thoughts.

   In conclusion I want to draw attention to a curious effect
brought about by historical study. To start with, it has often
been observed that the historian's genuine understanding reaches
as far as his own mind will expand. Benedetto Croce used to say
that we can only understand the Jacobins of the French Revolution if we are a bit Jacobin ourselves.[33] This is undoubtedly true
and can be formally demonstrated to be so in terms of the terminology of the first and second record and by the need for the
recourse to translation. When the historian falls back on pure
interpretation, of course, he dispenses with the need to share the
experiences of a Jacobin. One can interpret the Jacobins — as
distinct from explaining them — without being the least bit of
a Jacobin. Even interpretation can lead to self-knowledge, though
at first sight this sounds like a contradiction. Suppose a historian
is able to imagine himself a Jacobin. He may know how dangerous
Jacobins are, and to protect the world from himself, he may become obsessive in his determination to interpret the Jacobins
rather than to explain them. In such a case the historian can
gauge the strength of his own Jacobinism from the strength of
his determination to interpret rather than to explain them. Conversely, one often finds that a historian who is proof against
Jacobinism is as ready and as capable of interpreting Jacobinism
as a historian who is a genuine sympathiser. But interpretation
apart, the historian's efforts at understanding, be they translational or confined to pure explanation proper, will be something
of a test of the nature of his own personality, or, more precisely
and less psychologically, of the nature of his own second record.
The extent to which he can refrain from interpretation and the
distance he can go with explanation proper and translation will
indicate to him what sort of person he is, what his mind is capable
of, and what it contains. It will measure the elasticity of his mind.
Presumably there will be limits to even the most elastic mind.
These limits can be learnt from historical study and for this reason

historical study is not only mind expanding but also leads to self-knowledge.

Conversely, a historical effort to understand the Jacobins will not only test the historian's affinity with Jacobins. By studying the Jacobins he is running a risk. If he reads Robespierre over and over again he will end up by seeing the year 1793 as Robespierre saw it. Through the sheer pressure of psychological assimilation, he will tend to forget his own knowledge and assimilate that of Robespierre. In this sense the study of history leads not only to self-knowledge but is mind expanding. It not only tests the distance the historian can go; it also is likely to change his mind and transform him into something like a Jacobin. In a sense every historian takes his life in his hands when he studies a society or culture very distant from his own. I recall a very vivid and formative experience of my own. There was nothing in my secular- and classical-oriented upbringing to acquaint me with angels. I had heard of their existence but I had equated them with the fairies and with Father Christmas. When I spent years reading Richard Hooker and the books he had read, the force of the belief that angels do not really exist was considerably weakened. I had started to move in an intellectual climate in which everybody believed that angels existed and in which much time, and effort, and scholarship was spent in finding out the manner of their existence and the nature of their bodies or spirits. In short, by studying Hooker and his world I had exchanged the society I was living in for another and gradually I began to respond to my new companions. Eventually I returned to my own society and friends but I brought with me the conviction that their scepticism about angels was very relative to their own lives and technology. I came back as a traveller who had benefited from his life in foreign lands.

T. E. Lawrence wrote in *The Seven Pillars of Wisdom* that he came close to insanity when he realised how much of an Arab Bedouin he had become.[34] He knew he was English and he also knew he was not a Bedouin and yet he could understand the Bedouin both as a Bedouin understood himself and as an Englishman could understand a Bedouin and vice versa. Such experience can often come to the historian. It leads to a shattering doubt of personal identity. In the shelter of his study the historian can usually manage to keep a firmer grip on himself than T. E. Lawrence could in the sands of the Arabian desert. The historian can turn this kind of experience into something else. He can derive a great sense of superiority. Napoleon understood Napoleon and a great many things beside. Caesar understood Caesar, but knew

nothing of Napoleon. But the historian knows both Napoleon and
Caesar, and in addition to understanding himself, he can also
understand both Napoleon and Caesar. While all men are caught
up in a certain situation and have to make the most of it according
to their lights, the historian assumes, *ex officio*, a superior view.
He may lack riches and power, but he is one up on the richest
millionaire and the most powerful statesman or general. He understands them not only as they understood themselves but in addition he understands himself as well as all the others, which is
more than all the others were able to do. They suffered from lack
of leisure and lack of learning. In this sense the working historian,
provided he does not confine himself to counting the cabbage
patches of Ohio, is gradually pushed into some kind of omniscience. Since the future, relative to the past he is studying, is
known to him, the historian is also free from the anxieties and
uncertainties from which the people he studies, to whom the
future was not known, suffered. For this reason, the historian's
reenactment is essentially different from all enactment. If he falls
for the temptation and imagines he is God, so much the worse
for him. But he can turn the omniscience that is gradually forced
on him to good account. It can lead him to irony. He can develop
a vast sense of infinity, which he can encompass because he remains uncommitted to any one of the thoughts he surveys. Caesar
and Lenin may have laboured to gain power or to improve the
world; but the historian encompasses both personalities without
being identified with either because he is labouring to understand
both. In this sense the historian can achieve an ironical superiority
over all the single thoughts entertained by single people. Such
cultivated irony, provided it does not degenerate into *hybris*,
affords a taste of eternity denied to other mortals. The historian's
vision is very similar to that of the comic as described by Hegel:
an 'infinite geniality and confidence capable of rising superior to
its own contradiction and experiencing therein no taint of bitter-
ness or sense of misfortune whatever.'[35]

   This achievement of ironic perspective is of great practical
importance to the historian. I have argued above that the criterion
of relevance is derived not from the sources but from the knowledge the historian brings to bear on the sources. As the historian's
knowledge extends, however, he will learn to switch from one kind
of knowledge as a criterion of relevance to another kind of knowledge so that he can learn to do conjuring tricks. He can train
himself, as he is undergoing mind-expanding experience, to substitute pieces of knowledge he did not originally possess for those

he did originally possess. In this way his range and skill in interpretation will increase and he can make sources that first appeared
irrelevant appear relevant. An historian may go into the Middle
Ages a confirmed Marxist. But as his mind is expanding, he may
add a religious dimension to his Marxism and learn to switch
backwards and forwards. Such skill will in turn further confirm
the irony with which he must encounter both Marxism and a
religious standpoint, and the irony will help him to increase his
skill to switch even further. ' "History comprehended" ', as Walter
Kaufmann summed up Hegel's *Phenomenology of the Spirit*, 'must
replace theology'.[36]

Chapter Eight

THE NATURE OF THE STORY

At all times we must distinguish carefully between the totality of
everything that has happened in the past and a story about some
of the events that have taken place in the past. We shall call the
totality of all events *res gestae* and the story or any story of some
events *historia rerum gestarum.* It is immediately obvious that we
can portray *res gestae* graphically as a broad column and *historia
rerum gestarum* as a tiny, thin strand inside that column. Moreover, we can have innumerable thin strands of history inside that
broad column. These strands of stories can run parallel to each
other or cross and recross one another. There is no end of the
histories one can compose inside the broad column. *Res gestae*
means not only the totality of all recorded events — which would
be large enough and too large for any historian, even when he
works with a team. It means the totality of the past as a whole —
in its intuitively unsurveyable complex multitudinousness. It is,
by comparison with the sum total of all known or conceivable
narratives that give shape to time and to the past and that are so
many different appearances of the past, like Kant's noumenal
world. It may be a moot point whether it is noumenal in any
absolute sense, but it is so in comparison to any possible narrative.[1]

The distinction has a direct bearing on our notion of historical
truth. One cannot say that a historical account or narrative is true
if what it portrays actually happened. It is impossible to test the
truth of a narrative by looking at *res gestae.* The totality of everything that ever happened is immense. Any historical narrative is a
minute part of that totality. That minute part does not exist as a
part in its own right but only because somebody has put it together, defined it, delimited it, and by so doing has made it into a
recognisable part of the whole. The part by itself does not exist
and is not recognisable unless somebody has selected its elements
and linked them together. If we have a historical narrative, there is
nothing over and above that narrative to compare it with. It would
be quite wrong to think that we have on one side a history that

really happened and on the other a narrative of it. We have *only*
a narrative and nothing else. The most one can do is to check one
story against another story. One can compare the two and any
notion of 'truth' one can form must be related to such a comparison. Our historical knowledge, in short, is of historical knowledge — not of what actually happened.

Most readers will concede that this may well be so in the case
of a very large event. If we call World War II a large event, they
will admit that it is a highly composite event and that the composition is highly complex. They will agree therefore that any
decision whether it took place or not, that is, any decision as to
whether the event corresponds to something that actually happened or not, must depend on checking hundreds of lesser stories
of simpler events. One cannot possibly hope to check the statement that World War II occurred by looking at something called
'the Second World War'. But when it comes to smaller events,
most readers will think that one could indeed, at least ideally,
check whether they occurred by looking at them. Either Caesar
crossed the Rubicon or he did not cross the Rubicon. The truth
of the assertion of such a small event should be capable of a direct.
test. Either someone saw him cross or somebody saw that he did
not cross.

Closer examination will show that the distinction between
large-scale events and small-scale events makes no difference. In
both cases the truth of the statement that they occurred can be
checked only by looking at other accounts or stories or reports.
Suppose we want to find out whether Caesar actually did cross the
Rubicon. We have to rely either on his report or on somebody
else's report. All we can do is to check the story that he crossed
against another story.

The tough-minded defender of the view that history is a purely
empirical science that reports what actually happened will now
object that this peculiar circumstance is due to the fact that the
crossing of the Rubicon took place a long time ago and that all
eyewitnesses are dead. Hence, since we are dealing with the past,
we are confined to checking the truth of the statement by looking
at another statement rather than at the facts. A Methuselah,
present at the crossing, might conceivably still be alive today and
tell us whether the crossing took place or not. However, even if
there were a Methuselah, the position would not be different. Our
Methuselah could only report what he thought he saw. He would
tell us that he saw Caesar getting into a dinghy, that he saw him
rowing across the river and setting foot on the other side. He

would tell us that he connected the departure from one bank with
the arrival at the other bank. He would inform us that he put two
events together because he thought there was a link between them.
Our Methuselah would further admit that he linked these two
events because he understood the colossal importance for Roman
politics of the crossing. But let us imagine that our Methuselah
knew nothing of Roman politics and the law that forbade the
crossing of the river. He would then tell us that he saw Caesar
stepping into the boat and that in his mind this event was firmly
linked to the reeds growing by the shore and the current of the
river and that, being a fisherman himself, he was fascinated by the
progress of a dislodged pebble in relation to the progress of a
hundred other dislodged pebbles. Then he lost sight of Caesar and
could not tell us whether Caesar actually crossed or was carried
downstream. Here we find then that we will get one story from
one kind of Methuselah and another story from another kind of
Methuselah. The chain of events that actually took place is a chain
seen by somebody. One story can be compared to another, but no
story can be checked by looking at the actual sequence of events.
We can never get a particular *sequence* without an observer. Any
event, no matter how small, is an event only in virtue of an interested observer. 'Interested' here does not mean 'curious'. It means
that the observer must make use of a universal, either concrete or
abstract, to link any two of the many elements.

Our hard-headed empirical historian will concede our point
but ascribe the predicament to the fact that no Methuselah is a
wholly trustworthy observer. All eyewitnesses, he will say, are
fallible and give only a partial account of what actually happened.
Let us instead suppose that the crossing was filmed and that the
film was screened to an audience of modern historians. Here, our
tough-minded empiricist will insist, we can discover what took
place. But in practice the problem cannot be solved, not even with
a film camera or a video tape. When the historians watch the film
on the screen, they will again be in the position of the several
Methuselahs. Every historian watching the totality of events in
front of his eyes will come up with a different story of which
events are linked together. The dispute as to which events are
'really' linked together as against which events are linked together
in the eyes of the observer will be opened again, this time not at
the banks of the Rubicon but in a cinema in a twentieth-century
city. The predicament, if one can call it that, is not due to the fact
that people are unreliable observers — though they are that, too.
It is due to the fact that without an interested observer, there is

no earthly reason why the subevent of Caesar placing his foot into the water should be the cause of the crossing of the Rubicon. Given another general law than the one used by the observer, it can just as readily be the cause of the displacement of a pebble, which in turn displaces a fish, and so forth.

The record of the traces of what happened in the past has come down to us in the shape of stories that somebody put together, that is, in the shape in which things appeared to somebody. Hence, when we want to find out what actually happened, we mean that we want to find out how things appeared to somebody to have happened. It is tempting to make the mistake of thinking that this circumstance is fortuitous and entirely due to the fact that we are dealing with the past and depend on records and that it would not occur if we were dealing with the present or with a filmed record of the past. But this is not so. Even if the past had been handed down to us in the shape of a photograph on a platter or as a record made by a totally magic camera, the situation would not be different. We could then look at it and, to make an assertion about it, would have to put together stories about how various parts of it appeared to us. The only difference would be that we would then be in the position of an observer contemporary to the events that took place. But that is all. We would still have to do what the compilers and authors of the records of the past did in the past. And when we are writing contemporary history, we would still be doing the same. In all cases, there are only appearances and in all cases we can test any one appearance (i.e., a narrative) only by comparing it to another appearance.

No matter how we turn and no matter how much we introduce ideally the device of a filmed record of the past, we cannot get away from the fact that *res gestae* as such cannot be surveyed. When the film is screened, it might appear as a total mechanical record that has never been filtered through a human mind. But it would then merely duplicate the confusing totality and its incomprehensible multiplicity.[2]

Nevertheless, there would, in theory, be one difference. When Caesar's contemporaries watched him crossing the Rubicon, they made use of the laws they knew of to put the subevents together. If we were today watching a magic film — very different from Fellini's sequence in *Roma* in which a school teacher reenacts for his pupils the crossing of the Rubicon — which would be four dimensional and show the *res gestae* in question simultaneously from every conceivable angle, we would use the laws *we* know of to put the subevents into a mininarrative. Even when watching an ordinary film, members of the audience usually disagree on what they have seen, because they bring with them into the theatre different sets of universals and hence different expectations. This recalls a joke about Alain Resnais' film *Last Year in Marienbad.* When the London censor passed it for general exhibition, the distributor showed surprise. When questioned about his surprise he said, 'Well, after all, it does have a rape scene in it!' The censor, 'Did it?'

It requires a real intellectual wrench to accept the view that what we know as 'history' (i.e., the story of kings and empires and societies) is only one of an infinite possible number of the shapes of time. But one can make a strenuous experiment in thought. One can imagine *alternative* stories *ad libidem* with the same or even greater density of events for every span of time than the conventional series that we have come to identify as history *par excellence.* Many people might grant that alternative sequences are possible but they will then imagine that such alternative sequences are less densely filled with events and show greater gaps. But this is not correct. The only reason why we cannot imagine other shapes with equal density of events is that we are uncritically wedded to the idea that time can have only one shape and that that shape is identical with our conventional history. Indeed, the other possible shapes, without suffering the slightest diminution in density, need have no events in common, for the same span of time, with the conventional shape that we call history and that we believe to be the historian's business to discover.

Without committing himself to the full philosophical implications of this situation, Geoffrey Barraclough[3] once put the matter very simply. History will appear to every historian, he said, as the story that emerges from the sources he is most familiar with. History is not what happened but what people think happened. Our knowledge of very large events is obviously something that is put together. It is derived from a selection of smaller events that are believed to be linked. But the same is true of our knowledge of small events. Any small event is an assembly of subevents and there is no compelling reason why any two subevents have to be put together in one way and in one way only. Any subevent can be linked either with one subevent or another subevent so that it depends on the thought of the compiler whether one subevent is linked with one subevent or another. Exactly the same is true for the so-called eyewitness and for the person involved in the small event.

When one keeps the distinction between *res gestae* and *historia rerum gestarum* firmly in mind, one can see that the historian does not copy what happened. Nor does he select what he writes down from *res gestae*. *Res gestae* are unknowable, unsurveyable, and beyond grasp. When the historian selects, he selects from somebody else's *historia rerum gestarum*, even though this history he selects from may appear in his mind as 'the sources'. But those sources, as we have seen in chapter 7, are not substantially different from ordinary narratives. As far as *res gestae* is concerned, they are the reality. But this reality cannot be copied. There is nothing there to be portrayed. It is true that the historian has to select; but he does not select from anything that could be described as *res gestae*. He selects from *historiae rerum gestarum* to produce another *historia rerum gestarum*. His reasons for doing so are not that he wants to duplicate, but that he wants to use other universals. He wants to translate and interpret and, possibly, use explanations other than the ones that are contained in the sources.

This view forces us to revise our whole notion of historical truth. Traditionally it was believed that an historical narrative is true if it reports or portrays accurately what happened. But since the narrative is not a portrait of what happened (*res gestae*), it becomes clear that this simple notion of historical truth is nonsensical. The whole question whether a particular set of events occurred or not and whether a story about them is true *because* they occurred is a misplaced question, because there is no way in which we can look at *res gestae* and check, by looking, whether any particular narrative is true.

Any particular event, let alone any particular set of series of events, can be said to have occurred only because somebody thought it did. If nobody had thought it did, the subevents of which it consists could have been assembled into different ways or could not have been assembled at all, in which case there would be no source. Therefore the only sensible question we can ask is whether somebody thought the event to have occurred, that is, whether somebody assembled the subevents in this particular way or not. The problem of truth is therefore not the problem of whether a particular event occurred or not, but whether somebody thought that it occurred.[4]

Murray G. Murphey[5] distinguishes in his discussion of historical truth between the view of the classicists and that of the revisionists. The classical view is, he says on page 32, that internal criticism can evaluate the statements occurring in the documents

according to their meaning and their trustworthiness.[6] The
revisionists, he says on page 58, although they accept all the criteria for establishing the trustworthiness of the statements in the
documents, are aware that historians do not use all the facts established as trustworthy, but that they select facts. I agree that the
distinction between classicists and revisionists is, up to a point,
useful; but to me, they are all birds of the same feather. The
problem of truth has been discussed in these and similar terms for
two millennia from Lucian in the first century A.D. to Bodin and
Bacon in the sixteenth century. But the debate was started in
earnest when Descartes proclaimed his own definition of truth.
He said that truth was self-evidence. This requirement was so
austere that a half-century later, Vico realised that it could never
be satisfied by historical knowledge. If we follow Descartes, he
said, there can be no *historical* knowledge. Hence began his search
for a different criterion. He came up with the idea that *verum* is
factum. We call a statement true, he argued, if and only if it
describes something that has been made by man. A statement
about a rock or about the sun may be true in Descartes' sense.
But it cannot be true in the sense in which statements about
things that have been made and done by men are true. These latter
statements are true in a different sense, and precisely in the sense
that they correspond to the thoughts thought by the people who
made or did the things described in the statements. With this argument he inaugurated a new era in the history of thought — or, at
any rate, in the history of our thought about historical truth. His
insight has received the strongest possible confirmation by our
twentieth-century discovery that language and the structure of our
mind make it impossible for any report of any event to be 'accurate', unless that event is itself linguistic or mental. For the
medium of language or mental operation has its own form and is
not infinitely adaptable to an exact reproduction of things that
are made of stone or light. Since this is so, the only proper application of the word 'accuracy' or 'truth' is to a portrait of a portrait. If the object portrayed is not something material but
something made by man, a proper portrait is possible and the
term 'truth' is applicable. This insight is little more than an elab-
oration of Vico's famous doctrine. We cannot speak of the truth
of a portrait of an event. We can only speak of the truth of a portrait of a portrait. When we grasp the world of Roman politics as
Caesar grasped it, we can claim that our grasp is true. But it makes
no sense to ask whether Caesar's grasp was true, unless we mean
by this question that we want to compare Caesar's grasp with

Cicero's grasp. Under no circumstances can we test whether Caesar's grasp was true by looking at Roman politics in the raw. When a modern historian reports how Caesar saw the political situation in Gaul, his report can be true or false.

At this point we must introduce the old concepts of truth by correspondence and truth by coherence. It is clear from everything that has been said above that in historical knowledge we cannot have a correspondence view of truth in the sense that what the historian tells corresponds with reality, that is, with *res gestae*. It can only correspond with what other observers or other historians have said. With this qualification — and it is an extremely important qualification — there is room in historical knowledge for a correspondence theory of truth. However, a further qualification is needed. The correspondence theory of truth is applicable when the historian, describing Caesar's view of the politics and society of Gaul, uses the same universals that Caesar used. Possibly even when he uses the same universals that Caesar *might* have used but did not use — though here there is room for argument. But when the historian starts to interpret (i.e., when he starts to use universals that could not have been used by Caesar), we move away from truth in the correspondence sense. For any interpretation of what Caesar said about Gaul cannot possibly correspond to what Caesar said. In this case we move steadily and firmly toward a coherence theory of truth. If the historian's interpretation of what Caesar said about Gaul coheres with what Caesar said, it is true. If it does not, it is not true. We can see here the great importance of the requirement for typological relationships between explanations and interpretations outlined in chapter 4. If there is no typological relationship at all, there is next to no coherence between what Caesar said and what the modern historian says. And, since the presence of interpretation makes the correspondence notion of truth inapplicable, we are left high and dry when there is no typological relationship. For, in this case, there is no criterion of truth available at all.

To sum up. When we are doing explanation, we start with a correspondence theory of truth and as we are progressing toward interpretation, we are moving toward a coherence theory of truth. However, the employment of the two terms 'coherence' and 'correspondence' is somewhat arbitrary. The only thing that is really ruled out is the idea that there can be a correspondence truth in the sense that a narrative corresponds to *res gestae*.[7] This idea, an old favourite of textbook and classroom, must be dismissed forever. Once it is dismissed, it is legitimate to speak of a correspondence truth between the sources (provided they are understood in the sense explained in chapter 7) and the historian's narrative; and to speak of a coherence truth between the sources and the historian's narrative as soon as interpretation enters into it. Historians have usually believed that the correspondence between sources and narrative has a special magic of absolute truth, whereas a mere coherence between sources and narrative has not. But in the present view of the nature of the sources and of their relation to *res gestae* (the sources are *not* photographic records of *res gestae*), there can be no such magic in the correspondence between narrative and source.

Since there is a possibility of equivocation and since the belief that correspondence between narrative and source has special truth magic will die hard, it might be preferable to change the nomenclature and to expunge the word 'correspondence' from the historian's vocabulary. The word 'coherence' comes really closer to the heart of the matter. A narrative is true if it coheres with the sources. It can do so either by using the same universals as the sources or by using different universals. The only disadvantage of the rejection of the word 'correspondence' is that it makes it more difficult or cumbersome to distinguish narratives that are typologically related to the sources from those that are not. Alternately, if there are people who have strong resistance to giving up the word 'correspondence' when they are thinking of truth, we should insist that in historical knowledge the correspondence theory of truth applies to a correspondence between portrait and portrait, between narrative and narrative — but never to a correspondence between what is actually the case (if one could conceive of such a thing) and a narrative. There can be correspondence between different stories. There can be no correspondence between a story and *res gestae.*

Correspondence often tends to appear to be a correspondence between a narrative and reality, though it is merely a correspondence between narrative and narrative. The illusion that such correspondence is a correspondence between narrative and *res gestae* is created by the fact that so many narratives of the same century in the same place tell the same tale. This incidental similarity of narratives can be accounted for either by the continuity of a cultural tradition or by the presence of certain ideological types of thought.[8] The similarity is not due to the fact that these narratives actually portray *res gestae* and are so similar because they do. But since the similarity undeniably exists, it fosters the idea that there is genuine correspondence between the narratives and *res gestae* when, in reality, there is only coherence between sources and narratives and between narratives and narratives.

We must therefore rest content with the fact that historical truth depends on the comparison of historical narratives whether small or large. History as distinct from the totality of everything that ever happened does not exist apart from an observer's mind and therefore we can only ascertain historical truth by comparing the account of one observer with the account of another observer. The great debates of history, therefore, are, if you will, in-fights. They are not debates between historians about what took place, but debates between historians about the plausibility and consistency of their several narratives. The study of the history of historiography is therefore of the utmost importance. All discussions of historical truth are discussions about different ways of writing history. Basically these different ways depend on the different general laws that are employed to make single events hang together. One of the most instructive books ever written on this subject is S. Mazzarino's *The End of the Ancient World.*[9] Mazzarino describes not the end of the ancient world but the most important and striking narratives of the end of the ancient world. He shows that though all deal ostensibly with the same series of events each narrative tells a different story and links the events in a different way. Some narratives contain events that do not occur in others so that one could even think that they deal with different happenings. But they do not. They merely select different events from the myriads of events into which the large-scale event 'the end of the ancient world' can be subdivided. As a consequence, since every narrative contains events in different sequences, each narrative gives a different reason for the end of the ancient world. Some of these narratives employ general laws that were held to be true in the fourth century A.D. but are no longer believed to be true today. Other narratives employ general laws that are obvious today, but that would not have rung a bell in the fourth century A.D. Some are explanations proper and others are interpretations and some contain a mixture of both. But in every single case one cannot ascertain the truth of any of these narratives by looking at the end of the ancient world, for there is no such thing. One can only look at narratives of the end of the ancient world and compare one narrative with another. The very idea that the ancient world ended is actually a historical narrative. There must have been millions of peasants who lived through the centuries in question without noticing that the ancient world was ending. Even if they were molested by hordes of barbarian invaders from time to time, they would have attributed the calamity to one thing or another without necessarily thinking about the end of the ancient world.

If a story is not a portrait of *res gestae* and if its truth depends on its 'coherence' (to use the term that applies equally to narratives that use explanation and to narratives that use interpretation) with other narratives, how can one distinguish between fiction and history? The straight answer is that one cannot, but that that answer is no cause for concern.[10] For fiction should never be equated with untruth. Fiction differs from history by virtue of the mode of its actuality. In fiction, be it myth, epic, or novel, there is a high level of universal actuality and a low level of particular actuality. This means that the novelist, to make his novel acceptable and intelligible, has to use exactly the same kinds of universals and generalisations about human conduct and human expectations and about how one thing leads to another and about the connections between causes and effects as the historian. The only difference is that the particulars the historian uses are particular events that can be located in time and space. His story, therefore, has a high level of particular actuality. The story of the novelist has a high level of actuality of the universals and usually, except in historical novels, a low level of particular actuality. A story that is *really* fictitious cannot be invented, for it would have to be a story that has not only a low level of particular actuality but also a complete absence of universal actuality. Just as we have seen that it is impossible to produce a complete portrait of *res gestae*, it is also impossible to produce a story that is pure invention and bears no relation at all to *res gestae* (see note 15 below).

Literary critics of all centuries have argued as if one could take sides. Some have said that a story should be mimetic and describe what really happened — admittedly, if it is fiction rather than history, with a higher level of universal actuality than of particular actuality. Others have insisted that a story is an autonomous entity of pure design and that its value and meaning consists entirely in its internal form. Although the debate continues unabated, it seems to be lacking in meaning. Genuine mimesis, as we have seen, is not possible. This applies to history as well as to fiction. For this reason the upholders of mimesis or realism in literature and history cannot be taken very seriously. But we cannot so easily dismiss the formalists and their claim that a story stands entirely on the merits of its internal design or form. They cannot be dismissed because in the present argument I have

taken the view that the form, consisting of the medium of universals, abstract or concrete, as the case may be, is of very great importance and that the truth of any story, fiction or history, cannot
be assessed in terms of its correspondence with *res gestae*.

At the present time, the formalists are indeed putting forward
a very strong case. Structuralists like Jakobson, Lévi-Strauss, and
Barthes all tend to infer from the observation that dances and sets
of table manners or styles of fashion in garments are closed systems with meanings of their own that do not depend on any
reference to the external world that stories ought to be treated in
the same manner and that one can understand a story or a portrait
by internal criticism alone, even as one can understand a set of
table manners or of fashions in apparel without reference to the
external world. For R. Barthes, for example, there is a close
analogy between fashion and literature:

> both are what I should call homeostatic systems whose function is not to
> communicate an objective, external meaning which exists prior to the
> system but only to create a function of equilibrium, a movement of
> signification. . . . If you like, they signify 'nothing'; their essence is in
> the process of signification, not in what they signify.[11]

Speaking more directly about literature, Barthes contends that
Honoré de Balzac's *Sarrasine* is a story that provides structuration
because it allows the reader to read into it as many meanings
as he can, none of them being more right than any other.[12] This
way of looking at Balzac's story is a little surprising, for every
reader of *Sarrasine* knows perfectly well that the story, though
fictitious, makes use of all sorts of universals that he knows to be
actually true. The story tells how a sculptor falls in love with a
beautiful actress and discovers to his dismay that she is a castrato.
That particular sculptor and that particular castrato may never
have existed, or if they did, may never have fallen in love. But we
all know what falling in love is like and that the disappointment
consequent upon the awful discovery, is a very real disappointment. The same problem and consternation arises when we peruse
Lévi-Strauss' and Jakobson's famous interpretations of one of Baudelaire's sonnets.[13] The whole structuralist approach and its application to literature — it has an obvious significance when we are dealing with table manners and fashions, though even here one could
think of ways in which both of these systems are influenced by and
related to external systems other than themselves — have found
favour because they are so reminiscent of the fashionable philosophy expressed by Wittgenstein. Wittgenstein often argued that a

language is a system of rules, the meaning of which has nothing to
do with experience or ostensive definitions or with any other relation to the external world but that it depends entirely on itself.[14]
Barthes and Lévi-Strauss are not in the habit of invoking Wittgenstein and there is no reason why they should. But it is all the
same remarkable that these two schools of thought, one in France
and the other in Britain, should aid and abet each other.

What are we to make of this and how does it affect the present
argument that eliminates the formal distinction between historical
narrative and so-called fiction? To begin with, I believe that the
extreme form in which the structuralists state their case is unacceptable. It is indeed a fallacy. It does not follow from the
observation that a story has an inner, structural meaning, that it
has no *other* meaning. It is certainly impossible to believe, as the
older school of critics were wont to do, that Stendhal was right
('the novelist is a man who carries a mirror along the highway of
life') and that we can take Aristotle and Ranke at their face value
when they say that the historian simply reports what actually
happened. But the new, structuralist critic falls into the opposite
error. When it is denied in the present argument about historical
truth that a historical narrative is simply a mindless mirror carried
along the highway of time, it should not be taken to be implied
that a historical narrative is true because of its own inner structure
or that it is true because it is a closed homeostatic system. Barthes
has never tried his hand at historical criticism; but if he did, he
would, doubtless, come up with some such view. The truth of the
matter is that a historical narrative and any novel — always
allowing for the differences in the manner of their actuality — have
a reference to something other than themselves. They can be
tested and checked by reference to other narratives. The germ of
truth in the structuralist contention is that the narrative cannot be
checked against external reality, against *res gestae*. But since it
can be checked against other narratives and since there is a way in
which we can examine its truth and falsity by testing its coherence
(if it is interpretative) and its correspondence (in case it is explanatory) with other narratives, it does have a reference to something
other than itself. If one wants to remain in the context in which
the structuralists carry on their arguments, one should say that it
is quite wrong to assess Baudelaire's sonnet *Les Chats* only by its
internal structure. While it is true that there is no point in testing
it by looking at one's cat, it is also true that one should do literary
criticism by comparing *Les Chats* with another poem about cats
or Rilke's poem about Leda and the swan with Yeats' poem about

Leda or Goethe's *Osterspaziergang* with Horace's *Diffugere nives.*
It is a mistake to check a story internally and it is a mistake to
check a story by trying to peer at the reality it is alleged to represent. It is no more a closed system than it is a portrait of *res
gestae.* The proper procedure is to reject both methods and to test
it by looking at other portraits and other narratives that deal with
the same sort of thing. The other portraits and narratives can be
further checked, by comparing them to yet other portraits and
narratives, and so forth. This kind of testing must of necessity lead
to an infinite regress — unlike the two other procedures. But when
there is no acceptable finite regress, an infinite one is better than
none.

  If truth in historical narrative consists in the correspondence or
coherence, as the case may be, of one story with another, one can
distinguish three different types of truth among the various shapes
that time can assume. Or, to put it differently, different shapes of
time can be true in three different senses.

  1. Since there is always a discrepancy between nature and
human consciousness, men often tend to make up stories by reshuffling the elements of nature and by recombining them in a
nonnatural way. To close the gap, for example, between our
knowledge of the cycle of the seasons and our innermost feelings
about the relationship of winter to spring, we transfer our knowledge of a cruel old man from an old-age home to the coat of snow
that covers a forest in winter and thus we obtain a myth of a
dying, unpleasant, and undesirable Old Man Winter whose disappearance raises our hopes. The stories resulting from such trans-
position of the separate elements in our experience are called
myths and their truth consists in the symbolic force with which
they give meaning to our innermost feeling of hope. They are pregnant with meaning in a way in which the recital of the facts of
nature (in this case, the enumeration of the four seasons) is not.
These stories are true in the sense that they relate to states of consciousness or inner feelings even though they are not literally true.
Their truth consists in their ability to close the gap between the
inner feeling and our experience of the cycle of the seasons. They
are metaphors and they are often, literally, false. Nevertheless,
such stories make time have a recognisable shape. Any series of
events that is figured into such a shape derives its truth or, at least
a certain truth, from the mythical story into which it is figured.

  2. Other stories are true in the sense that the universals they
contain have actuality, even though none or hardly any of the
particular events in them can be said to have actually taken place.

Here, truth resides in the universal actuality of the story and such
stories are usually referred to as fiction. They can be novels, epics,
plays, or short stories.

3. Some stories are true in the sense that all the particular
events they contain can be said to have actually happened. Such
stories are histories and are nonfictitious; although we must recognise that insofar as they depend on universals, they are not portraits or mirror images or reports of what actually happened, but
stories as seen and understood by somebody. Such stories have
particular actuality. There is no reason why, in the scheme of
truths, they should be given pride of place, let alone a monopoly.
But ever since modern man has convinced himself that time has an
inherent and ineluctable shape (a conclusion that, as we have seen,
is both gratuitous and false), he has jumped to the conclusion that
the definitive shape of time is identical with those stories that have
particular rather than universal or symbolic actuality. This conclusion is an error of judgment because it ignores the role of the
universal (either concrete or abstract) in our cognition of any
event whatever and therefore remains oblivious of the multiplicity
of senses in which any story can be true. There is a multiplicity
because no story is a mirror portrait of time. Even when we are
dealing with particular actuality stories, truth appears in a twofold
sense. There is, first, the truth as seen by the agent or a contemporary observer; and, second, the truth as seen by a modern or
remote observer who does not share the contemporary observer's
universals. And as we have argued throughout and consistently,
there is no reason why the one truth should be preferred to the
other.

Every time we tell a story, time appears as a shape or assumes
the appearance of a shape. As we have just seen, there are many
different ways in which a story can be true or have actuality. It
would be very difficult to imagine a totally false story in every one
of the senses discussed above, though it is easy enough to conceive
that a story can have little or no particular actuality. But even a
lie — to take the most extreme example — must have an actuality
in one of the senses described above. If it had not, it would be so
absurd as to fail in its purpose. If, for example, it used the generalisation that all men have no eyes or that all men are physically
immortal, it would defeat any conceivable object the lie might
have.[15]

As long as stories were studied so that people could learn from
them, it did not necessarily matter which of the many possible
actualities the story had. One could learn from the story of

Heracles as soon as from Thucydides' story of the Peloponnesian War — though one would admit that for purely pragmatic politics, one might learn more from the latter than from the former. Even so, a story about Oedipus or Abraham, or a story like Shakespeare's Hamlet or his Richard III, though weighted on the side of universal actuality rather than on the side of particular actuality, could be deeply pedagogical. But when people started to seek more from stories than mere instruction and started to look at the past because they were scientifically curious rather than because they hoped to learn how to become and remain prime minister or dictator, they formed the idea — should we not rather say, they formed the illusion? — that time actually possesses a shape and that scientific curiosity can be satisfied by the discovery of that definitive shape. There was, of course, a very striking reason for the shift from considering history as the teacher of politics to the view that the study of history can satisfy our curiosity about the past. As long as political and social institutions and economic practices remained comparatively uniform from the days of the ancient Greeks to the decades immediately preceding the Industrial Revolution, there was good sense in assuming that the political experiences of the past were relevant to other people and that Thucydides and Tacitus could be studied to advantage. But when society and technology changed in a revolutionary way toward the end of the eighteenth century, the experiences of the past became obviously less relevant and therefore the study of history ceased to be a school of politics and became a matter of scientific curiosity.[16] With the shift in orientation, there came the idea that scientific curiosity could only be satisfied if the definitive shape of time could be discovered. Gradually historians even forgot, if they had ever known, that time has no definitive shape and that there is nothing to be discovered in that sense. As they blandly assumed that time had a shape and that that shape had to be discovered, they lost, more and more, their interest in stories that possessed universal actuality and set more and more store on stories that had particular actuality. Thus there appeared an ever-increasing number of histories that consisted of nothing but laconic recitals of particular events, the occurrence of which could be located in space and time. It was believed that these series of particular events represented the *real* flow of time in the past and therefore satisfied all scientific curiosity. We have seen in chapter 5 how meaning on many occasions tended to crowd out truth. Here we can watch the opposite process — how truth (understood in a very narrow way as truth of particular actuality) started to crowd out meaning. Just as some of the historians we discussed in chapter 5 veered toward a surfeit of meaning, we can now see that from the middle of the nineteenth century onwards there appeared schools of historians who veered towards a surfeit of truth. The growth of histories with a surfeit of truth is all the more reprehensible, though by no means incomprehensible, because their authors completely forgot or failed to inquire into the fact that even histories with a surfeit of particular truth are intelligible only in virtue of the universals that make the particular events by which they set so much store hang together. They also overlooked the fact that even a single event is an assembly of subevents and could not arise as an event in the human mind unless universals are employed to construct it. These various schools of historians thought that their truth-surfeit stories are genuine portraits of time and reflect the shape of the passage of time like mirrors. In this way and for this reason, the preoccupation with a narrow kind of truth tended to crowd out the preoccupation with meaning. This crowding out of meaning would have been bad enough by itself. It was made worse by the fact that it was based on insufficient insight into the nature of events so that, in the end, it proved self-defeating. As a consequence and oblivious of the self-defeating character of the whole enterprise, historians started to distinguish between history and fiction as if they were mutually and exhaustively exclusive. As a result of this false dichotomy, a whole *corpus* of stories came to be presented and paraded as history, that is, as portraits of the shape of time, when, in reality, they had no more to recommend themselves than that they were badly told, that they were lacking in imagination and meaning, and that the universals on which they depended, *pace* the protestations of their authors were tacit and unacknowledged. These were the history books against which Febvre and Bloch in France and Collingwood in England reacted. Febvre and Bloch founded the *Annales* to combat the pernicious influence of the historians' self-delusion. Collingwood coined the phrase 'scissors-and-paste-history' to expose the absurdity on which the enterprise was based. The school of the *Annales*, as I argued in chapter 2, overreacted and came up with an alternative that had little to do with history as the science of change. Collingwood reacted sharply and vehemently; but he did not overreact. He came up, instead, with an alternative that seems eminently viable and that I have used as the basis for my own analysis of historical knowledge in chapters 3, 4, and 5.

It must be clear by now that there is no absolute distinction between myth, fiction, and history and that all stories, be they

mythical, fictional, or historical can be assessed by looking at
other stories. They cannot be assessed — and this is as true of
history as of fiction — by looking at reality or *res gestae*. Stories
are, in this sense no exception to other compositions or artefacts.
As Henri Poincaré observed a long time ago, there is no time over
and above the various clocks we have. We can compare one clock
to another clock; but we cannot compare any clock to time and
it makes therefore no sense to ask which of the many clocks we
have is *correct*.[17] The same is true of any story, including historical
narratives. We cannot glimpse at history. We can only compare one
book with another book.

   We must accustom ourselves to a completely different conception of truth. Or rather, we must accept that historians cannot be
exempt from the notion of truth that is implicit in Poincaré's
account of the relationship between clocks and time. Historians
alone among all scientists still believe that the only reason why
truth eludes them is that they show too much bias, or that their
sources do, or that there are missing 'facts'. But this is all wrong.
The real reason why it must forever elude us is that it is not there.
There is nothing the case over and above what people have thought
(i.e., the sources) and think (i.e., the narratives), so that we can
have no statement of which we can say that it is true if and only if
what it asserts is the case.

   One of the most heated debates that has ever taken place in
the study of history broke out when F. Fischer published his
Deutschlands Griff nach der Weltmacht in 1962.[18] The heat of the
debate is understandable. Fischer argued that the German imperial
government had already aimed during World War I at hegemony in
Europe and the world. This thesis, which he amply supported by
extracts from the diaries of the German chancellor, Bethmann-
Hollweg, had all sorts of different implications, each one by itself
likely to arouse violent opposition or violent support. The thesis
not only altered the conventional picture of imperial Germany and
of the benign chancellor Bethmann-Hollweg. It also lent support
to the claim of the allies, written into the Treaty of Versailles,
that Germany had been responsible for the war. Furthermore, it
showed that Hitler was by no means the originator of the idea of
German hegemony. Hitler's enemies in Germany felt that Fischer
was trying to shift responsibility from the Nazis to the kaiser and
his adherents heaved a sigh of relief because they felt that Fischer
had exculpated Hitler from being the originator of Germany's
megolamania. Fischer's book was attacked and supported according to the ideological disposition of its readers. Everybody thought

that the question might be settled by an examination of what really had gone on in Bethmann-Hollweg's cabinet. That is, people wanted to decide whether Fischer was right or wrong by looking at *res gestae*. They did not succeed and the debate continued.[19] It has never been settled, but Golo Mann wrote a contribution to the debate that is relevant to our argument.[20] Mann, though he did not spell this out in so many words, suggested that there is no point in discussing the question by looking at history and at what happened. He suggested instead that we should look at another image of Bethmann-Hollweg and then compare Fischer's image with the other image. Mann suggested that we think of Bethmann-Hollweg as he might have thought of himself. In our terminology this means that Mann started by replacing Fischer's interpretation by an explanation. Mann then came up with the suggestion that Bethmann-Hollweg saw himself not as a leader but as a sort of central clearing house of all ideas that were being bandied about in the German political world. His diaries, therefore, do not represent what the chancellor himself thought or wanted, but what he had heard and what he had been told by others. Looked at in this way, the diaries, though they show that they lend support to Fischer's contention that some people urged the chancellor to gear Germany's war aims toward hegemony, do not necessarily prove that the chancellor was aiming at hegemony or was prepared to go along with the pressure groups who did. I do not know how many historians were convinced by Mann. But the point that matters is that Mann examined the truth of Fischer's thesis not by trying to look at *res gestae* but at a different *historia rerum gestarum* of Germany's chancellor during World War I. Truth, he seemed to be saying, cannot emerge when we compare Fischer's narrative with what happened. It can only emerge, such as it is, when we seek to substitute explanation for interpretation and compare the correspondence between two narratives.[21]

This method of looking at truth has been lucidly presented by J. Bronowski.

> One aim of the physical sciences has been to give an exact picture of the material world. One achievement of physics in the twentieth century has been to prove that that aim is unattainable.
>
> Take a good, concrete object, the human face. I am listening to a blind woman as she runs her fingertips over the face of a man she senses for the first time, thinking aloud. 'I would say that he is elderly. I think, obviously, he is not English. He has a rounder face than most English people. And I should say he is probably Continental, if not Eastern-Continental. The lines in his face would be lines of possible agony. I thought at first they were scars. It is not a happy face'.

This is the face of Stephan Borgrajewicz, who like me was born in Poland. It is seen by the Polish artist, Feliks Topolski. We are aware that these pictures do not so much fix the face as explore it; that the artist is tracing the detail almost as if by touch; and that each line that is added strengthens the picture but never makes it final. We accept that as the method of the artist.

But what physics has now done is to show that that is the only method of knowledge. There is no absolute knowledge. And those who claim it, whether they are scientists or dogmatists, open the door to tragedy. All information is imperfect. We have to treat it with humility. That is the human condition; and that is what quantum physics says. I mean that literally.

Bronowski then goes on to show how we can get different images by using light waves of different lengths. Each kind of wave will present a different picture. There is no sense in asking which wave length comes closest to the 'real' face. There is no 'real' face at all. There are only different pictures and there are as many different pictures as there are different lengths of light waves.

We are here face to face with the crucial paradox of knowledge. Year by year we devise more precise instruments with which to observe nature with more fineness. And when we look at the observations, we are discomfited to see that they are still fuzzy, and we feel that they are as uncertain as ever. We seem to be running after a goal which lurches away from us infinitely every time we come within sight of it.[22]

As Bronowski's lucid argument conclusively shows, it is not correct to think that truth eludes us because we are not in possession of all the necessary information or that it eludes us because we are too stupid or too biased. It is more correct to think that there is no truth to be grasped. We must accustom ourselves to thinking, even as other scientists have done by now, that our consciousness of history is a highly complex interplay of the relations between competing explanations, between competing interpretations, and between interpretations and explanations; and that in the last interplay, the interplay between interpretations and explanations, the interplay is not between competing universals in general but between explanatory and interpretative universals, so that that interplay is different in kind from the interplay in the first two cases.

For exactly the same reason we must consider some of the great and time-honoured debates of history as nondebates. There is first of all the great debate whether the past is a series of cycles or one straight line. This is not really a debate about the past but about the manner in which we write historical narratives. It all depends on one's method. If one explains the present with the help of universals used by men in the past, the present must of necessity appear as a repetition of the past. This is so not because it *is* a repetition but because it has been made to appear as a repetition by the choice of universals. If, on the other hand, one interprets (i.e., uses for preference universals that are used at the present time), then the past must appear to be very different to the way in which it appeared to the people in the past and therefore the large-scale narrative must appear as a straight line. Again, this does not prove that it *is* a straight line. Its appearance as a straight line results directly from the method employed and from the choice of the universals. Consider an example. If one uses the universal that men will always revolt against authority and that such revolts will lead to democracy and then to anarchy and that such anarchy will give rise to an autocratic monarch, all history will appear to be a series of cycles. But if one uses the generalisation that the application of technology to food production will raise the standard of living and that a raised standard of living must lead to populism or democracy, events in the past will not appear as repetitions of the events in the present, or the other way round. They will appear as antecedents in a straight line because in the distant past there was no large-scale application of technology to food production and therefore whatever populist developments might have occurred in the past, they must have derived from other causes. Hence, no cycles. Debates of this kind are not debates about *res gestae*, but about the kinds of *historia rerum gestarum* we choose to write.

Sooner or later every student of history will ask himself whether history is made by great men or whether great men are the mouthpieces of historical forces, economic developments, climatic changes, popular upheavals, and so forth. The most various answers have been given to this and to related questions. But the real answer is that the question is wrongly put.[23] History is not something that exists independently so that one can study, and probe, and watch it to find out whether its course is determined by Napoleon or whether Napoleon was successful for a short period because he 'represented' some force or was the right man for the occasion. History is a narrative composed by somebody. All one can ask is whether in any given narrative Napoleon appears to himself as the man who shapes history, or whether he appears to himself as the mouthpiece of a popular voice, or whether he did so to somebody else. There is no reason why we should attribute more importance to how Napoleon appeared to himself than to how he appears to a modern historian or vice versa. The most important book written about Napoleon is not his own *Memoires* any more than the countless biographies and histories of his reign, but P. Geyl's study entitled *Napoleon, For and Against*, which is a history of the history of Napoleon.[24] Or consider the age-old question whether Alexander was the founder of Hellenistic civilisation, whether he was a great man or a pawn of the forces of social and economic events. Callisthenes saw Alexander as the hegemonist of Greece. The Macedonians saw him as their folk leader. Innumerable historians since have seen him as this or that. Some say he was great and made history; others say he was pushed by forces he could not have controlled. It is absurd to ask what Alexander the Great *really* was and whether Callisthenes or the Macedonians or any of the many other, later historians were right. Even if one knew whether Alexander himself would have agreed with Callisthenes or with the Macedonians, the question could not be settled, for we know that Alexander's view of himself was only one of many possible views. There is no history, no *res gestae*, to be consulted or searched for an answer because the way in which Alexander appeared to himself and to others is, in the first place, an abstraction from and a composition of the several parts into which an observer divides the totality of *res gestae*. Without an observer, there would be no configuration known as Alexander the Great, let alone a story of his campaigns and their relationship to the rise of Hellenistic civilisation. There is no truth over and above the truths of how people appear to themselves and to others and this is where the matter must rest. One can, of course, debate whether a certain narrative about Napoleon is convincing, whether it is explanation proper or an interpretation. But one cannot decide whether its portrayal of Napoleon as the shaper of history corresponds to reality. It may correspond to what Napoleon thought of himself or to what somebody else thought of him. But it cannot correspond to what actually happened for the simple reason that whatever happened is such a colossal myriad of events capable of being split up into an infinitely greater myriad of subevents that it cannot possibly be described as history or as a story of any particular set of events.

It follows that the methodological debate whether historians should study single individuals or economic developments, whether they should concentrate on class struggles or child-rearing habits, is pointless. These problems owe their existence to a mistaken conception of the broad column of *res gestae*. If one believes that that column has a structure of its own, one could well wonder whether that structure is best reproduced in a history book in

which individuals or in which classes are the protagonists. But the
column has no structure beyond the passage of time. All definitions of the single events and the manner in which the inevitable
gaps between the events are covered are derived from an observer
who may be either the participant or a historian or both. Once
this is recognised, the debates whether history consists of the
history of child-rearing habits or of the history of modes of production, whether it is shaped by the masses or by individuals, are
beside the point because there is no history to be studied with a
view to detecting what its salient features are. History is composed
by historians, and whatever salient features it contains are those
put into it by its participants' and by historians' consciousness.
Res gestae is the reality; but it has no features. Each *historia rerum
gestarum* is one of the infinitely possible appearances of *res
gestae.* Historians must first of all decide whether to confine themselves to explanations proper or to attempt interpretation or translation. If they decide on interpretation or translation, they must
then abide by the general laws they consider true or plausible. But
in no case are they privileged to watch history and determine empirically whether it is the story of class struggles or whether it is
propelled by how babies are reared. The histories we know are the
narratives compiled by historians, and we should never speak of
history with a capital H but only of historical narratives, selected
from and composed of single events all contained in the broad
column we have called *res gestae.* A large event can be represented
in that broad column as a square inch; a small event, as a fraction
of a square inch. But these squares are not part of the column.
They appear as the result of self-conscious construction. We cannot even say that the broad column is the totality of events in the
sense of a summation of all events. For it depends entirely on the
historian or the observer of how large an event he picks out and
how he links it with other events. The definition and delimitation
of events is very much part of the historian's work performed on
the broad column.

There are no historical problems. There are only problems in
the writing of historical narratives.[25] This should not be taken to
mean that I deny that there are interesting historical debates or
that I mean to belittle their importance. It is supposed to mean
that the problems and the debates pertain to the method of composing the narrative, not to *res gestae.* Consider, for instance, the
long debate between historians who believe in methodological
individualism and the historians who believe in holism. The former
maintain that everything that happens in history is willed or

planned by individuals. They include in their conception of willing the possibility that some of the consequences willed are willed unintentionally and admit that one cannot deduce what happens by looking at what people will to happen. The holists, on the other side, believe that the course of history is not determined by individual intentions or plans but by larger configurations such as crowds, institutions, and societies, of which individuals are merely constrained members.

In view of the whole preceding argument, it must become clear that the debate is a debate about the method of writing history, not about the course of history or the way in which time passes. One can either use universals that are generalisations about individual purposes or one can use universals that are generalisations about the manner in which institutions, crowds, or societies push their individual participants. But in both cases, since one is employing universals, one is using thoughts. The view that a crowd constrains its members to behave in a certain way is a holistic view. But since it is a view, it is a thought. The view that individuals determine their behaviour, even though they are members of a crowd, is a generalisation and, as such, a thought. In either case, we are dealing with thoughts and in either case the question as to which thought we should choose to employ is a question about the method of composing a narrative. It is not a question about the nature of the process of time or the characteristics of *res gestae*.[26]

Consider a completely different kind of example. For many years now there has been a vehement debate about the reasons why the slave trade was abolished. The conventional opinions were upset with the publication of Eric Williams' book.[27] Williams argued that increased production costs, the overproduction of sugar, the glutting of wartime markets during the Napoleonic wars, and the bankruptcy of West Indian estates all played into the hands of rising capitalists who sought to dismantle the mercantilist system and to find the cheapest available labour in Asia and Latin America. The celebrated humanitarian crusade to abolish the slave trade, he argued, was mere propaganda and would have found no support had it not been for these other factors. As against this, there are the findings of Seymour Drescher,[28] who contends that the opposite was the case. He argues that during the abolitionist era the West Indies were becoming increasingly valuable to the British economy and that, as far as British trade was concerned, the potential of slavery was greater during the crucial years from 1804 to 1814 than it had been between 1788 and 1792 or at any

other time during the eighteenth century. It would follow, therefore, from Drescher's findings, that Williams is wrong and that
humanitarianism triumphed over economic selfishness. And now
there is another book on the subject by Roger Anstey[29] in which
it is argued that in 1806 an entirely accidental conjunction of
politico-economic circumstances enabled the abolitionists to argue
that it was in the national self-interest to abolish the slave trade.
They could base themselves on an appeal to the profit motive and
pretend that they had no humanitarian or moral or religious interest in the matter. It was because of this appeal, Anstey argues,
that they won their battle. The 1806 law, carried ostensibly by an
appeal to selfishness, destroyed well over half the British slave
trade and therefore it was possible by 1807 to argue successfully
that the remnant of the slave trade should be stopped because
it was immoral. Had it not become comparatively unprofitable by
1807, the belated appeal to moral principles would not have
carried the day.

Here we have a formidable array of conflicting opinions as to
what happened. But when one takes a closer look, one discovers
that the debate is not a debate about what happened — did the
abolitionists triumph because opinion was selfish or did they triumph because people were swayed by humanitarianism? Obviously,
some people were prompted by self-interest, others by moral
principles. There was no *res gestae* that we could describe as 'the
triumph of humanitarianism' and no *res gestae* that we could
describe as 'the triumph of economic selfishness'. There were
people, at the time, who saw it one way; and there were people,
at the same time, who saw it the other way. The whole debate,
though on the surface a debate about *res gestae* (i.e., about what
happened) is really a debate about what certain people thought.
And since it is ideally possible to identify the people even though
in practice we have not enough records to enable us to find out
what everybody concerned (as distinct from the several protagonists) thought, it is true that the debate will never be resolved.
Even if we had all the records, it would still be open to anybody to
argue that any one thought was a delusion or a case of false consciousness. But whether the debate will or will not be resolved,
we must be clear what the debate is about. It certainly is not about
whether humanitarianism rather than economic selfishness triumphed, for there simply was no string of events to be described as
the triumph of the one or the other so that we are not in a position
to look at those events and decide who is right — Williams, or
Anstey, or Drescher. All we can do is to compare what Williams,

Anstey, and Drescher say with what certain people at the time said and then decide that for person A, Williams is right; for person B, Anstey is right; and so forth. The real historiographical problem, then, is not how we can check the truth of Williams, Drescher, and Anstey by looking at the facts (i.e., *res gestae*). The real historiographical problem is, on the contrary, what is the relation between these three writers who offer competing universals and what is the relation between the universals they offer and the universals in vogue at the time they are writing about, and who is interpreting and who is explaining.

In *Man on His Past*,[30] H. Butterfield draws attention to the importance of the history of historiography. But I cannot agree with him that its study is merely desirable. Its study is a necessity. One cannot come to grips with any narrative one wishes to write unless one looks at all the other narratives that have been written on the same topic. The first narratives on that topic are the sources. All following narratives are elaborations and extensions of these sources. An interpretative narrative goes completely beyond them; but one cannot judge whether a narrative is interpretative or not and in what sense it is interpretative unless one has compared it to all other narratives.

Direct truth, nevertheless, plays a negative part in historical knowledge. If it is asserted that a certain event took place at a certain time and a certain place, it may be possible to establish that it did not. This is a negative test and it is the only direct test that is possible. Even here we are not confronted by a completely simple problem. If the event asserted to have taken place is a very large-scale event like the French Revolution, it is not easy to indicate what would count as a falsification of the assertion that it took place. There were thousands of people in remote corners of France hardly affected by it at all. And even in Paris itself there were many people who lived on the fringe of it. If one looks at them one could perhaps reach the conclusion that the French Revolution did not take place or that its character and shape was very different from what it is alleged to have been. Obviously, the larger the compass of the event, the more difficult a negative test becomes. This fact alone, if nothing else, shows that a historical narrative — and the statement that the French Revolution occurred between 1789 and 1795 is nothing if not a historical narrative — is not knowledge of something that really happened but knowledge of somebody's knowledge. The smaller the event, the easier a possible falsification. If we state that Robespierre walked on a certain day at a certain time from his lodgings to the

Convention, one could state very simply what would count as a falsification of that statement. But it is small comfort to be left with the knowledge that the only certain knowledge we have of Caesar is that he did not live in the twentieth century.

The problem of historical truth also has another aspect. So far we have always gone on the assumption that the simplest intelligible constellation is two events or subevents plus a general law to link them. But the historian is often confronted with a situation in which he can discover in his sources only one event and a general law and often enough he even has to surmise what that general law was or infer it from collateral evidence. Once he has one event and a general law, he can then infer the second event. His sources, for one reason or another, may be silent. They do not tell him that it occurred nor do they enable him to establish that it did not occur. In his narrative that event will be inserted, prefaced by the qualification that it 'must have occurred' or that 'it is likely to have occurred' or that we 'may imagine that something like that must have occurred'. Every narrative is full of such qualifying clauses and there is no objection to the insertion of such postulated events. Without such insertions, the narrative could not be intelligible because it would fail to link one event with another. A single event is unintelligible.

The matter becomes more complicated when the sources either do not enable the historian to surmise the general law necessary to postulate the second event or when they lead him to a general law that is so implausible to the historian and his readers that it fails to serve as an explanation. Here the historian faces a special dilemma. If explanation proper fails, he must translate. But translation, we have seen, has to be guided by knowledge of the other event. In translation there simply occurs the substitution of a plausible general law (plausible to the historian and presumed plausible to his readers) for the implausible general law. But for such substitution to be possible, one has to know the other event. If one does not, one does not know which general law to substitute. In the absence of the knowledge of the second event, then, even a translation becomes really an interpretation. The substitution cannot be typologically related to the general law found in the sources and the ice the historian is treading on is becoming fairly thin.

None of these reflections destroys the notion of historical truth. Historical narratives are clearly not arbitrary compositions. They are anchored in reality in all sorts of ways. These reflections merely establish that historical truth is not a simple matter. A historical narrative is not a mechanical reproduction of what happened; it is not a photographic portrait of a sequence of events; and its truth or truthfulness cannot be tested by looking at the actual events. Moreover one should repeat that the complexity of the notion of historical truth does not derive from the fact that the historian deals with events in the past, that is, with events of which the eyewitnesses are dead and cannot be consulted. Every one of the factors that cause this complexity of the notion of truth would be equally present when we are dealing with contemporary history.

History is not the totality of events, but what people think happened. The historian who selects from the totality is exactly in the same position as an eyewitness. Any two events selected are linked by a thought, not by time or nature. The historian as much as the eyewitness traces them by finding the thought, not by discovering their temporal or natural connection. Any event, no matter how small, is always *at least* a composite of two subevents. Without a thought in the mind of an observer, be he eyewitness or historian, the composite cannot be created. One might therefore come to the conclusion that historical research is not directed toward the establishment of a factual basis at all. This conclusion is in a sense inevitable. The most factual discovery a historian can make is the discovery of the thoughts that bind two events together or that make two subevents into one event. The most factual discovery is not the discovery that a certain event occurred but that a certain *Sinngebild* occurred — that is, that there was a certain intelligible constellation of events, where 'intelligible' refers to the people involved in the events. This kind of discovery is the most 'factual' discovery there is. 'Factual' here, includes 'thought'; but then, thoughts are facts. They happen as much as the collapse of a bridge or the summoning of a parliament. Any historical research that is confined to the discovery of physically noticeable facts and that leaves out the thoughts is incomplete and destined to come up with an unrealistic story. When Sir Lewis Namier tried to tell the story of King George III's early Parliament by using, basically, nothing but the physical facts of how the members voted and who got them their seats, he came up with a somewhat unrealistic picture because we *know* that many of the members had thoughts.[31] They may have been evil thoughts or corrupt thoughts and may have had little bearing on grand political theory. But they were thoughts nevertheless. Some of the members may have been too dumb to think. But insofar as they were human, we can presume what they might have thought or to which thoughts they might have given their assent. Historical research confined to physical facts has an air of objectivity. But it is an essentially false objectivity. I recall Percy Schramm telling me that he considered most books on Hitler that described Nazi philosophy and doctrines of master race and thoughts of world dominion to be pure speculation because they contained opinions, and opinions, even though they were the opinions of the people the books were about, were not the stuff of history; they were not facts. He was then planning to write his introduction to Hitler's table talk by sticking to what he described as the objective facts: Hitler's physical height, the number of dogs he owned, his collar size, and so forth.[32]

A historical narrative — any narrative, for that matter — cannot enumerate events without some kind of cogency. If it presents event after event as if one damned thing happened after another without rhyme or reason, the reader cannot follow the story. I have tried to show that every event is a mininarrative and that such a mininarrative, no matter how brief, is an intelligible unit. Being constructed by linking two events with the help of a covering law, every event one obtains possesses an in-built intelligibility. We must now examine how this intelligibility is built into a fairly long series of events, the story. The story must make sense. If the story makes sense, the reader must be made to feel that there is a beginning and an end; and he must be made to feel that once the story has started, one thing follows another with a certain necessity. The sense of a beginning and an ending gives a story coherence, and so does the feeling that the sequence of events is not entirely unpredictable. Given the beginning, one thing led to another and led, through some kind of inherent necessity, to the end. Many novelists have told of the manner in which their stories and characters, once the beginning is conceived, take over. The novelist starts with a certain character in a certain situation and finds that after a few pages he becomes aware of an inner logic that takes over and develops the plot as well as the characters of the story. The novelists say they are not really free to 'invent' once the initial situation is in front of them. It has its own inner momentum. As the reader or the writer becomes progressively acquainted with the plot and the protagonists, the next steps become almost predictable.

There is an apparent problem here. We are accustomed to think that history is unpredictable and that everything that happens is contingent, that is, that it could have happened in a different way or not at all. Napoleon might have died after Marengo and the duke of Wellington could have lost the battle of Waterloo. A

historical narrative must embody these contingencies and cannot
possibly present the career of Napoleon as if it were predictable
that he did not die after Marengo and that Wellington won the
battle of Waterloo. But if the historian tells his story as if there
were nothing but contingencies, no reader could follow the story
and no reader would get the impression that the story was in fact
a 'story'. If the historian's narrative simply reports 'one damned
thing after another', it is not a narrative one can follow. Is there,
then, a real problem or is the problem only apparent?

The problem is only apparent. If one probes the matter, one
will understand that the problem disappears — or at least that
the problem becomes less fundamental than it seemed at first
glance. The problem would be genuine if the writing of a historical
narrative were a matter of copying a real sequence of events. In
this case one would have to take it that the real sequence is
a sequence of largely contingent events and that the historian,
when he is telling his story, has to play down the contingencies
and make the sequence appear to be more necessary and intelligible and 'followable' than it actually is. The historian, in
other words, not only has to introduce a sense of beginning
and a sense of an ending but also has to pretend that the events
were more predictable than they actually were. But we have
shown again and again that to write a narrative is not to copy
what happened. The totality of what happened is so large and
broad that it cannot be surveyed, and the mere subdivision of that
totality into definable and specific events distinct from one another is part of the historian's activity. The narrative that results
from the historian's work is not a portrait of what happened, but
it *is* the story of what happened. There is not an identifiable sequence over and above the one presented by the historian. The
historian's narrative is history. When we remind ourselves of this
situation, the problem disappears. The historian does not introduce an air of predictability or necessity into the sequence of
events, but presents the story with an air of predictability because
without that air there would be no story. And at this point, we
need to remind ourselves again that the historian is only repeating
on a larger scale the mental activity already performed both by the
person he is writing about and by the person who compiled the
sources on which he is drawing. W. B. Gallie has devoted the most
important chapter in his book entitled *Philosophy and the Historical Understanding*[33] to this question. It is tellingly entitled
"What is a Story"? The story, he says on page 29, must be acceptable and yet unpredictable. As the historian takes his reader from

one event to the next, he must succeed in rendering the contingencies acceptable. If he succeeds, the story is followable. Gallie's discussion of the question is sensitive and cautious. In view of all preceding discussions, we can offer an explanation and some degree of justification of the procedures involved.[34]

We can explain why the historian, though he is dealing with contingent events, is offering them in a way that makes them seem somewhat predictable. The sequence of any two events depends on a general law. Once there is a general law, tacit or stated, the second event will appear to follow from the first event. The predictability of every step in the story is put together. The reason why the historian and his readers can 'follow' the story is simple. It is not that the historian relates contingent events and pretends they are not contingent. It is that the historian, for the most part, selects his events in such a way that they will be coherent in the sense that the second event is predictable. There is no need for the whole story to be predictable. Each story can consist of many subplots and often it is sufficient for any two or three events to be predictable. This is why it is preferable to speak of an air of predictability rather than to state blandly that the whole story must be predictable. Given the general law, at least any two events must be put together in such a way that the second follows from the first.

This procedure does not involve a falsification of any kind. To begin with, there is no story without an air of predictability to be copied. The construction of a narrative that has an air of predictability is therefore not a false report of what really happened. Second, the general laws, which provide the air of predictability, are not imported into the events by the historian. They are, we have shown, part and parcel of the source material. Third, every actor in history is capable or is presumed to be capable of *thinking* of what or about what he is doing. Such thinking involves the employment of some general laws. Hence he himself as he is engaged in action can, ideally, be taken to know what the outcome might be. His actions are therefore not just blind actions but more like projects, like plans made to bring about a certain result. The actor himself, therefore, even before any source material emerges, acts in a teleological manner. His plans might be frustrated by accident or by the plans of other people. But planning and projecting is an integral part of the role he is playing. If we therefore present him as doing things that are in some way predictable, we are not distorting his activities but merely stressing one important aspect of these activities.

The second observation requires further comment. We said that the general laws, which provide the air of predictability, are not read into the events by the historians. This is certainly true as far as explanations proper are concerned but not really true as far as interpretations are concerned. But when we are dealing with explanations proper, we are frequently stuck with general laws that do not seem true or even plausible to the modern historian and his readers. If a modern historian tells a story in which one event is shown to be followed by another because Zeus sent a message by Mercury, the reader might take note and recall that some ancient Greek might have considered the second event thus to be explained by the first; but he cannot follow the story. He will want a different kind of explanation why the second event followed the first. Here the need for translation and possibly even for interpretation becomes paramount. On the general laws provided in the sources, the second event does *not* follow plausibly and the modern reader cannot follow the story. Translation will help him. When translation is required, one kind of air of predictability is replaced by another. And when interpretation is necessary, the story itself will be altered because the new general law will lead to a different second event. But interpretation only changes the general law and the second event and thus the story. It does not introduce an air of predictability where there was none in the first place. It changes the reasons for predictability but not the phenomenon of predictability itself.

In a striking and pungent passage that is worth quoting in full, G. R. Elton has described the situation:

> The hallmark of the amateur is a failure of instinctive understanding. This expresses itself most clearly in a readiness to see the exceptional in the commonplace and to find the unusual ordinary. The amateur shows a tendency to find the past, or parts of it, quaint; the professional it totally incapable of this. On the other hand, the professional, truly understanding an age from the inside — living with its attitudes and prejudices — can also judge it; refusal to judge is quite as amateurish a characteristic as willingness to judge by the wrong, because anachronistic, standards. By all these criteria, Lord Acton was an amateur, and so he was, a prince of amateurs. Very wide reading and self-consciously deep thinking may have attended him; but he was forever expressing distress or surprise at some turn in the story, was alternately censorious and uncomprehending, suspected conspiracies and deep plots everywhere. In short, he lived in history as a stranger, a visitor from Mars. The professional lives in it as a contemporary, though a contemporary equipped with immunity, hindsight and arrogant superiority — a visitor from the Inquisition. How is such professionalism created? G. M. Young once offered celebrated advice: read in a period until you hear its people

speak. But this is amateurishness of a drastic kind because it is superficially professional. Who ever knew or understood people just because
he heard them speak? The truth is that one must read them, study their
creations and think about them until one knows what they are going
to say next.[35]

The passage requires only one comment. Elton is vague in his failure to pinpoint the reason for this sort of predictability. The
reason is the ubiquitous presence of general laws. They are in the
minds of the actors, in the minds of the compilers of the sources,
and in the minds of the modern authors of historical narratives.
The professional historian can learn to predict what a person is
going to say next because he can gauge the general law that was
or is in the mind of that person.

   J. H. Hexter too, in *The History Primer*,[36] discusses the matter and his conclusions are very similar to Elton's. He recalls his
argument with a professor of engineering to whom he successfully
predicted the future, that is, what the professor would most likely
be doing during the coming week, (pages 54–55) and on page 123
he writes 'the ordinary life of even quite stupid men . . . is based
on a dense and firm fabric of such predictions'. But true to his
general argument, Hexter fails to point out that this dense fabric
of predictions rests entirely on everybody's use of general laws.
Without an admittedly trivial general law (of limited universality)
that professors of engineering in a certain university do certain
things in term time, Hexter would not have been able to demonstrate to the professor that he could predict the future. Hexter's
example, though pertinent and telling, is however, not well chosen.
The historian is rarely really interested in predicting the future
where 'the future' means the future from the historian's standpoint. In practice the historian is interested in something much
more modest and therefore much more capable of achievement.
He is interested in predicting the future where 'the future' means
something that has really happened as far as the historian is concerned but which is in the future in regard to the person he is
studying. If one is studying the early career of Frederick Barbarossa, one is interested in predicting the future in the sense that
one could predict what would happen in, for example, 1160. In
other words, the historian is not, as Hexter's example might lead
one to think, interested in predicting what the consequences of
a given event will be. He can make such a prediction, theoretically,
with the help of a general law because he can deduce the second
event from the first event by using the general law and the first
event as the initial condition. In reality, however, since the histori-

an is concerned with the past, he knows *both* the first and the second event and uses the general law to show that the second event might have been expected to follow upon the first event. He is also implying that if Frederick Barbarossa had reflected on the situation, he might himself have come to the conclusion that, by 1160, certain things would happen. He could probably not have predicted exactly which of three or four things would happen; but he could have narrowed the choice to three or four things. The shift of emphasis in the two predictions is significant. In the second prediction the historian is not prophesying the future but merely establishing that the relationship between the first and the second event was predictable, that the two events stand in an intelligible relationship to one another, and that if they are thus put together, they make an intelligible story that the reader can follow.

Under no circumstances should anything in the preceding arguments be taken as a proof that there are no accidents in history. One might presume that if the story is told in such a way in which successive steps appear to be predictable one is implying that in such a story there can be no accidents. In a sense this is perfectly true. But to say this is not to say much. All one is saying is that it is the historian's business, if he sets out to tell an intelligible story, to play down the role of accidents. But this does not mean that if one were God and surveyed the whole broad column of *res gestae* in its entirety, one could not perceive accidents. All it means is that the historian is professionally predisposed to present the succession of the events he narrates in an intelligible manner and that that manner tends to preclude the insertion of accidents. The whole concept of accident, moreover, is relative. It was once argued in a famous essay that the shape of Cleopatra's nose changed the course of history and since the shape of that nose did not stand in a causal relationship to the Roman politics of the time, Roman politics was changed by an accident.[37] But the analysis is insufficient. Cleopatra's nose may have been an accident in any chain of events belonging to Roman politics; but it was not an accident in any chain of events belonging to the genetic history of the Ptolemies of Hellenistic Egypt. The accident that changed the course of history, in other words, was not an absolute accident but the result of the crossing of two series of events. One belonging to Roman politics or, if one will, to the erotic tastes of both Caesar and Mark Antony, and the other belonging to the genetics of the rulers of Egypt. From this analysis alone it appears that the question whether or not accidents play

a role in history is a senseless question. All one could ask is whether it is an accident that at one particular point in time two series
of events should cross. But this is not all. Just as we have argued
that the very existence of each chain of events is due to a composition made by a historian or by the people he is writing about, so
we must also argue that the choice whether these two particular
chains of events are made to cross or not is left to the observer,
be he contemporary or a later historian. If a contemporary observer or a later historian believes that men like Caesar or Mark
Antony can be deflected from their political ambitions by the
beauty of a woman's nose, he might well be inclined to narrate
his story by crossing the two chains of events. In any case, the
question is not whether accidents change the course of history
but whether historians or contemporary observers can persuade
themselves of the truth of a general law in terms of which the
shape of a woman's nose and the political ambitions of Roman
statesmen can be seen to stand in a causal relationship to one
another.

The view that a story has to contain the single events in such
a way as to make a certain degree of predictability possible might
seem incompatible with the view that all events are contingent
and that whatever happened in the past is a single series of single
events. Marxists, though outstanding in this matter, are by no
means the only historians who tend to dismiss the accidental and
the contingent and treat every career of a statesman as a mere
episode in a development that was bound to happen and that was
predictable. In this way they reduce any particular episode to the
level of nonimportance and the more large scale the history they
write is, the more unimportant contingency becomes. On this
view, one ends up by seeing history as a *vis a tergo* and by taking
all contingencies as a historian's failure to understand their necessity. In his *Critique de la raison dialectique*,[38] Jean-Paul Sartre has
addressed himself to this problem. He clearly bases himself on
Hegel. Hegel pointed out that the slave is one up on his master.
The master may exploit the slave; but the slave, since he is suffering exploitation, thinks of ways of putting an end to his suffering.
Since he is planning and plotting, he is a constant threat to the
master and the master, far from being in control of the situation,
has to be on his guard all the time. The slave is free to plot his
liberation. The master is not, because he has to parry the slave's
plots. Sartre takes this argument further and generalises it. He
says that man is always the master of his fate because he antici-
pates the future and plans it by trying to shape his circumstances

in accordance with his desires. Man defines himself as man by his projects. The historical process, he says, is both imposed by material pressure (i.e., *vis a tergo*, necessity) and willed by human beings, who cannot change the past but who have projects for the future.[39] He means that man is like both master and slave: looking back he is like the master, compelled to parry the blows of the slave; looking forward, he is like the slave, freely plotting his own liberation.

If we follow Sartre, we can see that the two views ('history is necessity and therefore predictable' and 'history is a series of contingent events and therefore unpredictable') are not incompatible. Indeed, the incompatibility is deceptive. Even though history is a series of single events and therefore unpredictable, it is actually made up of events of which men are conscious and which have been assembled from subevents. Such events presuppose the use of universals and the employment of universals creates some kind of predictability. For this reason, history as known to us — and there is no other — always must appear more predictable and less contingent than we have reason to believe that it was. This does not mean that there is no contingency in *res gestae*. It only means that in thinking about *res gestae* we are forcing ourselves implicitly and necessarily into thinking of it as predictable and inevitable. And as we are doing so, we are indeed tending toward playing down the importance of individual episodes. And, such playing down becomes more obtrusive the larger the scale of the narrative is. *Res gestae* may well be one damned thing after another. But it cannot possibly *appear* as such. Indeed, to think of it as such and to *make* it appear as such requires a great deal of effort and sophistication, for it necessitates the extrusion of meaning (no easy thing) and the elimination of the *Sinngebild*, which is inherent in every event that is *known*. We have referred above to Jean-Luc Godard's film *Breathless*, which inaugurated in the early 1960s the new wave in the cinema. It is no accident that the art of telling stories began with Homer and produced Godard three milennia later. It is quite inconceivable that it should have started with Godard's way of telling a story in which events are just one damned thing after another.[40]

All constructions of the flow of time into events, all our knowledge of both minievents and of maxievents, is *ex post facto* and therefore reflective. This means that the predictability is not substantially inherent in *res gestae*, but an essential and necessary ingredient in our knowledge of *res gestae*, that is, in any *historia rerum gestarum*. Every story, therefore, contains an air of predict-

ability and even of necessity and all reflection, after the *res gestae*
have taken place, tends to make it look as if it could not have been
otherwise. But necessity and predictability are predicated of reflection and are, therefore, compatible with the view that *before*
things have happened, they could not have been predicted. Sartre
is therefore right in insisting that there is a dialectic between freedom and necessity and that while our understanding of history involves a knowledge of necessity, the freedom of any individual
to act this way or that way is not curtailed. Or, if it is curtailed,
it is not curtailed by the fact that in retrospect everything that
has happened appears to have been necessary.

For this reason, the historian, when he is reflecting by looking
back, is not essentially in a different position from the agent who
is reflecting on what he has just done or is about to do. Historians
are indeed neither the first nor the last people to whom the past
or time appears in a certain shape. Before them it appeared as an
intelligible sequence to the actors when and if they reflected; and
after them, it appears so to the philosopher of history who composes narratives on a very large scale and whose method we shall
examine in the following chapter. At this point of the argument
we should note that, whatever the special features of a full-blown
philosophy of history are, both the making and the writing of
history contain the same ingredients and reflections. 'History' as
the incomparable Theodor Mommsen said in a slightly different
context, 'is neither *written* nor *made* without love or hate'.[41]

There remains then, if the story is to be an intelligible story,
the sense of a beginning and the sense of an ending.[42] Every historian with a feeling for literature will start his story at a point
where the reader can be made to feel that something is beginning,
and similarly he must conclude by leaving the impression that,
though other things kept happening, the particular story is coming to an end. A proper investigation of this whole question belongs perhaps to literary criticism rather than to the philosophy of
history. But there are two aspects to the matter that are particularly relevant.

The notion of 'in the beginning' is a difficult notion though
we use it glibly every day. What happened in the beginning is
impossible to say for the simple reason that in the beginning, by
definition, there cannot have been anybody to watch what was
happening. There can be no report and no knowledge. Any historian who begins his story in an appropriate point in time is not
really beginning at the beginning. Nevertheless his choice of where
to begin will be influenced by a general notion of what people

might think to be a good beginning, of the sort of thing people
expect of a 'beginning'. The authors of the Old Testament history
had a very sure eye for this problem. They realised that if they
told a story people would want to know how it really all began.
And so they hit upon the idea of beginning at the real beginning,
that is, with the creation of the world. They were familiar with
all sorts of stories of how the world was first created. Indeed,
creation stories are a very common part of almost all mythologies
and in the Middle East they were particularly well known through
both ritual and myth. But whatever story was told, it was told in
a way that put it beyond the reach of history. There was a beginning and then, for a long, long time, nothing in particular happened. And then history began. In ancient Sumer, lists of kings
were kept from a certain time onwards and we could perhaps
consider them as a rudimentary and very primitive form of story
telling. But there is no link between these lists and the Sumerian
creation myth.[43] The events reported in the latter happened at the
beginning, in time out of mind, once upon a time. The story was
reenacted in Babylon at the beginning of every year, thus recon-
firming the connection between the beginning of the year's solar
cycle and the origin of the world. But that was all. In Egypt, there
were many different creation stories,[44] but again, no indication
of when the creation happened and of what happened between
this act of creation and the First Dynasty and the reign of Menes
in about 3200 B.C. Whatever history we have of Egypt — and it
was first composed very late under Hellenistic influences by
Manetho in the third century B.C. — there is no connection with
the real beginning. Although here, it must be admitted, there is
a subsidiary story of how it began. It began, Manetho tells us, with
the union of upper and lower Egypt.

By contrast, the authors of the Old Testament history were
more precise in their literary instinct. They took the old Babylonian story of creation and historicised it. Instead of treating it
like a myth that happened once upon a time and that is period-
ically reenacted, they told it like a historical narrative and then
proceeded by linking legend to legend and tradition to tradition
to make it the beginning of their historical narrative.[45] When one
reads the Old Testament one is given the impression that the history of the children of Israel really began in the beginning. There
is no unfathomable gap between the creation of the world and the
subsequent story. There is a continuous narrative. The sense of a
beginning is complete and eventually people even got into the
habit of counting the years as from the creation of the world by

God — a habit that is still in everyday use among orthodox Jews.
This strong sense of a beginning was transferred from the ancient
Jewish historians to medieval Christian historians and chroniclers.
They all began at the complete beginning as it was narrated in the
Old Testament. Whatever history was told in the Middle Ages was
firmly anchored in and related to the absolute beginning.

The only other tradition of historical writing that anchored
itself in a similar absolute beginning is to be found in ancient
Rome. There was no attempt to start at the beginning of the
world. But Livy and his precursors did the next best thing. They
took the foundation of the city of Rome as their starting point.
They combined traditional stories about the origins of Rome with
the ritual of making a sacred impregnable circle to demarcate an
enclosed space against the outside profane world and then linked
the whole story to the sagas of Troy and, in particular, to the
legends of Aeneas' arrival in Italy. The ritual of using a plough to
make a circle that divides the sacred world from the profane
world outside the circle takes the existence of the world itself for
granted. But it is not unlike the Babylonian creation story in that
it was used to provide a proper sense of a beginning. As in the Old
Testament, the ritual was historicised. It was alleged to have taken
place at an identifiable time and place and the man who ploughed
the circle was the first king of Rome. The method was continued.
The ancient Romans took themes of Indo-European mythology
and assigned these stories actual historical position in the story of
Rome. The mythical characters that appear regularly in Indo-
European mythology emerge in Roman history as historical persons. Take, for instance, the embodiments of wisdom and violence,
the myths of Mitra and Varuna, of Manu and Pururavas. In ancient
Rome we find these mythical powers transformed into historical
kings, Romulus and Numa, the one representing violence and the
other wisdom. Similarly the story of Caius Mucius Scaevola and
of Horatius Cocles are stories of Indo-European mythology translated into historical events of early Roman history. In this way
the early history of Rome was made to appear not as an arbitrary
series of happenings but as a display of archetypal themes.[46]

One of the neatest and most telling examples of the manner
in which myth impresses itself upon story telling and helps to
provide a sense of beginning is the history of the story of Cain
and Abel. In very ancient times in Canaan people practised a
fertility ritual in the course of which somebody had to fertilise
the barren soil of a piece of land by a sacrifice, possibly the
sacrifice of man. The blood made the barren soil fertile and the

sacrificer, having broken a taboo against killing and shedding blood, albeit in a good cause, had to be marked with a special sign and kept away from his community for a ritual period. In very ancient times a shepherd was actually slain at a time of drought in summer, and his official slayer was obliged to flee in order to remove the ceremonial guilt. When the ancient Hebrew bards or priests or priest-bards composed their history, which began with the creation of man, they had also to account for the second generation. They took the myth of the ritual slaying of the shepherd and incorporated it into their story, but in incorporating it they had to adapt it to their general theme. Cain and Abel became Adam and Eve's children and Cain, the tiller of the soil, became the murderer of his shepherd brother. The part about the fertility ritual had to be left out because the worshippers of Jahweh did not practise this kind of primitive magic. They simply retold the story by saying that God accepted the shepherd's sacrifice and rejected the agricultural sacrifice and that this discrimination made Cain jealous and caused him to murder his brother. Next, they had to expunge the ritual flight and transform the ritual mark. They said that Cain was cursed by God and marked because of his guilt and forced to flee.[47] In this form, the story provided the necessary link between Adam and Eve and the following generations and suitably introduced the next chapter in the continuing story of how original sin was handed from generation to generation. Looking back now, we find that its incorporation into Hebrew history is very similar to the incorporation of the Romulus-Numa story into ancient Roman history or the impression of an Indo-European mythical archetype upon the 'historical' story about Horatius Cocles and Mucius Scaevola.

In dealing with the intrusion of myth into the historical narrative, it is useful to recall the difference between infiguration by myth and historicisation or conversion of myth. Both infiguration and historicisation are used to increase the meaning and intelligibility of the narrative; but they are very different processes. Infiguration takes place when an ordinary story is composed by following the pattern of a myth. But we speak of the conversion or historicisation of myth when a mythical event is inserted into a story as if it really had happened.

As to the sense of an ending, Christian eschatology, in one or the other of its many forms — Neoplatonic, Gnostic, Apocalyptic — has always provided a powerful suggestion for historians, dramatists and novelists.[47] Any story that ended with the advent of the Antichrist or other events foreshadowing the Second

Coming had a proper end rather than an arbitrary stop imposed
by the fact that the historian had run out of time or breath or
both. The sense that the ending would be a doom was powerfully
reinforced by the convergence of Germanic mythology about the
Twilight of the Gods with Christian apocalyptic imagination.
Conversely, the sense of an ending in hope was fed by the expectation of a new birth, the Second Coming, the age of the Holy
Spirit which, according to Joachim of Flores, was the Third Age
in the divine dispensation. Christian mythology, with or without
German mythology, provided ample opportunity for the end of
any tale — which could be either doom or hope. And often
enough, where the story is not carried forward to the actual ending
derived from myth, we can recognise in many writers the influence of that mythical sense of ending. Take for instance Boso,
an English cardinal who circa 1178 A.D. wrote the life of his
friend Pope Alexander III. Instead of taking the birth and death
of his hero as the beginning and end, he cast his whole story in
the image of Christian myth. Alexander was the Jesus figure,
persecuted by the emperor Frederick Barbarossa. The pope was
humiliated and almost crucified by his enemies only to be led back
in triumph at Easter to the city of Rome, thus restored to the
Kingdom of Heaven. In following the mythical pattern, Boso had
to make some compromises with the truth. But he made no more
than was necessary and one could argue that even those could have
been avoided. The point about Boso is that we have here a telling
example of how myth provided a sense of an ending and made the
story intelligible in a sense in which a mere report of Alexander's
diplomatic successes toward the end of his life would not have
been.

It is difficult to write any story if one does not know what
the end is.[49] Namier once coined the happy maxim that the historian is a man who knows the future and imagines the past.[50] He
meant to remind us with a jolt that we are wrong in taking the
commonsense and commonplace view that historians know the
past and imagine what the future might be. Namier, I presume, did
not mean that historians are prophets who know the future but
that, since they live after the events they describe, they know the
future in regard to the story they were writing. One cannot very
well write the history of the Persian Wars without knowing the
end. The knowledge of the 'future' must therefore be a fixed point
that helps to make the story intelligible. Here then we have a
conclusion that is different from our earlier investigation of the
meaning of 'making a story intelligible'. Earlier we argued that

the historian's efforts to play down pure contingency and to make events appear to have been predictable are not radically different from the way in which the actors of the story saw the situation themselves. Every one of their acts was undertaken on the assumption that the outcome is in some way predictable, even though the actors knew that events might prove the prediction wrong. But now we have a situation that clearly indicates that the historian who knows the future, that is, who knows what the outcome was, is in a slightly advantageous position and more likely to write an intelligible story than the actor who did not know what the outcome really would be. The historian's hindsight, at this point, distinguishes him from the actor of history. We have always tended to play down all differences and have sought to show that the historian, even when doing interpretation, is not doing something completely different from what the actors themselves must be presumed to have been doing. But as far as the sense of an ending is concerned and insofar as that sense bestows intelligibility on the historian's tale, hindsight is a superior quality of which the historian has a monopoly.

THE PHILOSOPHY OF THE STORY

It must now be abundantly clear that history is *not* what people think — but what people *think*. Conventionally, people think that history is an activity that transcribes facts from reality to a piece of paper, an activity that is solely guided by the concern for truth. I have tried to show that it is not an activity that can be guided by nothing but the concern for truth. For the effort to distinguish fact from fable is only a small part of the historian's business. The far larger part is concerned with putting subevents together into events and events into stories. I will now argue that the next step in this progression is to put stories together into philosophies of history and that in taking this last step the historian is not ceasing to be a historian but merely continuing the work that was begun when the first subevents were assembled into an event. The putting together can be carried out in many different ways, depending on the universals that are used to make the necessary connections. And since the universals are thoughts, history is basically about thoughts. It is the story of what people have thought and how one thought replaced another. One must amend the statement that truth is the only guide necessary by adding that though the thoughts that are the subject matter of history are not all true thoughts, the fact that they were thought at a certain time and place is either a true fact or not. But truth itself is not even in this wider sense the only guide the historian needs. I have shown that in many cases the historian has to translate and interpret these thoughts into terms that were not thought at the time he is writing about and that are not even necessarily true at the time he is writing. I conclude that the historian's relationship to truth is an important one — but not important enough to constitute a characteristic definition of his activity. Almost all books concerned with the method of history state that the most important function of the historian is to distinguish fact from fable. Lucian, in a very influential ancient treatise entitled *The Way to Write True History*, elevated truth into the prime requisite. Since he and other ancient historians were mainly concerned with source material embodied in myths and epics, they can be excused in mistaking the effort to sort fact from fable as the chief character of historical writing. But there can be no such easy excuse for later authors of textbooks on the methodology of history.[1] Not even so thoughtful a modern thinker as Karl Löwith was able to free himself from the view that plain history is a record of the things that happened and that that record (i.e., the 'facts') has no meaning. In his book entitled *Meaning in History* he writes that history is made meaningful only by the indication of some transcendent purpose *beyond the actual facts* (my italics).[2]

The reader might say now that he should be spared further argument. I have shown how a story is constructed; I have examined its relation to truth and probed the way the story emerges from the sources. One can now argue that we have seen enough and that once one understands that history is not what people think but what they *think*, our work is done. I would like nevertheless to go a little bit further and plead the case of a proper philosophy of history. One must grant that the nature of the story is highly complex and that that complexity alone will preserve us in future from all nonphilosophical, naive empiricism, which sees the historian as a sort of mechanical transcriber of facts, a recorder of events and, at best, as a sort of detective inspector from Scotland Yard. Why not leave it at that?

There are several reasons why this insight into the true nature of the story is not sufficient. The first was already stated in chapter 1 and is indeed the main reason for writing this book. The pressure of academic institutions is a reprehensible influence. Universities must recruit a large number of teachers. They must use some kind of guideline to determine whom to recruit. The possession of a Ph.D. degree in history is an obvious criterion for the selection of teachers. Hence the pressure of academic institutions has worked to elevate the Ph.D. exercise into a universal criterion of good scholarship. If the preceding arguments in this book are accepted, it must be clear that a successful Ph.D. candidate is far from being a qualified historian. He is nothing but a detective inspector and should seek employment at the local police station. But things being what they are, he is more likely to end up as an influential chairman of a large history department in a large university. There he will uphold the narrow and stultifying methods he has been trained to use in his historical detection work when he was a Ph.D. student and there he will perpetuate the Ph.D. mentality — a mentality that is quite inimical to genuine

historical understanding. I have often enough heard such a distinguished 'historian' with an equally distinguished career express
the opinion that all that matters is whether the facts are true. The
story they are made to tell, the opinion continued, was a matter
for debate and really neither here nor there. Sir George Clark once
described history as a hard core of fact surrounded by a pulp of
disputable interpretations. E. H. Carr, wittily and with greater
perspicacity, stood the statement on its head. 'History', he wrote
in *What is History?* 'is a hard core of interpretation surrounded by
a pulp of disputable facts'.[3] If the field is left to the Ph.D. can-
didates and to those who have never managed to recover from
their Ph.D. studies, history will die of inanition. A detective has
a very important role to play in society. But a historian-detective
has not. Unless we can relate the fact that Caesar crossed the
Rubicon to a wider series of events and that series to a very wide
perspective of Rome and its importance, there is no point whatever in solving the question whether he did or not. 'What a mean
thing a mere fact is', Coleridge once wrote, 'if it is not related to a
comprehensive truth'. The philosophy of history aims to provide
that comprehensive truth. Without the comprehensive truth the
field will first be left to the Ph.D. mentality and then become
desolate because that mentality will drive all lively intellects away
to seek nourishment somewhere else. The philosophy of history
unifies and directs the order of events, and if the study of sources
is extended not only to the composition of narratives but also to
the search for a unifying philosophy, the study of history will
once again be exciting and vital.[4]

There is also a completely different reason why we need a
philosophy of history over and above the historian's story. When
we survey the vast panorama of stories told by historians — and I
am not thinking here of the vast variety of stories told about one
'subject' such as the fall of the Roman Empire or the Nazi era but
of the panorama of stories about different epochs and areas — one
gains a peculiar feeling. Each story is full of horror and triumph. It
tells of Promethean tragedies, where human beings pitted themselves against fate, and of Odyssean shrewdness, where human
beings attempted to make ends meet and work the possible. It
tells of crimes and follies, of institutions and social systems and of
their growth and decline. And above all it tells or ought to tell of
the countless silent victims of greed, brutality, and aggression. All
in all, one will see that each story portrays a set of values, non-
values, and countervalues and that each story tells of events that
are, as Ranke once put it, equally close to God. However this may

be, once the panorama is surveyed, there comes the next step. How are these events related to each other? How do these systems or protestations of value relate to other systems and protestations? Often enough it is assumed that the philosophy of history is nothing but an idle speculation about the meaning of history. Since I have shown that there is nothing in the past that corresponds to anything that could be described as History with a capital H, this speculation is indeed idle. In reality the philosophy of history is something much more modest and concrete. It is an attempt to make sense of the observation that in any one society at any one time the values and the knowledge considered binding and plausible differ from those of other societies at other times. Hence, every society's value and knowledge are relative. In this sense one could almost agree with the view that all these systems are ideologies, that is, systems of values and knowledge that are not what they purport to be. They purport to be true and good, but are not. Or at least, they are good and true only in a certain social context at a certain time. They are not absolute knowledge and absolute goodness, but entirely relative. Insofar as they can be shown to be relative, they can be unmasked or exposed to be something other than they claim to be. This can be done in many ways. The early Christians sought to show that the ancient pagans were not justified in their belief in their gods and modern Marxists seek to demonstrate that the practice of democracy is merely an ideological disguise of the manner in which capitalists exploit the proletariat and so forth. In a more general way, the very invention of sociology as the science of society amounted to nothing more and nothing less than the insight that any custom or belief does not serve the purpose it purports to serve but the purpose of keeping the society in which it is practised going. But sociology is content to leave it at that. The philosophy of history, on the other hand, is an attempt to unravel the relationships between these relative systems and to show how they are related to absolute truth. Better, absolute truth consists in the unravelling of the relationships in which these relative systems stand to each other and in that sense, philosophy of history is a search for an absolute truth.

It has always been and still is tempting to think of the relationship of the various relativities or subjectivities (as I have called them) as a causal relationship. One could thus provide a philosophy of history if one could show how the way in which Caesar thought of himself is causally related to the way in which a modern historian thinks of Caesar. Such causal relationships

can be understood as a dialectical relationship or as an evolutionary relationship or both. Even though the number of the subjectivities involved is not infinite and is, in fact, quite limited, it seems
an unrealistic task to search for causal relationships between these
subjectivities. The idea is nevertheless very old. The historical
scheme underlying the concept of a *praeparatio evangelica* is a
good example. It sought to show that the pagan beliefs of the
ancients, though false, stood in a causal or possibly teleological
relationship to those of the Christians. Marx's scheme in which the
progression from feudalism to a society in which the state will
have withered away has to pass through bourgeois capitalism and
the dictatorship of the proletariat is another example. One's
obvious, first criticism of these systems is that they all operate
with the notion that in the end the various subjectivities not
only are seen as causally related to each other but come to be
dissolved in a mental event that is an absolute rather than one
more subjectivity. Even so, one should not underrate the viability
of these systems, especially when they conceive the relationship
between the several subjectivities as a dialectical one.

Dialectical reasoning is very much part and parcel of the subjectivities themselves. It is a mental event.[5] It is a form of trial
and error and in this form it is implicit, though often only ideally,
in the very act of thinking. If one imagines that there is a dialectical relationship between these subjectivities, one is not
foisting an alien character on them. One is merely bringing out
something they contain. Suppose one could meet Caesar and
point out to him that his belief that he was crossing the Rubicon
could have been a disguise of some deeper and unconscious
motive. Or suppose one could get him to admit that the explanation he had propagated was designed to hoodwink his followers
but that it had not hoodwinked Caesar. These suppositions
are within the realm of possibilities because Caesar was able to
think. And if he could think, he could think critically.[6] From
Vico onwards, philosophers of history have tried to account for
the relationship between all the various subjectivities in some such
causal-dialectical scheme of which Toynbee's theory that each
civilisation is the chrysalis of a higher, saviour religion that transcends the civilisation that gave it birth is only the last in a long
line.[7] Such speculations are extrapolations from the raw material
(thoughts) of history. They are perfectly legitimate even though
they are extrapolations. They are one way in which the philosophy
of history fulfills the important and necessary function of helping
us to come to terms with the knowledge that every thought

that is sported and propounded is relative. All the same, one must recall that in chapter 4 an attempt was made to show that the legitimate relationship in which the subjectivities stand to one another is not a causal-dialectical one, let alone an evolutionary one. It was argued there that the only legitimate relationship that can be established between different subjectivities is a typological relationship. The philosophies of history described above all presume that one can go beyond such typological ordering and that one can eventually even find relationships between subjectivities that belong to different and incompatible typological series. I doubt that this is possible and I would prefer a philosophy of history that accomplishes its task of relating the various subjectivities to each other by confining itself to the typology that is inherent in the subjectivities themselves. If one confines oneself in this way, one does not exclude the possibility of seeing all subjectivities related to all other subjectivities in a dialectico-causal manner. A typology of subjectivities and even a typology of typologies would exhibit structural rather than causal relations and thus enable us to relate subjectivities synchronically *as well as* diachronically and, moreover, to establish equivalences between synchronic and diachronic relationships. Any dialectico-causal scheme is unnecessarily tied to diachronic relationships, that is, to the passage of time, and is therefore historicist. The proposed philosophy of history would replace such historicist, dialectico-causal relations by structural relations and thus appear as a non-historicist philosophy of history.[8]

A historicist philosophy of history would endeavour to establish a causal-dialectical relationship between subjectivities as they followed one another in time. It would therefore seek to show how Caesar's explanations of himself are linked to a modern historian's interpretations of Caesar and also to take into account the reasons that might prompt a modern historian, even though he is modern, to confine himself to those explanations that Caesar would have used. But in all cases, the endeavour to investigate and fix these relationships would be ordered chronologically. Given the whole of the preceding argument, this would be a mistake or, at least, an unnecessary self-curtailment. Subjectivities relate to each other absolutely and not just in the order in which they succeed one another in time. Thus, for example, it is ideally just as important to make Caesar intelligible to the modern reader as it is to make the modern reader intelligible to Caesar. The relationship is all-important. The fact that Caesar's explanations of himself preceded the explanations or interpretations of a

modern historian makes no difference. A nonhistoricist philosophy
of history would not be bound by the time sequence of the
various subjectivities but take it as its business to fix the relationships between all of them, regardless which came earlier and which
came later. It would not only disregard the time sequences, but it
would consider the reversal of the time sequences as important as
the time sequence itself.

Whether we pursue a historicist or a nonhistoricist philosophy
of history, we must be careful to distinguish the philosophy of
history from the so-called sociology of knowledge. The latter
merely tries to unmask each system and show its relativity. The
former seeks to establish that each system, though relative, is
related to all other systems. There need be no high-sounding discoveries of a metaphysical nature about the manner in which
Christianity is related to paganism or feudalism to the proletarian
mode of production. One can and must, in the first instance, use
the philosophy of history in a very modest manner to show the
place of, say, Charlemagne or the first British Labour government
in a larger setting. It makes no sense to study either for its own
sake and to know all about Charlemagne or the Labour government if one cannot relate it to what went before and came after
and assign it a slot in a fairly large pattern of events. There is room
for ample misunderstanding here. When I say that there is no
point in studying Charlemagne for his own sake, I do not mean to
say that he ought to be studied for the light such study can throw
on the present. I mean that if we find out all there is to be found
out about Charlemagne, we end up by knowing no more than he
did. We end up by playing the detective inspector. The historian's
interest starts when we can relate everything that was known to
Charlemagne to things that were *not* known to him. The pursuit
of this interest does not mean that we study him for ulterior
reasons or extraneous purposes, such as the light Charlemagne's
experience can throw on semifeudal warfare or old-age pensions.
It means that we extend the explanations Charlemagne and his
friends offered to themselves and the significance they attributed
to their efforts and relate them to other efforts. The real purpose
of a philosophy of history is to make such extension possible and
to increase the number of intelligible relationships.

We must guard against another confusion — the confusion
between philosophy of history and contemporary anthropology.
As long as the British school of functionalism held complete sway
in anthropology, no confusion was likely to arise.[9] On the contrary, one of the most popular and widely known products of that

school, Ruth Benedict's book *Patterns of Culture*[10] made the relevance of functionalist anthropology to the philosophy of history very clear. Functionalism explained every society and every social order as a more or less closed system, and for some people's taste erred perhaps on the side of closedness. In the preface of her book, Benedict specially stressed the relevance of Spengler's philosophy of history because Spengler too had seen the task of a philosophy of history in seeking the relationship or nonrelationship between these closed systems. But at the present time the mood of anthropologists is changing fast. Instead of functionalism, they believe in structuralism. They have lost interest, as indeed they might, in tracing how one social order after another is a functionally integrated system. Instead they seek to find the 'language' common to all and to discover the structure they all share. In this way, contemporary anthropologists are seeking to find the common denominator rather than the differences. The exercises of translation they thus commit themselves to are not easy ones. It is not easy to translate the structure of Australian totemism into a language comprehensible to modern postindustrial man and to make the latter see that his own social order is structurally identical with that of Australian aborigines, the survivors of the oldest stone age. But it can be done and some considerable progress has in fact been made.[11] As a result it is easy to confuse philosophy of history with this search for the common structure. I have indicated in chapter 1 of this book that all historical thought from the compilation of very simple sources to the most speculative philosophy of history is based on one and the same faculty of human reasoning — that is, of reasoning in terms of universals. One can see in this faculty the common denominator because it is indeed the most general structure of all human thought, primitive as well as sophisticated. But this does not mean that the efforts of a philosophy of history are superfluous or should be absorbed into those of structural anthropology. I take it that structural anthropology sees the discovery of the common language as its goal. The philosophy of history sees the discovery of this common denominator merely as its general premise. It starts from this premise as an assumption and then hopes to use it to relate the substances or contents expressed in this way to one another. It is a moot point whether this aim is more or less ambitious than that of structural anthropology. But it clearly is different. The philosophy of history seeks to relate the relative subjectivities of values and ways of life to one another by using the common denominator and does not rest content with the mere discovery of the common denominator. For this reason it is perhaps prone to operate with a common denominator that is less sophisticated and less involved than those toward which structural anthropology is wrestling to evolve. But often a slightly rougher tool will help to do the trick more readily than one that has been endlessly refined. At any rate, to the structural anthropologist the refinement of the tool is the end of the voyage. Given the difference in goal, any debate between philosophy of history and structural anthropology should perhaps be kept at a minimum.

Many people believe that we need a philosophy of history to predict the future. I would prefer to call the prediction of the future either prophecy or futurology. Neither activity has any direct bearing on the philosophy of history though it is not difficult to see why many people should have jumped to the conclusion that it has. A philosophy of history, like ordinary historical narrative, is essentially concerned with the past, that is, with what happened and with a special manner of understanding what has happened. It enlarges and extends the rudimentary units of intelligibility that are part and parcel of what has happened. That is all.

It is true that the extension of the intelligible unit of meaning has led many people into the temptation to use such extension to predict the future rather than to understand the past. The temptation is understandable but not pardonable. People have often given way to this temptation so much that the prediction of the future has come to be identified as the main characteristic of the philosophy of history. In view of the whole preceding argument, however, such prediction of the future cannot be justified. The only thing that can be said about the future is that historians will be likely to use the same intellectual equipment they have used so far to understand the past. *Historiae rerum gestarum*, if they continue to be written, will be similar to the histories of the past. But it cannot possibly follow that *res gestae* will be determined by and can be predicted on the basis of what we know so far. The belief that an understanding of the past can lead to a prediction of the future is part and parcel of the belief that what we know as history is something that has been copied by the historian from reality. We have seen time and again that that belief is untenable.[12]

In some senses, however, the future is predictable, history or no history. The whole Popperian model of scientific explanation was based on the idea that one can, given certain initial conditions and a general law, make a prognosis; and a prognosis is nothing if not a prediction. On the level of commonsense and everyday life, we could not live unless we made predictions. If I rise from my desk to answer the telephone, it is predictable that I will do so unless there is an earthquake or I have a heart attack. And one does not have to be a necromancer to know in advance that two trains travelling in opposite directions on the same rail will collide unless they stop. Nor need one have recourse to black magic to predict that some people or whole societies will, under certain circumstances, destroy themselves. All one needs to know is the old epigram that the man whom the gods want to destroy, they first make mad. Perhaps the most remarkable prediction I have ever come across is the one implied in Tocqueville's *Democracy in America*, written before the middle of the nineteenth century. Tocqueville himself made no predictions but merely described American society. But he did it in such a way that he was able to pinpoint its most salient features and precisely those features that were to shape its history during the coming century. It has, therefore, often been observed that the best modern books written on American society read like glosses on extrapolations from Tocqueville.[13]

There are, apart from people who speculate about the future, talented prophets who thunder predictions to alter the course of events. They predict in the hope that people will not want these predictions to come true and that people will therefore change their behaviour. Often enough, they are disappointed in their expectation that people will alter their behaviour and their predictions, against all hope, do in fact prove to have been correct. Then there are predictions that are quite implausible but that, provided they are accepted by a sufficiently large number of people, will provide their own verification. If enough people believe in their truth, they will alter their behaviour to ensure that the situation predicted will come about.

I mention these examples to show that our desire to predict the future is not only legitimate but also, in certain cases, both salutary and possible. But the connections between the prediction of the future and a philosophy of history is accidental rather than essential, and when people pursue a philosophical understanding of history all the better to predict the future, they are doing so at their own risk and are pursuing the philosophy of history for illegitimate reasons. All history, even the philosophy of history, is concerned with the past. The predictive value of a philosophy of history lies somewhere else. It does not assist us to know what will happen in the future where the 'future' is tomorrow. But since it does make the past intelligible, it makes it seem as if what happened in the seventeenth century could have been predictable in the sixteenth century, if not earlier. In this sense, it does assist us to understand the future, where 'future' means a series of events that already have taken place but that were future with respect to what went before. It does not follow that since a twentieth-century philosopher of history can say that the seventeenth century was 'predictable' now that he is looking back on the sixteenth century, he is also able to predict what the twenty-first century will be like.[14] The philosopher of history can say that what happened in the seventeenth century was predictable because he knows what happened and can present a view of the sixteenth century that makes sense in terms of what happened in the seventeenth century. But he cannot possibly do such a thing without knowing both the sixteenth and seventeenth centuries. In short, he can only predict the past, never the future.

The extension of historical understanding to a philosophy of history is legitimate and it is natural that our very first thought should turn to the theory of progress. For a long time it has been assumed that mankind progresses and that the general framework of progress provides the comprehensive truth that can relate all the many stories that have been told about the past to one another. The shift from paganism to Christianity or Islam and the shift from parochial tribalism to ecumenical imperialism were all held to be signs of progress and made the concept of progress into a very plausible philosophy of history. Then came the time when the prospect of material improvements, of rapid scientific and technological discoveries, made the idea of progress seem an even more plausible explanation of the course of history. It was even held that awareness of progress would speed it up and that a rise in the standard of living would soften manners and morals and lead to a mental improvement of man. But pollution and over-population and two World wars, Vietnam, and Auschwitz have made us see progress through the matrix of Huxley's *Brave New World* and Orwell's *1984*. If such experiences have made the fact of progress appear doubtful, we have also recognised that progress is morally reprehensible because it leads invariably to the destruction of other races and to indigenous religious and ethnic parochialism.[15] Doubt in the reality of progress as well as moral scruples have conspired, therefore, to make the idea of progress a very outmoded philosophy of history.

Despite these doubts, one should not throw out the idea of progress without further careful examination. The conventional reasons discussed in the preceding paragraph amount to little more

than emotional reactions and ethical scruples. These reactions
and scruples come and go as political winds of change influence
the conscience of mankind. One should never underrate the
importance of that conscience; but one should not lightly allow it
to become the basis for the direction of an intellectual inquiry,
especially as one can notice that that conscience is always very
sensitive to the fortuitous drift of economic and political constellations, that is, to factors that are extraneous to an intellectual
enquiry.

J. H. Plumb, in his book entitled *The Death of the Past*,[16] has
quite recently argued that the study of history will atrophy unless
it can attach itself once more to the theory of progress. If by
'theory of progress' he means a philosophy of history, one must
agree with him. But he means something more narrow. He means
'progress' in the old sense. He does manage to give it a real meaning by focussing his attention on one very small development in
historical studies. He shows that modern critical historical scholarship emerged when European historians were confronted with the
fact that the semimythical traditions of what the past was like
were found to be inconsistent with one another. He considers the
sorting out of these inconsistencies to be a sort of progress —
which it undoubtedly was. Finally he comes up with the proclamation that the substitution of critical history for mythical tradition
is progress and that such an increase in critical rejection of mythical tradition is all we need to restore our confidence in progress.
To begin with, one must object that this view of progress is
narrow because it refers only to intellectual-critical progress. Next,
one must doubt Plumb's cogency because we know that the
opposition between myth and critical history is by no means
absolute and that at many times the one emerges into the other.
This has been explained in detail in chapter 5. And finally we
cannot see how Plumb's view can establish a simple belief in
progress because we know the nineteenth- and twentieth-century
historians were by no means the first to doubt the complete
veracity of the myths alleged to have taken place in the past.
If, therefore, Plumb means by progress the rejection of the past
(where 'past' means the view that one's knowledge of the past
is an uncritical acceptance of mythical fables), progress has taken
place many times and been followed by lack of progress. People's
criticism of traditions vary enormously and it is quite wrong to
see such criticism, as Plumb does, as a unique and irreversible
event. Plumb is really only a latter-day Voltaire, who thought of
the Middle Ages much as Plumb thinks of the past in general.

Nevertheless, if we must reject Plumb's derivation of the notion of progress, we might probe modern scepticism of progress and ask ourselves whether progress is in fact not much more real than our well-founded scepticism allows.

Modern scepticism of progress is quite unjustified. There is really much more meat in the concept of progress than most modern thinkers allow. To begin with, one must take care that one formulates clearly what one means by the notion of progress. If one takes it to mean that primitive societies that exist in the twentieth century are fossilised survivals of protohistorical or paleolithic times, the notion is nonsensical. At least, to become sensible, we would have to invoke a great many hypotheses other than the hypothesis that there is progress. In its original form[17] it says that all societies are under pressure to progress and that such progression is the key to our understanding of all societies. Unfortunately, the notion of progress is usually put forward in this nonsensical form in which it was so popular during the nineteenth century. But if one turns the formulation round, the nonsense disappears. One can formulate the idea of progress by saying that modern societies are a departure from primitivism and that, where primitive societies exist in the twentieth century, they are societies to which the idea of progress is not applicable. By standing the nineteenth-century formula of progress on its head, it becomes fruitful.[18] Moreover, by standing it on its head it loses its connotation of iron-clad law. When it is stood on its head, one can see that progress was not necessary and that it not only did not have to happen, but also that it could have happened in a completely different way.[19]

Next, we might add that whatever there is in the idea of progress as a philosophy of history, it is an interpretative device for shaping time. It is certainly not an explanation of what happened. If it were explanatory, it would amount to saying that the ancient Egyptians were consciously paving the way for the emergence of Greece and Rome — a view that is patently absurd. We know that the ancient Egyptians could not possibly have explained themselves to themselves in this way. Unfortunately, critics of the idea of progress as a viable philosophy of history usually assume that it is supposed to be explanatory rather than interpretative and then have an easy time in showing that it is absurd.

It is now almost certain that *homo sapiens* existed for half a million years, living in small bands kept together by nothing but the biological bonds of kinship, and inventing, throughout this long span of time, nothing more than fire and a few rudimentary

tools made of chipped flints. And then, about ten thousand years
B.C. men discovered agriculture and a sedentary life, and within
another four or five thousand years, they had organised themselves
in urban communities, institutionalised religion, and were beginning to invent writing and a dozen other devices. Then again there
was a pause of almost four thousand years, until the seventeenth
century, since which in rapid succession men discovered gravity,
electricity, relativity and quantum mechanics, and learnt to split
the atom.

Unfortunately this simple grand view of progress has become
completely confused by the writings of modern ethologists. They
all endeavour to draw our attention to the fact that modern man,
even though he can fly to the moon, has not yet mastered his
aggressive instincts and is therefore still inferior in many important ways to all sorts of animals who have. Hence modern ethology
lends support to the conventional view propounded jointly from
pulpits and newspapers that man is intellectually very clever but
morally hopelessly backward. It may well be true that man has
not mastered his aggressive instincts in the sense that genetically
there has been no great change. We have learnt, however, that it
is possible to repress and control them. In the oldest nomadic
hordes that used to roam the earth in search for food and animals
and even in the earliest agricultural sedentary communities,
membership was small. Obviously, the only bond capable of
keeping people together more or less peacefully was the bond
of blood relationship. When that was absent, a man was considered a stranger and had to be killed. He could not be trusted to
cooperate. Eventually there began the urban revolution, which
must have taken place within three or four milennia after the
development of agriculture. It consisted, among other things, in
the fact that people were beginning to live together in groups
larger than clans, that is, larger than communities based on blood
relationship. It was now possible for two or three clans to live
together and in some cases it was possible to find a formula for
the admission of complete strangers. In other words, the numerical
extension of the viable community was based on the discovery of
a social formula that superseded the biological fact of blood
relationship. People could now be held together and could cooperate either on terms of equality or on terms of master-slave relation
without actually being related to each other by blood. A sociocultural form of bonding had been invented. Within the new type
of bonding, violence and aggression was up to a point controlled
and moral imperatives were developed to underpin this control.

The progress was colossal. It made no difference that, failing the sociocultural sanctions, people were genetically just as aggressive as before. The invention of the new sociocultural bond made it possible for men to live together comparatively peacefully without having to wait for another step in evolution or for a genetic change. There always have been and will be throwbacks. But they are, from a social point of view, pathological cases. Here we have real progress in morals, which far outdistanced any progress that has ever been made in the intellectual field.

There has been progress also in a different sense. There has been obvious progress in consciousness. During the three centuries immediately preceding the Christian era, during the period that Karl Jaspers[20] called the 'Axis Period' of history, it was discovered in several places that there is a morality superior to the retributive morality that had been current in small tribal societies and in the larger empires that had replaced them. The old tribal morality was retributive in the sense that people took an eye for an eye and generally passed on any wrong done to them either to the wrong-doer if they could catch him or to somebody else who happened to be within reach. Eventually the sins of the fathers were visited on the children. The new morality, which was developed and which found its starkest expression in the Buddha and in Jesus, taught that men must become like shockabsorbers and *not* pass on every wrong they suffer. It is true that this enormous change in consciousness did not produce any world-shaking changes in behaviour. But the growth of moral consciousness was irreversible. Once posited, the knowledge continued to be available and when available but not heeded, people are forced to develop all sorts of strategies of evasion, resentment, repression, and apology to justify their refusal to avail themselves of that knowledge.[20]

Two thousand years later, there was another Axis Period — another leap forward in self-consciousness. It came to be understood that all knowledge is relative and that people can differ in their values and beliefs without being actually 'wrong'. Moreover, it was found that it is possible to establish large systems of social cooperation on the basis that men are equal and that they should share the fruits of labour equally. Again, as after the first Axis Period, these insights were not immediately translated into practice, though there is now in many parts of the world a more equitable distribution of the fruits of labour than there was before. Equally important during this last leap of progress was the discovery that it is possible to bond people socially in a manner that is so neutral that people of the most diverse religious beliefs and

racial backgrounds can live side by side sufficiently well to make
an unprecedented division of labour possible, thereby raising the
standard of living far beyond the wildest dreams of earlier generations and making possible the implementation of the most complex technological inventions to increase production. Last not
least, following the dictates of equality, men have moved far
toward building welfare states, which have reintroduced all those
principles of social care and cooperation and welfare that used
to be taken for granted in primitive societies but that were usually
neglected and lost during the centuries of transformation. Finally,
during the second Axis Period it has come to be recognised that
the system of neutral bonding makes religion superfluous. During
all preceding millennia religious ritual and, to a slightly lesser
extent, religious belief were necessary not so much for their own
sake as for the sake of a basis of social cooperation. Religious
ritual shaped a community. During the second Axis Period, men
discovered not only the possibility but the necessity of a secular
society. If they wanted to pursue equality and economic rationalisation, they had to bond themselves to each other in a neutral
manner and leave religious belief and ritual to private life. The
extrusion of religion will, eventually, create its own problems.
For the presence of religion as the basis for social bonding provided important by-products. It encouraged metaphysical doctrines
and instilled a sense of the meaning of existence. The disappearance
of religion as a basis for social cooperation has deprived men of
these by-products of religion and it remains to be seen whether
men can survive or how they can survive without them. Leaving
this last question aside, there can be no reasonable doubt that
there has been progress and that only a superficial observer will
keep on mouthing the platitude that men have advanced intellectually and remained morally backward.

If this is so, and if the conventional and temporarily fashionable reasons for dismissing the idea of progress as a philosophy of
history are wrong, why can we not use the theory of progress as a
unifying philosophy of history? The answer is unfortunately very
simple. On the older view of progress, progress was alleged to be
more or less steady and continuous. It was not necessarily uniform
in that it was admitted that there were periods of recession such
as the Middle Ages in Europe or the Dark Ages that intervened
between Mycenean culture and the rise of Greek civilisation. But
barring these interludes, the view that progress is the genuine
philosophy of history is only acceptable if one thinks of it as
slowly continuous. Now while I have argued that progress is very

real and especially real in the moral field, I must also admit that
it is far from continuous. There was progress when agriculture was
invented and sedentary life became possible. There was further
progress when a new form of social bonding was invented that
made urban life possible and that helped to create large communities in which a real division of labour became possible, leading
to a rising standard of living. There was more progress during the
first Axis Period. But between then and the eighteenth century,
when the modern technetronic age began, nothing happened.
There was a huge gap of five thousand years between the invention
of agriculture and the urban revolution; a second wide gap of three
thousand years between the urban revolution and the first Axis
Period; and a wide gap of over two thousand years between the
first and second Axis periods. These gaps are too large to afford
a pattern of historical progression. Progress, though real, is too
general a concept. We can use it as a philosophy of history only
if we are prepared to disregard everything that happened between
the time when Ur of the Chaldeans flourished and the age of Jesus,
and between the first and second Axis periods. Perhaps there is
something to be said for such a grand view. It would make all the
intervening gaps of several millennia into 'middle ages' during
which nothing in particular took place. But historians who are
interested in anything more detailed will find that the concept of
progress is unsuitable. There is so much more history to be studied
than mere progress. Progress only happens once every two or three
thousand years; but potential subject matter for history happens
all the time. A philosophy of history based on the concept of
progress is, therefore, not false but too thin.[22]

If we have to discard the idea of progress as a philosophy of
history after all, we have to fall back upon other philosophies of
history. To begin with there is the philosophy of history that was
widely accepted for many centuries. It is firmly Christian in that
it embodies a large part of the Christian myth. It does so not only
by shaping itself in the image of that myth but by retaining part
of that myth as part of the story. According to that philosophy
the meaning of history consists in the fact that the world was
created by God so that men could follow His law. When they
failed to do so, He eventually provided firmer support by incar-
nating Himself in a man who died a sacrificial death. That death,
ritually celebrated once a year, affords support for a guarantee of
redemption. Redemption finally is made available at the Second
Coming of Christ.

There is no need to go into details and to explain the many

possible variations. Almost everything in this story is capable of different interpretations: the meaning of redemption, the nature of the sacrifice, the operation of the yearly ritual, the effect of divine providence. It is clear that this philosophy of history affords ample opportunity to fit every event that happens into its appropriate slot, though it is equally clear that there will be much opportunity for argument as to which slot is appropriate for any event. It is also clear that this philosophy of history is completely dependent on the survival of the Christian myth, which appears in it as part of the actual sequence of events. When that myth ceased to command support, the philosophy of history was bound to lose appeal. In a more general sense all theologically oriented philosophies of history fall short of the requirements of the practising historian because they do not offer slots or patterns into which particular phases and stories can be fitted. Their main preoccupation is with religion — that is, they ask when the Messiah will come and when the *saeculum* will end. The pattern they offer is defined only at the end of the story and possibly at the beginning and the middle (e.g., Incarnation). But everything else in between is left as open as in the theory of progress. They are useless as philosophies of history not because of their large mythic content but because they are too general and too sweeping.

If we find that the ordinary theory of progress and even a theologically oriented philosophy of history are too sweeping to be of practical assistance to the historian when he tries to find a slot for any particular story that has happened, we must start by taking a look at Hegel. Hegel tried to put teeth into the theory of progress. He managed to do it in the following manner.

To understand the full import and scope of Hegel's idea of history, we must begin with his *Phenomenology of the Spirit* of 1806. It contains all the original thoughts and is the real starting point for an understanding of his philosophy of history — much more so than the lectures he delivered later on the subject in Berlin.[23] Unfortunately he wrote the *Phenomenology of the Spirit* under great pressure,[24] and the work is therefore no masterpiece of literature and presents his thoughts in an uninviting manner. The leading idea, that there is a profound and inner connection between the history of mankind and the logico-genetic development of human thinking, nevertheless, emerges clearly. Hegel had discovered that there is an essential relationship — not just a coincidental parallelism — between the way in which men have developed their powers of thought and the course of their historical development. When the earliest men started thinking,

they did so intuitively. They looked at objects but were unaware
that they were looking at something other than themselves. Next
they became more critical and observed that the object they were
looking at was an object other than their own mind. Next, they
became *conscious* of the fact that the object they were looking at
was different from their own mind. And, finally, they became
aware that human thinking had developed in this particular
way from intuitive awareness to self-conscious knowledge of the
nature of thinking. Since there was a parallelism between the
development of methods of thinking and the course of history,
Hegel came to the conclusion that the history of mankind is the
autobiography of the Idea. The Idea was, among other things, the
totality of all human thought hypostatised. The philosophy of
history, for Hegel, is therefore a historical consciousness that not
only knows itself as such but also reflects on the conditions of its
knowledge. In the end, the philosophy of history consists in the
confluence of the knowledge of the methodological principles and
the knowledge of what happened in the past. For every stage of
thinking, there is a stage in sociopolitical institutions and art and
religion.

Throughout the *Phenomenology of the Spirit* Hegel explained
that consciousness is an ultimate and that the primary concern of
philosophical understanding is to grasp how we experience consciousness.[25] Statements about consciousness have no referent
other than themselves. There is nothing over and above a statement about the quality of character of my consciousness that, if
the case, could make the statement true or false. If I say I am
sad, there is no 'sadness' other than the sadness I am referring to
in my statement. There is nothing at which I could look and
which could serve as a test whether my statement that I am sad is
correct or incorrect.

Hegel then recognised that there is an original or primitive,
unreflective consciousness in which sensibilities are not dissociated
and in which subject and object do not glower at each other in
the knowledge that they are not one and the same thing. Consciousness that is aware of the object of its consciousness, however,
is reflexive and subject to a dissociation of sensibilities. It is aware
of the object it is looking at as something different from itself.
But it longs to return to its original condition.

Hegel believed that it is impossible to retrace one's steps. Once
dissociation has taken place and reflection has begun, thinking
must move forward. Hence he surmised, as many other philosophers, mystics, and prophets had done before him, that though

our end is as our beginning, ultimate self-awareness is not a simple return to the primitive state of nonreflective consciousness. On the contrary, at the end of time, the dissociation of sensibilities and the subject-object confrontation will cease through a total self-awareness of the process consciousness has traversed.

It goes without saying that this history of the development of consciousness is a history that is figured into a well-known mythical scheme and there is no need in this context to examine in detail the manner in which this was done. One can suppose that Hegel's early preoccupations with theology had left their indelible mark.[26] The important point to notice, however, is that with this theory, Hegel saw that the life of consciousness has a history and that that history is the autobiography of the Idea. He underlined his knowledge of the historicity of consciousness by two arguments on which he worked for the rest of his life. First, he put forward an analysis of logical thinking in which he demonstrated that if one thinks of thought, one is recapitulating all the stages of consciousness so that the three stages are necessitated by, or parallel to, our very conception of what it means to think. We start off by knowing no more than that A equals A. Then we recognise that A is not the same as B. Next we understand that A *is* like B because we have become conscious of the fact that the object we think confronts us is really an extrusion of our own consciousness. And, finally, we end up by seeing that A is indeed the same as A, though by now we do not mean by this knowledge the same thing that we meant when this equation was first established. When it was first established it was an intuition and the equivalence was implicit and unknown. Now, in the end, the equivalence is known because we have come to understand that in thinking we are thinking thoughts[27] and we know that we have arrived at the stage at which we are thinking thoughts by a certain route.

Second, Hegel applied the theory that history is the autobiography of the Idea to historical knowledge as we understand it. In this philosophy of history he showed that the progress of consciousness is a progress from the East to the West, which displays a development from the freedom of one person to the freedom of all persons. But bluntly, he tried to show that viewed philosophically on a broad scale, the course of history runs from China to Prussia.[28]

If the last sentence is an anticlimax and suggests that Hegel's thinking on history moved from the sublime to the ridiculous, we should pause before we form hasty judgments. The reason why I have explained Hegel's approach to the philosophy of history at such length is that it bears out the analysis of historical knowledge presented in the present book. When Hegel finally concluded that history moves from east to west he did not mean to make (as his parallelism between history and the genesis of ultimate self-consciousness shows) a statement about *res gestae*. He meant to make a statement about *historia rerum gestarum*. He knew perfectly well that the past consisted of more things than were dreamt of in his philosophy and that time as a totality was infinitely larger than anything he or anybody else could ever know. He meant to say that there must be a parallelism between the growth of consciousness and the ultimately large-scale historical narrative we can put forward because our knowledge of time is constituted in such a way as to make no other kind of narrative possible.

He undoubtedly overstated his case. We have seen on many occasions in previous chapters that there is a vast variety of possible interpretations and that even when we confine ourselves to those that are typologically related to the explanations given by the people of the past, there are many more ways of interpreting what happened than Hegel thought. But this objection is neither here nor there. Although it detracts from the claim that his philosophy of history was the ultimate philosophy of history, it still leaves him with the enormous merit to have recognised that there is a connection between every historical narrative and the manner in which we are conscious of what has happened. His real contribution lies in the fact that he enlarged upon and explained in detail how it is possible that while *esse* is not *percipi* (as Berkeley had thought), *configuratio essendi* is *percipi*. This is precisely the view advanced in this book and Hegel has shown how one can transform this general insight into a concrete and tangible historical narrative.

This matter has already been discussed in chapter 4, where I tried to show how Hegel had helped us to understand why universals are subjectivities and why and how these subjectivities are interchangeable. We can now take his contribution a step further and see that Hegel meant to show that one subjectivity is related to another subjectivity in a necessary rather than in a random manner. The relationships between the several subjectivities, be they explanations or interpretations, are not random but are controlled by the steps that lead from consciousness to self-consciousness and from self-consciousness to reason, and from reason to the knowledge of the whole process, which knowledge is the Idea. Again, one may doubt whether one should consider his demonstration that the relations between these subjectivities and the gradual substitutions of interpretations for explanations and the final absorption of all substitutions in the Idea is the final truth or the only way of conceiving these relationships. There may be alternatives and there is even a possibility that Hegel was wrong in thinking that the relationships between the subjectivities were not random. All this will remain a matter for argument. But it cannot detract from the great merit of his contribution.

We ought to ask ourselves how he had managed to arrive at such understanding. With uncanny power of prophecy, Hegel saw, at the beginning of the nineteenth century that mankind was standing on the threshold of an entirely new epoch. He did nothing less and nothing more than to predict the step toward self-consciousness that we were about to take. So far people had been conscious of this and of that. From now on, he saw, people would be conscious of consciousness. This insight was indeed all the more remarkable because Hegel himself knew, at this point, no more than the Enlightenment. And his experience of the Enlightenment had taught him no more than that things were not quite what they had appeared to have been. Myth and theology had been called into question; the French Revolution had proposed the possibility of social equality; established churches seemed less absolutely founded in the will of God than people had thought and the age of the earth was probably greater than the Bible had taught. Extrapolating from these and similar doubts about the conventional wisdom of mankind, Hegel proceeded to generalise and predicted that in the final epoch of mankind, men would become conscious of self-consciousness. Today, we have had Marx ('people are not what they are but what they eat'), and Freud ('people do not think what they think they think, but think what they do not think they think'), and have been taught by Einstein that neither time nor space is an absolute system of coordinates. We have been taught by the study of language that sentences do not simply describe reality. Similarly we know that no observation is a mirror image and that the observer is as important a factor as the matter that is observed and that the methods of observation and the media of description are as vital a part of our knowledge of the world as the world itself. There is nothing we can know or think without knowing that our knowledge or action, over and above being knowledge and action, is also, in turn, an object of knowledge subject to the methods and media of all other kinds of knowledge. When we bear all this in mind, Hegel's original proclamation, if it has a fault, sounds too modest. We certainly accept it without further question. But whether it now appears too modest or commonplace or not, it was and still is the most general characterisation of the modern stage of thought we possess. And, as Hegel suggested, it is impossible at the present time to imagine how it can ever be transcended. For any transcension would merely confirm that we are being conscious of being conscious and that consciousness itself has become an object of experience. A transcension of transcension would merely be yet another transcension. Whichever way we turn, there is no getting away from the crucial role of Hegel.

What exactly does all this have to do with the philosophy of history? So far we have examined how Hegel laid the foundations for the possibility of deriving a philosophy of history from the consideration of the nature of historical knowledge, because he had understood that when we are talking of historical knowledge we are not talking of knowledge of *res gestae* but of *historia rerum gestarum*. Hegel thought, of course, that he had not only laid the foundations for the possibility of such a philosophy of history but that he had laid the foundations for the necessity of such a philosophy of history and that no other possibility was conceivable. As I said earlier, there is no need to follow him in this last conclusion. But let us now turn to an examination of the particular manner in which he presented his philosophy of history as a large-scale narrative. As the theory stands in *The Phenomenology of the Spirit*, it foreshadows modern existential psychology much more than a philosophy of history. But in time Hegel proceeded to expand his argument. The situation in which one consciousness confronts another is both preceded and succeeded by another. It is preceded by a situation in which consciousness simply reflects the outside world and succeeded by a situation in which philosophers understand that both the situation itself and the situation that preceded it are the natural history of the human spirit. The final stage of the spirit is therefore a situation in which one understands how one understands. There is, thus, a succession of three stages. First there is a situation of unconsciousness; then, a situation of consciousness in confrontation; and finally, a stage of complete self-consciousness, the object of which is the way in which we understand our own consciousness. Looking back from the last stage of complete self-consciousness, Hegel understood how other people had understood themselves and then proceeded to interpret history in terms of these three states.

The history he interpreted was, of course, the history he knew. He had started with Herodotus and learnt about the resistance of the free Greek city-states to Persian despotism. He knew of the quality of Athenian democracy from Thucydides and of the rise of Rome from Livy. He had followed the decline of Roman imperial power through Tacitus and derived his knowledge of the Christian church as the depository of an ethic that was more universal than that of the classical city-state largely from Gibbon.[29] And so on to the French Revolution, which demolished by violence the institutions that continued to stand in the way of the unfolding of the last period. The nineteenth-century Prussian state, finally, was being built up in direct response to the collapse of Napoleon, rationally organised in such a way as to obviate the need for another French Revolution. To Hegel the Prussian state in the era of the Restoration was the Enlightenment of the last stage translated into practice.[30]

It is easy today, looking back, to ridicule this whole conception. In retrospect, the ministers of the Prussian enlightenment do not seem to deserve the admiration Hegel protested for them. They were unaware of the impending Industrial Revolution and the eventual emancipation of the masses. In an important sense Hegel had understood that the stage of absolute spirit was reached when he understood that all there is to be understood is how people understand themselves. It was a historical accident that he hitched his grasp of the absolute spirit to the political conditions of early nineteenth-century Prussia. Nothing but confusion results when we overrate this historical accident and continue to discuss Hegel as the lackey of the Prussian monarchy. The advent of the absolute spirit, the final stage of self-consciousness, is a real and irreversible event. But its identification with the Prussian state of the early nineteenth century is not, and is, at worst, an excusable error of judgment.

When I say that Hegel proceeded to interpret the history he knew in terms of the growth of consciousness, I take 'interpretation' here to mean interpretation in the technical sense in which it was defined in chapter 4. He summed it all up in his *Lectures on the Philosophy of History* in one magnificent sweep. History, he said, is a progress from east to west. First there is the stage in which only one man is free — the Persian despot. Then comes a stage in which some men are free — the ruling classes of the ancient city-state. Next comes a thrust toward growing numbers of free men through the expansion of Christianity. And finally there comes a stage when all men are free because they are part of the rational organisation provided by the reformed constitution of the nineteenth-century Prussian state.

It is not too difficult to see what had happened in Hegel's
mind. First of all he had reached his understanding of the growth
of understanding. Then he had combined this growth with his
knowledge of the great historians, not with his knowledge of
History. His vision of the past was not a vision of the past but a
vision of the major historians from Herodotus to the medieval
chroniclers like Otto of Freising or Bossuet, who, following
Saint Augustine, had depicted the triumph of the church as the
tail-end of the story that had begun in the Garden of Eden. Finally
he had interpreted what Herodotus had said about the Persians
and their despotism as the stage in which consciousness was dumb
because it reflected nothing but objects and came up with the
doctrine that in the first stage of history freedom was limited to
one man. When every man's consciousness is a dumb reflection of
nonsentient objects, man cannot be aware of himself; therefore he
does not understand what is going on and is the willing slave of
a despot. Next is the stage in which men are conscious of each
other and are conscious that other men are conscious. Hegel
identified this stage with the condition in which some men are
free at the expense of others. Finally, Hegel interpreted the
reforms of the Prussian state in the early nineteenth century with
the stage of the absolute spirit in which all men understand how
understanding works and in which they can, therefore, live together only in open realisation of the laws necessary for peaceful
cooperation. It is often taken for granted that Hegel first worked
out his theory of understanding and then interpreted the history
he knew. But one could equally argue that it is no coincidence
that the history he knew suggested this particular interpretation
to him. It may look like an *a priori* attempt to write history but
may in fact be nothing but an interpretation of the historical
sequences he had learnt from the historians he knew. Wherever his
starting point, his philosophy of history is really a summary of
the stories told by the great historians with an interpretation
added to make it intelligible to the absolute spirit.

On closer examination this whole sweep of narrative runs
actually parallel to the narratives of the great historians Hegel
knew and is therefore much more 'empirical' than most people
think. The word 'empirical' is really a misnomer; but it serves
here to indicate that Hegel was not an *a priorist* or armchair
speculator. True, he did not spend time in archives. But he had
read the narratives of other historians and derived his own conception from them. And since they in turn did not observe *res
gestae* but other mininarratives, we can see that the process of

composition that culminated in Hegel's philosophy of history is merely an extension of the way in which our knowledge of history is constructed. He even went one stage further. He not only used the earlier historians like Herodotus and Thucydides for information, but also considered them as instances of a very early form of consciousness:

> To this category belong *Herodotus, Thucydides*, and other historians of the same order, whose descriptions are for the most part limited to deeds, events, and states of society, which they had before their eyes, and whose spirit they shared. They simply transferred what was passing in the world around them, to the realm of re-presentative intellect. An external phenomenon is thus translated into an internal conception. In the same way the *poet* operates upon the material supplied him by his emotions; projecting it into an image for the conceptive faculty. These original historians did, it is true, find statements and narratives of other men ready to hand. One person cannot be an eye or ear witness of everything. But they make use of such aids only as the poet does of that heritage of an already-formed language, to which he owes so much; merely as an ingredient.[31]

I think that Hegel was probably wrong in his judgment of Herodotus and Thucydides and that he underrated their self-consciousness. He was here obviously carried away by the momentum of his own theory. But since he believed that he was right, one cannot dismiss him as an armchair speculator but has to give him credit for studying history the only way in which it can be studied — that is, by studying other narratives. Indeed, his comments on Thucydides and Herodotus, true or not, are examples of very astute source criticism on which neither Ranke nor Seignobos could have improved and it is fair to surmise that they would not have been capable of such subtle critical reading of these Greek writers. On Hegel's critical view of these writers, there is, therefore, a parallelism between the earliness of the information they provide and the earliness of their method of comprehending and presenting this information. His view of these authors, translated into our terminology, amounts to saying that they provided explanations and that Hegel accepted these explanations and did not replace them by interpretations. He took them to work like poets who operate on material supplied by the emotions, projecting it into an image for the conceptual faculty. And Hegel took their method at its face value — as many a good historian would — and concluded that their method was characteristic of the manner in which the ancient Greeks of the sixth century saw themselves and explained themselves to themselves.[32]

Hegel, then, was no simple *a priorist* and I can do no better than quote in full a passage from Hayden V. White:

> It is noteworthy that these phases can be regarded as indicating existential relationships, as ways of explaining those relationships, as ways of representing them, or as ways of symbolizing their 'meaning' within the whole process of Roman historical development. The important point is that, to Hegel, what Rome *was* at any given stage of its evolution was not considered to be reducible to *what it did*, to an effect of an exhaustive set of causes, to merely a formal coherence (that is, generic case), or to a self-enclosed totality of relationships. In other words, the identification of a historical state of affairs as constituting a phase, the explanation of why it is what it is, the characterization of its formal attributes, and the relations which it sustains with other phases of the whole process are all conceived to have equal worth as elements of the total characterization of both the phases and the whole process in which they appear. Of course, to those who regard Hegel as nothing but a practitioner of a priori method of historical representation, all these ways of characterizing a phase in the history of a civilization appear as nothing but *projections* of the categories of the dialectic: the in itself (thesis), the for itself (antithesis), and the in and for itself (synthesis), followed by a negation of the synthesis, which itself implies a new thesis (which is nothing but a new in itself), and so on, without end.
>
> It is true that one could effect such a conceptual reduction of Hegel's method of analysis, and in a way that might not have offended Hegel himself, since he regarded these categories as fundamental to both logic and ontology and as the key to the comprehension of any process, whether of being or of consciousness.
>
> But, in accordance with my way of characterizing his thought, in terms of the linguistic modes utilized in his characterizations, not only of the stages of being and logic, but also of history, I prefer to view these phases as conceptualizations of different modes of relationship in general as generated by Hegel's insight into the levels on which language, and therefore consciousness itself, had to operate.[33]

It is true that Hegel did argue that particular information does not matter, provided one grasps the principles of change and development (i.e., the shape time assumes when one omits irrelevancies and links relevant event to relevant event). This argument has caused him to be held up to ridicule and academic historians, ever since Ranke, have dismissed him as an *a priorist*. But far from denying sound historical method, as Ranke thought, Hegel only went a little bit further than all ordinary historians. His *a priorism* is not substantially different from the *a priorism* of all ordinary historians. The real difference between him and his academic detractors is that he was aware of his *a priorism*. The academic historian's air of superiority is therefore completely unjustified. It is perfectly true, as we have seen on several occasions in the preceding pages, that his theory sometimes ran away with him and that he may have even erred a little by failing to keep a reasonable balance between truth and meaning as discussed in chapter 5. But the unqualified dismissal of Hegel as a philosopher of history by historians who profess to write empirically grounded narrative is absurd.

After Hegel, one ought to consider Marx. But Marx, according to the argument here presented, is disqualified as a philosopher of history. To avoid misunderstanding, I would like to state expressly that this disqualification applies only to his philosophy of history, which says that history is the history of class struggles, that the authority of the state exists to assure the exploitation of one class by another, that religion and culture are ideologies supposed to disguise the harshness of such exploitation, and that communalism was succeeded by feudalism, feudalism by capitalism, and that capitalism will be succeeded by communism during which last phase the state will wither away. Marx's contributions to the social sciences and to our understanding of politics are both fertile and influential. But I am not concerned with this aspect of his thought.

Marx's philosophy of history, at first sight, recalls the infiguration into a mythic pattern. It exhibits the same form as the myth in which the end is like the beginning. If Marx had appealed to myth and had been aware of his debt, one would have to take his philosophy of history seriously because it would then have taken its place beside all historical narrative and all other philosophies of history. Even if Marx had not openly acknowledged his debt, it would have to be taken seriously. The reason why it is disqualified is that Marx explicitly propounded his philosophy of history and all the lesser narratives it contains as the result of an empirical study of *res gestae*. He was not only unaware of the *a priori* assumptions that have to go into the construction of narrative; he made it a vital point of his argument that there were none and that he had discovered the real nature of *res gestae* and had not written yet another *historia rerum gestarum*.

This point follows directly from his famous dictum that he had stood Hegel on his head. He had indeed stood him on his head. But Hegel is not the sort of philosopher one *can* stand on his head.[34] In Hegel's thought everything depends on the insight that all knowledge depends on our experience of consciousness. If one turns this insight round and stands it on its head, it becomes nonsensical. If our knowledge of being (*res gestae*) depends on our consciousness, one can construct historical narratives and eventually, a philosophy of history. But if one believes, as Marx did, that being cannot be reduced to consciousness and that one can,

nevertheless, have real knowledge of real being — then, whatever
one can do with such a belief, one cannot use it to make historical
narratives, let alone a philosophy of history. One does not have to
go so far as Hegel and use the changing modes of our experience of
our consciousness as the matrix for the stages of historical development. But if one denies that our knowledge of the historical past
depends on thought and that history is the history of thought, one
cannot build historical narratives. This denial is precisely the
cornerstone of Marx's thinking. He set great store by it because he
believed that by denying that history is the history of thought he
could form an absolute and final picture of *res gestae.* In a sense,
he considered this belief to be his greatest contribution. And now
we see, as far as the philosophy of history is concerned, that it
was the fatal flaw the presence of which forces us to pass his philosophy of history by as a nonphilosophy of history. For it is
based on the methodologically untenable assumption that we can
know what *res gestae* is like.

One could, of course, reinterpret Marx and argue that his
materialism (we can have knowledge of *res gestae*; *historia rerum
gestarum* is an ideology fabricated to embellish and disguise
politico-economic aspirations) is one of the many possible interpretations of *res gestae* and that it must take its place among all
the other possible interpretations. But if we believe that it is one
subjectivity among others, we would go so completely against the
whole thrust of Marx's own argument that the reinterpretation
would lose its point. Marx, we must recall, because we owe respect
to his own thought, believed that the materialist philosophy of
history was not just a possible interpretation and therefore a
historia rerum gestarum, but that it was the ultimate and absolute
explanation of *res gestae.*[35] I propose to take him by his word.
And, since we have shown at great length that the notion of an
explanation of *res gestae* is methodologically nonsensical, we must
abide by the verdict that Marx's philosophy of history is disqualified.

Lest such a dismissal of one of the most fruitful and stimulat-
ing theories of society appear too rigid, one can add the following
argument. The most general law employed by Marx is the law that
all societies are rent by class struggle and that political coercion
exists to facilitate the economic exploitation of one class by
another. All covering laws used by Marx to fill the gaps between
events so that one can obtain a coherent story are derived either
directly or indirectly from this law. In this way the class struggle
becomes the motive force of history or the most general description of the passage of time. Now we have seen in chapter 6 that

any understanding of primitive societies, of ancient, medieval, and early modern societies in terms of classes as the sociologist understands 'class' differs from the way the members of these societies understood themselves and is therefore excessively interpretative. If it were just interpretative one would have little to quarrel with it. But since there is no typological link between the notion of class and any of the notions employed in those societies, the interpretation becomes excessive. When we then come to modern industrial society, Marx is on perfectly safe, explanatory ground when he claims that these societies are to be explained in terms of class struggle. But Marx then goes on to argue that that class struggle must issue in a revolutionary situation. Here he is again mistaken because of an insufficient understanding of revolutions and of the effect of his own explanation on revolutions. A revolutionary situation arises not in response to poverty and despair, but in response to excessive social atomisation. But when people are class conscious, they are not atomised. Consciousness of class provides the firmest possible remedy for revolution no matter how poor the class one is a member of is. Marx, therefore, failed to understand that the advent of his own analysis of the class struggle in the modern world where it was explanatory rather than interpretative provided the very factor that would minimise the trend toward revolution.[36] Marx's philosophy of history, quite apart from its materialism, proves self-defeating because for pre-modern societies it is excessively interpretative and simply imposes our own way of understanding ourselves on them; and for modern societies it is so explanatory that it alters the thrust of the class struggle because once people accept themselves as class-conscious proletarians they cease to be alienated and as they cease to be alienated their revolutionary impetus is diminished.

Having disqualified Marx, I propose to omit Spengler's *Decline of the West* from this cursory survey of philosophies of history. There is no denying Spengler's touch of genius. He wrote his book during World War I and anticipated a great many ideas that have since become widely current. The main objective of the whole book was to explain that traditional European civilisation was coming to an end because of the rise of modern bureaucracy, of the managerial revolution, of other-directed man, of organisation man and the technetronic society. None of these terms was used by Spengler. They are due to Weber, Riesman, Burnham, Whyte, and Brzezinski.[37] Spengler's real importance lies in his intuitive ability to sense the changes that the middle of the twentieth century was to produce and to pinpoint these changes long before anybody else did as qualitative leaps that could not stand comparison with any previous change.

It is, however, no injustice to Spengler to say that his book was not a philosophy of history at all. He distinguished a number of cultures in world history and proceeded to describe each one. He claimed that each culture was subject to a cycle of change, to a biological law of rise and decline. But the course of the cycle was something independent of the nature of the culture and had no relation to that nature. Each culture was seen by him as a functionally integrated system of thoughts and institutions. If anything, this way of regarding each culture as a functionally integrated system of politics, institutions, and religion and philosophy denies historical narrative and makes complete nonsense of the philosophy of history. But one must grant that in his descriptions of societies Spengler showed remarkable intuition. He could not possibly have heard of Malinowski and of functionalism. But he practised functionalism long before Malinowski and Radcliffe-Brown had given currency to the concept and was independent of Malinowski's strenuous and consistent effort to understand every culture as a self-regulating system in which each part was functionally interrelated with every other part. Despite his shrewd insights, almost everything Spengler said is highly questionable. But this cannot detract from the importance of his grasp of functionalism. Unlike Malinowski, who first applied it carefully in his minutely detailed study of the Trobriand Islanders, Spengler applied his functionalism in a grand sweep to cultures so large both in temporal and spatial extension that the whole enterprise hardly makes sense. Spengler's work was an ambitious exercise in functionalism. It was ethnography on an immense scale, enriched in understanding by the use of functionalism before functionalism was invented as an explicit theory of understanding cultural systems. But for this very reason, it was no philosophy of history. Spengler failed completely to explain why, for example, Apollonian culture preceded Faustian culture and how the two could be related. In fact, being a thorough functionalist, he made a special point of insisting that no one culture could be related to another, let alone understood by it.[38]

It is of the essence of historical knowledge as the science of change, to show how and why one event, no matter how small or large, led to another. But it is of the essence of Spengler's theory that it is impossible to do this. His one proviso, that inside each system one phase must lead to the next because of an inexorable biologico-cosmic law, does not help. At best it affords ground for

believing that he has provided a set of separate philosophies of
the history of certain cultural systems. Under no circumstances
can one take his theory as a philosophy of history. If Spengler is
right, then there is no philosophy of history and we must forever
remain baffled why Appollonian culture preceded Faustian culture
and why Magian culture succeeded Apollonian culture.

After Hegel, then, the first major new development comes
with Arnold Toynbee. He tells a completely different story. His
knowledge of sources and historians is incomparably greater than
Hegel's. It was therefore impossible for him to attempt to sum it
all up in one consecutive story.

Toynbee's starting point was his contention that the smallest
intelligible unit of study is a civilisation. Most of his critics have
taken this as an admission of holism — which they dislike — or as
a concession to, or borrowing from, Spengler — whom they dis-
approve of. The truth, however, is that Toynbee in choosing civilisations was reacting strongly against nationalism as a political
creed and as a methodological criterion for writing history. During
the nineteenth century most historians had been preoccupied
with the histories of nations and Toynbee realised that this
preoccupation was too narrowly determined by political aspirations, most of which he understandably condemned. His critics
were all wrong. Whatever his sources and whatever his personal
convictions, Toynbee chose civilisations as the units of study
because he meant by 'civilisation' no more and no less than a
macroevent — a *Sinngebild* on a very large scale. As we have seen
in chapter 3 a Sinngebild is an intelligible unit of study. There
can be very small ones. When John slips on ice and breaks his leg,
we have a meaningful unit that consists of subevents. When Toynbee focusses his attention on civilisations, he focuses on very large-
scale intelligible units of study. If one looks at a civilisation as a
Sinngebild one is doing interpretation rather than explanation;
for the people in that civilisation were usually not able to arrive
at a knowledge of such an intelligible event. The concept itself,
however, as formulated by Toynbee, is merely a problem of size
and of interpretation. It is, formally, not essentially different from
any other *Sinngebild* we have discussed. There is nothing holistic
about it and it has nothing to do with an attempt to fix attention
on mysterious entities over and above the configurations that arise
when one puts very large-scale events together to form a super-
event. The confusion to which his critics have fallen victim is
understandable; but it is nevertheless a confusion. This does not
mean that one cannot advance criticisms of Toynbee's contention

that civilisations are the smallest possible intelligible units. I
think that it is demonstrably wrong to maintain that they are the
smallest such units. For practical purposes one can understand
much smaller units perfectly well. However this may be, Toynbee
seems to me perfectly right in drawing attention to the fact that
his choice of what is an intelligible unit is conceptually continuous with the much smaller units that we have called *Sinngebild*.

Toynbee spent much time in working out identifiable civilisations whose story he could tell. Eventually he produced twenty-
one separate civilisations and told their histories. But he told
the stories in such a way that he could discern remarkable likenesses in their developments. In each case, the story begins when
people rise to a challenge. The first phase in every civilisation is
represented by a response to a challenge. This is clearly an interpretation in the technical sense because the ancient Sumerians
when they first built their canals did not think of themselves as
responding to a challenge. More likely they thought that they
were carrying out the instructions of a god represented by a priest-
king. After the age of creative response comes usually a time of
troubles and then a phase of universal peace that ushers in a phase
of 'universal monarchy' in which a dictator or emperor exercises
vast power. Eventually there sets in a stage of fossilisation in which
people fail to respond creatively, and in this condition they are
vulnerable to attacks from internal as well as from external
'proletariats'. Superficial readers of Toynbee have done him a great
injustice by jumping to the conclusion that he discerns these
similarities inthe stages of development of his twenty-one civilisations because he thinks that each civilisation is like a living organism subject to biological laws of development, growth and decay.
Readers are encouraged in this superficial understanding of Toynbee because they often remember the philosophy of history of
Spengler, which does indeed draw heavily upon biological anal-
ogies. But Toynbee derives the entire inner momentum of every
history of every civilisation from the challenge-response pattern.
He distinguishes very carefully between the kinds of challenges
that are too great, too little, and those that are 'optimum'; and he
distinguishes equally carefully between the various possible responses. There are creative responses, imitative responses, and
fossilisations. The whole story of each civilisation is thus unfolded
like a vast exercise in problem solving. If one compares Toynbee
to Hegel, one should perhaps start such a comparison by stating
that Hegel's philosophy was a kind of transcendental idealism.
Toynbee's philosophy was a form of British empiricism. On one

side there was the vast unfolding of the spirit toward a state of total self-awareness; on the other side, there was a philosophy of problem solving and experimentation. In both cases the sequence of events is presented as hanging together by the strings of the general philosophy and in both cases the stories are highly interpretative.

If Hegel weakened his case by equating the reign of absolute spirit with the Prussian state, Toynbee weakened his case by claiming to have derived his philosophy from an empirical study of History. The very title of Toynbee's work *A Study of History* is designed to deceive and, unfortunately, many of his critics have taken him at the face value of that title. They have had no difficulty in demonstrating that his book is not what it purports to be. In Toynbee's case such a demonstration amounts to no more than a criticism of his method. In the case of Marx, I have argued, it was fatal. For Marx claimed to have established an ultimately objective knowledge of *res gestae.* As soon as one has demonstrated that it is not, one has destroyed the foundation on which his materialism rests. With Toynbee the situation is different. Although he claimed to have been an empiricist and to have studied *res gestae*, it was not an essential part of his argument that the results of his studies have revealed that there could be no other results and that if other results were to be revealed they had to be unmasked as ideologies designed to make the exploitation of somebody by somebody else palatable. Marx believed that the result of his empirical study of *res gestae* was the only result that was not an ideology and that could therefore not be unmasked. There is no comparable claim in Toynbee. His work would have been improved by more clear-sighted recognition of the nature of historical knowledge and the role of interpretation. But despite this criticism, his work is the most powerfully suggestive philosophy of history ever thought out and, what is more, it covers a wider field than Hegel's and tells a story that is sufficiently detailed to afford effective debating points. Working with Hegel, one can never proceed beyond general views that must remain vague.[39] Working with Toynbee, the historian can actually use him to find slots for almost everything he studies. And this is, after all, exactly what we expect of a philosophy of history.

On reflection Toynbee is very much more subtle than appears at first sight. The notion that all development in history takes place because there is a response to a challenge sounds very trivial. I think it is indeed trivial. But not all trivial notions are false or superfluous. Toynbee uses the notion in a very subtle way. To

begin with, he tries his hand at something that we might even
consider an instance of 'explanation proper'. When he considers
the origins of civilisations he says that they arose because people
responded to a challenge, and he tries to use the most ancient
myths to show that these people themselves understood their
efforts in this manner. He examines many ancient myths and seeks
to demonstrate that they are, though in appearance cosmic myths,
stories of responses to challenges. He claims, therefore, that people told these myths to explain how they themselves had risen to
the challenge of desiccation or overpopulation or whatever the
challenge had been. I have great doubts whether Toynbee's interpretation of these myths is correct and whether he is right in
claiming that his view that the origin of every civilisation lies in a
response to a challenge must be right because the people concerned
explained the origin in the same way. Unless one interprets these
cosmic myths in a Toynbeean manner, they do not constitute
'explanations proper' of what people thought happened, and in
this case one must classify Toynbee's challenge-response model
as an interpretation. But it would be unfair not to give him credit
for trying to start his philosophy of history with a genuine attempt
at historical explanation proper. He may not have succeeded; but
the measure of Toynbee as a historian must be taken in relation
to this attempt.

As histories proceed, the challenge-response pattern becomes
less and less trivial. Toynbee shows that there are many different
forms of responses and that the variations in the responses explain
the stages through which each civilisation changes. He contrasts,
for instance, a creative response with a merely imitative response
and shows that there are good reasons why people initially respond
creatively and eventually tend to respond by imitation. But the
most important point about the whole model is that Toynbee
seeks to explain the course of change in terms of the variations of
responses so that the challenge-response pattern, being subject to
continuous variation, provides the explanation of change. The
final discovery with which he comes up is the discovery that there
is a philosophy of history. It consists in the fact that the variations
to which the challenge-response pattern are subject in every one
of the twenty-one civilisations are the same.

All philosophies of history, of course, must of necessity suffer
from one fatal flaw. They are based on a circular argument. First
they devise a pattern of sequence; then they select the facts that
fit into that pattern; then they present the story of events in that
sequence; and finally their authors turn round and invite the reader

to believe that that sequence is the real story of events. The fatal flaw is that the particular sequence was selected by and constructed according to that pattern to prove that the pattern is correct. At first glance one might therefore be tempted to dismiss the whole enterprise, no matter how urgent the need for it is.

The usual argument, accepted both by philosophers of history and by their critics, is that 'events' are given by nature and are hard facts. The philosopher of history studies them, or so he says, and then reaches his conclusions. The critic of the philosophy of history objects because the facts are first selected with the philosophy as a criterion, and then the selection is used to prove that the philosophy is correct. The philosophy of history is then dismissed by him because it is based on a circular argument. My argument is different both from that of the philosophy of history and from that of the critic. It starts with the observation that the 'events' themselves are constructs and that the philosophy of history, in selecting, merely continues a process of selection already implicit in our very knowledge of the events. There is circularity; but such circularity as there is is nothing new introduced by the philosopher of history. It is already present in the compilation of sources and in the writing of quite ordinary narratives.

I want to urge two important considerations. First of all, one can devise two postulates to attenuate the fatal flaw of circularity. There are the Postulate of Sufficient Variety and the Postulate of Sufficient Specification.

The Postulate of Sufficient Variety demands that in the writing of any philosophy of history there should be sufficient variety between the criterion of selection and the pattern of events propounded as the philosophy. If the two are identical, the circularity of the argument is complete and fatal. But if there is one criterion of selection and a completely different philosophy in any one narrative, the philosophy of history can claim to stand on its own feet. For practical purposes this can mean that if one has a historical narrative composed by a historian and in reading it one comes across a pattern that does *not* stem from the explanations and interpretations used by the historian, one can confidently believe it to be a genuine philosophy of history. Complete variety is impossible. Everything I have said about the nature of the story and the methods of explanation and interpretation involved in its construction goes to show that complete variety is merely an ideal and that in practice the best one can expect is a partial fulfillment of this postulate.

Let us turn to an example. In a recent debate, Christopher

Hill has stated that the aim of much of his work on seventeenth-century English history has been to find out how 'traditional structures of ideas were modified to meet the new economic and political circumstances: to understand how traditional Christianity became Lockean liberalism'.[40] Hill states, in other words, that he wants to find something approaching a philosophy of history. At any rate, something that is a very large event. He not only says that in seventeenth-century England there was a transition; but he also puts forward an interpretation. The change, he says, consisted in the transformation of people's minds from traditional Christianity to Lockean liberalism.

J. H. Hexter has launched a broadside attack against Hill's method.

> It is the professional gambler's dream — the no-lose wager, like being able to place your bet after the results of the race are in. For given Dr. Hill's method there was no way that in his source-mine he could miss finding fifteen pages of fragments that seemed to support his case, indeed to support whatever case he chose.

Hill defended himself by stating that there was nothing disreputable in tackling big questions.[41] So far, so good. But then he goes on to say that he is not guilty of selecting evidence to support his thesis. This part of his defence makes only partial sense. The right defence would have been to say that since one cannot study *res gestae* one has to select in order to write any *historia rerum gestarum* and that in order to select, one has to have a criterion of selection. Such an argument would have rebutted Hexter's accusation that Hill was behaving like a man in a gambler's dream. But Hill did not put forward such a rebuttal. He recalled instead that his selections were always reasonable and judicious and that some of the evidence he has included in his history books does not even support the general thesis he makes. In other words, Hill takes Hexter at his face value and defends himself on the ground chosen by Hexter. Hill, like Hexter, appears to assume that there is such a thing as *res gestae* and that if the historian peers at it long enough he will come up with a description of what it is like. Hill believes that *res gestae*, in seventeenth-century England, is the change from traditional Christianity to Lockean liberalism. Hexter believes that the nature of *res gestae* is different and criticises Hill for the method he employs to produce evidence that it is not. Hexter is just as wrong as Hill. The sensible criticism of Hill would have been to charge that there is insufficient variety between the criterion of selection and the philosophy of history

Hill has put forward. But it is not sensible to say that out there, there is something called *res gestae* and that its true nature can be discovered by total portraiture. Hill, in reply, ought to have examined the degree of variety between his criterion of selection and the thesis he hopes his selected evidence will support. Instead he too, like Hexter, believes that he has discovered what *res gestae* in seventeenth-century England was really like. He believes that it can best be described as the change from traditional Christianity to Lockean liberalism. This change is not the character of the totality of everything that happened in seventeenth-century England; but one of the many possible shapes time in seventeenth-century England can be seen to assume. The real problem is who first saw it in that shape. Is this shape an explanation or an interpretation? What contemporary narratives does it correspond to? This debate, like so many others, would have been much more fruitful if it had been based upon the correct methodological assumptions and steered clear of the untenable view that the historian has to make an empirical study of an external reality called History so that he can tell us what History is like.

The Postulate of Sufficient Specification operates in a different way to make a philosophy of history more credible. It demands that any philosophical pattern should be sufficiently specified as to time and place. If there is no specification at all, it is not only conceivable but also quite likely that, given the enormous variety of events that have actually taken place, some events somewhere should sometimes exhibit the pattern put forward by the philosophy. If it merely claimed that there are class struggles or that people sometimes respond to challenges creatively, it cannot come as a great surprise if one is able to select some events from somewhere that can be put together to bear out the truth of such a pattern. But if the alleged pattern has a precise specification of time and place and one can come up with events that have taken place at that time and that place that bear it out, one can have considerable confidence in the truth of the pattern. In the ideal satisfaction of this postulate there must be complete specification of time and place. But such ideal satisfaction is self-defeating. If the time and place is minutely specified, one could, at best, discover one set of events that exhibit the particular pattern in question. But if one comes with only one set, one does not have a philosophy of history but merely a particular story. If, on the other hand, the postulate is completely unsatisfied and if one is free to choose one's illustrations of a certain pattern from ancient China as soon as from modern America, the pattern cannot claim a high degree of credibility. To steer carefully between the Scylla of particular narrative and the Charybdis of incredibility, the historian has to seek a judicious compromise. A complete satisfaction of this postulate is as useless as a complete disregard.

Here then we have the beginning of a rational and critical approach to the philosophy of history. In every case we can start by asking whether and to what extent these two postulates are satisfied. Toynbee has had a large number of critics. He has been rejected on theoretical grounds by both Popper and Geyl; subject to personal abuse and ridicule by Trevor-Roper; and attacked for his political and religious opinions by Walter Kaufmann.[42] Today there is hardly a single academic historian prepared to take him seriously, and it is an encouraging sign that S. Andreski in his book entitled *The Social Sciences as Sorcery*, respects his serious scholarship.[43] Perhaps there can be a genuine Toynbee revival if one can show that he scores very well on both postulates and that the circularity is somewhat mitigated because there is both variety and specification, even if one can argue that it is not sufficient.

Almost all attacks on Toynbee start at the wrong end. They begin with the presumption that there is an absolute gulf between ordinary history and a philosophy of history. They dismiss Toynbee because he produces a historical narrative in which laws and patterns of development are very explicit and, if I may use this expression, larger than life. They reject him not because these patterns are wrong, but because the patterns are there. History, they argue, must not make sense. If it does, it must be bad history. But with such an argument a good historian not only reduces Toynbee *ad absurdum;* he also reduces himself *ad absurdum —* and, what is worse, he reduces the people he studies *ad absurdum.* For they too thought about the meaning of their actions and the developments of which these actions were part. History, to them, made sense. If it makes sense to the historian and even more sense to the philosopher of history, the difference is only a difference of degree.

A genuine criticism of Toynbee must start with an examination of the degree to which he violates the two postulates. If it can be shown that his argument is completely circular and that that circularity is nowhere attenuated by a partial satisfaction of the two postulates, his arguments will lose some of their force. But there is no point in criticising him *a priori*, that is, for the mere fact that he presents a narrative that is intelligible and that makes sense. It is perfectly true that there is much to be said in criticism of Toynbee when one meets him on his own ground. In most cases, the Postulate of Sufficient Variety is satisfied. He takes most of his material from other historians and shows that on their own reading of the events, certain interpretations are possible and certain patterns exhibited. He is still selective in the sense that he chooses now one historian now another. But the narrative itself is predigested, so to speak, and the 'discovery' of the possible interpretations is therefore distinct from the selection of the raw material. How distinct it may be in every case is a matter for argument and examination. But I would like to suggest that it is precisely here that an intelligent criticism of Toynbee must begin. Or consider the Postulate of Sufficient Specification. At first glance, Toynbee scores well because he does not assert that there is a 'time of troubles' at any time and in any place. He specifies both place and period when it occurs and we must therefore accord considerable respect to the fact that he does come up with evidence to show that it did occur at the time and place where he said it is to be expected. A second glance will show that there is a certain lack of precision in his formulation of what constitutes a 'time of troubles' or a 'universal monarchy'. This lack of precision enables him to look upon one and the same set of occurrences as evidence for quite different phases of development. His treatment of Charlemagne is a case in point. In one place the Carolingian régime figures as a creative response and in another place as an imitative response and as a worship of an obsolete institution. On page 117 of the first volume of the abridged edition, entitled *A Study of History*,[44] Charlemagne appears as the first manifestation of cultural and intellectual energy in our Western world, while on page 320, Charlemagne is described as 'providentially unsuccessful'. I would insist that any intelligent criticism of Toynbee must start at this end of his narratives rather than with the laconic prejudice that his narratives are full of exaggerated interpretations and therefore nonsensical. What arouses one's doubts in regard to Toynbee is what arouses one's doubts in regard to any historian. We are all liable to mistakes and guilty of equivocation and lack of precision. Toynbee, being more bold in his claims, is more so than most. But it is absurd to dismiss him on principle. His method of composition is no different than the method by which every human being composes facts. There is a desire to make sense, to explain, to interpret.

The satisfaction or partial satisfaction of the two postulates is only the first step. The next step is to recall that the difference between a philosophy of history and an ordinary narrative is only a difference in degree and that the two do not represent completely different aspects of our knowledge of the past. We have shown that Löwith's contrast between fact and meaning is completely wrong (see page 247). We can also show that every major feature of any philosophy of history is merely an extension of or exaggeration of a feature inherent in the nature of the narrative, so that we may conclude that the philosophy of history is nothing but a special kind of narrative and that the philosophy of the story is contained in the nature of the story. The difference between ordinary historical narrative and a philosophy of history is therefore only a difference in degree. This observation and this observation alone really justifies the pursuit of the philosophy of history. The difference between the ordinary historian and the philosopher of history is therefore no more than the difference between a microhistorian and a macrohistorian. If we say that the investigation of any particular event can only make sense if it can be shown where the slot in the philosophy of history is into which it can be fitted, we are saying no more than that any microhistorical investigation ought to be carried out in such a way that it can be, if required, extended into a macrohistorical investigation.

This follows without the need for further argument from our analysis of events and of the construction of narratives. There is only one thing we should add. One can arrive at any one event one cares to pinpoint as an effect by an infinite number of series of events of any level of size. There is no privileged level.[45] If one wants to show that the outbreak of World War II was the effect of something, one can either trace the crossing of the German troops of the Polish border back to Hitler's command or to Germany's resentment of the Treaty of Versailles and the economic depression of the later 1920s, or to the Teutonic presence in central Europe and to efforts to contain it in a trough between the Rhine and the Oder. One can also causally link the crossing of the Polish border in September 1939 to the friction of the soldier's boots on the surface of the road — although admittedly in this last case, one would have to have a complex of interlocking series to establish a meaningful unit that contains, at the far end, the outbreak of this particular war. This shows that any causal explanation of an event can be derived from a high level philosophy of history (i.e., a macroevent) as soon and as plausibly as from an account of the minute events immediately preceding it.

The demonstration of this thesis is, in view of all the preceding chapters, not very difficult. Even a cursory observation of any philosophy of history must show that it is marked by two essential characteristics. First, it deals almost exclusively with very large-scale events, and second, it consists almost entirely of interpretations. But we have seen that the differences among small-scale events (Napoleon brushed his teeth at a certain moment in time), large-scale events (World War II ended with the defeat of Nazi Germany), and very large-scale events (the Roman Empire declined from the third century A.D. onwards) are not substantial and that all events, no matter how small, are composed of sub-events with the help of general laws, that is, with the help of thoughts. We have also seen that interpretations as distinct from translations and explanations proper are very much part of all historical narrative work. Neither of these two features so characteristic of the philosophy of history brings us up against something new, something that was not already familiar from the writing of ordinary historical narratives.

Apart from the allegedly fatal flaw of circularity, there is another stumbling block. Philosophies of history, it is alleged, depend on the belief in a developmental law or a law of succession. Such a law asserts that one single series of events was inevitable and that in that series one event had to follow upon its predecessor. If philosophies of history really depended on such developmental laws, then, no matter what strength all our previous arguments possess, they would have to be dismissed, for Karl Popper has shown convincingly that the very notion of 'developmental law' as distinct from an ordinary general law is nonsensical.[46] A law is a statement of observed or of observable regularities — not quite the same things. But whether it is the one or the other, it cannot possibly be a statement of a mere progression or succession of two or more particular events. One may have observed that two or more events followed upon one another. But having observed this once, one cannot, under any circumstances infer that they had to and call such an observation a 'developmental law'. Moreover, the absurdity of describing a sequence as a developmental law is fully revealed when one recalls that it is in fact impossible to observe such a sequence unless one has a genuine general law up one's sleeve. The general law must be of the 'all A's are B's' type. This applies to history as well as to geology and biology. The emergence of a continent is not due to the operation of one single developmental law that states that there had to be one particular sequence of events that resulted in the appearance of a certain land mass at a particular place. The proper way to describe the emergence of the continent is to make any two single events hang together with the help of a general law about the effect of volcanic upthrust or the effect of rain on soil, the law of gravity, laws governing the movements of rocks and lava of different viscosities relative to each other, and so forth. In other words, instead of one single developmental law, one uses a whole set of ordinary general laws the combined effect of which is to bring about the emergence of the continent. It is perfectly true that general laws about minievents are more easily testable than general laws about macroevents. Since we can observe every day that John is likely to break his leg when he slips on ice, the generalisation involved is easily open to inspection. When the generalisation concerns the fall of the Roman Empire, it is obviously not as easily open to inspection, for empires do not fall every day and no two empires are so obviously alike that one could generalise about the way they fall. But such difficulties are practical difficulties. They do not concern the heart of the matter. The heart of the matter is that philosophies of history do not use laws other than ordinary general laws. They do not depend on developmental laws any more than geology or the the theory of biological evolution does. One cannot find fault with Popper's criticism of developmental laws; but one can find fault with his view that they are indispensable for philosophies of history and that if they have to be dismissed, philosophies of history have to be dismissed.[47]

The crucial part of Popper's argument is his demonstration, on page 117, that there can be no laws of succession or developmental laws that determine 'a sequence of historical events in the order of their actual occurrence'. Any actual succession of phenomena, he says, proceeds according to the laws of nature, but *'practically no sequence of, say three or more causally connected concrete events proceeds according to any single law of nature'.* There can be no doubt that this argument is correct. But one must doubt whether it really demolishes the justification for those seemingly developmental laws that are employed in speculative philosophies of history as explained in this chapter. Popper appears to think that such developmental laws are very large laws determining the unique sequence of events ('Human societies develop from simple societies to complex societies' or 'creative periods are followed by universal monarchies'). My argument takes a different view of the matter. The things that are big in the laws employed by speculative philosophies of history are not the general laws — or, at any rate, they are no bigger than other general laws. The things that are big in such speculative philosophies of history are the events linked by these laws. The philosopher of history will not link the accession of King Henry VIII with the death of King Henry VII but will link the new monarchy with the decline of feudalism. The general laws he employs are ordinary general laws. The feature that distinguishes his narrative from the ordinary narrative is the size of the events he links with the help of the law. Now we have seen in the preceding pages that the size of the events any historian deals with is a matter of choice and perspective. All events are composite events. This applies to the smallest conceivable events as much as to the largest conceivable event. Since there is no logical limit to the smallest event the historian can deal with, there is also no logical limit to the largest event he wishes to deal with. The difference between an ordinary story and a philosophy of history consists in the sizes of the events linked together, not in the logical form of the general laws employed to do so. Since the ordinary historian deals with small events one has no objection to his general laws (e.g., 'all living things die when exposed to heat'), whereas the philosopher of history, since he is dealing with very large-scale events, creates the impression that he is using unjustifiable developmental laws. In reality the latter is using equally justifiable general laws; but since they are used to link very large-scale events, which, by the nature of the case, occur comparatively infrequently, they are easily mistaken for laws determining a unique sequence of events. My contention, in brief, is that the speculative philosophy of history does not make use of those laws that Popper, rightly, condemns as laws of succession but uses those general laws that he, rightly on page 145, accepts as legitimate general laws, although it uses them to link causally very large-scale events.

The larger the events, the more they must appear to be unique. When one is dealing with the stabbing of Caesar, one is concerned with a small event and the general laws employed to compose it as well as the general laws employed to link it with other events of comparable size will be general laws that cover a vast number of similar events. But when one is dealing with events so large as the decline of the Roman Empire, the general laws that will link them with other events of comparable size will cover fewer instances and will therefore tend to be regarded as less general. And, clearly, when one is dealing with the largest event conceivable, that is, 'the world exists', the general law that one might invent to link it causally to another event of similar size (provided one could imagine that there is one) must of necessity describe a unique sequence. It follows therefore that philosophies of history ought to stop short of using for their narration extremely large events lest they be forced to employ general laws that will assume the appearance of laws of unique succession and thereby reduce them-

selves to absurdity. In this way there ought to be a limit to the
macrocity of the events the historian can employ. The differences
between minievents and macroevents is a difference of degree.
Once one understands the nature of the composition of ordinary
narratives and once one understands the concept 'event', one can
see that a philosophy of history is nothing but an extension of the
composition of events and their sequential assembly in narratives.
But when the events in a historical series surpass a certain size,
they will force the employment of a general law that will assume
the guise of a developmental law or a law of succession in Popper's
sense. At this point the philosophy of history ceases to be legitimate. To my knowledge there are no philosophies of this kind; but
to guard against their appearance and to make sure that nothing in
the present argument should be constructed as a legitimisation of
philosophies of history of this kind, I would put forward the Postulate of Maximum Permissible Macrocity. It states that while it is
legitimate to increase the size of the events that form the units in a
narrative sequence to the point where the sequence assumes the
shape of a philosophy of history, it is not permissible to increase
their size to the point at which they cover almost everything that
ever happened and at which they make it necessary, to be linked
to the next event, to employ a covering law that will look, given
the comparative uniqueness of the macroevents, like a law of
unique succession. It is easy enough to detect the extreme cases
that violate this postulate. But there are marginal macrocities and
in such cases one will have to examine each case on its merits. A
philosophy of history that links the event 'all men are always evil'
with the event 'in the year 2000 there will be Armageddon' is
prohibited by the Postulate of Maximum Permissible Macrocity,
regardless of the fact whether the occurrence of Armageddon in
the year 2000 is ascertainable or not. But a philosophy that deals
with events such as the appearance of postindustrial civilisation
is not necessarily ruled out and will have to be examined on its
merits. The Postulate of Maximum Permissible Macrocity is not a
rule of thumb but a guideline that draws our attention to the
margin beyond which philosophies of history become nonsensical.
The postulate must therefore not be taken as an admission that all
philosophies of history, as many historians and philosophers have
maintained, are nonsensical if pushed beyond a certain point. The
weakness of all criticisms of philosophies of history put forward
so far, from Ranke to Popper, is that they have drawn the line of
demarcation far too soon.

Earlier in this chapter, Marx was disqualified as a philosopher of history. The reasons for such disqualification differ completely from the reasons advanced by Popper, on page 51, and other critics. Marx was disqualified because his doctrine of historical materialism, if taken seriously, makes the construction of a historical narrative impossible long before such a narrative is developed into a philosophy of history. Marx's materialism contradicts the view that all history is the history of thoughts and that thoughts are the ultimate raw material of our knowledge of the past and commits one to the view that provided one stares at *res gestae* with sufficient attention, one will be able to detect their true nature. Most critics of Marx are not concerned with these objections but seize upon his use of a developmental law as a ground for rejecting him. But it seems to me that this is the one charge he must be acquitted of.

Let us take a close look at a stark example of what most people would describe as Marx's developmental law. In the *Communist Manifesto*,[48] Marx tells the following story:

> 1. From the serfs of the Middle Ages sprang the chartered burghers of the earliest towns. From these burgesses the first elements of the bourgeoisie developed.

> 2. The feudal system of industry . . . now no longer sufficed for the growing wants of new markets. The manufacturing system took its place. The guild masters were pushed to one side; division of labor between the corporate guilds vanished in the face of division of labor in each single workshop.

> 3. Meantime the markets kept ever growing; the demand ever rising. Even manufacture no longer sufficed. The place of manufacture was taken by the giant, modern industry, the place of the industrial middle class by industrial millionaires, the leaders of whole industrial armies, the modern bourgeois.

At first reading, one certainly gains the impression that Marx is stringing the sequence of events together because there is a developmental law that leads from the first event to the last. But closer examination shows that all this can also be expressed in terms of general laws affecting or governing the relationships between very large-scale events (e.g., the bourgeoisie and their behaviour). Marx's own presentation of the narrative looks as if he had made use of a developmental law. But the appearance is deceptive once we understand that the concept 'event' is relative and fluid and that the existence of the bourgeoisie and its behaviour is simply a large-scale event and nothing less than an ordinary narrative. In principle it is not different from a small-scale event, which nobody would deny to be linked to another small-scale event with the help of a causal law. Marx himself, of course, would never have allowed anybody to guess this, let alone to demonstrate it. For he thought that the single events he had strung together were not themselves narrative constructions. He thought that he had discovered them in the stream of *res gestae* as one might discover a nugget of gold. I have argued above that he was grossly mistaken in this belief. But having called his bluff in general, we should not allow him to provide us with a demonstration that his narrative of the history of the class struggle was dependent on a developmental law.

It is perfectly true that the idea of a developmental law that applies to a unique set of events is unintelligible. We have now also seen that not even Marx employed a developmental law. He merely thought he did. It is interesting to note that people who defend the idea that there are developmental laws usually like to invoke organic developments or the story of evolution as a model. But as I have shown in chapter 2, the story of the evolution of species and the story of the development of the earth and of cells and other organisms does not depend on developmental laws but on specifically stated ordinary general laws. Hence the appeal to organicism and the invocation of an organic model to justify the viability of developmental laws is particularly inappropriate.

Developmental laws have received their unenviable reputation first because they were mistaken for special laws determining the development of any given entity, especially of an organism. Second, having been mistakenly identified as something special, they assumed the reputation that they bestowed the power of prophecy on whoever knew them. For if they determine the course of the development in the past, they can be held to determine the course of the development in the future. In this way they appeared to be expressions of iron-clad necessity. All this was a chimera and in the shape of this chimera they were held by Popper to have been responsible for countless atrocities. But once they are cut down to size and classed with ordinary, general laws, their power of prophecy is also cut down to size. General laws can predict the future in a very limited sense. If one knows that people who slip on ice might break their legs, one can predict that John might break his leg if one sees him slipping on ice. This power of 'limited prophecy',[49] if one wants to use this term, is inherent in all generalisations and does not disappear once we have shown that there are no developmental laws as distinct from ordinary laws or lawlike statements. In the light of this analysis there is nothing more remarkable, let alone prophetic, about Toynbee's law that a time of troubles will be followed by a universal monarchy than about the law that if I jump off a twenty-foot tower, I am likely to break my leg. The notion that general laws that are mistaken for developmental laws are reprehensible because there is something specially 'iron-clad' about them is absurd. In a sense all laws are iron-clad. This does not mean that they cannot be wrong. It means that when I strike a match to light my pipe, I rely on an iron-clad necessity to predict the future, that is, that a lit match will light the tobacco in my pipe. If there was nothing iron-clad about the law, I would never bother to strike my match.

Nevertheless, there is a difference between the general laws that link minievents and the general laws that link macroevents. The former can be accorded a certain truth value in the sense that they are generalisations of frequently observed phenomena; or, better, that they are hypotheses with the help of which we can construct from the infinite multiplicity of *res gestae* a finite set of events that will support them. The truth value of the latter is much more precarious, though not radically different. But as the events increase in macrocity, they require generalisations that are not nearly so well supported because the greater the macrocity of an event the less frequent its occurrence. For this reason one should approach them with greater care. An ordinary generalisation can safely be used to predict the future. When I stand on the Eiffel tower it will be reasonable to predict my death if I jump off. But when there is a time of troubles, it is not nearly so reasonable to predict an age of universal monarchy. And when I ascertain that the world exists, no particular prediction at all can be considered reasonable. Since the truth values of the general laws vary in proportion to the macrocity of the events concerned, one has to admit that the predictions legitimised by the general laws also vary. Beyond a certain macrocity of events, general laws should not be used for prediction. This admission, however, is no argument against a philosophy of history that employs such general laws. For all philosophies of history are concerned with the past, with our understanding of the past, and, particularly, with an increase in our ability to link the several and separate stories about the past into coherent sequences. The question about the future and the power of predicting the future does not arise and we should end this particular part of the argument with a fourth postulate, the Postulate of Absolute Praeterity. This postulate demands that every philosophy of history should contain exclusively narratives about the past and that none of the general laws employed in such narratives, regardless of the macrocity of the events involved, should ever be held to have the power to predict the future. This does not mean that they should not be employed to predict the future of the sixteenth-century observer. It only means that they should not be employed to predict the future relative to the time in which the historian or philosopher of history is writing. If this postulate is observed, the question whether there are certain general laws in the philosophy of history the truth value of which is so precarious that any prediction made with their help becomes pernicious is obviated. Furthermore, the observance of this postulate eliminates, as far as the writing of philosophies is concerned, an important moral problem. It has often been argued that when people know, from their philosophy of history, that a universal monarchy is bound to happen next, they will do little to oppose its emergence so that in such a case belief in the truth of a philosophy of history will diminish the determination to resist so undesirable a thing as a universal monarchy. In this way, the philosophy of history, by weakening the power to resist something that is held to be bad, is likely to produce its own verification. The observance of the Postulate of Absolute Praeterity will prevent the operation of all philosophies of history in this direction. The need for this postulate is, however, not primarily moral. In the first instance it is necessary to observe this postulate because of the admitted precariousness of general laws that link events that exceed a certain macrocity.

Many thoughtful and reflective historians, mindful of what they were doing and how they were doing it, have been aware of the fact that the transition from ordinary historical narrative to a philosophical evaluation of that narrative and to an extension of that narrative into a philosophy of history is a comparatively small step. If one focusses one's attention on the general laws employed in explanations proper and considers that even in quite ordinary interpretations general laws are used, one will start to wonder whether there is a pattern to be found in the manner in which explanations are superseded by interpretations. It is therefore almost inevitable that the writing of good narrative history will — imperceptibly at first and self-consciously later — develop into a philosophy of history. This point was lucidly made and explored in a book that deserves to be much better known than it is. Carlo Antoni in his book entitled *Dallo storicismo alla sociologia*[50] examined the intellectual careers of historians like Troeltsch and Weber, Wölfflin and Huizinga, to show how their historical researches of necessity developed into philosophies of history. The book has a title that was likely to mislead most English-speaking

readers and this may account for its comparative neglect. When we
speak of 'sociology' we are thinking of a social science and not of
a philosophy of history. Antoni's title therefore was bound to confuse the English reader, for the point of the book was not that
historians predictably transformed themselves into sociologists
but that they could be expected to develop into philosophers of
history and that the historians he examined lived up to this
expectation.[51]

Let us be more specific. If we examine the properties of a
philosophy of history in detail, we will note that they are all contained in the ordinary narrative.

1. Every philosophy of history is a thought about the meaning
of what happened in the past. We have seen that our knowledge of
any event at all depends on our thought about that event and upon
the relation of that thought to the thought of the person who
experienced that event in the first place, who was responsible for
its finding its way into a source or who was an actor of that event.
The historical actors themselves speculated about the possible
meaning or were bigotedly certain as to what that meaning was.
And if they were not, they could have been — which, from our
point of view, comes to the same thing. The philosopher of history,
therefore, in establishing the meaning of a series of events is
merely carrying on the process of thinking about events.

2. Every philosophy of history is in competition with other
philosophies of history and it is admittedly impossible to establish
the 'truth' of any one philosophy of history.[52] This is due to the
circularity of the argument by which it seeks to justify itself, and
it remains so even if that circularity is softened or qualified by
the partial satisfaction of the Postulates of Sufficient Variety and
of Sufficient Specification. We have shown that in this regard the
historical narrative is not in a very different situation. The truth of
any one narrative cannot be established by comparing it to what
actually happened. *Historia rerum gestarum* is a selection and abstraction from the totality of events that have taken place and its
'truth' can therefore not depend on whether what it tells did or did
not happen in that particular way. Any one event, provided it is small
enough, can be falsified if it did not actually happen. But any
event in any narrative, provided it is a fairly large-scale event, is
no more capable of such potential falsification than any very
large-scale event that occurs in any philosophy of history. Truth,
therefore, is precarious at all times, whether we have a simple
narrative or whether we have a full-blown philosophy of history.

3. Every philosophy of history has a meaning in the sense that

it presents a series of events that has a beginning and an end. We have shown that the sense of a beginning and the sense of an ending are very important ingredients in any story telling. Admittedly, they are not essential. But if they are entirely absent from the ordinary narrative, there will be a loss in intelligibility. Again, therefore, we find that the difference between a philosophy of history and an ordinary narrative is in degree only.

4. Every philosophy of history claims to be able to predict. Often it does so in the sense that it claims to predict the unknown future. But more often it does so in the sense that it claims to be able to predict that one set of events that have actually taken place could have been expected to have taken place. We have seen that this sort of predictiveness is inherent in any narrative and, what is more, also inherent in any reflection on quite small sets of events. It depends on the employment of universals, be they concrete or abstract. It can be derived entirely from the simple fact that any actor in acting has certain expectations of the results of his actions and can be thought of undertaking these actions in the expectations that they will bring about these results. He does so because he makes use of universals. The philosophy of history makes use of universals in the same way and in doing so does not introduce a new feature into our knowledge of the past.

5. Every philosophy of history selects. It does so with a vengeance, usually using its own philosophical pattern as the criterion of selection. Here again, the philosophy of history is not basically different from ordinary history. No historical narrative can be written without selecting events from the totality of everything that has happened. The ordinary historian is more cautious and modest. He selects what the sources suggest to him and he considers himself bound in an important sense by the general laws contained in or implied by the sources. The philosophy of history goes beyond the sources in the sense that it deals freely with interpretations and does not allow the sources to dictate. The difference is again a difference in degree. The mere fact that a philosophy of history is highly selective does not distinguish it from an ordinary narrative.

6. Every philosophy of history contains the suggestion, and often more than a suggestion, that events had to follow a certain course and that certain stages of progression of developments were bound to follow upon one another. In every philosophy of history there is therefore something that looks like a law of development, a law that asserts that there is some kind of iron-clad necessity for one phase to be followed by another. After the phase

in which one man was free, there follows one in which some men are free. After a period of 'creative response' there comes a 'time of troubles'; after feudalism, there comes the rule of the bourgeoisie. Such sequences are not basically different from the sequence 'John slipped on ice' and 'John broke his leg'. In both kinds of sequences, contingencies are eliminated by the operation of causal laws. It is perfectly true that all such sequences will look deceptively like sequences governed by a developmental law. The larger the events, the more unique they will look. Since pure contingency has been driven out from the composition of the smallest mininarrative onward, the sequence of the very large events will tend to look like a unique sequence necessarily determined by a developmental law. But we ought not to be deceived. The covering law model of the origin of the conception of an event and of the composition of ordinary narratives commits us to the acceptance of the fact that in a properly intelligible narrative there is next to no contingency. This is not the same as saying that there is no contingency in *res gestae*. It merely says that when we select particle events to join them with other particle events into a mininarrative, and so forth, we are always selecting in such a way as to extrude contingency and fabricate the highest possible degree of predictability. Since this process of fabrication continues into the largest conceivable macroevents, a philosophy of history that links macroevents is, in its extrusion of contingency, in no way different from an ordinary narrative. The absence of contingencies is not due to the presence of a developmental law anymore than it is due to the fact that there *are* no contingencies. It is due to the manner in which we look at time and make it appear to us.[53]

7. Every philosophy of history, and this is as true of Hegel's and Toynbee's as it is of theologically orientated philosophies, contains a strong mythic flavour. By the nature of the case, a philosophy of history must deal with the beginning and the end of the whole story. It must explain how civilisations began and how they will end or how some have ended. The mere setting up of a number of events under the descriptive term 'civilisation' creates an entity that has both borders and a beginning as well as an end. Absolute beginnings and absolute ends are, of course, removed from all kinds of observation. At the beginning there cannot have been an observer anymore than there will be an observer capable of surviving the end and reporting it. All absolute beginnings and ends must therefore be mythical. One could argue that a philosophy of history need not concern itself with absolute

beginnings and ends but that it could construct the pattern of
events starting at a point after the beginning and stopping short
of the actual end; and that in the case of many civilisations in a
Toynbeean sense, one could expect reports of their beginnings
and ends from observers in other civilisations. But then civilisations are not easily identifiable entities like chairs and tables.
Everybody knows where a chair begins and where it ends. But
the definition of a civilisation is complex. In fact, one cannot define a civilisation and then examine its beginnings. One must first
form a notion of a beginning and with its help then try to define a
civilisation. It is therefore clear that even if one does not concern
oneself with absolute beginnings and endings, one must nevertheless have a sense of beginning and a sense of an ending independent
of empirical observation and indeed prior to empirical study.
Unless Toynbee had a sense of an ending he would not be able to
say where Hellenism had ended. A historian who has a sense of
ending different from Toynbee's will almost certainly come up
with a very different tale of the ending of Hellenism.

Here again we must conclude that the difference between a
good history and a philosophy of history is in degree only. A story
must have a beginning and an end; and we have sought to show
that mythical patterns have often provided suggestions as to how
stories began and how they ended. Philosophies of history too are
under the influence of these mythic patterns, and the mythic
flavour is often stronger than in ordinary histories. Hegel's vision
of a progression from despotism to freedom is a special instance
of the progression from unsentient consciousness to complete
self-consciousness. This pattern of development, in turn, is only
a special instance of the progression from pure, undifferentiated
potency to complete actuality. Hegel's progression of history is
therefore conceived entirely in terms of the progress from undifferentiated Chaos to Godhood; or from the closed Lotus to the
unfolded Lotus. If we can recognise the archetype behind the
myth and the myth behind the philosophy, and the philosophy
behind the knowledge of the historical development from ancient
Persia to nineteenth-century Prussia, have we added to Hegel's
vision or detracted from it? If the spirit can understand itself as an
instance of the archetype, so much the better for the spirit. And
the chances are that since it was presumably the archetype that
propelled the development and progression of the spirit, such
understanding is indeed a correct understanding. And if not,
what exactly could we mean by a 'correct' understanding?

In summary: philosophies of history are only slightly different from ordinary narratives. They make meaning more explicit. They deal almost exclusively with very large-scale events. Therefore they have less opportunity to use explanations proper and give much wider scope to pure interpretation. And since they are concerned with the meaning of the past to the modern reader, they are not concerned with translation. This disregard of translation often gives them an air of arrogance and contempt for the past and invites antagonism. And finally, the general laws they employ often assume the appearance of developmental laws because they connect very large-scale events.

The gulf that separates ordinary history from the philosophy of history is not unbridgeable. If we become more sceptical about ordinary history and cease to believe that it is a transcript of what actually happened and if we become less dogmatic about philosophies of history, we will see that the gulf can be bridged — that, in fact, it will bridge itself. There are important differences between the two. But the analytical philosophers who have branded the philosophy of history as an irresponsible pursuit have, first of all, been very mistaken in their view of the nature of ordinary history. And secondly, they have rendered a disservice to ordinary history by condemning it to becoming a senseless pursuit in which the antiquarian ultimately replaces the historian. If the philosophy of history is a precarious pursuit because it exploits too heavily the speculative elements in ordinary historical writing, the latter cannot be considered meaningful unless it is related to the former.

Nor can ordinary historical writing be simply truthful unless it is constantly related to a wider perspective. Since the truthfulness of any account does not consist in a correspondence with the facts but in the coherence of sources with accounts and narratives because narratives are extensions of sources, and since wider perspectives are usually inherent in the sources, the extrusion of these wider perspectives amounts eventually to falsification. In this sense the presence of a philosophy of history not only increases meaning but also truthfulness, and its absence, far from increasing truth, as is so widely believed, actually diminishes it.

NOTES

Chapter One: Introduction

1. Gerald Holton's phrase in 'The Mainsprings of Discovery', *Encounter* 247 (1974). The following quotations from Copernicus and Einstein are to be found on pp. 90 and 91 of the same article.
2. Karl-Georg Faber, *Theorie der Geschichtswissenschaft* (Munich, 1974), pp. 109–46.
3. P. Gardiner, ed., *Theories of History* (Glencoe, 1959); S. Hook, ed., *Philosophy and History* (New York, 1963); W. H. Dray, ed., *Philosophical Analysis and History*, New York, 1966; P. Gardiner, ed., *The Philosophy of History*, London, 1974.
4. The great monument to this approach is H. G. Gadamer, *Wahrheit und Methode: Grundzüge einer philosophischen Hermeneutik* (Tübingen, 1960). It is now available in English as *Truth and Method* (New York, 1975). Unfortunately the translation is so totally literal that it is very difficult to understand unless one knows enough German to retranslate almost every sentence into the original.
5. I have been preceded in this attempt by Haskell Fain, *Between Philosophy and History* (Princeton, 1970). His book bears the subtitle *The Resurrection of Speculative Philosophy of History Within the Analytic Tradition*. Although I am very much in sympathy with Fain's goal, I feel that he does not probe the analytic tradition hard enough, or, at least, not hard enough to reach his avowed goal.
6. Ranke expressed great contempt for Hegel's philosophy of history and is usually given the credit for having freed history from philosophy. See his seminal paper 'Geschichte und Philosophie' (ca. 1830) in Leopold von Ranke, *Geschichte und Politik*, ed. H. Hofmann (Leipzig, s.d.), pp. 133ff. But the matter is not simple. Ranke himself showed a permanent interest in universal history. See H. Butterfield, *Man on His Past* (Cambridge, 1969), pp. 103–05. E. Troeltsch, 'Der Historismus und seine Probleme', *Gesammelte Schriften*, 3 (Tübingen, 1922), argued that Ranke was closer to Hegel than he and his followers were prepared to admit. In 1928, however, E. Simon, *Ranke und Hegel*, Beiheft 15 of *Historische Zeitschrift* (Munich, 1928), showed conclusively that Troeltsch was wrong and that if Ranke had general ideas, they were those of German Romanticism and not of Hegel. However this may be, Ranke's modern admirers forget that his own proud denunciation of Hegel — a fateful moment in the history of historical thought — owed much to a very special factor. At that time most of the archives were being opened up for the first time and Ranke could look forward to historical research as its own reward for many decades to come. In those and the following years he could have 'love affairs' with documents in the Vatican Archives or the State Archives of Vienna and his disciples were able to spend their summer holidays tramp-

ing with boots and knapsack from monastery to monastery to unearth new and ever new documents. In those halcyon days of research one did not necessarily have to have a philosophy of history to find research rewarding. But times have changed since then and a historiography that cuts itself off from the philosophy of history is not likely to flourish today as it did until the early years of the present century. In those days every historian was a sort of *Wandervogel* and *Wandervögel* need no philosophy of history to keep them going. As against Ranke, Johann Gustav Droysen was always conscious of the fertilising importance of a speculative philosophy of history. See his *Historik*, 4th ed. (Darmstadt, 1960), pp. 404ff.

7. Cp. G. Barraclough, *History in a Changing World* (Oxford, 1955), p. 1:

> we stand at the end and outside of the traditional history of the schools and universities, . . . we are beset by a new sense of uncertainty because we feel ourselves on the threshold of a new age to which previous experience offers no sure guide.

and R. Aron, *The Dawn of Universal History* (New York, 1961), pp. 15-16:

> From the beginning of the nineteenth century every European generation has believed in the uniqueness of its own period. Does the very persistence of this conviction in itself indicate that it was unfounded? Or was it rather a kind of premonition, the truth of which has been borne out by our own generation, and which must, therefore, have been false in the case of our predecessors? If we hesitate to ascribe error . . . to every generation but our own, can we suggest a third hypothesis, namely, that all of them have been right, not individually, but regarded as a whole . . . ?
>
> In other words it would seem to be a fact, or at least a plausible hypothesis, that the last century has seen a kind of revolution, or more precisely a *mutation* which began before the nineteenth century, but whose rate of change has accelerated during the past few decades.

8. First published as a series of papers in *Economica* 11 (1944) and as a book in London, 1957.
9. Thus, e.g., P. Gardiner, 'The Philosophy of History', *International Encyclopaedia of the Social Sciences*, (New York, 1968) 6:428-34. If one bears the literature that appeared at the beginning of this century in Germany in mind, one will be less sure than Gardiner that analytical philosophy of history is comparatively recent.
10. '. . . what *ultimately* makes the perfect account unfeasible is precisely what makes speculative philosophy of history unfeasible'. A. C. Danto, *Analytical Philosophy of History* (Cambridge, 1968), p. 115. I agree with Danto that the perfect account is unfeasible and will start my own discussion with a similar argument. But, unlike Danto, I will try to show that this very unfeasibility, interpreted correctly, provides justification for a great many speculative philosophies of history.
11. See the fine reflections by Golo Mann, 'The History Lesson', *Encounter* 227 (1972).
12. *Sincerity and Authenticity* (London, 1972), p. 136. Many other writers have commented on the down-right rejection of the past by modern man.

See, for example, Alfred Weber, *Farewell to European History*, (London, 1947), A. Heuss, *Verlust der Geschichte* (Göttingen, 1959); H. Schelsky, *Einsamkeit und Freiheit* (Hamburg, 1963); A. Mitscherlich, *Auf dem Weg zur vaterlosen Gesellschaft* (Munich, 1963); and F. Wagner, 'Begegnung von Geschichte und Soziologie bei der Deutung der Gegenwart', *Historische Zeitschrift* 192 (1961). Unlike Trilling, some of these authors think that psychoanalysis has become a substitute for an interest in history.

13. *Political History: Principles and Practice* (London, 1970), p. 158f.
14. *The Death of the Past* (London, 1969), pp. 14–15, 77, and 86.
15. 'The Burden of History', *History and Theory* 5 (1966): p. 115. White might have added as a further example of the belief in the essential contemporaneity of human experience the French *nouveau roman*, i.e., Natalie Sarraute, Butor, Robbe-Grillet. This contemporaneity has been beautifully portrayed on the screen by Alain Resnais in *Hiroshima, mon amour* and *Last Year in Marienbad*. The film is a better medium for the portrayal of such contemporaneity than a literary narrative.
16. I must confess, though, that there is at least one idiosyncratic German playwright who did; Peter Weiss in his *Hölderlin* had a great success in Germany in 1971 when he added Hegel, on the stage, to the long list of historians with repressed sensibility.
17. C. Lévi-Strauss, *The Scope of Anthropology* (London, 1967), p. 47.
18. (London, 1972).
19. For the contributions made by Popper and Hempel, see ch. 3, n. 3.
20. This fairly obvious point and the dubiousness and precariousness of all such enterprises has been argued at great length by G. Steiner, *After Babel* (London, 1975).
21. Although aesthetically of no great interest, it must be admitted that Andy Warhol made a philosophically interesting point when he exhibited a Coca-Cola bottle instead of painting of one.
22. J. P. Stern, *On Realism* (London, 1973), p. 67.
23. Renford Bambrough, 'Principia Metaphysica', *Philosophy* 39 (1964):p. 98. The problem is dealt with in the famous Japanese film *Rashomon* and by Salvador de Madariaga in his book entitled *A Bunch of Errors* (London, 1954). In the Japanese film it is naively supposed that there is a face behind the mask but that human mendacity makes it impossible to see it correctly. Madariaga tells his story on the assumption that there is no reality behind the various stories or versions of a set of events and that there is nothing to be found over and above these different versions.
24. 'To understand a sentence means to understand a language. To understand a language means to be master of a technique'. Wittgenstein, quoted by J. Culler, *Structuralist Poetics* (London, 1975), p. 113. It is remarkable how close Wittenstein's statement comes to R. Barthes' description of 'homeostatic systems' in his *Essais critiques* (Paris, 1964), p. 156 and to Lévi-Strauss' characterisation of mythological structures and kinship structures. In a slightly different vein Karl Kraus too believed that speech is to be assessed internally and that there is an ideal way of expressing oneself linguistically the truth of which would be apparent without reference to any facts. Cp. J. P. Stern, 'Karl Kraus', *Encounter* 263 (1974):43–44. The later Wittgenstein really stood positivism on its head. The positivists had argued that the meaning of a proposition is the

method of its verification. The later Wittgenstein said that meaning is
independent of verification.
25. Barthes, *Essais*, p. 156.
26. Contemporary philosophers as far apart as Hans Georg Gadamer and Karl
    Popper are in complete agreement on the inevitable and fundamental
    ubiquity of universals of some kind or other. See for example, H. G.
    Gadamer, *Truth and Method* (New York, 1975), pp. 15 and 278; K. R.
    Popper, *The Logic of Scientific Discovery* (London, 1959), pp. 94-95.
27. (Baltimore, 1973).

Chapter Two: The Time Sequence

1. J. Finegan, *Light from the Ancient Past* (Princeton, 1946), 1:254.
2. For the *Annales* school, see L. Febvre, *Combats pour l'histoire* (Paris,
   1953); F. Braudel, *Écrits sur l'histoire* (Paris, 1969); and F. Wagner,
   Moderne Geschichtsschreibung (Berlin, 1960), ch. 5. There is a brief
   history of the school and their journal by M. Aymand, 'The *Annales*
   and French Historiography', *Journal of European Economic History*
   1 (1972):491-511. See also M. Siegel, 'Henri Berr's *Revue de Synthèse*',
   History and Theory 9 (1970); and W. H. Sewell, 'Marc Bloch and the
   Logic of Comparative History', *History and Theory* 6 (1967). Many
   critics have expressed the opinion that F. Braudel's renowned masterpiece
   The Mediterranean and the Mediterranean World in the Age of Philip II
   (London, 1972-73) is weak when it seeks to deal with change. Cp. G.
   Parker, 'Braudel's *Mediterranean*', *History* 59 (1974):240-41.
3. *Journal of Modern History* 44 (1972):495, has a map of the influence of
   the school.
4. For the meaning and the pervasive influence of the famous textbook on
   historical method by Langlois and Seignobos, see D. Thomson's review
   of a new edition in *History and Theory* 6 (1967):236.
5. M. Bloch, *The Historian's Craft* (Manchester, 1954), pp. 8-9.
6. My assertion that narrative is the best and only appropriate form of
   doing justice to and of shaping time is a bold assertion that has often been
   challenged. Cp. the searching discussions by A. C. Danto, 'Narrative
   Sentences', *History and Theory* 2 (1962); M. Mandelbaum, 'A Note on
   History as Narrative', *History and Theory* 6 (1967); The symposium on
   Mandelbaum, ibid. 8 (1969):275-94; and W. H. Dray, 'Narrative in Historiography', ibid. 10 (1971). It seems to me that these discussions all
   suffer from a total defect. They do not recognise that any event, no
   matter how small, is divisible and that we can therefore think of any
   event only as a construction or a putting together of other events. In
   this sense the concept 'narration' is really implicit in the concept 'event'.
7. Although thoughtful philosophers have never subscribed to this view
   and although thoughtful historians know from their professional practice
   that this view is untenable, it is still considered the hallmark of professional respectability among historians and their public to believe that
   sound detective work can uncover the facts (cp., e.g., Th. Schieder,
   'Unterschiede zwischen historischer und sozialwissenschaftlicher
   Methode', in *Festschrift für Hermann Heimpel* 1 [Göttingen, 1971])
   and that one can then, according to one's taste, inclination, conscience,
   or ideology try one's hand at explaining or interpreting them at one's
   peril. Most academic historians nowadays, as the pages of the learned

journals of almost all countries attest, prefer to leave them as they stand. Even so skillful and experienced an historian as Miss Wedgwood, to mention a random example, can speak of the 'solid structure of fact' ('Tragic Wallenstein', *Encounter* 278 [1976]:65). Although this view is so absurd and so patently false, there is no point in invoking authority to prove it. But it is well to remind ourselves that no less an historian than Carl L. Becker drew the attention of historians in 1926 to the absurdity of the belief in 'hard facts' (P. L. Snyder, ed., *Detachment and the Writing of History: Essays and Letters of Carl Becker* [Ithaca, 1958], pp. 141f.). So did Hayden V. White in 'The Burden of History', *History and Theory* 5 (1966): 131. On the philosophical side I would like to refer to Gregory Bateson, *Steps Towards an Ecology of Mind* (London, 1973), p. 456: there are no facts in nature, he states, only an infinite number of potential facts; and F. Waismann, *How I See Philosophy*, ed. R. Harré (London, 1968), p. 64: "Language contributes to the formation and participates in the constitution of a fact. . . ."

8. Samuel Richardson has the unenviable reputation of being the novelist who left nothing out. But not even he gave a full account. His reputation of leaving out nothing is only relative to other novelists who left out more.

9. Darwin, too, was very restrictive in his choice of general laws and for this reason was able to make the story of evolution look like a time sequence. In fact it is not a story of the succession of events in time but a story of events that are linked by a given set of general laws such as *natura non facit saltum* and 'the fittest always survive' among others. The great debate between Darwin and, for example, Lamarck or Bergson is not a debate about the evidence but a debate about the laws to be employed to turn the evidence into a story of cause and effect. The dependence of both biology and geology on this recognition was clearly noticed by James Hutton and Charles Darwin. Cp. F. J. Teggart, *Theory and Process of History* (Berkeley, 1941), pp. 137f. For James Hutton and geology , see G. J. Whitrow, *What Is Time?* (London, 1972), p. 24f.: 'He [Hutton] realized that the true scientific approach is not to invite such *ad hoc* hypotheses [a unique series of sudden catastrophes] but to test whether or not the same agents as are operating now [i.e. the general laws of physics and chemistry known to us] could have operated all through the past'. In these and all such subsequent cases the possibility of establishing a historical series of events depends on a prior agreement to confine oneself to a given set of general laws. In ordinary history such prior agreement is neither possible nor desirable.

10. In book form, first published in London, 1957.

11. The importance of general laws in Darwin's story of evolution and his conception of the chain of causation is explained by M. T. Ghiselin, *The Triumph of the Darwinian Method* (Berkeley, 1969), pp. 28-9, 112, 126-27.

12. R. Nisbet, *Social Change and History* (London, 1969), does not distinguish between change that is observable and change that is not. He argues correctly that nobody has ever seen a civilisation die (p. 3) and that talk of change in that context is metaphorical. But he is wrong in assuming that no change is observable and that therefore all talk of change is metaphorical. Although proverbially watched kettles never boil, it is nevertheless possible to watch a kettle come to the boil. Nisbet, however, is

right in the sense that when we deal with large-scale change and large events we are dealing with abstractions or constructs that cannot be observed. Indeed, his comment applies not only to change but also to the entities that are changing. Every single entity is an abstraction or construction and when we reduce it, we are never reducing it to a sense-datum, but always to yet another abstraction and construction. In no case is there an unbroken sequence from the stimulation of a nerve cell to anything we know to exist or to have happened. There is always at least one hiatus, and usually more than one.

13. *Memories of My Life*, ed. G. A. Bonnard (London, 1966), p. 136.

14. P. Janet, *L'Evolution de la mémoire* . . . (Paris, 1928), pp. 495-97, remarks that philosophers have a particular dislike for time.

15. See S. Shoemaker, 'Time Without Change', *Journal of Philosophy* 66 (1969). Shoemaker discusses the possibility that we might be able to think of time without change, but distinguishes such possibility from the truism that we cannot think of change without time.

Chapter Three: The Covering Law

1. The example of the ice and the broken leg is a very unpolished one. I have chosen it because I first heard it in a lecture by Popper. Popper was no doubt aware that it was an insufficiently analysed example, but I think he used it for didactic purposes. The lecture was part of an ordinary course and he was interested in drawing the attention of his students to the stark simplicity of the model, and I have always felt since that this is precisely what he achieved. Every important and seminal idea must be simple, at least at first sight. With this rough and simple example Popper admirably succeeded in drawing the attention of his students to the all-important fact that there is nothing to link the slipping with the broken leg, not even repeated observation of the sequence, and that the two events remain separate until one has recourse to a general law, even though in this case it might be no more than a lame generalisation. It is indeed Popper's main contribution to philosophy to have shown that we need a general law or generalisation *before* we can even start to observe sequences.

2. This model of what constitutes a causal explanation was first put forward by K. R. Popper, *Logik der Forschung* (Vienna, 1935), pp. 26ff. It is now available in English as *The Logic of Scientific Discovery* (London, 1959). See also idem, *The Open Society and Its Enemies* (London, 1945), 2:248-52, 342-43.

3. Popper's model was made available in English and first applied specifically to historical explanation by C. G. Hempel, 'The Function of General Laws in History', *Journal of Philosophy* 39 (1942). Since Hempel first introduced the model in English and applied it to history, it has also become known as 'Hempel's model'. During the years there has grown up an enormous controversial literature on the subject and I can only single out the following important discussions of the matter. A. Donagan, 'Historical Explanation: The Popper-Hempel Theory Reconsidered', *History and Theory* 1 (1964); M. Mandelbaum, 'Historical Explanation: The Problem of "Covering Laws"', *History and Theory* 1 (1961); R. H. Weingartner, 'The Quarrel about Historical Explanation', *Journal of Philosophy* 58 (1961); A. Donagan, 'Explanation in History', in *Theories*

of History, ed. P. Gardiner (Glencoe, 1959). The literature is not only vast but the participants in the debate as well as the readers appear to have come to treat the matter as sort of football game and the frequent discussions that continue unabated are often concerned not with the problem but with misunderstandings and misquotations and imputations of views that their authors modify or deny to have held. For the reader, the debate is more reminiscent of the progress of the Harlem Globetrotters or of Manchester United than of a sensible attempt to come to terms with an intellectual problem. People are said to have advanced from positions or to have retreated from views that they held earlier and the spectacle is much more like an in-game than an intelligent debate. The more people write, the greater the confusion. Some scholars have tried to label the different contestants and thus one has come to distinguish between idealists (supporters of Collingwood, who is alleged to be against covering laws) and Hempelians, also known as 'the covering-law theorists'. See Murray G. Murphey, *Our Knowledge of the Historical Past* (Indianapolis, 1973), p. 76; M. Mandelbaum, 'Historical Explanation', p. 229 (now reprinted under the title 'The Problem of "Covering Laws"' in *The Philosophy of History*, ed. P. Gardiner [London, 1974]) labels Dray and Donagan 'the reactionists' because they react against the unity of science in believing that history is *sui generis* and not part of the unity of science. The covering law theory is alleged to be part of the unity of science. But the reactionists are said to react against the model for reasons that differ from the criticisms of the model advanced by the idealists. J. Passmore reviewing William Dray's *Laws and Explanation in History* (Oxford, 1957) in the *Australian Journal of Politics and History* 4 (1958):269 wonders whether Dray should not be called an idealist.

4. I am not sure why this particular name was chosen. It is a good name because it indicates that the law is the factor in the story that covers the gap between one event and the next and thus draws attention to the fact that the two events that make the minimal story are not temporarily contiguous but separated by a gap.

5. Historians have been known to be so certain about the truth of their general laws or theories that they use them not only as a heuristic device but also to deduce from them events for which there are no sources. See J. Habakkuk, 'Economic History and Economic Theory', *Daedalus* 100 (1971):305–22. While almost all historians, past and present, have used theories tentatively and hesitatingly for such purposes in cases of extreme necessity, the deductive method has become a major strategy for econometric historians. One must wonder whether there is something special about *economic* theories that justifies such procedures. There is a vast literature on the subject. For a brief bibliography, see H. U. Wehler, *Geschichte als historische Sozialwissenschaft* (Frankfurt, 1973), p. 80.

6. This consideration should eliminate the force of M. Scriven's objections to the covering law model as stated in his 'Truisms as Grounds for Historical Explanations' in *Theories of History*, ed. P. Gardiner (Glencoe, 1959).

7. We obviously need and can afford a very liberal construction of the notion of general law because we are not concerned with explanation but with narration. In this special context, therefore, the very elaborate scruples and detailed examinations of the various types of general laws by Morton White, *Foundations of Historical Knowledge* (New York,

1965), esp. pp. 72ff. are superfluous. Morton White is a defender of the
covering law model and insofar as he is concentrating on explanation
rather than on narration, his examinations and qualifications are extremely valuable. The same applies to chapter 3 of Murphey, *Historical Past*.
Further problems and scruples are introduced when it is alleged that
general laws have to support counterfactual statements, that is, statements
that will be true in the future. Obviously, a strictly general law would
have to apply to the future. But there is legitimate doubt whether this
requirement is all that obvious, for since Popper it is no longer possible
to believe that the truth of a general law is dependent on what we know
of the future and Popper would not require of a general law that it
support counterfactual statements. All general laws are true until they
are falsified, and any counterfactual statement is a potential falsifier of
a general law. If this is borne in mind, we do not have to be overscrupu-
lous as to which generalisation deserves the title 'general law'.

8. See, e.g., P. C. Suppes, *A Probabilistic Theory of Causality* (Amsterdam,
1970).

9. Maine de Biran (1766–1824) proposed that we should think of causation
as a volition force or treat it on the analogy of an expectation. An effect,
he argued, is something we expect to happen just as we expect our arm
to move when we will to move it. For a lucid presentation of the proposal,
see Philip P. Hallie, *Maine de Biran* (Cambridge, Mass., 1959), ch. 4. It is
of great interest that two contemporary philosophers have now taken up
this argument and presented it in two recent books. David Pears, *Questions in the Philosophy of Mind* (London, 1975), discusses the causal
framework of our thinking and suggests that our notion of causality is
directly derived from our knowledge of what we are going to do and our
experience of the force of our own motives within ourselves. Similarly
G. H. von Wright, *Causality and Determinism* (New York, 1974), states
that out concept of causality is intrinsically linked with our conception
of action and agency. He argues that our view of causal necessity is to be
understood in terms of our own experience of our ability to *make*
changes in nature or to interfere with nature. In one way or another these
lines of thought about causation all go back to Vico, who maintained
that human beings, through reflection, have direct access to the causes of
their own mental activity and that that access constitutes a vital difference
between the intelligibility we have of causation in the human or mental
sciences and the intelligibility or, rather, nonintelligibility, of causation
in the natural sciences. In this form the distinction is also fundamental
in the works of W. Dilthey. See *Gesammelte Schriften* (Leipzig and
Berlin, 1927), 7:156.

10. *The Problem of Historical Knowledge* (New York: 1939), p. 200. For
similar views, see W. H. Dray, *Laws and Explanation in History* (Oxford,
1957), pp. 157–58 and W. H. Walsh, *An Introduction to the Philosophy
of History* (London, 1951), p. 23. This view is reminiscent of A. N.
Whitehead, *Process and Reality* (Cambridge, 1929), ch. 8, although
Whitehead presented it in a more complex and sophisticated form. Whitehead was anxious to deny that there are permanent and stable substances. He saw the whole world as sets of genetic processes and argued
that the categories of development of these processes reflect a very
primitive experience of causality. Events, he said, are temporal interac-
tions with identifiable phases. If one wishes to see the world in terms of

process rather than in terms of substance, this is a good approach. But if one analyses it formally, one will find that it too must be reduced to the covering law model. The only reason why we can perceive a genetic *process* and why we have primitive experience of causality is because we can leap from subevent to subevent with the help of a general law. Take the general law away and the leap becomes impossible and the perception of the genetic process evaporates. Whitehead should therefore not be considered as an alternative to the covering law model but as a different version of it. See the interesting paper by Dale H. Porter, 'History as Process', *History and Theory* 14 (1974).

11. 'Collingwood's Historicism: A Dialectic of Progress', in *Critical Essays on the Philosophy of R. G. Collingwood*, ed. M. Krausz (London, 1972). A. Donagan, *The Later Philosophy of R. G. Collingwood* (Oxford, 1962), tends to conclude from Collingwood's choice of examples that Collingwood was a kind of methodological individualist, though he does admit that the acts of groups are included (pp. 207–09). It seems that he has mistaken the examples with which Collingwood, for the sake of a straight argument, has chosen to illustrate his case for the substance of Collingwood's ideas.

12. *Analytical Philosophy of History* (Cambridge, 1965), p. 143.

13. See ch. 1, n. 9.

14. This was a widely held distinction. See esp. H. Rickert, *Die Grenzen der naturwissenschaftlichen Begriffsbildung* (Leipzig, 1896; 5th ed., Tübingen, 1929).

15. It is now often suggested that even in nature many laws may hold only in certain places at certain times and it is believed that gravity is diminishing. See the review article by J. Taylor, 'Revolution in the Heavens', *Encounter* 244 (1974):82–86. Cp. S. Toulmin and J. Goodfield, *The Discovery of Time* (Harmondsworth, 1967), p. 334: 'The "laws of nature" themselves turn out to change slowly from one cosmic epoch to another'. See also Peter Wiles' remarks in *The Historian Between the Ethnologist and the Futurologist*, ed. J. Dumoulin and D. Moisi (Paris, 1973), p. 96: 'After all political explanation of this type is indeed a kind of generalisation, but is valid only for an epoch, and the politician, or the political economist, faces daily the nightmare of the astronomer and the astrophysicist, namely the super-heavy star . . . of which the natural elements have lost their ordinary properties.'

16. 'All laws are general, but there are different degrees of generality; and what may be a fact about a particular society may also be a law governing the behaviour of members of that society'. See Murphey, *Historical Past*, p. 81 and the excellent discussion preceding this passage in which Murphey shows that lawlike statements *can* contain uneliminable reference to individual things or to particular times and places. Cp. also White, *Foundations*, p. 48. These passages support in detail my summary reference to general laws with limited universality.

17. Cp. Popper, *Logic of Scientific Discovery*, p. 82f.

18.   To correct the interpretation of an individual work of art by a 'history of style', which in turn can only be built up by interpreting individual works, may look like a vicious circle. It is indeed, a circle, though not a vicious, but a methodical one [cf. E. Wind, *Das Experiment und die Metaphysik* (Tübingen, 1934), p. 6; idem, 'Some Points of Contact between History and Science', *Philosophy and*

History: Essays Presented to Ernest Cassirer (Oxford, 1936), pp. 255 ff.] Whether we deal with historical or natural phenomena, the individual observation assumes the character of a 'fact' only when it can be related to other, analogous observations in such a way that the whole series 'makes sense'. This 'sense' is, therefore, fully capable of being applied, as a control, to the interpretation of a new individual observation within the same range of phenomena. If, however, this new individual observation definitely refuses to be interpreted according to the 'sense' of the series and if an error proves to be impossible, the 'sense' of the series will have to be re-formulated to include the new individual observation. This *circulus methodicus* applies, of course, not only to the relationship between the interpretation of motifs and the history of style, but also to the relationship between the interpretation of images, stories, and allegories and the history of types, and to the relationship between the interpretation of intrinsic meanings and the history of cultural symptoms in general. E. Panofsky, *Meaning in the Visual Arts* (New York, 1955), p. 35. Idem, *Studies in Iconology* (New York, 1962), p. 11.

See also the remarks on hermeneutic circularity by K. Hübner in *Die Funktion der Geschichte in unserer Zeit,* ed. E. Jäckel and E. Weymar (Stuttgart, 1975), pp. 41–58. The concept of the hermeneutic circle goes back to Dilthey and still plays an important part in H. G. Gadamer, *Wahrheit und Methode* (Tübingen, 1960). 'Dilthey', writes E. D. Hirsch, *Validity in Interpretation* (New Haven, 1967), p. 259, 'called this apparent paradox the hermeneutic circle and observed that it was not vicious because a genuine dialectic always occurs between our idea of the whole and our perception of the parts that constitute it. Once the dialectic has begun, neither side is totally determined by the other.'
19. (Oxford, 1957).
20. (London, 1972).
21. Cp. J. Passmore, 'Explanation in Everyday Life, in Science and in History', *History and Theory* 2 (1962–63):105.
22. *The Nature of Historical Explanation* (London, 1952).
23. For Dray, see *Laws and Explanation*, and for Donagan, 'Explanation in History', in *Theories of History,* ed. P. Gardiner (Glencoe, 1959).
24. Cp. the discussion in Murphey, *Historical Past*, p. 71.
25. *Between Philosophy and History* (Princeton, 1970), p. 298.
26. L. O. Mink, 'The Autonomy of Historical Understanding', *History and Theory* 5 (1966), writes that the narrative mode is 'synoptic' and involves an act of understanding that is not accessible to deductive analysis. W. B. Gallie, *Philosophy and the Historical Understanding* (London, 1964), pp. 105ff, says that the historian's narrative style is supposed to reveal growth and development and that historians who use the covering law model for their explanation must fail in showing the genetic nexus between events. See the interesting article by Porter, 'History as Process', where an attempt is made to bring 'Hempelians and geneticists' together with the help of A. N. Whitehead. The attempt is interesting; but the alleged rift between Hempelians and geneticists is based on a misunderstanding all round, for without the model there can be no genetic narrative.

27. 'I did not, however, regard this particular analysis', writes Karl Popper, 'as especially important for *historical* explanation'. *Unended Quest,* (London, 1976), p. 176. I hope that I will be forgiven for putting the analysis to a use for which it was not intended. As T. S. Eliot once remarked, a poem has meanings other than those intended by its author. 'We may gain more knowledge', writes Popper, 'from our children or from our theories than we ever imparted to them'. Ibid., p. 196.

Chapter 4: Explanation and Interpretation

1. See F. Meinecke, *Die Entstehung des Historismus* (Munich, 1936); now available in English as *Historism: The Rise of a New Historical Outlook* (London, 1972); E. Troeltsch, *Der Historismus und seine Probleme* (Tübingen, 1922). Cp. the review of Meinecke's book by F. Gilbert in *History and Theory* 13 (1974):59–64. For the whole history of this matter, see G. G. Iggers, *The German Conception of History* (Middletown, Conn., 1968), chs. 6 and 7.

2. *The Poverty of Historicism* (London, 1957), p. 3, where historicism is defined as the belief that the task of the social sciences is to propound historical prophecies and that we need such prophecies if we are to conduct politics in a rational way. Originally *Historismus* meant almost the exact opposite and was certainly not supposed to be a social science or the method *par excellence* of the social sciences. But there is a point of contact between Popper's use of the term and its original meaning. *Historismus* implied that as entities endured through time, they did so in obedience to an *innere Gesetzlichkeit* — an inner law. The German term for inner law is very suggestive and fraught with significant meaning, but untranslatable. When rendered in English and examined in the cool light of reason it becomes something like a 'unique developmental law' and in this sense it deserves all the criticism which Popper raises against it. On the other hand, it is only fair to remember that the German *innere Gesetzlichkeit* was largely derived from the first of Goethe's *Orphische Urworte*, '. . . das Gesetz nach dem du angetreten,' and in that sense it is far removed from the notion of developmental law and from all of Popper's criticisms. See A. Donagan, 'Popper's Examination of Historicism', in *The Philosophy of Karl Popper*, ed. P. A. Schilpp (La Salle, Ill., 1974). For a detailed history of 'historism' and 'historicism', see Iggers, *German Conception of History*, pp. 287–90.

3. Meinecke did believe that historism frees our historical understanding from all ideology and makes it completely scientific and objective because it grasps the uniqueness of the unique and does not force it into or subsume it under an alien, that is, a general, concept. It dispenses with the universal. In this sense historism is a chimera for the very use of the word 'grasps' involves one in universals of some kind or other. Cp. M. C. Brands, *Historisme als Ideologie* (Assen, 1965). See especially the doubts expressed by H. G. Gadamer, *Truth and Method* (New York, 1975), p. xiv and p. 6. On pp. 15 and 278 Gadamer explicitly stresses the universality of universalisation.

4. Collingwood used the term 'reenactment' of other people's thoughts to refer to our understanding of the *Sinngebild*. Some of his readers have assumed that he meant by reenactment 'rethinking' and once one supposes that this is what he meant, one comes close to the idea that he

assumed that rethinking is tantamount to explanation. But I agree with
Leon Goldstein, 'Collingwood on the Constitution of the Historical Past',
in *Critical Essays on the Philosophy of R. G. Collingwood*, ed. M. Krausz
(London, 1972), that any attempt to explain an action *presupposes*,
rather than undertakes, the rethinking of the agent's thought. All the
same, Goldstein somewhat overstresses the difference between reenactment and explanation. But this is a problem for Collingwood exegesis. In
my present argument the two operations, though not identical, are
certainly connected.

5. See for example ch. 10 of *An Autobiography* (London, 1944), and *The
   Idea of History* (Oxford, 1946), pp. 217ff.

6. It is a moot point, again to be resolved by exegesis, whether Collingwood
   did or did not mean by reenactment something like 'intuition'. His
   positivist critics say he does, so that they can have a stick to beat him
   with. Other, more idealist, readers often insist, on the contrary, that he
   overintellectualised the process of historical understanding. See A.
   Donagan, *The Later Philosophy of R. G. Collingwood* (Oxford, 1962),
   pp. 191ff, for a comparatively positivist exegesis. Whatever doubts one
   may have about the term 'reenactment' it is preferable to such terms as
   'intuitive grasp', 'empathy', 'historical vision', and the like as used by
   Herder, Dilthey, Ranke, Troeltsch, and others.

7.   Thus generalisation enters indirectly, as a consequence of the
       applicability of 'ideal types'. Generalisations of a different kind also
       enter in as far as they are invoked to explain the connections be-
       tween items within various models or ideal types. These kinds of
       generalisations, borrowed rather promiscuously from anywhere, are
       admittedly invoked *ad hoc* and in a rough and ready manner.
           Thus generalisation enters somewhat indirectly. On the other
       hand, the ideal types themselves are an essential, integral part of the
       method, and indispensable. There is no alternative to using them. The
       alternative is not some brave, tough-minded history, a pure un-
       adorned narrative of 'what really happened', but only a childish narra-
       tive which takes the nexus between events for granted. E Gellner,
       'Our Current sense of History', in *The Historian Between the Eth-
       nologist and the Futurologist*, ed. J. Dumoulin and D. Moisi, (Paris,
       1973), p. 10.

8. *Autobiography*, ch. 10; *Idea of History*, pp. 217–28.

9. It has been shown in n. 6 that there is room for disagreement as to the
   exact meaning of Collingwood's intuitionism. I doubt very much whether
   Collingwood really intended to imply that a historian had to possess the
   gifts of Caesar or Rembrandt to reenact their thoughts, as Popper, *Objective Knowledge* (Oxford, 1972), p. 188, suggests. I would like to
   think that Collingwood meant by reenactment more or less what Popper
   means by situational analysis. 'The historian's task', writes Popper, in
   Objective Knowledge, p. 189, 'is, therefore, so to reconstruct the problem situation as it appeared to the agent, that the actions of the agent
   become *adequate* to the situation. This is very similar to Collingwood's
   method, but it eliminates from the theory of understanding and from the
   historical method precisely the subjective . . . element which for Collingwood and most other theorists of understanding (hermeneuticists) is its
   salient point'. I would prefer not to bracket Collingwood with the other

hermeneuticists, as Popper does. And when one looks at the quotation from Troeltsch in ch. 4, n. 11, one must have one's doubts whether the other hermeneuticists were as firm in their rejection of situational analysis as Popper claims. They lacked the beautiful lucidity of Popper's precision; but may have meant something much closer to him than he admits. This applies especially to Collingwood, whose choice of the word 'reenactment' is indicative of his intention to depsychologise the process involved and to get away from various forms of intuition. Collingwood was not given to think in terms of metalanguage, metaproblems, and metatheories. He therefore chose the term 'reenactment' as the next best thing to describe the thoroughly intellectual nature of the process. However this may be, Popper's use of the term 'adequate' introduces a new difficulty; or, more exactly, glosses too readily over an old difficulty. The Saxon historian Widukind (late tenth century) explained the rise of the Saxon house by the fact that it possessed relics. It is easy enough to reenact his thought or to carry out the necessary situational analysis and to formulate the metatheory that Widukind had a theory that the possession of relics causes dynastic power. No doubt, this theory was adequate for him. But while our metatheory is adequate for our understanding of Widukind, Widukind's theory is *not* adequate for *our* understanding of the reasons for the rise of the Saxon house. For further discussion of the difference between what is adequate for Widukind and what is adequate for us, see p. 80.

10. Ibid., p. 188.
11. The gap between intuitive grasp and rational situational analysis was already narrowed by E. Troeltsch, *Gesammelte Schriften* (Tübingen, 1923) 3:59, 'Historical intuition, the real essence of historiography, is at the same time thought'. Troeltsch was very careless in his expression and simply glossed over such differences as there might be between historical intuition and thought. The fact that he did shows that he did not think it important to distinguish and that he was unaware of the quite considerable differences of opinion that might arise. I think that Popper's description of situational analysis deals once and for all with everything that is referred to variously as empathy, historical intuition, or reenactment.
12. During the last few decades philosophers have reacted against the hermeneuticists, who believed that one explains when one enters into somebody's mind or interprets it, with a vengeance. They have, in England and America, concentrated entirely on the problem in terms of social science by asking the question how one explains something to us. This should not be taken as a criticism of that literature but merely as a comment on the limits of its relevance. For an example of this literature, see P. Gardiner, *The Nature of Historical Explanation* (Oxford, 1952). Even though this book defends the covering law, it does so for purposes different from the purposes for which it is used here. For other examples, see W. Dray, 'The Historical Explanation of Actions Reconsidered', in *The Philosophy of History*, ed. P. Gardiner (London, 1974); A. C. Danto, *Analytical Philosophy of History* (Cambridge, 1968), chs. 10 and 11; R. R. Brown, *Explanation in the Social Sciences* (London, 1964); Qu. Boyce Gibson, *The Logic of Social Inquiry* (London, 1960); M. Mandelbaum, 'Historical Explanation', *History and Theory* 1 (1961); and the excellent chapter 3 in Murray G. Murphey, *Our Knowledge of the Historical Past* (Indianapolis, 1973); Morton White, *Foundations of*

Historical Knowledge (New York, 1965), chs. 2 and 3; A. Donagan, 'Historical Explanation', *History and Theory* 1 (1964). Some of these authors support and some attack the covering law model, but all follow in the original footsteps of Hempel; see idem, 'The Function of General Laws in History', *Journal of Philosophy* 39 (1942) and the large number of papers he has published on this topic. Since he saw the problem of explanation in history as nothing but a special instance of the problem of explanation in general, this literature is entirely concerned with the question as to the formal conditions that have to be fulfilled for any law or story to count as an explanation. My own argument is not concerned with the logico-formal conditions that have to be satisfied if a narration can be accepted as an explanation, but with the content the laws and generalisations have to have to make the narrative hang together and to make it intelligible. It is therefore not encumbent on me, for the present argument, to discuss this literature.

13. In this sense the concept of 'historical explanation' is supremely important because under no circumstances must one simply set aside people's homemade explanations. They are part and parcel of the historian's raw material and are to be treated with the greatest respect. Even if one accepts Ranke's aim that we have to find out what actually happened, one has to include these homemade explanations for they are in a simple positivist sense, part of what actually happened. Cp. C. Lévi-Strauss, *Structural Anthropology* (New York, 1963), p. 282, 'Culture's homemade models cannot be set aside. . . . '

14. The present example is largely made up to illustrate the argument. For a scholarly investigation of Caesar's intentions, see Victor Ehrenberg, 'Caesar's Final Aims' in *Man, State, and Deity* (London, 1974). I have on purpose not drawn on Ehrenberg.

15. I have chosen this example on purpose to draw attention to the ambiguity necessarily involved in this question. It so happens that we have grounds for supposing that Caesar was interested both in his mother (Suetonius, ch. 7: Caesar dreamt he had sexual intercourse with his mother) and in the story of Oedipus (Suetonius, ch. 56: Caesar wrote a play about Oedipus). However, there is a far cry from these interests, strange though they may be, to a fully Freudian way of interpreting Caesar. Nevertheless, Suetonius' testimony does provide reasons for wondering how much interpretation and how much explanation there is in the present example.

16. (London, 1972).

17. The histories of Alexander the Great by Arrian and Plutarch are very much concerned with this aspect.

18. W. W. Tarn, 'Alexander the Great and the Unity of Mankind', in *Alexander the Great: The Main Problems* ed. G. T. Griffiths (Cambridge, 1966). Cp. P. A. Brunt, 'The Aims of Alexander', *Greece and Rome* 12 (1965).

19. E. Badian, 'Alexander the Great and the Loneliness of Power', in *Studies in Greek and Roman History* (Oxford, 1964).

20. For further comments on our understanding of Alexander the Great, see ch. 7, n. 10.

21. In a number of widely read books, E. Betti has argued that the sole legitimate purpose of historical study is to dispell such incomprehensions. See, e.g., *Die Hermeneutik als allgemeine Methodik der Geisteswissenschaften* (Tübingen, 1962), p. 49.

22. *The England of Elizabeth* (London, 1951), p. 464f. and esp. p. 487,

'There is no nonsense that human beings have not been prepared to die for at all times. . . .'

23. *Archbishop Laud* (London, 1940).
24. For a discussion of the difficulties the historian encounters in understanding strange passions, superstitions, and the like, see F. West, *Biography as History* (Sydney, 1973), p. 7, n. 5. West points out that historians often get around this problem by adding the adjective 'surprisingly' to whatever somebody did or thought. But I would comment that if that adjective occurs too often, the historian is obviously not doing his job. It is extraordinary how rapidly a historian's acceptance of what is credible or intelligible can change and how easily a new political experience or a mere headline in a newspaper can change one's attitude from incredulity to acceptance. E. Badian remarked very properly, in his review of R. L. Fox, *Alexander the Great* (London, 1973), that Fox is probably wrong in surmising, when royal pages conspired to kill Alexander, that they did so because their fathers had been demoted. To Fox, whose experience is confined to what one can pick up in Eton and Oxford, Badian says, it is incredible that young boys might act from genuine political motives because he has never heard of boys of fifteen throwing hand grenades from very political motives. See idem, *New York Review of Books* (Sept. 19, 1974), p. 10.
25. The example is taken from Widukind, the historian of the ancient Saxons. Cp. R. Southern, 'Aspects of the European Tradition of Historical Writing', *Transactions of the Royal Historical Society* 20 (1970):191.
26.   The philosophical significance of the scientific industrial 'form of life', whose rapid global diffusion is the main event of our time, is that for all practical purposes it does provide us with a solution of the problem of relativism . . . The cognitive and technical superiority of one form of life is so manifest . . . that it simply cannot be questioned. E. Gellner, 'The New Idealism', in *Problems in the Philosophy of Science*, ed. I. Lakatos and A. Musgrave (Amsterdam, 1968), p. 405.

27. *An Economic Interpretation of the Constitution* (New York, 1913). The purely 'interpretative' character of Beard's story is analysed by R. E. Brown, *Charles Beard and the Constitution* (Princeton, 1956). Brown, however, does not do justice to the importance of interpretation. Once he has shown that Beard transposed a model of society from his own day to the eighteenth century, he thought he had made an end of Beard. I think this is plainly false. Beard is as entitled to his general law as the fathers of the Constitution were to theirs. There is no telling where the *real* truth lies. For further discussion of the problem of truth, see ch. 8.
28. (New York, 1975).
29. *Piété baroque et déchristianisation en Provence au XVIIIe siècle* (Paris, 1973).
30. *Western Attitudes Towards Death* (Baltimore, 1974).
31. Peter Munz, 'John Cassian', *Journal of Ecclesiastical History* 11 (1960).
32. Hexter's term is new in this context. But the phenomenon it describes was first observed by B. Croce when he wrote that 'historicism . . . is the truth of humanism'. See idem, *History as the Story of Liberty* (London, 1941), p. 315. See also chapter 10 of Collingwood, *Autobiography*. 'Humanism', as the old saying goes, is the conviction that 'I am a man and

that nothing human is alien to me'. Cp. also Collingwood, *Idea of History*, p. 218, middle paragraph.

33. For an English translation and full bibliographical details, see Peter Munz and G. M. Ellis, *Boso's Life of Pope Alexander III* (Oxford, 1973).

34. They are printed in Jacques Migne, *Patrologiae . . . Series Latina* (Paris, 1844-1864) 200.

35. The presence of the mythical scheme has eluded historians, who have, without exception, accepted the verdict of A. Brackmann that the story of Pope Alexander III by Boso is a *Life* of Alexander. See his 'Der *Liber Pontificalis*' in *Gesammelte Aufsätze* (Weimar, 1941), p. 393 and 'Die Handschriften des *Liber Pontificalis*', *Neues Archiv* 26 (1901).

36. Cp. W. H. Auden, *The Enchafed Flood: Or the Romantic Iconography of the Sea* (London, 1951).

37. *Western Society and the Church in the Middle Ages* (Harmondsworth, 1970), p. 36. Southern, here, is on firm ground in following the views of M. Pacaut, *Alexandre III* (Paris, 1956) and G. Le Bras, 'Le Droit Romain au service de la domination pontificale', *Nouvelle revue historique de droit français et étranger* (1949).

38. *Geschichte Alexanders III und der Kirche seiner Zeit* (1st edition, Berlin and Leipzig, 1845; 3 vols. 1860-64).

39. 'Strictly speaking the concept of illusion has no place in psychology because no experience actually copies reality'. E. Boring, *Sensation and Perception* (New York, 1942), p. 238. The remark is equally applicable to history. Boso, Reuter, and Southern supply three very different visions of Alexander III. It is idle to speculate which is correct because none is copied from reality.

40. (Wien, 1949), ch. 8.

41. See Th. Mayer's review of Heer, *Aufgang Europas*, in *Historische Zeitschrift* 171 (1953):462.

42. (New York, 1958).

43. The same and similar considerations apply to another of Erikson's substitutions. On p. 97 of *Luther*, Erikson writes that Luther's entry into the monastery was a moratorium. He needed a respite from the pressures he had been exposed to. But H. H. Boehmer, *Martin Luther* (New York, 1957), pp. 89ff, writes that Luther became a monk to 'work' for salvation. There can be no doubt that Boehmer's universal ('monks work for salvation') is a proper explanation and that Erikson's universal ('young people need a moratorium') is an interpretation. But since it may well be that Erikson tells us what *really* happened as opposed to what Luther thought happened, part of what really happened is taking place in the minds of twentieth-century psychologists who understand the institution of a moratorium as Erikson does on pp. 100-04.

44. See, e.g., J. H. Rüsen, ed., *Historische Objektivität* (Göttingen, 1975).

45. 'Everyman his own Historian', *American Historical Review* 37 (1932). This line of argument has a very respectable ancestry in the famous book on the theory of history by J. G. Droysen, *Historik*, 4th ed. (Darmstadt, 1960).

46. 'The Objectivity of History', *Philosophy* 33 (1958).

47. Cp. R. G. Collingwood, *The Principles of Art* (Oxford, 1938), p. 43; S. Langer, *Problems of Art* (London, 1957); W. Nowothny, *The Language Poets Use* (London, 1962), p. 45: 'The nature of language is such that there can be no such thing as a neutral transcription of an object into

words'. André Malraux *Les Voix du silence* (Paris, 1951), p. 451 and André Gide, *Les Faux Monnayeurs* (Paris, 1925), p. 255, speak of the 'rivalry' between reality and a story about reality. All in all, when one thinks one is describing events, one is really adding more events by one's description. This would be very disconcerting were it not for the fact that one can have no conception of the events in the first place and a story one tells is therefore hardly an addition — for it cannot be thought of as an addition to something if that something is something one has no conception of. All this is quite commonplace among literary critics and art critics. It is strange that of all story tellers historians alone keep imagining that they are exempt and that these insights into the nature of reality, and of 'realism', and into the operation of our imagination do not apply to the stories *they* tell.

48. The present denial of the concept of absolute objectivity should neither be mistaken as pessimistic resignation in the face of insuperable odds nor as an open invitation to reckless subjectivity according to which one wild guess is as good or as bad as another. It follows directly from the view that the particles of which events consist are not temporally contiguous and that they must be connected to each other by a factor other than time. There is an infinite number of possible ways of connecting them and and hence no one 'objective' way. Such objectivity as can be reached does not consist in finding the one and only way in which they are linked but in tracing the relationship between the many possible links. The search for such objectivity, as contrasted to the search for a nonexisting mindless absolute objectivity, must be strictly controlled by the consideration that any link offered should stand in a detectable and intelligible relationship to all the other links that have been offered. In this sense the links that have been thought of in the past must limit the field in which links to be found or thought up in the future will have to lie. See R. Unger, 'The Problem of Historical Objectivity: A Sketch of its Development to the Time of Hegel', *History and Theory* 11 (1971).

49. Cp. E. Jones, *Sigmund Freud* (London, 1956) vol. 1, ch. 3.

50. 'Concluding Address' in *The Explanation of Culture Change*, ed. C. Renfrew (London, 1973), p. 769.

51. M. Weber, *The Protestant Ethic* (London, 1930). R. Tawney, *Religion and the Rise of Capitalism* (London, 1926).

52. 'Concepts and Society', *Transactions of the Fifth World Congress of Sociology* 1 (Louvain, 1962).

53. Victor White, *God and the Unconscious* (London, 1952), p. 57. Cp. Mary Douglas, *Natural Symbols* (London, 1970), p. 55: 'It fits the Durkheimian premise that society and God can be equated: to the extent that society is impoverished and confused in its structure of relations, to that extent is the idea of God poor and unstable in content'. Durkheim had thought that the equation works only in one way and that all religious phenomena can be reduced to social events. Mary Douglas, without rejecting Durkheim, points out that if God is the social, one can equally presume that the social is God.

54. *Lotte in Weimar* (London, 1947), p. 336.

55. Given that we can have no definition of reality, the concept of mask is relative. Appearances mask reality as readily as reality, so called, masks appearances. Cp. Peter Munz, *When the Golden Bough Breaks* London, 1973), p. 90.

56. I shall never forget the spark of illumination when I first read White, *God and the Unconscious*, p. 57, where he says that there is no reason why we should see God as a father-figure rather than our father as a God-figure.

57. In modern times we take it for granted that reality consists of such substances as sex and money and that its relations should be quantitative ones. Everything else tends to be regarded as appearance behind which the reality lies hidden. It seems worth pondering why we take it for granted that it is so and not the other way round. Similarly, when examining bias, we should not confine ourselves to examing whether the grounds for attributing bias are true or false, but with questioning the form of life and society in which bias is regarded as a fault. On this last point see P. McHugh et al., *On the Beginning of Social Inquiry* (London, 1974).

58. P. Goubert, *L'Ancien Régime*, 2nd ed. (Paris, 1969), p. 257 and R. Mousnier, *La Plume, la faucille et le marteau* (Paris, 1970); J. H. Shennan, *The Parlement of Paris* (London, 1968), p. 297; E. F. Heckscher, *Mercantilism* (London, 1955), 1:217. See also the polemical discussion by F. Furet, 'Le Catéchisme révolutionnaire', *Annales* 26 (1971), pp. 255–88.

59. A. Cobban, 'The Myth of the French Revolution', in *Aspects of the French Revolution* (London, 1968) and *The Social Interpretation of the French Revolution* (Cambridge, 1964).

60. The classic examples are G. Lefèbvre, *Les Paysans du nord pendant la révolution française* (Paris, 1924), pp. 48–50; A. Mathiez, *La Vie chère et le mouvement social sous le terreur* (Paris, 1927); A. Soboul, *The Parisian Sans-Culottes and the French Revolution* (Oxford, 1964) and *Précis d'histoire de la révolution française* (Paris, 1962). See also R. Robin, *La Société française en 1789: Sumer-en-Anvois* (Paris, 1970) and C. Mazauric, *Sur la révolution française* (Paris, 1970). One of the most sensitive attempts at bridge building is G. Rudé, 'The Origins of the French Revolution', *Past and Present* 8 (1955).

61. The following statement is a typical example of such a thought: 'The important and basic spring of action for man is his relationship to the alignment of classes in the economic struggle . . . . It would be impossible to arrive at a judgement about an individual by noting only his own view of himself', Karl Marx, *A Contribution to the Critique of Political Economy*, trans. N. I. Stone (Chicago, 1913), pp. 11f.

62. There is a parallel controversy in seventeenth-century England. Interpretative theory presumes that the people who spearheaded the Puritan Revolution were 'bourgeois' and that the gentlemen, impropriators or yeoman farmers who actually did spearhead it, though rural people, must be called 'bourgeois', simply because they started the revolution. On the other side, historians argue that since the people who started the revolution were demonstrably not 'bourgeois' in our sense of the term, the revolution was not started by bourgeois people. The whole question revolves round the problem as to whether one can define 'bourgeois' independently or whether one simply applies the word to whoever happens to start a revolution against a political order that has its roots in feudalism. Cp., e.g., J. H. Hexter, 'The Burden of Proof', *Times Literary Supplement* 3841 (1975): 1250, col. 5 and Christopher Hill's reply, 3843 (1975): 1333, col. 2.

63. Though a commonplace in existentialist psychiatry from Binswanger to R. D. Laing, this insight is rarely given sufficient weight by social scientists.

Unfortunately even existentialist psychiatrists ready to protest against labelling certain people as sick and of thus reducing them to objects incapable of making valid statements about themselves, tend to overlook the fact that the process of objectification begins long before psychiatrists get hold of 'patients'. Any such potential patient, when asserting something about himself, looks upon himself as an object. Objectification is not something terrible done by psychiatrists or social scientists to 'patients', but something that is inflicted by man on himself. See ch. 8, n. 40.

64. Cp. Peter Munz, *Frederick Barbarossa: A Study in Medieval Politics* (London, 1969), pp. 30-32.

65. Ibid., p. 336.

66. See R. Horton and R. Finnegan eds., *Modes of Thought* (London, 1973), p. 32 and the references to Evans-Pritchard cited, for the anthropologists' concern with the problem of translation. Murphey, *Historical Past*, pp. 33ff., has a searching discussion of this problem.

67. See C. Lévi-Strauss, *Tristes Tropiques* (New York, 1974), ch. 38, 'A Little Glass of Rum', for a discussion of the moral and epistemological aspects of this matter.

68. 'The Copernican revolution in our conception of history amounts to this. In the past, the past was taken to be the past. The present merely endeavoured to approach this fixed point as best it could. But now the relationship between past and present has been inversed. The past is bebecoming the dialectical precipitate of the enlightened consciousness of the present' [my translation]. Walter Benjamin, quoted after R. Tiedemann, *Studien zur Philosophie Walter Benjamins* (Frankfurt, 1965), p. 125.

69. First published by J. A. Goebhardt in Bamberg and Würzburg in 1807 as the first part of a projected *System der Wissenschaft*.

Chapter Five: Myth: An Alternative Coverage

1. (Baltimore, 1973), pp. 34-38.

2. This does not prevent the reader from making substitutions and any reader may wish to examine any shape in terms of the explanation-interpretation dichotomy.

3. Cp. L. Wittgenstein: The paradigm case is 'not something that is represented, but a means of representation'. *Philosophical Investigations* (Oxford, 1958), par. 50. A. Boyce Gibson, *Muse and Thinker* (Harmondsworth, 1972), p. 75, comments that Wittgenstein blends with Hegel in this presentation of the concrete universal.

4. This was well observed by E. Auerbach, *Mimesis: The Representation of Reality in Western Literature*, trans. W. R. Trask, (Princeton, 1968), p. 20: 'To write history is so difficult that most historians are forced to make concessions to the technique of legend'. But Auerbach considers such inevitable recourse to legend as a necessary evil, as some sort of fall from grace. There runs, through the whole of his book, the view that myth is some kind of naïve simplification of truth and that history is prior to myth. His view is diametrically opposite to that of Jan de Vries who believes that myth is prior to history. See his 'Das Motiv des Vater-Sohn-Kampfes im Hildebrandslied', *Germanisch-Romanische Monatsschrift* 34 (1954). See Peter Munz, 'History and Myth', *The Philosophical Quarterly* 6 (1956), for a discussion of the interdependence of myth and

history. 'It is doubtful', wrote Michael Grant, *Roman Myths* (London, 1971), p. 262, 'if either history or myth could exist without the other'.

5. F. Jacoby, 'Griechische Geschichtsschreibung', *Die Antike* 2 (1926): 1–8. See also A. Momigliano, 'Il razionalismo di Ecateo di Mileto', *Terzo contributo alla storia degli studi classici e del mondo antico* (Rome, 1966), 1:323ff.

6. See D. S. Wallace-Hadrill, *Eusebius of Caesarea* (London, 1960).

7. For a clear rehabilitation of Herodotus, see A. Momigliano, 'The Place of Herodotus in the History of Historiography', *History* 43 (1958), now reprinted in his *Studies in Historiography* (London, 1966), pp. 127–42.

8. M. I. Finley, 'Myth, Memory and History', *History and Theory* 4 (1964–65).

9. (New York, 1953).

10. (London, 1960).

11. For this reason Wörringer's absolute dichotomy of geometric and empathic art, though suggestive, is not likely to be exhaustive. It must be certain, and all early works of art seem to confirm this, that geometric art preceded empathic art and that the latter was derived from the former. See S. Giedion, *The Eternal Present: The Beginning of Art*, Bollingen Series, 35, 6, 1, (New York, 1962).

12. (New York, 1954).

13. Cp. S. G. F. Brandon, 'The Ritual Perpetuation of the Past', *Numen* 6 (1959).

14. H. W. Wolff, *The Old Testament* (Philadelphia, 1973), p. 25. Cp. also W. O. E. Oesterley, 'Early Hebrew Festival Rituals', in *Myth and Ritual*, ed. S. H. Hooke (London, 1933).

15. Eliade is not alone in this rigid distinction between profane and sacred history. It is also to be found in H. and H. A. Frankfort in their 'Conclusion' and their 'Introduction' to H. and H. A. Frankfort, J. A. Wilson, and Thorkild Jacobsen, *Before Philosophy* (Harmondsworth, 1949) (also known as *The Intellectual Adventure of Ancient Man* [Chicago, 1946]), where Hebrew historical thinking is depicted as an emancipation from the cyclical mythology of the ancient Babylonians. It is true that Hebrew historical thinking was not cyclical; but it was none the less profoundly influenced by mythological figures and moulds.

16. The case made by Jacoby, 'Griechische Geschichtsschreibung', for Hecataeus as the first historian is therefore only a very partial case. There is more to the writing of history than the criticism of traditional myths and for this reason Herodotus must be kept in the place that convention has assigned to him. Cp. R. Drews, *The Greek Accounts of Eastern History* (London, 1974), who stresses the importance of the experience of the Persian Wars rather than Ionian rationalism. See the charming story about an imaginary encounter between Herodotus and the author of Genesis by J. T. Shotwell, *The Story of Ancient History* (New York, 1961), pp. 122–23.

17. 'Aspects of the European Tradition of Historical Writing', *Transactions of the Royal Historical Society* 20 (1970):178–79.

18. Ibid., p. 181. Southern gives other telling examples. For Saint Augustine, see ibid. 21 (1971): p. 161; for Bede, p. 161; for Hugh of Saint Victor, pp. 166 and 171; for Anselm of Havelberg, p. 175 and 22 (1972): p. 165.

19. (London, 1964).

20. (Berlin, 1967).

21. (London, 1970).
22. See Peter Munz, *Frederick Barbarossa: A Study in Medieval Politics,* (London, 1969), pp. 130ff.
23. (New York, 1960), p. 204. Apart from Snell the *locus classicus* of a description of how people identify themselves with the help of a mythical paradigm is Thomas Mann, 'Freud and the Future' in *Essays of Three Decades,* trans. H. T. Lowe-Porter (New York, 1968), pp. 424f.

> The ego of antiquity and its consciousness of itself were different from our own, less exclusive, less sharply defined. It was, as it were, open behind; it received much from the past and by repeating it gave it presentness again. The Spanish scholar Ortega y Gasset puts it that the man of antiquity, before he did anything, took a step backwards, like the bullfighter who leaps back to deliver the mortal thrust. He searched the past for a pattern into which he might slip as into a diving-bell, and being thus at once disguised and protected might rush upon his present problem. Thus his life was in a sense a reanimation, an archaizing attitude. But it is just this life as reanimation that is the life as myth. Alexander walked in the footsteps of Miltiades; and ancient biographers of Caesar were convinced, rightly or wrongly, that he took Alexander as his prototype. But such "imitation" means far more than we mean by the word today. It was a mythical identification, peculiarly familiar to antiquity; but it is operative far into modern times, and at all times is psychically possible. How often have we not been told that the figure of Napoleon was cast in the antique mould! He regretted that the mentality of the time forbade him to give himself out for the son of Jupiter Ammon, in imitation of Alexander. But we need not doubt that — at least at the period of his Eastern exploits — he mythically confounded himself with Alexander; while after he turned his face westwards he is said to have declared: "I am Charlemagne." Note that: not "I am like Charlemagne" or "My situation is like Charlemagne's," but quite simply: "I am he." That is the formulation of the myth. Life, then — at any rate, significant life — was in ancient times the reconstruction of the myth in flesh and blood; it referred to and appealed to the myth; only through it, through reference to the past, could it approve itself as genuine and significant. The myth is the legitimization of life; only through and in it does life find self-awareness, sanction, consecration. Cleopatra fulfilled her Aphrodite character even unto death — and can one live and die more significantly or worthily than in the celebration of the myth?

24. (New Haven, 1950).
25. Toward the end of the book, when Mishkin is travelling back to Switzerland, he meets an old friend in the train. The friend is all eager to explain how and why things have happened the way they did and mouthes one abstract universal platitude about Mishkin's love for Mother Russia and his consequent disappointment and how this disappointment was transferred to the women he met during his sojourn in Russia after another. Mishkin listens thoughtfully and in a way agrees, because he knows that this is how the whole story must hang together, even in his own mind.

But eventually he keeps wondering and asks whether any of these abstract
universals *really* hits the nail on the head. The mirror image, that is, the
story of his sojourn in Russia, is a concrete universal and no attempt to
sum it up in a set of abstract generalisations can really do justice to it.

26. (Oxford, 1963), p. 201.

27. In the twelfth century, Cardinal Boso wrote a Life of Pope Alexander III.
    It is not really a story of Alexander but a narrative of the struggle
    between Alexander and Frederick Barbarossa. Boso cast the whole narra-
    tive in a mythic mould. The mould he selected was the myth of the
    battle between good and evil. For a detailed examination of the effect of
    the mould on the story as we know it from other sources, see Peter
    Munz's "Introduction" to Peter Munz and G. M. Ellis, *Boso's Life of
    Pope Alexander III* (Oxford, 1973).

28. See M. Frisch, *Wilhelm Tell für die Schule* (Frankfurt, 1971) and F. Graus,
    Lebendige Vergangenheit (Cologne, 1975), pp. 61–72. Cp. also E. J.
    Hobsbawm, *Bandits* (London, 1969), in which he shows how the story
    of Robin Hood is a mould into which the lives of social bandits of many
    ages and many countries are poured regardless of their 'actual' conduct.
    Hobsbawm, it is fair to add, believes that it is possible to distinguish
    precisely between the mould and the actual conduct.

29. F. M. Cornford, *Thucydides Mythistoricus* (London, 1907), p. 132. In
    his play *Les Mains sales* (Paris, 1948), Jean-Paul Sartre has dramatised the
    story and shows the unerring certainty with which the myth outlines the
    real springs of human action. Sartre's hero, trained and commissioned to
    assassinate a dictator, cannot get himself to do so until he discovers that
    his wife is the dictator's mistress.

30. *A Study of History*, vols. I–VI, abridged by D. C. Somervell (London,
    1946–57), pp. 217ff. It is easy to think of other examples of infigurations.
    In the Old Testament, David's arrival at Saul's palace is figured into the
    story of the giant who threatens a nation and of the small but cunning
    hero who saves the nation. See M. A. Beek, *Geschichte Israels* (Stuttgart,
    1961), p. 53. Th. H. Gaster, *Myth, Legend and Custom in the Old Testa-
    ment* (London, 1969), is a systematic survey of the mythic moulds used
    in the construction of the Old Testament narrative and brings Sir James
    Frazer's classic *Folklore in the Old Testament* (London, 1923) up to
    date. It would be absurd to discuss this subject without reference to the
    story of Jesus. The reports of his trial and death are figured into the
    story of the dying god who comes to life again and into the whole
    Mediterranean resurrection mythology. And Jesus himself, during his own
    lifetime, had figured both his behaviour and his thoughts about that
    behaviour into the Messiah mythology of the Old Testament. There is no
    need to dwell on this subject. When Frazer thought he had shown the
    connection and the process of infiguration, he concluded that he had
    disposed of the myth of Jesus. But one might equally conclude that the
    real meaning of the myth of Jesus is finally confirmed by the proof that
    his life was figured into the older myths. At any rate, Frazer thought he
    had disposed of the historical Jesus Christ and left us, at best, with the
    man Jesus. But since the original reports and sources are completely shot
    through with infiguration, the whole notion of a profane Jesus as distinct
    from a mythical Jesus Christ is very dubious. For this reason, one must
    consider the whole theological enterprise, first set in motion by A.
    Schweitzer, *The Quest of the Historical Jesus* (London, 1910), misguided.

Schweitzer assumed that Jesus was a historical figure and that as such he could be divorced from the myths into which he had been figured and that a careful scrutiny of the sources together with a criticism of other historians less careful with the sources would reveal the historical Jesus and what he had come to reveal of God.

31. Infiguration takes place when an ordinary story is composed by following the pattern of a myth. G. v. Rad has shown how the story of David in the Old Testament was composed by infiguration. The story as it stands, he points out, is a peculiarly secular portrait and contrasts to the naive miracles that form part of the heroic epic. But the mythic pattern cannot be mistaken. In the story's profane narrative there is a clear evidence of God's providence. Such secular story telling that bears identifiable traces of the mythic mould into which it was figured was a revolutionary innovation in the age of Solomon. See idem, 'Der Anfang der Geschichtsschreibung im alten Israel', *Archiv für Kulturgeschichte* 32, (1944):40–41 and the same author's *Der heilige Krieg im alten Israel* (Göttingen, 1958), p. 63.

32. *Thucydides Mythistoricus.*

33. In his *Thucydides and the Science of History* (London, 1929), Ch. N. Cochrane has provided a diametrically opposed account of Thucydides' method. He considers that Thucydides was, above all, a clinician who aimed at and very largely succeeded in giving us an unemotional and unbiased and realistic account of what actually happened. Cochrane's evidence is largely based upon a paradigm, that is, upon Thucydides' clinical description of the plague. Cochrane's analysis of Thucydides' method may well be true or, at least, be a salutary corrective to that of Cornford. But there is one part of the argument that cannot stand up to examination. As Cochrane's title indicates, there is the assumption that history can be a science in the sense that it can be a clinical description of events that take place in the outer world and that the valour and quality of a historian is to be assessed by his ability to describe it clinically. Cornford has had many critics besides Cochrane and his book does not enjoy the prestige it deserves. For the practically only balanced assessment of Cornford, see F. W. Walbank, 'History and Tragedy', *Historia* 9 (1960). The unpopularity of Cornford's book on Thucydides is ironical for his critics forget that Cornford did not praise Thucydides' practice of infiguration. On the contrary, Cornford considered such infiguration a failing and took pains to show how the dependence on myth obliged Thucydides to neglect the economic aspects of imperialism. His critics simply bristled when they read about infiguration and the importance of myth and completely forgot that Cornford, wrongly, was really on their side in insisting that there is an objective reality of economic imperialism that remained obscured to Thucydides because of his dependence on myth. H. Strasburger, 'Die Wesensbestimmung der Geschichte durch die antike Geschichtsschreibung', *Sitzungsberichte der wissenschaftlichen Gesellschaft an der Johann Wolfgang Goethe-Universität* (1966), pp. 62–65, shows the importance of the epic model for Thucydides.

34. First published in Cambridge, Engl., 1961. I am using here the 2nd edition of 1972.

35. See *On Social Ideas and Ideologies*, ed. and trans. E. G. Jacoby (New York, 1974), pp. 206ff.

36. *The Failure of the Roman Republic* (Cambridge, Engl., 1955).
37. *Richard II* (Cambridge, Engl., 1963).
38. (Baltimore, 1967).
39. *The Crisis of the Early Italian Renaissance* (Princeton, 1955).
40. Cp. J. H. Whitfield, *Petrarch and the Renaissance* (Oxford, 1943), p. 11. Burckhardt most probably derived the idea that refinement presupposes corruption from Rousseau.
41. Cp. the standard works by H. M. Chadwick, *The Heroic Age* (Cambridge, Engl., 1926); J. de Vries, *Heldenlied und Heldensage* (Bern, 1961); M. Bowra *Heroic Poetry* (London, 1952).
42. Cp. L. Woolley, *Abraham* (London, 1936).
43. G. Weber, *Nibelungenlied* (Stuttgart, 1968), pp. 31–32. See also K. F. Stroheker, 'Studien zu den historisch-geographischen Grundlagen der Nibelungendichtung', *Deutsche Vierteljahrschrift für Literaturwissenschaft und Geistesgeschichte* 32 (1958) and K. Hauck, 'Heldendichtung und Heldensage als Geschichtsbewusstsein', in *Alteuropa und die moderne Gesellschaft*, O. Brunner Festschrift (Göttingen, 1963). See also Graus, *Lebendige Vergangenheit*, pp. 275–89.
44. Vries, *Heldenlied*, pp. 310–11.
45. Cp. F. R. Schröder, 'Mythos und Heldensage', *Germanisch-Romanische Monatsschrift* 36 (1955); O. Höfler, *Siegfried, Arminius und die Symbolik* (Heidelberg, 1961); and W. Mohr, 'Geschichtserlebnis im altgermanischem Heldenliede', in *Zur germanisch-deutschen Heldensage*, ed. K. Hauck (Darmstadt, 1961). It is well known that the famous and influential German philologist A. Heusler completely denied and, where he could not deny, belittled the 'historical' material in epic literature. See his 'Geschichtliches und Mythisches in der germanischen Heldensage', Deutsche Akademie der Wissenschaften, Berlin. *Sitzungsberichte* 47 (1909).
46. *Mythe et épopée* (Paris, 1968).
47. Ibid., pp. 261ff. Cp. J. Heurgon, *The Rise of Rome* (London, 1973), pp. 132–33.
48. Heurgon, *Rome*, p. 133, writes that it is 'impossible to believe that traditional ideology, if it existed, could have exercised this constraint and control, through long ages constantly modified by historical events, over intellects so diverse, in which ideology was so exposed to the erosion of history'. There is much evidence that the blending of myth and truth was much greater than Dumézil allows; but it is not in the least 'impossible' to believe that the traditional ideology should have had a powerful hold for many centuries. On pp. 134–35 Heurgon himself provides a subtle and sensitive account of the blending.
49. *Greece before Homer* (London, 1956), pp. 162–64. A. Heusler held the strange view that the German epics, unlike the *Iliad*, had no historical kernel and were solely and exclusively concerned with tragic fates and artistic mood and had no connection with history and the memory of ancestors. See his *Die altgermanische Dichtung*, 2nd ed. (Potsdam, 1943), p. 155. Whatever Heusler's motives, it is even stranger that E. Curtius, *Europäische Literatur und lateinisches Mittelalter* (Bern, 1948), p. 175, should have endorsed Heusler's view without qualification and added that, in contrast to Homer, the German epics were irreligious, Curtius takes this as further proof that they had no historical kernel. But, surely, the correct explanation of their irreligiosity is the fact that they were written down at a time when their authors and their audiences had be-

come Christians and could not see a simple way of weaving the older, pagan religious motifs into the story. The best account of the relation of myth to epic and history is by J. Markale, *Le Roi Arthur* (Paris, 1976), 'L'épopée et l'histoire'.
50. (Chicago, 1970).
51. On this topic, cp. H. Weisinger, *Tragedy and the Paradox of the Fortunate Fall* (London, 1953).
52. *Anatomy of Criticism* (Princeton, 1971), p. 136.
53. See R. F. Treharne, *The Glastonbury Legends* (London, 1971), pp. 74ff. and E. K. Chambers, *Arthur of Britain* (Cambridge, 1964), p. 106f.
54. For the core of truth in the traditional myth of the origin of Rome, see Heurgon, *Rome*, pp. 130ff and part two, chapter 4: 'From Hypercriticism to the Rehabilitation of the Tradition'. See also A. Momigliano, 'An Interim Report on the Origins of Rome', *Journal of Roman Studies* 53 (1963).
55. H. v. Einem, *Michelangelo* (Stuttgart, 1959), p. 171.
56. Marcel Proust is another rewarding example. As. G. D. Painter, *Marcel Proust*, 2 vols. (London, 1959-65), has shown, there is nothing in his novel that is 'invented'. Jean-Francois Revel, *On Proust* (London, 1972), rightly comments on p. x: 'The only story that Proust ever invented is that his book is a novel'. But both Painter and Revel are wrong in thinking that this discovery is the end of the matter. The one element that Proust did not copy from life or reality is the pattern in which the single events are arranged and that provides the meaning as explained in the last volume. R. Shattuck, *Proust* (London, 1974), p. 149, shows perceptively that one can actually date the change in Proust's method. In 1909 he shifted away from a description of reality (autobiography) and from the writing of pure 'fiction' to produce his amalgam of truth and poetry, that is, something like Michelangelo's unfinished statues.
57. (London, 1969).
58. *The Scope of Anthropology* (London, 1967), p. 47.
59. Cp. Peter Munz, 'The Purity of Historical Method', *New Zealand Journal of History* 5 (1971):6-7.
60. (London, 1966).

Chapter Six: The Taxonomy of Universals

1. 'Our Current Sense of History', in *The Historian Between the Ethnologist and the Futurologist*, ed. J. Dumoulin and D. Moisi (Paris, 1973), pp. 4-6. Mary Douglas, *Natural Symbols* (London, 1970), suggests a different taxonomy. On p. 65 she writes that the social body constrains the way the physical body is perceived and on pp. 140-41 she sketches the following alternatives:

> Of the three extreme types of cosmology surveyed, it appears that none is intellectually free. Each social form and its accompanying style of thinking restricts individual thought and action, even when it most seems to celebrate the value of the individual as such. First, the position near zero. However charming its world view and rosy its concept of human nature, it is barren. All opportunities of individual development are limited by the lack of organisation. The range and quality of personal interaction are restricted. The possibilities

of knowing the self are reduced by the limited contact with other selves. Intellectually it is as null as it is ineffective in organisation.

Second, the closed community with its intolerance of imperfections: its focus on an impossible good is limiting in another way. The failure to confront the menacing idea of evil is as complete here as in the first case. At zero point evil is implicitly ignored, here it is explicitly shunned and rejected. Thus both systems allow the individual to cherish an inadequate view of the self and its capacities and dangers.

Third, the grid of ego-focussed categories: this society allows all the possibilities of large-scale organisation to be taken, but at the expense of personal relationships. Again, in the extreme form, there is a sterile exaltation of the self in isolation from other selves. Other persons are treated as things, instruments, pawns in a game. So the individual caught up in this system is incapable of reflecting on the nature of the self, or of symbolising it as a complex agent. Here we have an equal impoverishment of the symbolic life and deadening of metaphysical curiosity.

2. (London, 1969).
3. (London, 1972).
4. (London, 1951), p. 111.
5. 'The Family', *Past and Present* 27 (1964).
6. *The Passing of Traditional Society* (Glencoe, 1958). The tendency of many sociological laws to oscillate between tautology and falsity has been well observed by R. R. Brown, *Rules and Laws of Sociology* (London, 1973).
7. (London, 1972), p. 115.
8. (London, 1969).
9. Elton, *Practice of History*, pp. 29–30.
10. Although we have been well supplied with histories of peasants and workers for many decades, P. Laslett, *The World We Have Lost* (London, 1965), has tried to elevate this kind of history into a question of principle and make it the starting point of a 'school'. As the book stands, it reads more like a pedantic imitation of Proust.
11. There is a vast literature in defence of quantified methods in history and a plea for more generalisation. See, e.g., L. Gottschalk ed., *Generalisation in the Writing of History* (Chicago, 1963). The idea goes back to the French *Annales*, in the pages of which it has been practised with usually enlightening effects for many decades. Each case, it would seem, has to be examined on its merits and there seems no occasion for discussing whether quantification and generalisation is permissible in principle. But cp. H. Heimpel, 'Geschichte und Geschichtswissenschaft', *Vierteljahrschrift für Zeitgeschichte* 5 (1957); and S. M. Lipset and R. Hofstadter eds., *Sociology and History Methods* (New York, 1968).
12. Cp. e.g., the following recent references to the topic, none of which probes beneath the surface. Elton, *Practice of History*, Asa Briggs, as reported in *Past and Present* 27 (1964):103; G. Leff, *History and Social Theory* (London, 1969); H. Trevor-Roper, 'The Past and the Present: History and Sociology', *Past and Present* 24 (1969) and S. M. Lipset, *Revolution and Counter-Revolution* (London, 1969), ch. 1. See the

thoughtful discussion by H. U. Wehler, *Geschichte als historische Sozial-wissenschaft* (Frankfurt, 1973), pp. 9–44.

13. See, e.g., D. Martindale, *The Nature and Types of Sociological Theory* (London, 1961), p. 127, 'Sociology comes into being with the extension of the scientific method . . . to the social world of man himself'. Also J. Goldthorpe, *An Introduction to Sociology* (Cambridge, Engl., 1968), p. 4: 'Sociology is the scientific study of society'.

14. *De la Démocratie en Amérique*, ed. A. Gain (Paris, 1951) 2:7.

15. See, for instance, J. Madge, 'The Contribution of Sociology', in *The Frontiers of Sociology*, ed. T. R. Fyvel (London, 1964), p. 90; and P. Willmott, 'A Code for Research?', *Times Literary Supplement* 3449 (1968):341. Madge, it is worth noting, displays a certain amount of innocence in this matter. Oblivious of both Whewell and Popper, he writes on p. 89 that in view of this prevalent method of assembling facts it can be safely assumed that sociology is taking on 'the typical features of a science'.

16. *The Rules of Sociological Method* (Glencoe, 1964), p. liii. It is instructive to compare Marx, Sixth Feuerbach Thesis: 'The human essence . . . is the totality of social relationships'. Marx recognised, as the Utilitarians had not, that interests are structured and are rarely distributed at random. Hence his 'great interest to sociology' (Talcott Parsons, *Essays in Sociological Theory* [Glencoe, 1964], p. 321). The fact that he is thus of interest, defines the scope of sociology: that is, sociology is the science of those societies in which the members are divided into classes, or, at least, the members of which can be grouped according to external criteria and in which the social is, therefore, primary. It is worth noting that Marx found it notoriously difficult to arrive at a concept of class. One should view his attempts to define class as a sociological constant that is in terms of identity of sources of income in the light of his growing awareness that objective criteria do not yield the desired concept. See esp. idem, *Capital* (Chicago, 1915), 3:1031–32. One is almost forced to suspect that he was working up to the formulation of T. H. Marshall, *Citizenship and Social Class* (Cambridge, Engl., 1930), p. 92, that 'the essence of social class is the way a man is treated by his fellows (and, reciprocally, the way he treats them), not the qualities or the possessions which cause that treatment'. In this formulation, 'class' is not an objective sociological constant, but the result of how people interpret themselves and are interpreted by others: that is, class depends on consciousness — and not the other way round. If such an un-Marxist meaning can be given to Marx's own wrestling with the objective criterion, Marx is firmly established in the sociological thought as here defined.

17. *The Methodology of the Social Sciences* (Glencoe, 1949), pp. 90, 93.

18. This approach goes back to the writings of George Herbert Mead. For modern variants, see, e.g., W. Aubert, *Elements of Sociology* (London, 1968), pp. 63ff and for the whole concept of 'legitimate expectation', the writings of Talcott Parsons. It seems to me that the writings of E. Goffman, *Where the Action Is* (London, 1969), *Stigma* (Englewood Cliffs, N.J., 1963), among others tend to push this approach into somewhat insensitive cast-iron mouldings.

19. For these and similar views, see the writings of S. F. Nadel and Max Gluckman, and for the form here presented, see P. S. Cohen, *Modern*

Social Theory (London, 1968), pp. 152ff. The distinction between elementary and complex societies has also been endorsed by C. Lévi-Strauss, *The Elementary Structures of Kinship* (London, 1969), p. xxiii: 'Elementary structures of kinship are those systems in which the nomenclature permits immediate determination of the circle of kin and that of affines'. Complex systems are those that limit themselves to defining the circle of relatives and leave the determination of spouses to other mechanisms — the prevalent operation of which, he might have added, has to be ascertained empirically and the findings of which must lead to class groupings, e.g., middle-class blondes tend to marry university graduates.

20. I am confident that a systematic investigation of all varieties of sociological theory would bear me out. The one outstanding difficulty for this view is the functionalism of Talcott Parsons. His theory of role expectation fits in; but his idea that in a society all roles are functionally integrated does not. It has been suggested recently by T. B. Bottomore, *New York Review of Books* 15, 6 (1970):20–21, that Talcott Parsons' functionalism was largely inspired by the interwar years when Anglo-American opposition to the Axis made him think that 'Democracy' was a static form of society. However, this may be, on the whole one gains the impression that the differences between sociologists are usually being exaggerated, not least by the adherents of the several 'schools'. But on examination, the differences are more apparent than real. See my review article of R. W. Friedrich's *A Sociology of Sociology* in *History and Theory* 10 (1971).

21. For Bonald, cp. R. Spaemann, *Der Ursprung der Soziologie aus dem Geist der Restauration* (Munich, 1959), p. 200; for Comte, O. Massing, *Fortschritt und Gegenrevolution* (Stuttgart, 1966), p. 122. Although it is almost universally accepted that sociology originated in the intellectual aftermath of the French Revolution, most writers see in the beginnings of sociology an attempt to restore, or at least to justify, the *ancien régime*. While the conservative interest was often undeniable, this narrow view makes the origin of sociology into a more or less political issue and thus fails to account for the specific features of sociological method. See R. A. Nisbet, 'The French Revolution and the Rise of Sociology', *American Journal of Sociology* 49 (1943) and 'Conservatism and Sociology', ibid. 58 (1952). F. A. Hayek, *The Counter-Revolution of Science* (Glencoe, 1952), also takes the narrow view. He is not so much concerned with the fact that despite the revolution society survived and that Burke's gloomy prophecy had been falsified and that that falsification required an explanation. He concentrates on the 'hybris' of scientism and on the social scientist's effort to ape the successful natural sciences. Concentrating entirely on Comte, he makes only the most cursory remarks about Durkheim. But if one alters the perspective, a very different interpretation appears.

22. The classical study is D. Riesman, *The Lonely Crowd*, first published in 1950. Although it purports to be no more than a description of modern American society, the concept of 'other-direction' makes it the sociological study *par excellence*. There is a strange ambivalence in Riesman's attitude to Tocqueville. On p. 19 (New Haven, 1961) Riesman states that modern Americans are decisively different from those observed by Tocqueville. And yet a great many chapters are prefaced by telling quotations from Tocqueville and Riesman would have found no difficulty

in quoting from ch. 20, vol. 2 of *De la Démocratie en Amérique* to find
support for the concept of other-direction. S. M. Lispet, *Political Man*
(New York, 1963), p. 411, points out that already Harriet Martineau
seems to have been 'paraphrasing' Riesman's description of other directed
men in her book *Society in America* (New York, 1837), 2:158–59. It may
be argueable that Riesman's ambivalent attitude to his great precursor is
due to his strenuous attempt to interpret the emergence of other-
directedness not in terms of quality and not in terms of Tocqueville's
analysis of the absence of feudalism and the growth of democracy, but in
such narrower, quantitative (supposedly scientific?) terms of population
growth. When *The Lonely Crowd* is stripped of its demography, there
remains, essentially, a brilliant disquisition on Tocqueville's 'equality'.
And, what is more, it is a genuine advance on Tocqueville, for Tocqueville
concentrated on the loneliness that is brought about by an increase in
equality, whereas Riesman has discovered that beyond a certain point an
increase in equality impels men to seek an end to loneliness through
other-direction. H. Schelsky, observed in *Ortsbestimmung der deutschen
Soziologie* (Cologne, 1959), p. 27, that sociology is an instrument of the
much discussed Americanisation of European society. The crux of the
matter is not whether and how one tradition is being replaced by another,
but whether European society is becoming post-*ancien régime* in the sense
in which American society is. 'Americanisation', here, is not an ethnic
but a sociological concept. Tocqueville saw America as the future of
Europe; Riesman describes America as other-directed and Schelsky sees
sociology, the science of other-directedness, as the instrument for making
European society more other-directed.

23. Cp., for instance, R. Dahrendorf, *Die angewandte Aufklärung* (Munich,
1963), p. 120. S. M. Lipset, *Political Man*, believes that the immense
popularity of sociology in the modern world is due to a decline of a preoccupation with politics. This is certainly correct if one thinks of politics
as the conflict resulting from the attack on the traditional order. However
this may be, sociology is the ideology of modern mass society, because if
sociology amounts to neighbour-watching and if neighbour-watching is
the principle that makes mass society hang together and prevents it from
dissolving into atoms, sociology is indeed the ideology of this kind of
society. Cp. Th. W. Adorno, 'Soziologie und empirische Forschung', in
Wesen und Wirklichkeit des Menschen, H. Plessner Festschrift (Göttingen,
1957); also Peter Munz, 'The Concept of the Middle Ages as a Sociological
Category', Inaugural Address, Victoria University of Wellington, 1969,
p. 8.

24. Cp. Peter Munz, 'Historical Understanding', *Philosophical Quarterly* 3
(1953); idem, 'The Skeleton and the Mollusc', *New Zealand Journal of
History* 1 (1967); and ch. 2, above.

25. This view goes back to Croce and Collingwood but is here presented,
stripped of its Hegelian ancestry, on the purely logical grounds that
every fact is a composite phenomenon and therefore divisible.

26. This view goes back to the celebrated standpoint of Ranke that 'every
period is equidistant from God'; but as here formulated its truth is quite
independent of the Romantic theology that first inspired it.

27. The expression is due to R. Dahrendorf, *Homo Sociologicus* (Cologne,
1958). If one equates Riesman's other-directed man with *homo sociologicus*, one obtains a working definition of sociology.

28. There is a celebrated work by G. C. Homans, *English Villagers of the Thirteenth Century* (Cambridge, Mass., 1942), that purports to be a 'sociological' study of a part of medieval society. But if one peruses it carefully, one will discover that it is a very ordinary historical account of an English medieval village and that the sociological terminology is thrown in gratuitously, and, I may add, misleadingly, in the last chapter.

29. Cp. M. Eliade, *The Myth of the Eternal Return* (New York, 1954), for the normative character of such myths. If such myths have normative character, they must be considered as universals that constrain individuals. But since they are concrete and particular stories, they must be distinguished from abstract universals such as laws and customs, which constitute Durkheim's 'objective reality'.

30. There is an interesting difference between the manners in which concrete and abstract universals constrain. Cp. B. Snell, *The Discovery of the Mind* (New York, 1960), pp. 204ff. See also chapter 5, above.

31. It is a great pity that Elton, *Practice of History*, p. 47, has seen fit to gloss over this important subject with nothing more than a dogmatic gibe. It goes without saying, and nobody would quarrel with him, that historians must always remain aware of the difference between nineteenth-century Bantus and ancient German forest tribes. But the all-important matter is that both Bantus and Germanic tribesmen were given more likely to concrete universals than to abstract universals. Hence the relevance of social anthropology to medieval history, for example. For other reasons for such relevance see Peter Munz, 'Medieval History in Australasia', *Historical Studies* 11 (1963) and idem, 'Early European History and African Anthropology', *New Zealand Journal of History* 10 (1976).

32. Cp. L. O. Mink, 'The Autonomy of Historical Understanding', *History and Theory* 5 (1966).

33. J. H. Plumb, *The Death of the Past* (London, 1969), pp. 112, 136.

34. *Memoirs of My Life*, ed. G. A. Bonnard (London, 1966), p. 117.

35. See Peter Munz, 'India: Homo Hierarchicus or Generalised Exchange of Souls', *Pacific Viewpoint* 11 (1970):190.

36. *Structural Anthropology* (New York, 1963), p. 18.

37. 'We can understand . . . that natural species are chosen (as totems) not because they are "good to eat" but because they are "good to think"'. *Totemism* (Boston, 1963), p. 89.

38. For the criticism of Durkheim, see ibid., esp. p. 70. It is interesting to note that in this case Lévi-Strauss, for once, attributed greater merit to Radcliffe-Brown than to Durkheim. On p. 91, he credits the former's second theory, though not his first (p. 61), about totemism with a real attempt to come close to the unconscious foundations.

39. In a different controversy, Lévi-Strauss can claim with greater justification to have laid bare the unconscious determinants of behaviour. He has argued that matrilateral cross-cousin marriages are more frequent than patrilateral ones (*Structures of Kinship*) because a society that practices this kind of marriage achieves a better integration; whereas a society in which patrilateral cross-cousin marriage is practised cannot achieve similar integration. Therefore, although the inventors of matrilateral cross-cousin marriage cannot have been aware of this, matrilateral cross-cousin marriage societies are more frequent than patrilateral cross-cousin societies. As against this it has been argued on psychological grounds by

G. C. Homans and D. M. Schneider, *Marriage, Authority and Final Causes* (Glencoe, 1955), that a young man is more likely to prefer the mother's brother's daughter than the father's sister's daughter because the former presents part of the side of warmth, love, and affection whereas the latter presents part of the side of harsh paternal authority. This explanation of the greater frequency of matrilateral cross-cousin marriage is based on the operation of conscious psychological preference. In Lévi-Strauss' distinction, he is here doing anthropology by laying bare the unconscious determinants of behaviour and Homans and Schneider are doing history by investigating the conscious determinants. There may be some value in this distinction since the latter base their generalisation about matrilateral cross-cousin marriages on psychologically determined sequences of events; but Lévi-Strauss bases his generalisation on an analysis of unconscious and unknown structure. If the distinction holds, then R. Needham, *Structure and Sentiment* (Chicago, 1962), is misguided in his attempt to resolve the controversy between Lévi-Strauss and Homans and Schneider by massive investigations of kinship structures and the distinction between 'preferential' and 'prescriptive' marriages.

Chapter Seven: Sources and Raw Material

1. Murray G. Murphey, *Our Knowledge of the Historical Past* (Indianapolis, 1973), p. 57, describes this unrealistic precept offered in the conventional handbooks for historians as follows: 'As classical historiography conceived its method, internal criticism was to yield the historian a set of statements weighted according to their probability of being true, on the basis of which the "synthetic" task of the historian was to be carried out'. I entirely agree with Murphey's criticism of this unrealistic approach.
2. The examples are taken from L. Gottschalk, *Understanding History* (New York, 1965), p. 90 and from Ch. V. Langlois and Ch. Seignobos, *Introduction to the Study of History* (London, 1912), p. 168. There is more such advice in N. F. Cantor and R. I. Schneider, *How to Study History* (New York, 1967). It requires very little perspicacity to see that these and similar guidelines must fail in their objective, for they are based on bad psychology. An expert may be all the more expert in disguising the truth than a nonexpert observer. Many detective thrillers are based on this simple knowledge. The plot often turns upon the employment of a professional detective by a criminal; for the criminal knows that if he is seen to employ an expert, he, the criminal, will appear more innocent than he is. There is no end to the degree of subtlety one can bring to bear on the critical scrutiny of the sources and on the inferences they may legitimise. If one literally followed the advice of D. H. Fischer's *Historian's Fallacies* (New York, 1970), one would have to give up writing history. Luckily, all these prescriptions, from Seignobos to Fischer, are no guarantee of grasping the flow of the totality of the past and need therefore not be taken too seriously. The past as such eludes us anyway, whether or not we apply the standards of Seignobos, or of Ernst Bernheim's equally famous *Lehrbuch* (Leipzig, 1889), or of Fischer. Not even Fischer's exacting standards, though more subtle than those of Bernheim and Seignobos are foolproof. On p. 189, Fischer advises, for example, that psychoanalysis has little or no value in the investigation of the 'motivation in stable, integrated personalities'. To begin with, it is clear that the concept 'integrated per-

sonality' is derived from psychoanalysis or allied studies and that we cannot follow Fischer's advice without first taking seriously what he advises us to neglect. Second, there is endless room for argument as to who is and who is not an 'integrated stable' personality. I mention all this not to belittle Fischer but to show that no amount of sophistication can help us to arrive at truth by the conventional methods of source criticism, whether we follow the conventional rules of thumb or Fischer's seemingly impeccable instructions. Truth eludes us. But it does so not because we are too careless in our source criticism. Once we understand the real reason why it *does* elude us, we are fortunate that we no longer have to put all our money on the one horse of source criticism.

3. See Stuart Piggott, *The Druids* (New York, 1974), p. 6ff.

4. As recently as 1928, the famous prehistorian G. Kossinna, in what can only be described as a desperate attempt to salvage material evidence without thought for the purpose of writing history, proclaimed his famous law that 'all distinct cultural province, no matter how limited, bears witness to a distinct race' (*Ursprung und Verbreitung der Germanen* [Leipzig, 1928], p. 4). This assumption is completely gratuitous and most probably completely false, and there can be no doubt that G. Childe, *Prehistoric Migrations in Europe* (Oslo, 1950), p. 1. is right: 'Culture and race do not coincide.' On Childe's principle it is impossible to write a history when nothing but material remains are available. Halfway between Kossinna and Childe there stands a principle suggested by G. Patroni, 'L'indoeuropeanizzazione dell'Italia', *Atheneum* 17 (1939): 215: if one supposes that in primitive societies pottery is left to women, the appearance of new pottery types shows the presence of foreign women and hence of foreign families. Cp. H. Hencken, 'Indoeuropean Languages and Archeology', *American Anthropological Association* 84 (1955), p. 3. The principle, of course, is doubtful. But even if one accepts it, it yields only the most rudimentary guideline for putting silent material remains together into a story. See the lucid remarks on the whole problem by C. Renfrew, 'Models in Prehistory', *Antiquity* 42 (1968):132-34.

5. (London, 1972). Renfrew supplements the general postulate by the models, derived from cybernetics, of deviation amplification and of the multiplier effect. In regard to the general postulate, however, one should bear in mind C. Lévi-Strauss' epigram: 'It is a truism that every society functions; but to say that everything in a society functions is an absurdity'. (*Structural Anthropology* [New York, 1963], p. 13). In his "Concluding Address" in *The Explanation of Cultural Change*, ed. Colin Renfrew (London, 1973), p. 767, E. Leach points out that the general postulate appears to legitimise all sorts of inferences about X from Y and is used to extend the study of X to a point at which one can reconstruct the whole structure of an internal social organisation. 'This', he continues, 'is an illusion. There are always an indefinitely large number of alternative ways in which particular human social systems might be adapted to meet particular ecological and demographic situations. It is quite untrue that forms of social organization are somehow "determined" by the environmental situation and the cultural repertoire with which a particular group is equipped to encounter that environment'.

6. (London, 1972).

7. E. Gibbon, *Memoirs of My Life*, ed. G. A. Bonnard (London, 1966), p. 117.

8. Peter Munz, *The Place of Hooker in the History of Thought* (London, 1952), pp. 107–11.

9. 'A candid admission of the purpose of one's own study', writes A. Momigliano, *Studies in Historiography* (London, 1966), p. 110, 'a clear analysis of the implications of one's own bias helps to define the limits of one's own historical research and explanation. To take the example of a great book, if Ronald Syme had clearly asked the question that was at the back of his mind when he wrote his *Roman Revolution* (Oxford, 1939) — was Augustus' revolution a fascist revolution? — his research would have been more clearly directed to a definite aim'. It is unlikely though, one should add, that he could have improved upon the precision of style and narrative.

10. If the experience of university professors and Oxbridge dons is confined to the world described by C. P. Snow in *The Master* (London, 1952), one must applaud their wisdom in confining themselves to the documents. The limitations of the second record can mislead even the best of historians. W. Giesebrecht, *Geschichte der deutschen Kaiserzeit* (Brunswick, 1860) 5, i:27, for example, was convinced that there could be no truth in the well-attested rumour that Frederick Barbarossa's first wife had committed adultery with a member of her husband's household of very inferior class because in his experience (he was writing in Munich in the middle of the nineteenth century, the Munich of Lola Montez and of the mad Ludwig and of Wagner!) noble women do not commit adultery and especially not with members of the lower orders. One of the most fascinating opportunities for a comparative study of second records is the history of Alexander the Great. E. Badian depicts him as a ruthless and irrational megalomaniac. See his 'Alexander the Great and the Loneliness of Power' in *Studies in Greek and Roman History* (Oxford, 1964). W. W. Tarn, *Alexander the Great* (Cambrdige, Engl., 1948), saw him as a Scottish laird. F. Schachermeyr, *Alexander der Grosse: Ingenium und Macht* (Vienna, 1949), sees him as a Nietzschean superman and U. Wilcken, *Alexander the Great* (New York, 1967), as a missionary of Greek culture. J. R. Hamilton, *Alexander the Great* (London, 1973), shows him as an efficient and reasonable, if hard-drinking, realist and to the eye of R. L. Fox, *Alexander the Great* (London, 1974), far from being as sexually innocent and/or virtuous as Tarn's Scottish laird, Alexander was not only sexually promiscuous but both homosexual and heterosexual. For the history of the history of Alexander, see the following: G. Walser, 'Zur neueren Forschung über Alexander den Grossen', *Schweizer Beiträge zur allgemeinen Geschichte* 14 (1956); F. Schachermeyr, *Alexander der Grosse* (Vienna, 1949), chs. 14–15; F. Pfister, 'Alexander der Grosse, Die Geschichte seines Ruhmes im Lichte seiner Beinamen,' *Historia* 13 (1964). One of the finest and most searching studies of the role of the second record is H. Stretton's analysis of the many possible explanations of why Joseph Chamberlain, the best-known protagonist of social reform in the British Cabinet, changed his mind about old-age pensions in December 1899: *The Political Sciences* (London, 1969), pp. 23–51. This book also contains a splendid analysis of the second records employed by Eli Halevy and by E. H. Carr. For an examination of the second record used by Gerhard Ritter, see A. Dorpalen, 'Historiography as History: The Work of Gerhard Ritter', *Journal of Modern History* 34 (1962); and by Croce, see A. R. Caponigri,

History and Liberty: The Historical Writings of Benedetto Croce (London, 1955). For the importance of the historian's horizon of experience see H. U. Wehler, *Geschichte als historische Sozialwissenschaft* (Frankfurt, 1973), pp. 90–91 and H. G. Gadamer, *Truth and Method* (New York, 1975), pp. 299.

11. *Réalité*, 175 (June 1965):51, col. 1.

12. Cp. M. de Certeau, *L'Écriture de l'histoire* (Paris, 1957), and F. Graus, *Volk, Herrscher und Heiliger im Reich der Merowinger* (Prague, 1965), pp. 25–59. Graus surveys the history of the methods employed by historians to deal with the problem. The Bollandists confined themselves to the distinction between false legends and genuine legends, that is, they avoided the problem of whether levitation is credible. A. Bernouilli solved the problem by looking upon legends of implausible happenings as the religion of the masses. H. Delehaye argued that legends lead us to the places of the cult and that the rest, that is, stories of levitation, are to be discounted. During the Enlightenment it was argued that incredible legends were the lies put forward by priests to deceive the masses and during the nineteenth century such legends came to be regarded as proof of superstition among priests and masses alike.

13. 'The Rise and Function of the Holy Man in Late Antiquity', *Journal of Roman Studies* 61 (1971):80–101. Peter Brown shows that the belief that saintliness causes levitation is today unacceptable. His substituted interpretation, however, though very intelligible to us, is not more necessarily true than the belief that saintliness causes levitation. The same comment can be made about Keith Thomas' *Religion and the Decline of Magic* (London, 1971). Today nobody believes that these women really practised witchcraft because today we believe that witchcraft is not something that *can* be practised. Keith Thomas, therefore, shows that the belief in witchcraft in sixteenth- and seventeenth-century England marks a change in society. When the state-administered poor law entered the village, people got into the habit of turning indigent old women away from their doors. This breach with the customs of neighbourliness made people feel guilty and they tried to assuage their guilt feelings by persuading themselves that the old women they were treating badly were really witches. The belief in witchcraft, therefore, though it may appear as repressive and a sign of hate, was really a method of social adjustment that helped people to make the transition from the village community spirit to the intrusion of the state in the form of the poor law. Keith Thomas' interpretation of what happened is plausible to us because we always think in terms of social adjustment and similar concepts. It is markedly different from what people said and believed at the time. So we might ask ourselves who knows best what really happened — the people of the seventeenth century or our modern sociologists? There is no telling because we know of no reality against which we can check the two conflicting universals. We have an explanation and an interpretation. We can substitute the one for the other. But nobody can claim to have discovered what really happened. The explanation tells us what really happened in the minds of some people in the seventeenth century and the interpretation, what is happening in the minds of some people in the twentieth century. See also Keith Thomas, 'The Relevance of Social Anthropology to the Historical Study of English Witchcraft', in *Witchcraft Confessions and Accusations*, ed. Mary Douglas (London, 1970).

14. *Die Entstehung des Historismus* (Munich, 1936); now translated by J. E. Anderson as *Historism: The Rise of the New Historical Outlook* (London, 1972).

15. *Medioevo e Rinascimento* (Bari, 1954), pp. 105, 158, 168. See my 'Introduction' to E. Garin, *Italian Humanism* (Oxford, 1965), pp. xxii-xxiii.

16. The term 'uniformitarianism' was used by A. O. Lovejoy, *Essays in the History of Ideas* (Baltimore, 1948), pp. 78ff. The concept was introduced by James Hutton in the eighteenth century to describe geological processes. It became accepted in the nineteenth century, with Charles Lyell probably its most famous proponent. Uniformitarianism was an important concept in the development of evolutionary theory.

17. Cp. Gadamer, *Truth and Method* (New York, 1975), p. 18.

18. See G. H. Nadel, 'Philosophy of History Before Historicism', in *The Critical Approach to Science and Philosophy*, ed. M. Bunge (Glencoe, 1964).

19. It includes also what French historians call the study of *mentalité*, that is, the study of the intellectual history of nonintellectuals. Cp. R. Darnton, 'French History', *New York Review of Books* (April 5, 1973):26, cols. 3-4. It is important to understand that the net is cast widely, for one also has to take into account the thoughts that Caesar could have had but did in fact not have.

20. If we were dependent on a knowledge of the actual motives for establishing the links between events or for making subevents into events, psychology would have to be the ultimate basis of all history. The current vogue of psychohistory is based on the mistaken belief that the linking of events depends on knowledge of actual motives rather than on subsequent reflection on motives. For literature on the subject, see B. Mazlish, *Psychoanalysis and History* (Englewood Cliffs, N.J., 1963); B. B. Wolman ed., *The Psychoanalytic Interpretation of History* (New York, 1971); R. J. Lifton and E. Olson eds., *Explorations in Psychohistory* (New York, 1974). Psychohistory is a misconception because it aims to psychoanalyse dead people. As Freud always said, psychoanalysis depends on free association and free association is impossible when the person who is supposed to associate freely is dead. The whole attempt to reduce history to psychology was an interesting, tempting, and understandable project. It is, however, completely misconceived and nothing in the present argument should be construed to give it the slightest support. Further discussion in Wehler, *Historische Sozialwissenschaft*, pp. 85-123; A. Besancon, 'L'inconsciente', in *Faire de l'histoire*, ed. J. and Nora P. le Goff (Paris, 1974), vol. III; Certeau, *L'Ecriture de l'histoire*, chs. 8-9.

21. There is a colloquial statement that history is about chaps. Taken literally, it is not true. Institutions, movements, psychic forces, and the like, all play their part in history. But figuratively the statement suggests the important truth that history is the history of thought, since only chaps can think.

22. *An Autobiography* (Harmondsworth, 1944), p. 75.

23. This is true of *The Idea of Nature* (Oxford, 1945) and of *An Essay on Metaphysics* (Oxford, 1940).

24. The idea that thoughts belong to a certain social or intellectual environment to which they are functionally related and that their truth must be assessed entirely in relation to that environment was, to my knowledge,

first clearly enunciated by Spengler. It plays a large part in the work of
Malinowski. I could imagine that Collingwood was influenced by Spengler
in whom he showed, for an Englishman, a strong interest. See his article
'Oswald Spengler and the Theory of Historical Cycles', *Antiquity* 1
(1927). The Collingwood of *Essay on Metaphysics,* in turn, has become
the ancestor of both M. Foucault, *Les Mots et les choses: Une Archéologie des sciences humaines* (Paris, 1966), and Th. S. Kuhn, *The Structure
of Scientific Revolutions* (Chicago, 1970). Both Foucault and Kuhn
follow Collingwood in the belief that thoughts are dislodged and that,
once dislodged, they cease to be relevant to the thoughts that have taken
their place. Cp. the spirited discussion of Foucault by Hayden V. White,
'Foucault Decoded', *History and Theory* 12 (1973).

25. *England in the Age of the American Revolution,* 2nd ed. (London,
    1961), pp. 147–49.

26. Psychologically speaking, Namier may be perfectly right. When men are
    part of a crowd and when men act in a thoroughly institutionalised
    situation, and in most other situations in between these two extremes,
    men mostly act without thinking and without plan. But this is not the
    point. We are not doing psychology here but are concerned with the
    mode of understanding. Men always can and often do reflect on their
    actions; and as far as the mode of understanding is concerned it makes
    no difference whether they reflect on their actions before or after they
    carry them out. For the purpose of the present discussion all that matters
    is that men are ideally capable of reflection. The *psychology* of their
    behaviour is irrelevant. In his *The Origins of the Second World War*
    (London, 1961), p. 69, A. J. P. Taylor wrote: 'In my opinion, statesmen
    are too absorbed by events to follow a preconceived plan. They take one
    step, and the next follows from it. The systems are created by historians.
    . . .' This is pure Namier and, like Namier, Taylor confuses psychology
    with the ideal faculty of reflection. Psychologically, Taylor sounds quite
    plausible. But he is wrong in concluding that the 'systems' are created by
    the historians. The first authors of the 'systems' are the statesmen who
    act, because, ideally, they are also capable of thinking about their actions.
    The 'systems' created by the historians are only the continuation of the
    'systems' created ideally, if not actually, by the actors themselves. Even
    when the actors confess to a hard-boiled pragmatism and pride them-
    selves of having no plans or thoughts, they reveal by such a proclamation
    what their thoughts or 'systems' are.

27. *George III and the Historians* (London, 1957), p. 296. See the amusing
    description of the Tory interpretation of history by A. J. P. Taylor in
    the *New Statesman* (May 6, 1950):p. 517–18.

28. There is reason for believing that Namier's theory, which has become so
    influential, was really a counsel of despair. '"Shall we get any nearer to
    explaining the senseless irrelevancy of so-called human thought and
    action?", he wrote in answer to a question about the possibility of
    writing an impartial history of World War II. "Behind your question
    seems to lurk a very justifiable doubt . . . whether we shall ever know
    anything which is worth knowing." This doubt lies at the basis of all of
    Namier's work. It is the real heresy against which his critics contend'
    (John Brooke, 'Namier and His Critics', *Encounter,* 137 [1965]:48,
    col. 2).

29. H. Butterfield, 'George III and the Constitution', *History* (42–43),
    1958, p. 21.

30. Ibid., pp. 15, 33.
31. Butterfield, *George III*, p. 298.
32. See, e.g., *Conflicts* (London, 1942); *The Revolution of the Intellectuals* (London, 1946); *Vanishing Supremacies* (London, 1958); *Europe in Decay* (London, 1950); *In the Margin of History* (London, 1939).
33. *Theory and History of Historiography* (London, 1921), pp. 134–35. Cp. also H. G. Gadamer, *Truth and Method*, Engl. transl., (New York, 1975), p. 299. This gave rise to Croce's famous theory that all history is contemporary history because in the act of understanding the past becomes the present, or, more correctly, the past becomes something that is happening in the present. The point was well put by R. G. Collingwood in *The Idea of History* (Oxford, 1946), p. 284: 'All history is contemporary history: not in the ordinary sense of the word, where contemporary history means the history of the comparatively recent history of the past, but in the strict sense: the consciousness of one's own activity as one actually performs it. History is thus the self-knowledge of the living mind. For even when the events which the historian actually studies are events that happened in the distant past, the condition of their being historically known is that they should vibrate in the historian's mind'. It is worth recalling Georg Lukács' comment on Croce, written with the dogmatism only a blindly prejudiced mind is capable of: 'In all these theories one sees the convulsive attempts of the ideologists of the period to turn their gaze away from the real facts and tendencies of history, deny them recognition and at the same time to find an illuminating, up-to-date explanation in the "eternal essence of life". History as a total process disappears; in its place there remains a chaos to be ordered as one likes. This chaos is approached from consciously subjective view-points' (*The Historical Novel* [Harmondsworth, 1969], p. 215). Lukács seeks to make his point by the innuendo that subjectivity is intolerable. He believed that history is an object of knowledge. See H. Védrine, *Les Philosophies de l'histoire* (Paris, 1975), pp. 91–2. In view of the whole argument of this book, there is not one sentence of his comment that can stand up to criticism. Moreover, 'subjectivity', far from being bad, is anything but uncontrolled arbitrariness. Our appreciation of it is constantly controlled by the strict rules for the substitution of one subjectivity for another.
34. (London, 1935), p. 125.
35. *The Philosophy of Art*, trans. F. P. B. Omaston (London, 1920), vol. 4, p. 302. More curtly and clumsily, Ranke described such knowledge of history as *Mitwisserschaft des Alls*, that is, co-omniscience of the universe; quoted by E. Curtius, *Europäische Literatur und lateinisches Mittelalter* (Bern, 1948), p. 12. This frame of mind is very similar to Hegel's description of stoicism in *Phänomenologie des Geistes* (Frankfurt, 1973), p. 156: 'When I am thinking, I am free because I am not inside another but completely appropriated by myself. Insofar as I am operating with concepts, it is I who is operating inside myself'.
36. *Hegel* (New York, 1965), p. 162.

Chapter Eight: The Nature of the Story

1. After this chapter was written I came across H. M. Baumgartner, *Kontinuität und Geschichte* (Frankfurt, 1972), who argues along very similar lines. See esp. pp. 247, 249, 292, and 308.

2. 'A copy of the universe is not what is required of art; one of the damned things is ample'. Rebecca West, quoted by M. H. Abrams, *The Mirror and the Lamp* (Oxford, 1953), p. 100.
3. I am quoting from memory a remark I heard in a lecture.
4. I have always had doubts about Alfred Tarski's famous definition of truth: a statement is true if and only if, what it asserts is the case. Logicians claim that it applies only to the relation between statements, not to the relation between statements and 'facts'. If they are right, the definition is applicable, with a large number of qualifications, to the present argument. The qualifications are necessary because, as will become apparent in the following pages, one cannot simply decide whether a statement is true by looking at another statement that asserts what is the case.
5. *Our Knowledge of the Historical Past* (Indianapolis, 1973).
6. If one takes a close look at Charles Seignobos' criteria of trustworthiness, one will see that they are formulated by a scholar in his ivory tower who knew very little of the wiliness of human nature and nothing whatever of depth-psychology and the tricks our unconscious can play on us.
7. Such a narrative would have to be what A. C. Danto, *Analytical Philosophy of History* (Cambridge, 1968), p. 2, calls an 'Ideal Chronicle'. It should be stressed that Danto and I reject the possibility of an Ideal Chronicle for very different reasons.
8. *Metahistory* (Baltimore, 1973), pp. 22–31.
9. Trans. G. Holmes (London, 1966).
10. Orthodox opinion has it that fiction is invention of the past and that history is a story about the past that is based on evidence. Even so idealist a philosopher as H. Bradley, *The Presuppositions of Critical History*, ed. L. Rubinoff (Chicago, 1968), p. 89, thought that as long as a narrative is based on documents, it is verifiable. It seems that he completely forgot to ask himself how the document can be verifiable and how it can portray *res gestae*. The argument on which the rigorous distinction between history and fiction is based presumed that there is something magical in the evidence of the documents so that it reflects or mirrors what happened. We have seen in chapter 7 that this is not so and that the records (evidence) are subject to exactly the same vicissitudes of story telling as all other story telling. Predictably, I have a great sympathy with H. Toliver, *Animate Illusions* (Lincoln, Nebr., 1974), in which he demonstrates how the exigencies of story telling impose their shape on how we see the past. But Toliver is quite wrong in thinking that these exigencies poison the springs of true knowledge. Since there is no true knowledge as distinct from what the sources tell us, since the *res gestae* as such forever elude our grasp, and since the sources are subject to the same or similar exigencies as the narrative, there is nothing we can compare the narrative to any more than there is nothing we can compare the sources to — except other narratives and other sources. The idea that the exigencies of story telling and of the sources *distort* truth would presuppose that we know truth independently. But we do not. In this context we should reflect on Vico (Tasso's Godfrey is truer than the real one, *New Science* 47) and on Ranke's declaration that he determined to devote his life to finding out what had really happened after he had read Sir Walter Scott. To Vico, the truth of fiction is preferable to mere 'reality'; to Ranke, the truth of reality is preferable to

'fiction'. Admittedly, Tasso was a greater poet than Sir Walter Scott and more deserving of the respect with which Vico treated him.

11. *Essais critiques* (Paris, 1964), p. 156. The translation is by J. Culler, *Structuralist Poetics* (London, 1975), p. 32. I can endorse his critical discussion of Barthes' view on pp. 33ff completely.

12. *S/Z* (New York, 1974). Cp. M. Merleau-Ponty, as quoted in *Encounter* 262 (1975):54: 'There is nothing over and above the story told. Speech is is not a means in the service of an external end'.

13. R. Jakobson and C. Lévi-Strauss, '"Les Chats" de Charles Baudelaire', *L'Homme* 2 (1962):5–21.

14. E. Leach has drawn attention to the similarity between Wittgenstein and Malinowski's functionalism. Where Wittgenstein said that meaning is use, Malinowski assumed that use is meaning (*Times Literary Supplement* [July 14, 1974]:759, col. 5). Cp., for Wittgenstein, R. Needham, *Belief, Language and Experience* (Oxford, 1972). E. Gellner, 'Concepts and Society', *Transactions of the Fifth World Congress of Sociology* (Louvain, 1962), 1:1, also observes that Wittgenstein held this view and adds that it is already implicit in E. Durkheim's *The Elementary Forms of the Religious Life,* first published in English translation in 1915. More remarkable still is the attempt by P. Winch, *The Idea of a Social Science* (London, 1958), to turn the 'use is meaning' equation into the foundation of all sociological knowledge. Wittgenstein never mentions either Durkheim or Malinowski. But C. Lévi-Strauss, *Tristes Tropiques* (New York, 1974), p. 59, in professing a structuralism that is very concerned with the meaning inherent in closed systems declares that he is faithful to the Durkheimian tradition. The precise pedigree of this idea does not really matter. What matters is the fact that the idea that a system of thought or behaviour or symbols can be a closed system and that one can understand it without reference to anything external to itself is today very widespread.

15. To my knowledge the Surrealists, between the two World wars, were the only people who really put their mind to discovering a way of writing genuine fiction. See F. Alquié, *The Philosophy of Surrealism* (Ann Arbor, 1965), ch. 2, iii, 'Derealisation'. I will quote a passage by Apollinaire, who was not, in the strict sense, a member of the movement, to show the sort of story one could come up with. Despite its initial impression of genuine fictitiousness, a second or third reading will reveal even here that universals are used that give the story some kind of actuality. Not even Apollinaire was able to succeed completely in this strange enterprise of inventing genuine fiction:

> The coals of heaven were so near that I became afraid of their smell . . .
> Two animals of different species began to mate and the shoots of roses
> turned into grape-vines, hanging heavily from the moons' bundles.
> Flames shot up from the throats of monkeys and decorated the world
> with lilies. The monarchs were amused . . . and towards evening . . .
> my Self multiplied a hundred times. The herd which I was, sat down
> by the sea. The sword quenched my thirst . . . A whole nation, in-
> carcerated in a wine-press, bled while singing. Uneven shadows lovingly
> obscured the scarlet of the sails while my eyes were multiplying in
> rivers, in the cities over the snow and over the mountains. *Oneirocriti-
> cism*, opening sentences.

16. This blanket generalisation should not be taken literally. In the middle of the last century, when it became clear in Oxford that the study of theology would fail in its educational purpose as the core of the curriculum because the theologians kept quarrelling too much, it was finally decided, after much heart-searching, that theology ought to be replaced by history. Obviously, history was then still supposed to have pedagogic value. See R. Southern, *The Shape and Substance of Academic History* (Oxford, 1961), p. 11.
17. Quoted by G. J. Whitrow, *What is Time?* (London, 1972), p. 97.
18. *Germany's Aims in the First World War* (London, 1967).
19. F. Fischer, *World Power or Decline* (New York, 1974). For the whole controversy, see J. Moses, *The Politics of Illusion* (London, 1975).
20. '1914: The Beast in the Jungle', *Encounter* 182 (1968):70ff.
21. The same should be done for the controversy about A. J. P. Taylor's *The Origins of the Second World War* (London, 1961). There is no point in discussing whether Taylor depicted reality. There is no reality of which the sources are true, or more or less true, accounts. There are only the sources, each of which is one of the possible ways in which time appeared.
22. J. Bronowski, *The Ascent of Man* (London, 1973), pp. 353–56.
23. This applies particularly to the discussion of the problem of historical inevitability by I. Berlin, *Historical Inevitability* (London, 1954). Berlin fails to distinguish between *res gestae* and *historia rerum gestarum*. He therefore fails to see that the question whether history is a sequence of inevitable events should be asked of *historia rerum gestarum*. He writes and examines all the different views held on this matter as if the question concerned *res gestae*. In reality, the question concerns *historia rerum gestarum* and the viability of any answer depends on how the narrative is written; not on the nature of History.
24. (London, 1949).
25. H. M. Baumgartner, 'Thesen zur Grundlegung einer transzendentalen Historik', in *Seminar: Geschichte und Theorie*, ed. H. M. Baumgartner and J. Rüsen (Frankfurt, 1976), pp. 295–98, has provided examples to show that the answers to so-called historical problems depend on the narratives one consults and not on the inspection of history. All conceivable answers to these and similar questions about the character of history are 'metanarrative predicates'. Cp. idem, *Kontinuität und Geschichte*, p. 308.
26. See, e.g., J. Agassi's discussion of the controversy of holism *versus* individualism, 'Methodological Individualism', *British Journal of Sociology* 11 (1960). Even if one does not share his conclusions, his paper shows that the problem is a problem of *method*, not a problem of substance.
27. *Capitalism and Slavery* (Chapel Hill, 1944).
28. Quoted by D. B. Davis, 'The Ideology of Anti-Slavery', *Times Literary Supplement* 3841 (1975):1263, col. 4.
29. *The Atlantic Slave Trade and British Abolition* (London, 1975).
30. (Cambridge, Engl., 1955), p. 24. There are many encyclopaedic compilations of the history of historiography, from J. Wachler, *Geschichte der historischen Forschung und Kunst* (Göttingen, 1812) to J. W. Thompson, *A History of Historical Writing* (New York, 1943) and H. E. Barnes, *A History of Historical Writing* (Norman, 1937). To my knowledge the first

book ever to approach historical knowledge as the sum of varying interpretations was F. Gundolf, *Caesar: Geschichte seines Ruhms* (Berlin,
1925); English translation by J. Wittmer with the title *The Mantle of
Caesar* (London, 1928). There are many important treatments of history
of this kind now. As an example one should mention H. Butterfield,
George III and the Historians (London, 1957). There are not nearly enough.
The *Revision* articles, which were a regular feature in *History*, are an
extremely important contribution to this kind of historical thought. Unfortunately many undergraduates have tended to misunderstand them as
attempts to 'rubbish' older views. The historicity of our understanding
of the past is the main burden of the argument in H. G. Gadamer, *Truth
and Method* (New York, 1975).

31. H. Butterfield, 'George III and the Constitution', *History* 42-3, (1958):
33.
32. P. E. Schramm, *Hitler: The Man and the Military Leader* (London, 1972).
33. (London, 1964).
34. Cp. E. Gellner, 'Our Current Sense of History', in *The Historian Between
Ethnology and Futurology*, ed. J. Dumoulin and D. Moisi (Paris, 1973),
p.7.
35. *The Practice of History* (London, 1969), p. 30.
36. (London, 1972).
37. 'Cleopatra's Nose', in *The Selected Essays of J. B. Bury*, ed. H. Temperley
(Cambridge, Engl., 1930).
38. (Paris, 1960).
39. I follow G. Lichtheim, 'Sartre, Marxism and History', *History and Theory*
2 (1963). 'L'essentiel n'est pas ce que l'on fait de l'homme, mais ce qu'il
fait de ce qu'on a fait de lui' (Jean-Paul Sartre, quoted by H. Védrine,
Les Philosophies de l'histoire [Paris, 1975], p. 98). I suspect that Sartre's
generalisation and possibly even Hegel's master-slave analysis are romanti-
cised versions of Kant's observation that man as an agent is a member of
the noumenal world and therefore free, and that when he observes himself he sees himself through the categories of understanding and thus is
part of the phenomenal world and appears as unfree, that is, determined
by causes.
40. The story of Godard's film is very subtle and by no means the result of a
simple photographic trick. Godard wanted to leave out all universals that
might have connected the events as they succeed one another, because he
believes that the introduction of universals leads to inauthenticity.
He underlines this belief in one sequence in the film where the heroine
interviews an American journalist on his arrival in Paris. The American's
answers consist of nothing but generalisations and his appearance in the
film is held up as a demonstration of inauthentic existence. Godard's tale
is constructed so as not to hang together and not to be predictable.
However, each single event, since it is an assembly of particular subevents, clearly depends on the presence of tacit universals. But this
presence does not interfere with the purpose of Godard's dismissal of
universals on the level on which the tale as distinct from the separate
events of which it consists is placed.
41. Quoted by G. P. Gooch, *History and Historians in the 19th Century*, 2nd
ed. (London, 1952), p. 462. Since the historian's activity is a continuation of the potential self-reflective activity of the actors he is dealing with,
the story he tells is not an arbitrary story. History is therefore not just

what historians are doing, as I. Berlin, 'History and Theory', *History and Theory* 1 (1960):1, once suggested; but what historians are doing in continuation of the thoughts of the people who 'made' (or suffered) history. I can think of no better description of the difference between acting/living and *thinking* about acting/living — a difference that applies to the actor/liver as much as to the historian who comes *after* the event — as the chapter entitled 'Saturday, Noon' in Jean-Paul Sartre, *Nausea* (Harmondsworth, 1965), pp. 61-63.

42. Cp. J. F. Kermode, *The Sense of an Ending* (Oxford, 1967). The following discussion owes much to this book. The possible and likely narrative movements are explored by Northrop Frye, *The Secular Scripture* (Cambridge, Mass., 1976).

43. S. N. Kramer, *History Begins at Sumer* (Garden City, N.Y., 1959), ch. 6. For Sumerian myths of origin, unconnected with history, the same author's *Sumerian Mythology* (New York, 1969), ch. 2. For an attempt at a rudimentary Mesopotamian transformation of the past into a history, see E. A. Speiser, 'Ancient Mesopotamia', in *The Idea of History in the Ancient Near East*, ed. R. C. Dentan (New Haven, 1955), pp. 50-55 and L. Woolley, *The Sumerians* (New York, 1965), p. 29ff. For the conversion or the historicisation of myth, consult also the following: Chester G. Starr, *The Awakening of the Greek Historical Spirit* (New York, 1968); P. Vidal-Naquet, 'Temps des dieux et temps des hommes', *Revue de l'histoire des religions* 157 (1960); A. Momigliano 'Time in Ancient Historiography', *History and Theory* 6 (1966); M. I. Finley, 'Myth, Memory and History', *History and Theory* 4 (1964).

44. See R. T. Rundle Clark, *Myth and Symbol in Ancient Egypt* (London, 1959), ch. 1. There is even less connection between these stories and actual events than in Mesopotamia. See L. Bull, 'Ancient Egypt' in *Ancient Near East*, ed. R. C. Dentan; H. Frankfort, *Ancient Egyptian Religion* (New York, 1948), explains that the ancient Egyptians not only did not transform time into history but actually went out of their way to persuade themselves that not even time kept passing. If the transformation of the past into history is one way of dealing with the past, the ancient Egyptians actively dealt with the past in the diametrically opposite way.

45. There is a vast literature on this subject. The best brief accounts are Ch. R. North, *The Old Testament Interpretation of History* (London, 1946), ch. 2 and M. Burrows, 'Ancient Israel' in *Ancient Near East*, ed. R. C. Dentan. See also the interesting comments by A. Momigliano, 'Fattori orientali della storiografia Ebraica post-esilica e della storiografia Greca', *Terzo contributo alla storia degli studi classici e del mondo antico* (Rome, 1966) 2:807ff. See also W. den Boer, 'Graeco-Roman Historiography in its Relation to Biblical and Modern Thinking', *History and Theory* 7 (1968).

46 See the many works by G. Dumézil as well as M. Grant, *Roman Myths* (London, 1971), passim and esp. pp. 217-23.

47. S. H. Hooke, *The Siege Perilous* (London, 1956), pp. 66-73. For similar analysis of, for example, the Passover feast see W. O. E. Oesterley, 'Early Hebrew Festival Rituals', in *Myth and Ritual* ed. S. H. Hooke (Oxford, 1933).

48. When there was no thought of the final end, Christian historians liked to end stories in terms of God's punishment for sins. Outside Christianity the sense of ending was often provided by metaphors of old age (*fracta*

est aetas or *mundus senescens*) or by thoughts of doom or by images of how all life must come to an end. Polybius, for example, tells us that Scipio Africanus the younger, as he was watching the destruction of Carthage in 146 B.C. thought of Rome and quoted Homer: 'The day will come when even holy Troy will be destroyed'.
49. W. Kaegi, *Chronica Mundi* (Einsiedeln, 1954).
50. *Conflicts* (London, 1942), p. 70. Cp. the opposite comments by E. H. Carr, *What is History?* (London, 1961), p. 117: 'It is at once the justification and the explanation of history that the past throws light on the future, and the future throws light on the past'.

Chapter Nine: The Philosophy of the Story

1. See two of the older, most influential textbooks of historical method: Ch. V. Langlois and Ch. Seignobos, *Introduction aux études historiques* (Paris, 1908), with many subsequent editions and translations and E. Bernheim, *Lehrbuch der historischen Methode* (Leipzig, 1889) with many later, revised editions. Admittedly, these books are rarely used today but there are modern substitutes. See ch. 7, n. 2. The frame of mind they represent is far from dead. It was severely criticised by R. G. Collingwood, who christened it the 'scissors and paste method' (*The Idea of History* [Oxford, 1946], pp. 257-61). Despite Collingwood, the method survives.

2. (Chicago, 1949), p. 5. Such meaning as history possesses is imposed on it by the transcendental knowledge of a goal. Though Löwith's book is a most sympathetic introduction to fourteen philosophies of history, he makes it quite clear that all of them are imposed upon or read into the 'facts' by some kind of superhistorian. This view is diametrically opposed to the view taken in the present book. If Löwith is right, a philosophy of history is not the last step in a procession of reflections and thoughts that begins with the composition of the mininarrative (i.e., what Löwith calls the 'facts'), but an adjunct one can do without. On the same page Löwith writes that 'history is a movement in time'. His conclusions about the meaning of history are derived from this failure to see that history is not something that flows through time but that consciousness and reflection are necessary if time is to be transformed into history. Löwith starts with the mistaken assumption that a mere observation of the passage of time will provide 'the facts of history'.

3. (London, 1961), p. 2.

4. One could cite many examples of the seminal and fruitful influence of philosophies of history on historical research. I am thinking, for instance, of the works of Gordon Childe. In his case the Marxist philosophy of history enabled him to transform the study of mere archeology into prehistory. Most of the concepts of our knowledge of the period are due to him and are used by prehistorians even if they do not now follow his Marxist philosophy of history. Or look at the fruitful way in which Durkheim's rudimentary philosophy of history has been used for the study of ancient Greek history by Jane Harrison and F. M. Cornford. Or take a completely different field. Lawrence Stone, reviewing a series of books on the history of childhood, *New York Review of Books* (Nov. 14, 1974), remarked that all the books under review were written with the help of a model, that is, a philosophy of history. Only in a comparatively

new field of historical research, he might have added, are there historians who are conscious of their debt to something other than their researches. Or consider Max Weber's philosophy of history and its fertile effect on the study of sixteenth- or seventeenth-century religion and economics.

5. Hegel once remarked to Goethe that all he meant by dialectics is the method of contradiction inherent in every human being. *Goethes Gespräche mit Eckermann*, October 18, 1827.

6. In *Knots* (London, 1970), R. D. Laing throws very ingenious doubt on this faculty. But the knots he presents make one doubt *only* the psychological capacity to carry out such criticism. The mere fact that Laing can formulate what cannot be carried out psychologically shows that the resolution of the knots (and thus critical thought and reflection) is logically conceivable. This is all that is necessary for the present argument.

7. Cp. Peter Munz, *When the Golden Bough Breaks* (London, 1973), ch. 13.

8. I hope to complete a book on the philosophy of history along these lines soon. This perspective owes an obvious debt to C. Lévi-Strauss *The Savage Mind* (London, 1966), ch. 9, 'History and Dialectic'.

9. The influence, let alone the dominance, of functionalism is diminishing fast. See the remarks by E. E. Evans-Pritchard, 'Fifty Years of British Anthropology', *Times Literary Supplement* 3722 (1973):763 col. 5 and by E. Leach, 'Concluding Address', in *The Explanation of Culture Change* ed. Colin Renfrew (London, 1973), p. 762: 'Functionalism is "old hat" in social anthropology'.

10. (London, 1935).

11. Lévi-Strauss, *Savage Mind*, p. 124 and *Totemism* (Boston, 1963).

12. 'Futurology' is an ugly word and the notion it expresses has a bad press. K. R. Popper rightly inveighed it in both *The Open Society* (London, 1945) and *The Poverty of Historicism* (London, 1957). But one can carry the hostility to futurology too far. R. Nisbet, 'Has Futurology a Future?' *Encounter* 218 (1971), argues vehemently against it and yet, though he does not notice it, refers approvingly both to Tocqueville and to the Marquis de Custine, who 'futurologised' quite successfully about America and Russia. See n. 13, and also J. Dumoulin and D. Moisi eds., *The Historian between the Ethnologist and the Futurologist* (Paris, 1975). It is unfortunate that so many writers identify speculative philosophy of history with futurology. See, e.g., A. C. Danto, *Analytical Philosophy of History* (Cambridge, Engl., 1968), p. 182.

13. R. Nisbet, *The Social Bond* (New York, 1970), p. 205; Henry Steele Commager, *The American Mind* (New Haven, 1959), pp. 3, 365; H. Laski, *The American Democracy* (London, 1949), p. 712; M. Lerner, *America as a Civilisation* (London, 1957), pp. 62, 72; D. Bell, *The Coming of Post-Industrial Society* (London, 1974), p. 318: 'on the reasons why the predictions of Tocqueville . . . are still so cogent . . .' M. Lerner, *Tocqueville and American Civilisation* (New York, 1969): 'In reading *Democracy* today, one has the uncanny feeling of reading not about Jackson's America but one's own'. D. Riesman, *The Lonely Crowd* (New Haven, 1950), is quite explicit about his debt to Tocqueville for his concept of other-direction. In many places, however, Riesman is critical of Tocqueville. It seems that this ambiguity in his attitude to Tocqueville stems from the fact that Riesman tries to argue that other-directedness is a modern development and not originally endemic in American society; whereas Tocqueville, though he did not use the term, saw it as a natural

consequence of American equality. I owe this explanation to my colleague J. O. C. Phillips.

14. It was to be expected that sooner or later the computer would be resorted to. Professor Meadows and the Club of Rome have cashed in on the sensation that we were able to produce by feeding a model of development into a computer. I am certain that the shock sensation will have important and salutary moral consequences. But it cannot be taken seriously as historical prediction. See, e.g., the incisive comments by J. Naughton, 'A Little Global Difficulty', *Encounter* 244 (1974):76.

15. 'The first thing we see as we travel around the world is our own filth, thrown into the face of mankind'. C. Lévi-Strauss, *Tristes Tropiques* (New York, 1974), p. 38.

16. (London, 1969).

17. The idea of progress is very old and came in many different shapes. It gathered enormous momentum as a tool of science during the nineteenth century. See J. B. Bury, *The Idea of Progress* (London, 1932) and, more recently, S. Pollard, *The Idea of Progress* (London, 1968).

18. The following two quotations define the distance between primitivism and modernity:

> There is no more thrilling prospect for the anthropologist than that of being the first white man to visit a particular native community. Already in 1938, this supreme reward could only be obtained in a few regions of the world — few enough indeed to be counted on the fingers of one hand. Since then, the possibilities have diminished still further. I was about to relive the experience of the early travellers and, through it, that crucial moment in modern thought when, thanks to the great voyages of discovery, a human community which believed itself to be complete and in its final form suddenly learned, as if through the effect of a counter-revelation, that it was not alone, that it was part of a greater whole, and that, in order to achieve self-knowledge, it must first of all contemplate its unrecognizable image in this mirror, of which a fragment, forgotten by the centuries, was now about to cast, for me alone, its first and last reflection. (Lévi-Strauss, *Tristes Tropiques*, p. 326).

> The philosophical significance of the scientific-industrial 'form of life', whose rapid global diffusion is the main event of our time, is that for all practical purposes it does provide us with a solution of the problem of relativism — though a highly unsymmetrical one. (It is for this reason that no symmetrical solution can be entertained.) The cognitive and technical superiority of one form of life is so manifest, and so loaded with implications for the satisfaction of human wants and needs — and, for better or worse, for power — that it simply cannot be questioned. E. Gellner, 'The New Idealism', in *Problems in the Philosophy of Science*, ed. I. Lakatos and A. Musgrave (Amsterdam, 1968), p. 405.

19. See Thomas S. Kuhn, *The Structure of Scientific Revolutions*, 2nd ed. (Chicago, 1970), p. 170: 'The developmental process described in this essay has been a process of evolution *from* primitive beginnings. . . . But nothing that has been or will be said makes it a process of evolution *toward* anything'.

20. *The Origin and Goal of History* (London, 1953).
21. Thus, e.g., one can see the history of all Christian churches and of their influence as so many strategies for the evasion of the Sermon on the Mount.
22. This applies also to all derivatives of the theory of progress: social integration–anomy; status–contract; *Gemeinschaft–Gesellschaft;* inner-direction–other-direction; tradition–modernity; ascription society–achievement society; traditionalism–economic rationalisation, and so forth. It also applies to the opposite of the theory of progress, to Freud's view of civilisation. Freud argued that men first repress libido and then punish themselves, often excessively so, both for inflicting such a sacrifice on themselves and for wishing to avoid such a sacrifice. Civilisation is the compound of repression and of the consequent punishments. The theory is probably true, but too thin to explain what happened in the past. Similarly thin is the medieval scheme of progress that divides the past into the old and the new dispensation, even when it comes in the fuller version of Joachim of Flores. The same applies to Comte's scheme of progress.
23. The lectures on the philosophy of history were edited and published posthumously by E. Gans in 1837. A revised second edition by Karl Hegel appeared in 1840. The standard English translation is by J. Sibree 1858, from the third German edition of 1843.
24. For the extraordinary circumstances in which the book was written, see W. Kaufmann, *Hegel* (New York, 1965), pp. 108ff.
25. I follow Ch. Taylor, 'The Opening Arguments of the *Phenomenology*', in *Hegel* ed. A. MacIntyre (Garden City, N.Y., 1972).
26. For Hegel's early theological studies, see G. Lukács, *Der junge Hegel* (Zürich, 1948).
27. I follow Qu. Lauer, *Hegel's Idea of Philosophy* (New York, 1971), p. 20.
28. Not even Hegel took the view that history ends in nineteenth-century Prussia literally. He knew perfectly well that the future extended to America. For his fascinating speculations about the future of America and the dependence of its history with population growth, see I. Fetscher, *Hegel: Grösse und Grenzen* (Stuttgart, 1971), pp. 16ff.
29. Jean Hyppolite, *Genesis and Structure of Hegel's 'Phenomenology of Spirit'* (Evanston, Ill., 1974), p. 366.
30. Cp. E. Weil, *Hegel et l'état* (Paris, 1950).
31. *The Philosophy of History*, trans. J. Sibree (New York, 1956), p. 1.
32. For Hegel's parallelism between thought and form of life, see both Ch. Taylor, *Hegel* (Cambridge, Engl., 1975), p. 156 and Lukács, *Hegel,* p. 572.
33. *Metahistory* (Baltimore, 1973), p. 124.
34. For one, there can be a dialectical way of thinking. But one cannot stand dialectics on its head and assert that things other than thought behave dialectically and that dialectic thinking is copied from the dialectical behaviour of things other than thought.
35. F. Jameson, *Marxism and Form* (Princeton, 1971), has made the interesting attempt to relativise Marx and to treat his philosophy of history as one among others. Jameson tries to show that the mode of production, which Marx saw as the irreducible character of reality (i.e., *res gestae*), is really an intellectual construction and not the socioeconomic reality itself. If Jameson's reduction is correct, and I think it is, then Marx's philosophy of history is all wrong for it consisted precisely in the doc-

trine that, though other reductions are imperative, this particular reduction is not permitted.

36. See Peter Munz, *Reflections on the Theory of the Revolution in France*
(Wellington, N.Z., 1972), p. 8.

37. Marianne Weber, *Max Weber* (Tübingen, 1926), p. 685f; Riesman, *Lonely
Crowd;* J. Burnham, *The Managerial Revolution* (London, 1941);
W. Whyte, *The Organization Man* (New York, 1956); and Z. Brzezinski,
'America in the Technetronic Age', *Encounter* 172 (1968).

38. Quite recently this method has been given a new lease of life by M.
Foucault, *The Archeology of Knowledge* (London, 1972). In this book
Foucault divides the history of Europe into three epochs, each informed
by its own *episteme* so that each is so completely self-contained that one
cannot develop into another and that one cannot understand one if one
is an inhabitant of another. It is not clear how Foucault has persuaded
himself to be able to take such a comprehensive view when he too must
be the captive of an *episteme.* Cp. Hayden V. White 'Foucault Decoded:
Notes from Underground', *History and Theory* 12 (1973).

39. Hegel, for example, on the first page of his *Lectures on the Philosophy
of History* said that the ancient Greeks were a society in which unreflective morality held sway. This is so general that it makes little sense.
But there are societies of which such an assertion would be true and it
might even be true of the Greeks before the full emergence of the city-
states. It is a pity that Hegel had no chance of reading George Thomson's
Aeschylus and Athens (London, 1941).

40. 'The Burden of Proof', *Times Literary Supplement* (Nov. 7, 1975):1333,
col. 3.

41. 'The Burden of Proof', *Times Literary Supplement* (October 24, 1975):
1252, col. 5.

42. Popper, *Poverty of Historicism,* where the criticism and total rejection is
implicit throughout, even though Toynbee is mentioned only four times;
P. Geyl, *Debates with Historians* (London, 1962), chs. 5, 7, and 8. This is
the most rational criticism I know of. See also W. Dray, 'Toynbee's
Search for Historical Laws', *History and Theory* 1 (1960); H. Trevor-Roper,
"The Toynbee Millennium', *Encounter* 45 (1957). Written with verve, this
article carries the criticism beyond all reason by playing on certain mystical tendencies in the very last of the ten volumes; and W. Kaufmann,
From Shakespeare to Existentialism (Boston, 1959), chs. 19–20.

43. (London, 1972), p. 77.

44. (London, 1946).

45. One of the leading ideas in F. Braudel's work is the distinction between
different durations of events. Some sociologists use durations that are too
short; others, durations that are too long. Historians, Braudel thinks, use
durations of just about the right length to capture change. If the durations
are too short, one is dealing with the instantaneously present. If they are
too long, one is dealing with what appears perenially immobile. But even
in the middle range, where the historian operates, Braudel distinguishes
between short duration, medium duration, and long duration. He system-
atises the threefold distinction by showing that short duration is an *événe-
ment;* medium duration, a *conjoncture;* and long duration, a *structure.*
I am not attempting a translation of these terms because, though the first
and third are intelligible, the term *conjoncture* is not. To my knowledge

it was first introduced into the history of literary criticism by Chrétien de Troyes in the twelfth century. Chrétien announced in the opening pages of *Erec et Énide* that he was about to 'draw from a tale of adventure a very fine *conjointure*'. The general meaning is clear: he was about to turn a tale of an adventure into an entertaining romance. But scholars have ever since pondered the exact meaning of '*conjointure*' and it is extremely interesting that it crops up again in the twentieth-century in the thought of F. Braudel. For the term, see E. Vinaver, *The Rise of Romance* (New York, 1971), pp. 34ff. For Braudel's classification, see also E. Kedourie, 'New Histories for Old', *Times Literary Supplement* 3809 (1975):240, col. 2; and J. H. Hexter, 'Fernand Braudel and the *monde Braudellien*', *Journal of Modern History* 44 (1972):502–05.

46. *Poverty of Historicism.*

47. One can criticise Popper for being too ready to take the opposing parties at their own word. The upholders of developmental laws have always claimed that their detection of these laws in *res gestae* does not depend on universals, and ordinary historians are fond of claiming that they only record contingencies. One can hardly blame Popper for making it easy for himself when both parties to the dispute make such and similar protestations. After all, why should he not take them at their own word? Real criticism should therefore begin with the demonstration that both the upholders of developmental laws and the ordinary historians are wrong in their belief that their activities do not depend on universal laws. Once the widespread self-delusion on both sides is dispelled, Popper's criticism seems less appropriate. Its cogency is directed at the conventional accounts of developmental laws rather than at developmental laws as such. To make the gap between historicists (i.e., philosophers of history and social scientists who believe in developmental laws or laws of succession) and ordinary historians appear as wide as possible, Popper, *Poverty of Historicism,* has chosen for the historicist case T. H. Huxley (p. 108), Comte (p. 116), Mill (p. 72), Marx (p. 51), and Plato (p. 73); and in one sweep such philosophers of history as, Machiavelli, Vico, Spengler, and Toynbee (p. 110). For the ordinary historian's case, he cites H. A. L. Fisher's famous sentence from *A History of Europe* (London, 1936), p. V, that history is one emergency following upon another. The philosophers of history are treated very summarily, except Comte. Huxley and Mill are hardly representative of the speculative philosophy of history and, on the other side, the quotation from Fisher is taken from a book that is so cogent a narrative of the determined progression toward liberalism as to be almost indistinguishable from a proper philosophy of history so that one is forced to conclude that Fisher himself did not believe his own argument; or, if he did, that he did not live up to it. This leaves one with the impression that Popper, to clinch his argument, set up straw men on both sides and that closer examination would have shown that the gap between what philosophers of history are really doing and what ordinary historians are really doing is not nearly as wide as Popper claims. In fairness to Popper one has to admit that most philosophers of history, in claiming to have discovered laws of development, tend to misrepresent the nature of their activity as much as H. A. L. Fisher does. The present comment, therefore, is no criticism of Popper's case against what he calls historicism, but merely a criticism of its applicability to the study of history.

48. English translation in Karl Marx, *Basic Writings on Politics and Philosophy* ed. L. S. Feuer (New York, 1959), p. 8.
49. The distinction between limited and unlimited prophecy is based on and corresponds to Popper's distinction between prediction and prophecy; see *Poverty of Historicism*, ch. 1.
50. (Florence, 1940).
51. The book has been translated into English by Hayden V. White as *From History to Sociology* (Detroit, 1959). It is unfortunate that the literal translation of the title is likely to perpetuate the misunderstanding. In his book entitled *Thought and Change* (London, 1964), p. 20, E. Gellner considers this same problem in a different context. 'When we have real explanations', he writes, 'the specification of the path is redundant'. When we work through to a philosophy of history, he seems to be saying, the sum total of the smaller narratives becomes superfluous. 'The tracing of the Path itself is a mere summary of the findings'. The tendency to work forward to an overall scheme is a tendency that no real historian can resist. When he has arrived there and looks backward, the single narratives and series of events that went into the scheme will lose their independent importance.
52. This is the reason why Marx's philosophy of history is disqualified. He believed that his philosophy of history was not just one among many possible philosophies, but a philosophy of history to end all philosophies of history by exposing them as ideologies. With this view he went against the nature of historical knowledge.
53. This argument is based on Kant's account of man's freedom. See ch. 8, n. 39.

SELECT BIBLIOGRAPHY

This list contains all the works cited and discussed in this book as well as a small number of relevant and informative works on the philosophy and methodology of history not referred to in the text. It is hoped that their inclusion will prove useful to the reader. The entries are in all cases the editions actually quoted or referred to in the text and the notes, not necessarily the first editions. This list was compiled with the help of Mrs. Dorothy Freed, Reference Librarian, Victoria University of Wellington.

Abrams, Meyer Howard. *The Mirror and the Lamp*. New York: Oxford University Press, 1953.

Acham, Karl. *Analytische Geschichtsphilosophie*. Freiburg: Alber, 1974.

Adorno, Theodor W. 'Wesen und Wirklichkeit des Menschen'. In *Wesen und Wirklichkeit des Menschen*. Festschrift für Helmuth Plessner. Edited by Klaus Ziegler. Göttingen: Vandenhoeck and Ruprecht, 1957.

Agassi, Joseph. 'Methodological Individualism'. *British Journal of Sociology* II (1960): 244-70.

Alquié, Ferdinand. *The Philosophy of Surrealism*. Translated by Bernard Waldrop. Ann Arbor: University of Michigan Press, 1965.

Amerio, Franco. *Introduzione allo studio di G. B. Vico*. Torino: Società editrice internazionale, 1947.

Anderle, Othmar F. 'A Plea for Theoretical History'. *History and Theory* 4 (1964): 27-56.

———. 'Theoretische Geschichte'. *Historische Zeitschrift* 185 (1958): 1-54.

Andreski, Stanislav. *The Social Sciences as Sorcery*. London: Deutsch, 1972.

Anstey, Roger. *The Atlantic Slave Trade and British Abolition, 1760-1810*. London: Macmillan, 1975.

Antoni, Carlo. *From History to Sociology*. Translated by Hayden V. White. Detroit: Wayne State University Press, 1959.

Ariés, Philippe. *Western Attitudes Towards Death: From the Middle Ages to the Present*. Translated by Patricia M. Ranum. Baltimore: John Hopkins University Press, 1974.

Aron, Raymond. *The Dawn of Universal History*. Translated by Dorothy Pickles. New York: Praeger, 1961.

———. *Introduction to the Philosophy of History*. Translated by George T. Irwin. London: Weidenfeld & Nicolson, 1948.

Aubert, Wilhelm. *Elements of Sociology*. London: Heinemann, 1968.

Auden, Wystan Hugh. *The Enchafed Flood: Or The Romantic Iconography of the Sea.* London: Faber, 1951.

Auerbach, Erich. *Mimesis. The Representation of Reality in Western Literature.* Translated by Willard R. Task. Princeton: Princeton University Press, 1968.

Aymand, Maurice. 'The *Annales* and French Historiography (1929–1972)'. *Journal of European Economic History*, 1 (1972):491–511.

Badian, Ernst. 'Alexander the Great and the Loneliness of Power'. In his *Studies in Greek and Roman History.* Oxford: Blackwell, 1964.

———. Review of *Alexander the Great* by R. L. Fox. *New York Review of Books* (Sept. 19, 1974):8–10.

Bambrough, Renford. 'Principia Metaphysica'. *Philosophy* 39 (1964):97–109.

Barnes, Harry Elwes. *A History of Historical Writing.* Norman: University of Oklahoma Press, 1937.

Baron, Hans. *The Crisis of the Early Italian Renaissance.* Princeton: Princeton University Press, 1955.

Barraclough, Geoffrey. *History in a Changing World.* Oxford: Blackwell, 1955.

Barthes, Roland, *Essais critiques.* Paris: Editions du Seuil, 1964.

———. *S/Z.* Translated by Richard Miller. New York: Hill & Wang, 1974.

Bateson, Gregory. *Steps Towards an Ecology of Mind.* London: Paladin Books, 1973.

Baumgartner, Hans Michael. *Kontinuität und Geschichte.* Frankfurt: Suhrkamp, 1972.

———. 'Thesen zur Grundlegung einer transcendentalen Historik'. In *Seminar, Geschichte und Theorie.* Edited by H. M. Baumgartner and J. Rüsen. Frankfurt: Suhrkamp, 1976.

Beard, Charles. *An Economic Interpretation of the Constitution of the United States.* New York: Macmillan, 1913.

———. 'Written History as an Act of Faith'. *American Historical Review* 39 (1934):219–29.

Becker, Carl Lotus. *Detachment and the Writing of History: Essays and Letters of Carl Becker.* Edited by Phil L. Snyder. Ithaca: Cornell University Press, 1958.

———. *Everyman His Own Historian.* New York: F. S. Crofts, 1935.

———. 'Everyman His Own Historian'. *American Historical Review* 37 (1932): 221–36.

Becker, Marvin B. *Florence in Transition.* Baltimore: Johns Hopkins University Press, 1967.

Beek, Martinus Adrianus *Geschichte Israels.* Stuttgart: Kohlhammer, 1961.

Bell, Daniel. *The Coming of Post-Industrial Society: A Venture in Social Forecasting.* London: Heinemann, 1974.

Benedict, Ruth. *Patterns of Culture.* London: Routledge & Kegan Paul, 1935.

Berlin, Isaiah. *Historical Inevitability.* London: Oxford University Press, 1954.

———. 'History and Theory: The Concept of Scientific History'. *History and Theory* 1 (1960):1–31.

———. *Vico and Herder.* London: Hogarth Press, 1976.

Bernheim, Ernst. *Lehrbuch der historischen Methode und der Geschichtsphilosophie.* Leipzig: Duncker & Humblot, 1889.

Besançon, Alfred. 'L'inconsciente'. In *Faire de l'histoire.* Edited by J. Le Goff and P. Nora. Paris: Gallimard, 1974.

Betti, Emilio. *Die Hermeneutik als allgemeine Methodik der Geisteswissenschaften.* Tübingen: Mohr, 1962.

Bloch, Marc L. B. *The Historian's Craft.* Translated by Peter Putnam. Manchester: Manchester University Press, 1954.

Boehmer, Heinrich. *Martin Luther.* Translated by John W. Doberstein and Theodore G. Tappert. New York: Meridian Books, 1957.

Boer, Willem den. 'Graeco-Roman Historiography in its Relation to Biblical and Modern Thinking'. *History and Theory* (1968):60–75.

Bollhagen, Peter. *Soziologie und Geschichte.* Berlin: Deutscher Verlag der Wissenschaften, 1966.

Bollnow, Otto Friedrich. *Dilthey.* 3rd ed. Stuttgart: Kohlhammer Verlag, 1955.

Boring, Edwin G. *Sensation and Perception in the History of Experimental Psychology.* New York: D. Appleton-Century Company, 1942.

Born, Karl Erich. 'Neue Wege in der Wirtschafts- und Sozialgeschichte in Frankreich. Die Historikergrupper der *Annales.*' *Saeculum* 15 (1964): 189–209.

Bowra, Cecil Maurice. *Heroic Poetry.* London: Macmillan, 1952.

Brackmann, Albert. 'Die Handschriften des *Liber Pontificalis*'. *Gesellschaft für ältere deutsche Geschichtskunde. . . . Neues Archiv* 26 (1901):15–37.

———. 'Der *Liber Pontificalis*'. In his *Gesammelte Aufsätze.* Weimar: H. Böhlaus Nachfolger, 1941.

Bradley, Francis H. *The Presuppositions of Critical History.* Edited by Lionel Rubrioff. Chicago: Quadrangle Books, 1968.

Brand, Gerd. *Gesellschaft und Geschichte: Die mythologische Sinngebung sozialer Prozesse.* Stuttgart: Kohlhammer, 1972.

Brandon, Samuel G. F. *History, Time and Deity: A Historical and Comparative Study of the Conception of Time in Religious Thought and Practice.* Manchester: Manchester University Press, 1965.

———. 'The Ritual Perpetuation of the Past'. *Numen* 6 (1959):112–29.

Brands, Maarten Cornelis. *Historisme als Ideologie.* Assen: Van Gorcum, 1965.

Braudel, Fernand. *Écrits sur l'histoire.* Paris: Flammarion, 1969.

———. *The Mediterranean and the Mediterranean World in the Age of Philip II.* Translated by Sian Reynolds. London: Collins, 1972–73.

Bronowski, Jacob. *The Ascent of Man.* London, British Broadcasting Corporation, 1973.

Brooke, John. 'Namier and His Critics'. *Encounter* 137 (1965):47–49.

Brown, Peter. 'The Rise and Function of the Holy Man in Late Antiquity'. *Journal of Roman Studies* 61 (1971):80–101.

Brown, Robert Eldon. *Charles Beard and the Constitution.* Princeton: Princeton University Press, 1956.

Brown, Robert R. *Explanation in the Social Sciences.* London: Routledge & Kegan Paul, 1964.

———. *Rules and Laws in Sociology.* London: Routledge & Kegan Paul, 1973.

Brunt, Peter Astbury. 'The Aims of Alexander'. *Greece and Rome* 12 (1965): 205–28.

Brzezinski, Zbigniew K. 'America in the Technetronic Age'. *Encounter* 172 (1968):16–26.

Bull, L. 'Ancient Egypt'. In *The Idea of History in the Ancient Near East.* Edited by Robert C. Dentan. New Haven: Yale University Press, 1955.

Burnham, James. *The Managerial Revolution or, What is Happening in the World Now.* London: Putnam, 1941.

Burrows, Millar. 'Ancient Israel'. In *The Idea of History in the Ancient Near East.* Edited by Robert C. Dentan. New Haven: Yale University Press, 1955.

Bury, John Bagnell. *The Idea of Progress.* London: Macmillan, 1932.
——. *Selected Essays of J. B. Bury.* Edited by Harold Temperley. Cambridge:
    Cambridge University Press, 1930.
Butterfield, Herbert. 'George III and the Constitution'. *History* 42-43 (1958):
    14-33.
——. *George III and the Historians.* London: Collins, 1957.
——. *Man on His Past.* Cambridge: Cambridge University Press, 1955.
Cahnman, Werner Jacob, and Boskoff, Alvin, eds. *Sociology and History.*
    Glencoe: Free Press, 1964.
Cantor, Norman F., and Schneider, Richard I. *How to Study History.* New
    York: Crowell, 1967.
Caponigri, Aloysius Robert. *History and Liberty: The Historical Writings of
    Benedetto Croce.* London: Routledge & Kegan Paul, 1953.
Carr, Edward Hallett. *What is History?* London: Macmillan, 1961.
Certeau, Michel de. *L'Écriture de l'histoire.* Paris: Gallimard, 1957.
Chadwick, Hector Munro. *The Heroic Age.* Cambridge: Cambridge University
    Press, 1926.
Chambers, Edmund Kerchever. *Arthur of Britain.* Reprinted with supple-
    mentary bibliography. Cambridge: Speculum Historiale, 1964.
Childe, Vere Gordon. *Prehistoric Migrations in Europe.* Oslo, Aschehoug,
    1950.
Clark, Robert Thomas Rundle. *Myth and Symbol in Ancient Egypt.* London:
    Thames & Hudson, 1959.
Cobban, Alfred. 'The Myth of the French Revolution'. In his *Aspects of the
    French Revolution.* London: Cape, 1968.
——. *The Social Interpretation of the French Revolution.* Cambridge: Cam-
    bridge University Press, 1964.
Cochrane, Charles Norris. *Thucydides and the Science of History.* London:
    Oxford University Press, 1929.
Cohen, Percy S. *Modern Social Theory.* London: Heinemann, 1968.
Collingwood, Robin George. *An Autobiography.* Harmondsworth: Penguin,
    1944.
——. *An Essay on Metaphysics.* Oxford: Clarendon Press, 1940.
——. *The Idea of History.* Oxford: Clarendon Press, 1946.
——. *The Idea of Nature.* Oxford: Clarendon Press, 1945.
——. 'Oswald Spengler and the Theory of Historical Cycles'. *Antiquity* 1
    (1927):311-25.
——. *The Principles of Art.* Oxford: Clarendon Press, 1938.
Commager, Henry Steele. *The American Mind.* New Haven: Yale University
    Press, 1950.
Conze, Werner, ed. *Theorie der Geschichtswissenschaft und Praxis des
    Geschichtsunterrichts.* Stuttgart: Klett, 1972.
Cornford, Francis MacDonald. *Thucydides Mythistoricus.* London: Routledge
    & Kegan Paul, 1965 (1907).
Croce, Benedetto. *La filosofia di Giambattista Vico.* Bari: Laterza, 1911.
——. *History as the Story of Liberty.* Translated by Sylvia Sprigge. London:
    Allen and Unwin, 1941.
——. *Theory and History of Historiography.* Translated by Douglas Ainslie.
    London: Harrap, 1921.
Culler, Jonathan. *Structuralist Poetics.* London: Routledge & Kegan Paul,
    1975.
Curtius, Ernest Robert. *Europäische Literatur und lateinisches Mittelalter.*
    Bern: Francke, 1948.

Dahrendorf, Ralf. *Die angewandte Aufklärung.* Munich: R. Piper, 1963.
——. *Homo Sociologicus.* Cologne: Westdeutscher Verlag, 1958.
Danto, Arthur Coleman. *Analytical Philosophy of History.* Cambridge: Cambridge University Press, 1968.
——. 'Narrative Sentences'. *History and Theory* 2 (1962-63):146-79.
Darnton, R. 'French History: The Case of the Wandering Eye'. *New York Review of Books.* (Apr. 5, 1973):25-30.
Davis, David Bryon. 'The Ideology of Anti-Slavery'. *Times Literary Supplement,* 3841 (1975):1263.
Dilthey, Willhelm. *Der Aufbau der Geschichtlichen Welt in den Geisteswissenschaften.* Introduction by Manfred Riedel. Frankfurt: Suhrkamp, 1970.
——. *Wilhelm Diltheys Gesammelte Schriften.* Vol. 7. *Einführung in die Geisteswissenschaften.* Leipzig and Berlin: Teubner, 1927.
——. *Wilhelm Diltheys Gesammelte Schriften.* Vol. 8. *Weltanschauungslehre.* Leipzig and Berlin: Teubner, 1927.
Donagan, Alan. 'Explanation in History'. In *Theories of History.* Edited by Patrick Gardiner. Glencoe: Free Press, 1959.
——. 'Historical Explanation: The Popper-Hempel Theory Reconsidered'. *History and Theory,* 1 (1964):3-36.
——. *The Later Philosophy of R. G. Collingwood.* Oxford: Clarendon Press, 1962.
——. 'Popper's Examination of Historicism'. In *The Philosophy of Karl Popper.* Edited by Paul Arthur Schilpp. La Salle, Ill.: Open Court, 1974.
Dorpalen, Andreas. 'Historiography as History: The Work of Gerhard Ritter'. *Journal of Modern History* 34 (1962):1-18.
Douglas, Mary. *Natural Symbols.* London: Cresset Press, 1970.
Dray, William Herbert. 'The Historical Explanation of Actions Reconsidered'. In *The Philosophy of History.* Edited by Patrick Gardiner. London: Oxford University Press, 1974.
——. *Laws and Explanation in History.* Oxford: Oxford University Press, 1957.
——. 'Narrative and Historiography'. *History and Theory* 10 (1971):153-71.
——, ed. *Philosophical Analysis and History.* New York: Harper & Row, 1966.
——. 'Toynbee's Search for Historical Laws'. *History and Theory* 1 (1960): 32-54.
Drews, Robert. *The Greek Accounts of Eastern History.* Washington D.C.: Distributed by Harvard University Press, 1973.
Droysen, Johann Gustav. *Historik.* Edited by Rudolf Hübner. 4th ed. Darmstadt: Wissenschaftliche Buchgesellschaft, 1960.
Dumézil, Georges. *From Myth to Fiction: the Saga of Hadingus.* Translated by Derek Coltman. Chicago: University of Chicago Press, 1970.
——. *Mythe et épopée.* Paris: Gallimard, 1968.
Dumoulin, Jerome, and Moisi, Dominique, eds. *The Historian Between the Ethnologist and the Futurologist.* A conference sponsored by the International Association for Cultural Freedom, by the Giovanni Angelli Foundation and by the Giorgio Cini Foundation. Paris: Mouton, 1973.
Durkheim, Émile. *The Elementary Forms of the Religious Life: A Study in Religious Sociology.* Translated by Joseph W. Swain. London: Allen & Unwin, 1915.
——. *The Rules of Sociological Method.* Translated by Sarah A. Solovay and John H. Mueller and edited by G. E. G. Catlin. Glencoe: Free Press, 1964 [1938].

Ehrenberg, Victor. 'Caesar's Final Aims'. In his *Man, State and Deity*. London: Methuen, 1974.

Einem, Herbert von. *Michelangelo*. Stuttgart: Kohlhammer, 1959.

Eliade, Mircea. *The Myth of the Eternal Return*. Translated by Willard R. Trask. New York: Pantheon Books, 1954. (Bollingen series, 46.)

Elton, Geoffrey Rudolph. *Political History: Principles and Practice*. London: Penguin, 1970.

———. *The Practice of History*. London: Fontana, 1969.

Ely, R. G. et al. 'Mandelbaum on Historical Narrative: A Discussion'. *History and Theory*, 8 (1969):275-94.

Erikson, Erik Homburger. *Young Man Luther*. New York: W. W. Norton, 1958.

Evans-Pritchard, Edward Evan. 'Fifty Years of British Anthropology'. *Times Literary Supplement* 3722 (1973):763-64.

Faber, Karl-Georg. *Theorie der Geschichtswissenschaft*. Munich: C. H. Beck, 1974.

Fain, Haskell. *Between Philosophy and History: The Resurrection of Speculative Philosophy of History Within the Analytic Tradition*. Princeton: Princeton University Press, 1970.

Febvre, Lucien. *Combats pour l'histoire*. Paris: Colin, 1953.

Fetscher, Iring. *Hegel: Grösse und Grenzen*. Stuttgart: Kohlhammer, 1971.

Finegan, Jack. *Light from the Ancient Past*. Princeton: Princeton University Press, 1946.

Finley, Moses I. 'Myth, Memory and History'. *History and Theory* 4 (1964-65):281-302.

Fischer, David Hackett. *Historians' Fallacies: Toward a Logic of Historical Thought*. New York: Harper & Row, 1970.

Fischer, Fritz. *Germany's Aims in the First World War*. London: Chatto & Windus, 1967.

———. *World Power or Decline: The Controversy over Germany's Aims in the First World War*. Translated by Lancelot L. Farrar, Robert Kimber, and Rita Kimber. New York: W. W. Norton, 1974.

Fisher, Herbert A. L. *A History of Europe*. London: Arnold, 1936.

Forsdyke, Edgar John. *Greece before Homer*. Edited by Wilfrid J. Millington Synge. London: Parrish, 1956.

Foucault, Michel. *The Archeology of Knowledge*. Translated by A. M. Sheridan-Smith. London: Tavistock, 1972.

———. *Les Mots et les choses: Une Archéologie des sciences humaines*. Paris: Gallimard, 1966.

Fox, Robin Lane. *Alexander the Great*. London: Allen Lane, 1974.

Fraisse, Paul. *The Psychology of Time*. Translated by Jennifer Leith. New York: Harper & Row, 1963.

Frankfort, Henri. *Ancient Egyptian Religion*. New York: Columbia University Press, 1948.

——— et al. *Before Philosophy*. Harmondsworth: Penguin, 1949. (Also published as *The Intellectual Adventure of Ancient Man*. Chicago: University of Chicago Press, 1946.)

Frazer, James George. *Folklore in the Old Testament: Studies in Comparative Religion, Legend and Law*. Abridged ed. London: Macmillan, 1923.

Frisch, Max. *Wilhelm Tell für die Schule*. Frankfurt: Suhrkamp, 1971.

Frye, Northrop. *Anatomy of Criticism*. Princeton: Princeton University Press, 1971.

——. *The Secular Scripture*. Cambridge, Mass.: Harvard University Press, 1976.

Furet, François. 'Le Catéchisme révolutionaire'. *Annales* 26 (1971):255–89.

Gadamer, Hans Georg. *Truth and Method*. Translation edited by Garrett Barden and John Cumming. New York: Seabury Press, 1975.

——. *Wahrheit und Methode: Grundzüge einer philosophischen Hermeneutik*. Tübingen: J.C.B. Mohr, 1960. 2nd ed., 1965.

Gallie, Walter Bryce. *Philosophy and the Historical Understanding*. London: Chatto & Windus, 1964.

Gardiner, Patrick. *The Nature of Historical Explanation*. London: Oxford University Press, 1952.

——. 'The Philosophy of History'. In *International Encyclopaedia of the Social Sciences*. Edited by David L. Sills. New York: Macmillan, 1968.

——, ed. *The Philosophy of History*. London: Oxford University Press, 1974.

——, ed. *Theories of History*. Glencoe: Free Press, 1959.

Gargan, Edward J., ed. *The Intent of Toynbee's History*. Chicago: Loyola University Press, 1961.

Garin, Eugenio. *Medioevo e Rinascimento*. Bari: Laterza, 1954.

Gaster, Theodor Herzl. *Myth, Legend and Custom in the Old Testament*. London: Duckworth, 1969.

Gellner, Ernest. 'Concepts and Society'. In *Transactions of the Fifth World Congress of Sociology*. Washington, 1962, v. 1. Louvain: International Sociological Association, 1962.

——. 'The New Idealism'. In *Problems in the Philosophy of Science*. International Colloquium in the Philosophy of Science, edited by Imre Lakatos and Alan Musgrave. Amsterdam: North-Holland, 1968.

——. 'Our Current Sense of History'. In *The Historian Between Ethnology and Futurology*. Edited by Jerome Dumoulin and Dominique Moisi. Paris: Mouton, 1973.

——. *Thought and Change*. London: Weidenfeld & Nicolson, 1964.

Gentile, Giovanni, 'The Transcending of Time in History'. In *Philosophy and History*. Edited by R. Klibansky and H. J. Paton. Oxford: Clarendon Press, 1936.

Geyl, Pieter. *Debates with Historians*. London: Collins, 1962.

——. *Napoleon For and Against*. Translated by Olive Renier. London: Jonathan Cape, 1949.

Ghiselin, Michael T. *The Triumph of the Darwinian Method*. Berkeley: University of California Press, 1969.

Gibbon, Edward. *Memoirs of My Life*. Edited by George A. Bonnard. London: Nelson, 1966.

Gibson, Alexander Boyce. *Muse and Thinker*. Harmondsworth: Penguin, 1972.

Gibson, Quentin Boyce. *The Logic of Social Inquiry*. London: Routledge & Kegan Paul, 1960.

Gide, André. *Les Faux Monnayeurs*. Paris: Gallimard, 1925.

Giedion, Sigfried. *The Eternal Present: The Beginning of Art*. New York: Pantheon Books, 1962. (Bollingen series, 35.)

Giesebrecht, Wilhelm von. *Geschichte der deutschen Kaiserzeit*. Brunswick, C.A. Schwetschke, 1860.

Gilbert, Felix. Review of English translation of *Historism* by Friedrich Meinecke. *History and Theory* 13 (1974):59–64.

Goffman, Erving. *Stigma: Notes on the Management of Spoiled Identity.*
    Englewood Cliffs, N.J.: Prentice-Hall, 1963.
———. *Where the Action Is.* London: Allen Lane, 1969.
Goldstein, Leon. 'Collingwood on the Constitution of the Historical Past'.
    In *Critical Essays on the Philosophy of R. G. Collingwood.* Edited by
    Michael Krausz. London: Clarendon Press, 1972.
Gombrich, Ernest Hans Josef. *Art and Illusion.* London: Phaidon Press, 1960.
Gooch, George Peabody. *History and Historians in the 19th Century.* 2nd
    ed. London: Longmans, 1952.
Gottschalk, Louis Reichenthal, ed. *Generalisation in the Writing of History.*
    Chicago: University of Chicago Press, 1963.
———. *Understanding History: A Primer of Historical Method.* 2nd ed. New
    York: Knopf, 1965.
Goubert, Pierre. *L'Ancien Régime.* 2nd ed. Paris: Colin, 1969.
Grant, Michael. *Roman Myths.* London: Weidenfeld & Nicolson, 1971.
Graus, Frantisek. *Lebendige Vergangenheit.* Cologne: Böhlau, 1975.
———. *Volk, Herrscher und Heiliger im Reich der Merowinger.* Prague:
    Nakladatelstvi Ceskoslovenské Akademie Ved, 1965.
Groh, Dieter. *Kritische Geschichtswissenschaft in emanzipatorischer Absicht.*
    Stuttgart: Kohlhammer, 1973.
Gundolf, Friedrich. *The Mantle of Caesar.* Translated by Jacob Wittmer
    Hartmann. New York and London: The Vanguard Press, 1928.
Habakkuk, John. 'Economic History and Economic Theory'. *Daedalus* 100
    (1971):305–22.
Hallie, Philip Paul. *Maine de Biran.* Cambridge: Harvard University Press,
    1959.
Hamilton, J.R. *Alexander the Great.* London: Hutchinson, 1973.
Hauck, Karl. 'Heldendichtung and Heldensage als Geschichtsbewusstsein'.
    In Universität Hamburg, Historisches Seminar. *Alteuropa und die
    moderne Gesellschaft.* . . . Göttingen: Vandenhoeck & Ruprecht, 1963.
Havelock, Eric Alfred. *Preface to Plato.* Oxford: Blackwell, 1963.
Hayek, Friedrich August. *The Counter-Revolution of Science.* Glencoe: Free
    Press, 1952.
Heckscher, Eli Filip. *Mercantilism.* Translated by Mendel Shapiro. 2nd ed.
    Edited by E. F. Söderlund. London: Allen & Unwin, 1955.
Hedinger, Hans-Walter. *Subjektivität und Geisteswissenschaft.* Berlin:
    Duncker & Humblot, 1969.
Heer, Friedrich. *Aufgang Europas.* Wien: Europa Verlag, 1949.
Hegel, Georg Wilhelm Friedrich. *Phänomenologie des Geistes.* Frankfurt:
    Suhrkamp, 1973.
———. *The Philosophy of Fine Art.* Translated by F.P.B. Omaston. London:
    G. Bell and Sons, 1920.
———. *The Philosophy of History.* With prefaces by Charles Hegel and the
    translator, J. F. Sibree, and a new introduction by C. J. Friedrich. New
    York: Dover, 1956.
Heimpel, Hermann. 'Geschichte und Geschichtswissenschaft'. *Viertel-
    jahrshrift für Zeitgeschichte* (1957):1–17.
Hempel, Carl G. 'The Function of General Laws in History'. *Journal of
    Philosophy* 39 (1942):35–48.
Hencken, Hugh. 'Indoeuropean Languages and Archeology'. *Memoirs of the
    American Anthropological Association* 84 (1955). 68 pp.

Heurgon, Jacques. *The Rise of Rome to 264 B.C.* Translated by James Willis. London: Batsford, 1973.

Heusler, Andreas. *Die altgermanische Dichtung.* 2nd ed. Potsdam: Akademische Verlagsgesellschaft Athenaion, 1943.

——. 'Geschichtliches und Mythisches in der germanischen Heldensage'. Deutsche Akademie der Wissenschaften, Berlin. *Sitzungsberichte* 47 (1909):920-45.

Heuss, Alfred. *Verlust der Geschichte.* Göttingen: Vandenhoeck & Ruprecht, 1959.

Hexter, Jack H. 'The Burden of Proof'. *Times Literary Supplement* 3841 (1975):1250-52.

——. 'Fernand Braudel and the *monde Braudellien*'. *Journal of Modern History* 44 (1972):480-539.

——. *The History Primer.* London: Allen Lane, 1972.

Hill, Christopher. 'The Burden of Proof'. Letter to the Editor. *Times Literary Supplement* 3843 (1975): 1333.

——. *The Century of Revolution.* Edinburgh: Nelson, 1961.

——. *Change and Continuity in 17th Century England.* London: Weidenfeld & Nicolson, 1974.

——. *Puritanism and Revolution: Studies in Interpretation of the English Revolution of the 17th Century.* London: Secker & Warburg, 1958.

——. *The World Turned Upside Down: Radical Ideas During the English Revolution.* London: Temple Smith, 1972.

Hirsch, Eric Donald. *Validity in Interpretation.* New Haven: Yale University Press, 1967.

Hobsbawm, Eric John. *Bandits.* London: Weidenfeld & Nicolson, 1969.

Hodges, Herbert Arthur. *The Philosophy of Wilhelm Dilthey.* London: Routledge & Kegan Paul, 1952.

Höfler, Otto. *Siegfried, Arminius und die Symbolik.* Heidelberg: C. Winter, 1961.

Holton, Gerald. 'The Mainsprings of Discovery'. *Encounter* 247 (1974):85-92.

Homans, George Caspar. *English Villagers of the 13th Century.* Cambridge: Harvard University Press, 1942.

——. *The Human Group.* London: Routledge & Kegan Paul, 1951.

——, and Schneider, D. M. *Marriage, Authority and Final Causes. . . .* Glencoe: Free Press, 1955.

Hook, Sydney, ed. *Philosophy and History: A Symposium.* New York: New York University Press, 1963.

Hooke, Samuel Henry. *The Siege Perilous.* London: SCM Press, 1956.

Horton, Robin, and Finnegan, Ruth, eds. *Modes of Thought.* London: Faber, 1973.

Hübner, Kurt. 'Erkenntnistheoretische Fragen der Geschichtswissenschaft'. In *Die Funktion der Geschichte in unserer Zeit.* Edited by Eberhard Jäckal und Ernst Weymar. Stuttgart: Klett, 1975.

Hyppolite, Jean. *Genesis and Structure of Hegel's 'Phenomenology of Spirit'.* Translated by Samuel Cherniak and John Heckman. Evanston: Northwestern University Press, 1974.

Iggers, Georg Gerson. *The German Conception of History.* Middletown: Wesleyan University Press, 1968.

Jacoby, E.G., ed. See: Tönnies, Ferdinand.

Jacoby, Felix. 'Griechische Geschichtsschreibung'. *Die Antike* 2 (1926): 1–30.

Jakobson, Roman, and Lévi-Strauss, Claude. *'Les Chats* of Charles Baudelaire" *L'Homme* 2 (1962):5–21.

Jameson, Fredric. *Marxism and Form.* Princeton: Princeton University Press, 1971.

Janet, Paul Alexandre René. *L'Évolution de la mémoire et de la notion de temps.* Paris: Chahine, 1928.

Jaspers, Karl. *The Origin and Goal of History.* Translated by Michael Bullock. London: Routledge & Kegan Paul, 1953.

Jones, Ernest. *Sigmund Freud: Life and Work.* London: The Hogarth Press, 1956.

Kaegi, Werner. *Chronica Mundi.* Einsiedeln: Johannes Verlag, 1954. (Christ heute, 3. Reihe, 6.)

Kaufmann, Fritz. *Geschichtsphilosophie der Gegenwart.* New ed. Darmstadt: Wissenschaftliche Buchgemeinschaft, 1967.

Kaufmann, Walter Arnold. *From Shakespeare to Existentialism: Studies in Poetry, Religion and Philosophy.* Boston: Beacon Press, 1959.

——. *Hegel: Reinterpretation, Texts and Commentary.* Garden City, N.Y.: Doubleday, 1965.

Kedourie, Elie. 'New Histories for Old'. *Times Literary Supplement* 3809 (1975):238–40.

Kermode, John Frank. *The Sense of an Ending.* Oxford: Oxford University Press, 1967.

Klibansky, Raymond, and Paton, H. J., eds. *Philosophy and History.* Oxford: Clarendon Press, 1936.

Knowles, David. *The Monastic Order in England.* Cambridge: Cambridge University Press, 1941.

——. *The Religious Orders in England.* Cambridge: Cambridge University Press, 1941.

Kon, Igor Semenovic. *Die Geschichtsphilosophie des 20. Jahrhunderts.* Berlin: Akademie Verlag, 1964.

Koselleck, Reinhart. 'Historia Magistra Vitae'. In *Natur und Geschichte.* Edited by Hermann Braun et al. Stuttgart: Kohlhammer Verlag, 1967.

——. 'Wozu noch Historie?' *Historische Zeitschrift* 212 (1971):1–18.

—— and Stempel, Rolf-Dieter, eds. *Geschichte: Ereignis und Erzählung.* Poetik und Hermeneutik, 5. Munich: Fink, 1973.

Kossinna, Gustav. *Ursprung und Verbreitung der Germanen in vor- und frühgeschichtlicher Zeit.* Leipzig: C. Kabritzsch, 1928.

Kramer, Samuel Noah. *History Begins at Sumer.* Garden City, N.Y.: Doubleday, 1959.

——. *Sumerian Mythology.* New York: Harper, 1969.

Kuhn, Thomas S. *The Structure of Scientific Revolutions.* 2nd ed. Chicago: University of Chicago Press, 1970.

Laing, Ronald David. *Knots.* London: Tavistock, 1970.

Landes, David Saul. *History as Social Science.* Englewood Cliffs, N.J.: Prentice Hall, 1971.

Langer, Susanne Katherina. *Problems of Art: Ten Philosophical Lectures.* London: Routledge & Kegan Paul, 1957.

Langlois, Charles Victor, and Seignobos, Charles. *Introduction to the Study of History.* Translated by G. G. Berry. London: Duckworth, 1912.

Laski, Harold Joseph. *The American Democracy: A Commentary and an Interpretation.* London: Allen & Unwin, 1949.

Laslett, Peter. *The World We Have Lost.* London: Methuen, 1965.

Lauer, Quentin. *Hegel's Idea of Philosophy, with a New Translation of Hegel's 'Introduction to the History of Philosophy'.* New York: Fordham University Press, 1971.

Lawrence, Thomas Edward. *The Seven Pillars of Wisdom. A Triumph.* London: Cape, 1935.

Leach, Edmund Ronald. 'Concluding Address'. In *The Explanation of Culture Change: Models in Prehistory.* Proceedings, Research Seminar in Archaeology and Related Subjects, University of Sheffield, 1971. Edited by Colin Renfrew. London: Duckworth, 1973.

Le Bras, Gabriel. 'Le Droit Romain au service de la domination pontificale'. *Nouvelle Revue historique de droit français et étranger* 27 (1949):377–98.

Lefèbvre, Georges. *Les Paysans du nord pendant le révolution française.* Paris: F. Rieder, 1924.

Leff, Gordon. *History and Social Theory.* London: Merlin Press, 1969.

Le Goff, J., and Nora, P., eds. *Faire de l'histoire: Nouveaux problèmes.* Paris: Gallimard, 1974.

Lerner, Daniel. *The Passing of Traditional Society: Modernizing the Middle East.* Glencoe: Free Press, 1958.

Lerner, Max. *America as a Civilisation: Life and Thought in the United States Today.* New York: Simon & Schuster, 1957.

——. *Tocqueville and American Civilisation.* New York: Harper & Row, 1969.

Lévi-Strauss, Claude. *The Elementary Structures of Kinship.* Rev. ed. Translated by James Harle Bell, John Richard von Sturmer; edited by Rodney Needham. London: Eyre & Spottiswoode, 1969.

——. *The Savage Mind.* London: Weidenfeld & Nicolson, 1966.

——. *The Scope of Anthropology.* Translated by Sherry O. Paul and Robert A. Paul. London: Cape, 1967.

——. *Structural Anthropology.* Translated by Claire Jacobson and Brooke Grundfest Schoepf. New York: Basic Books, 1963.

——. *Totemism.* Translated by Rodney Needham. Boston: Beacon Press, 1963.

——. *Tristes Tropiques.* Translated by John and Doreen Weightman. New York: Atheneum, 1974.

Lichtheim, George. 'Sartre, Marxism and History'. *History and Theory* 2 (1963): 222–46.

Lifton, Robert J., and Olson, Eric, eds. *Explorations in Psychohistory: The Well-fleet Papers.* New York: Simon & Schuster, 1974.

Lipset, Seymour Martin. *Political Man: The Social Bases of Politics.* New York: Doubleday, 1963.

——. *Revolution and Counter-Revolution.* London: Heinemann, 1969.

——, and Hofstadter, Richard, eds. *Sociology and History: Methods.* New York: Basic Books, 1968.

Lovejoy, Arthur Oncken. *Essays in the History of Ideas.* Baltimore: Johns Hopkins Press, 1948.

Löwith, Karl. *Meaning in History.* Chicago: University of Chicago Press, 1949.

Lukàcs, György. *The Historical Novel.* Translated by Hannah and Stanley Mitchell. Harmondsworth: Penguin, 1969.

——. *Der junge Hegel.* Zürich: Europa Verlag, 1948.

Madariaga, Salvador de. *A Bunch of Errors.* London: Cape, 1954.

Madge, John Hylton. 'The Contribution of Sociology'. In *The Frontiers of*

Sociology. Edited by Tosco Raphael Fyvel. London: Cohen & West, 1964.

Makkreel, Rudolph A. *Dilthey: Philosopher of the Human Studies*. Princeton: Princeton University Press, 1975.

Malraux, André. *Les Voix du silence*. Paris: NRF, 1951.

Mandelbaum, Maurice. 'Historical Explanation: The Problem of "Covering Laws" '. *History and Theory* 1 (1961):229–42.

——. 'A Note on History as Narrative'. *History and Theory* 6 (1967):413–19.

——. *The Problem of Historical Knowledge: An Answer to Relativism*. New York: Liveright, 1939.

Mann, Golo. 'The History Lesson'. *Encounter* 227 (1972):23–30.

——. '1914: The Beast in the Jungle'. *Encounter* 182 (1968):70–77.

Mann, Thomas. 'Freud and the Future'. In his *Essays of Three Decades*. Translated by H. T. Lowe-Porter. New York: Knopf, 1968.

——. *Lotte in Weimar*. Translated by H. T. Lowe-Porter. London: Secker & Warburg, 1947.

Manuel, Frank Edward. *Shapes of Philosophical History*. Stanford: Stanford University Press, 1965.

Markale, Jean. *Le Roi Arthur*. Paris: Payot, 1976.

Marrou, Henri Irénée. *The Meaning of History*. Translated by Robert J. Olsen. Baltimore: Helicon, 1966.

Marshall, Thomas Humphrey. *Citizenship and Social Class, and Other Essays*. Cambridge: Cambridge University Press, 1950.

Martindale, Don Albert. *The Nature and Types of Sociological Theory*. London: Routledge & Kegan Paul, 1961.

Martineau, Harriet. *Society in America*. New York: Saunders & Otley, 1837.

Marx, Karl. *Capital: A Critique of Political Economy*. Translated from the 3rd German edition by Samuel Moore and Edward Aveling and edited by Frederick Engels and Ernest Untermann. Chicago: Kerr, 1915.

——. *A Contribution to the Critique of Political Economy*. Translated from the second German edition by N. I. Stone. Chicago: Kerr, 1913.

——, and Engels, Friedrich. *Basic Writings on Politics and Philosophy*. Edited by Lewis S. Feuer. Garden City, N.J.: Doubleday, 1959.

Marx, Werner. *Hegel's Phenomenology of Spirit*. Translated by Peter Heath. New York: Harper & Row, 1975.

Massing, Otwin. *Fortschritt und Gegenrevolution*. Stuttgart: Klett, 1966.

Mathiez, Albert. *La Vie chère et le mouvement social sous le terreur*. Paris: Payot, 1927.

Mayer, Theodor. Review of *Aufgang Europas* by F. Heer. *Historische Zeitschrift* 171 (1951):449–72.

Mazauric, Claude. *Sur la Révolution française*. Paris: Editions sociales, 1970.

Mazlish, Bruce. *Psychoanalysis and History*. Englewood Cliffs, N.J.: Prentice-Hall, 1963.

——. *The Riddle of History: The Great Speculators from Vico to Freud*. New York: Harper & Row, 1966.

Mazzarino, Santo. *The End of the Ancient World*. Translated by George Holmes. London: Faber, 1966.

McHugh, Peter et al. *On the Beginning of Social Inquiry*. London: Routledge & Kegan Paul, 1974.

Meinecke, Friedrich. *Historism: The Rise of the New Historical Outlook*. Translated by J. E. Anderson. London: Routledge & Kegan Paul, 1972.

Mink, Louis O. 'The Autonomy of Historical Understanding'. *History and Theory* 5 (1966):24–47.

——. 'Collingwood's Historicism: A Dialectic of Progress'. In *Critical Essays on the Philosophy of R. G. Collingwood*. Edited by Michael Krausz. London: Clarendon Press, 1972.

——. *Mind, History and Dialectic: the Philosophy of R. G. Collingwood*. Bloomington: Indiana University Press, 1969.

——. 'Philosophical Analysis and Historical Understanding'. *Review of Metaphysics* 21 (1968):667-98.

Mitscherlich, Alexander. *Auf dem Wege zur vaterlosen Gesellschaft*. Munich: R. Piper, 1963.

Mohr, Wolfgang. 'Geschichtserlebnis im altgermanischen Heldenliede'. In *Zur germanisch-deutschen Heldensage*. Edited by Karl Hauck. Darmstadt: Wissenschaftliche Buchgesellschaft, 1961.

Momigliano, Arnoldo Dante. 'Fattori orientali della storiografia Ebraica post-esilica e della storiografia Greca'. In his *Terzo contributo alla storia degli studi classici e del mondo antico*. Roma: Edizioni di storia e letteratura, 1966.

——. 'An Interim Report on the Origins of Rome'. *Journal of Roman Studies* 53 (1963):95-121.

——. 'The Place of Herodotus in the History of Historiography'. In his *Studies in Historiography*. London: Weidenfeld & Nicolson, 1966.

——. 'Il razionalismo di Ecateo di Mileto'. In his *Terzo contributo alla storia degli studi classici e del mondo antico*. Roma: Edizioni di storia e letteratura, 1966.

——. *Studies in Historiography*. London: Weidenfeld & Nicolson, 1966.

——. 'Time in Ancient Historiography'. *History and Theory*, Beiheft 6 (1966):1-23.

Mommsen, Wolfgang J. *Die Geschichtswissenschaft jenseits des Historismus*. Düsseldorf: Droste, 1972.

Montagu, Ashley, ed. *Toynbee and History: Critical Essays and Reviews*. Boston: Sargent, 1956.

Morgan, Edmund Sears. *American Slavery, American Freedom*. New York: W. W. Norton, 1975.

Moses, John Anthony. *The Politics of Illusion: The Fischer Controversy in German Historiography*. London: G. Prior, 1975.

Mousnier, Roland. *La Plume, la faucille et le marteau*. Paris: Presses Universitaires de France, 1970.

Munz, Peter. '*The Concept of the Middle Ages as a Sociological Category*'. An Inaugural Address. Wellington: Victoria University of Wellington, 1969.

——. 'Early European History and African Anthropology'. *New Zealand Journal of History* 10 (1976):37-50.

——. *Frederick Barbarossa: A Study in Medieval Politics*. London: Eyre & Spottiswoode, 1969.

——. 'Historical Understanding'. *The Philosophical Quarterly* 3 (1953): 193-210.

——. 'History and Myth'. *The Philosophical Quarterly* 6 (1956): 1-16.

——. 'India: Homo Hierarchicus or Generalised Exchange of Souls?' *Pacific Viewpoint* 11 (1970):188-99.

——. 'Introduction'. In *Italian Humanism*, by Eugenio Garin. Translated by Peter Munz. Oxford: Blackwell, 1965.

——. 'Introduction'. In *Life of Alexander III* by Cardinal Boso. Translated by G. M. Ellis. Oxford: Blackwell, 1973.

——. 'John Cassian'. *Journal of Ecclesiastical History* 11 (1960): 1-22.

——. 'Medieval History in Australasia'. *Historical Studies* 11 (1963):1–17.

——. *The Place of Hooker in the History of Thought.* London: Routledge & Kegan Paul, 1952.

——. 'The Purity of Historical Method: Some Sceptical Reflections on the Current Enthusiasm for the History of Non-European Societies'. *New Zealand Journal of History* 5 (1971):1–17.

——. *Reflections on the Theory of the Revolution in France.* Wellington, N.Z.: Victoria University of Wellington, 1972.

——. Review of *A Sociology of Sociology* by R. W. Friedrichs. *History and Theory* 10 (1971):359–69.

——. 'The Skeleton and the Mollusc'. *New Zealand Journal of History* 1 (1967):107–23.

——. *When the Golden Bough Breaks: Structuralism or Typology?* London: Routledge & Kegan Paul, 1973.

——, and Ellis, G. M., eds. *Boso's Life of Pope Alexander III.* Oxford: Blackwell, 1973.

Murphey, Murray G. *Our Knowledge of the Historical Past.* Indianapolis: Bobbs-Merrill, 1973.

Nadel, George Hans. 'Philosophy of History Before Historicism'. In *The Critical Approach to Science and Philosophy.* Edited by Mario Augusto Bunge. Glencoe: Free Press, 1964.

Nagel, Ernest. 'Determinism in History'. *Philosophy and Phenomenological Research* 20 (1959–60):291–317.

Namier, Lewis Bernstein. *Conflicts: Studies in Contemporary History.* London: Macmillan, 1942.

——. *1848: The Revolution of the Intellectuals.* London: Oxford University Press, 1946.

——. *England in the Age of the American Revolution.* 2nd ed. London: Macmillan, 1961.

——. *Europe in Decay: A Study in Disintegration, 1936–1940.* London: Macmillan, 1950.

——. *In the Margin of History.* London: Macmillan, 1939.

——. *The Structure of Politics at the Accession of George III.* 2nd ed. London: Macmillan, 1957.

——. *Vanished Supremacies: Essays on European History, 1812–1918.* London: Hamilton, 1958.

Naughton, John. 'A Little Global Difficulty'. *Encounter* 244 (1974):72–77.

Needham, Rodney. *Belief, Language and Experience.* Oxford: Blackwell, 1972.

——. *Structure and Sentiment: A Test Case in Social Anthropology.* Chicago: University of Chicago Press, 1962.

Nietzsche, Friedrich. *The Use and Abuse of History.* Translated by Adrian Collins. Indianapolis: The Bobbs-Merrill Company, 1973.

Nisbet, Robert Alexander. 'Conservatism and Sociology'. *American Journal of Sociology* 58 (1952):167–75.

——. 'The French Revolution and the Rise of Sociology in France'. *American Journal of Sociology* 49 (1943):156–64.

——. 'Has Futurology a Future?' *Encounter* 218 (1971): 19–28.

——. *The Social Bond.* New York: Knopf, 1970.

——. *Social Change and History.* London: Oxford University Press, 1969.

North, Christopher Richard. *The Old Testament Interpretation of History.* London: Epworth Press, 1946.

Nowothny, Winifred. *The Language Poets Use.* London: Athlone Press, 1962.

Oesterley, William Oscar Emil. 'Early Hebrew Festival Rituals'. In *Myth and Ritual*. Edited by Samuel Henry Hooke. London: Oxford University Press, 1933.

Pacaut, Marcel. *Alexandre III*. Paris: Vrin, 1956.

Painter, George Duncan. *Marcel Proust: A Biography*. London: Chatto & Windus, 1959-65.

Panofsky, Erwin. *Meaning in the Visual Arts: Papers in and on Art History*. Garden City, N.Y.: Doubleday, 1955.

———. *Studies in Iconology: Humanistic Themes in the Art of the Renaissance*. New York: Harper & Row, 1962.

Parker, Geoffrey. 'Braudel's *Mediterranean:* The Making and Marketing of a Masterpiece'. *History* 59 (1974):238-43.

Parsons, Talcott. *Essays in Sociological Theory*. Rev. ed. Glencoe: Free Press, 1964.

Passmore, John Arthur. 'Explanation in Everyday Life, in Science and in History'. *History and Theory* 2 (1962-63):105-23.

———. 'The Objectivity of History'. *Philosophy* 33 (1958):97-111.

———. Review of *Laws and Explanation in History* by W. H. Dray. *Australian Journal of Politics and History* 4 (1958):269-75.

Patroni, G. 'L'indoeuropeanizzazione dell' Italia'. *Atheneum* 17 (1939):209-38.

Pears, David Francis. *Questions in the Philosophy of Mind*. London: Duckworth, 1975.

Perelman, Ch. *Let catégories en histoire*. Brussels: Editions de l'Université de Bruxelles, 1969.

Pfister, Friedrich. 'Alexander der Grosse: Die Geschichte seines Ruhmes im Lichte seiner Beinamen'. *Historia* 13 (1964):37-79.

Pickering, Frederick Pickering. *Augustinus oder Boethius?* Berlin: E. Schmidt, 1967.

———. *Literature and Art in the Middle Ages*. London: Macmillan, 1970.

Piggott, Stuart. *The Druids*. Harmondsworth: Penguin Books, 1974.

Plumb, John Harold. *The Death of the Past*. London: Macmillan, 1969.

Pollard, Sidney. *The Idea of Progress: History and Society*. London: Watts, 1968.

Pompa, Leon. *Vico: A Study of the New Science*. London: Cambridge University Press, 1975.

Popper, Karl Raimund. *The Logic of Scientific Discovery*. London: Hutchinson, 1959.

———. *Objective Knowledge: An Evolutionary Approach*. Oxford: Clarendon Press, 1972.

———. *The Open Society and Its Enemies*. London: Routledge & Kegan Paul, 1945.

———. *The Poverty of Historicism*. London: Routledge & Kegan Paul, 1957.

———. *Unended Quest*. London, Fontana, 1976.

Porter, Dale H. 'History as Process'. *History and Theory* 14 (1974):297-313.

Powicke, Frederick Maurice. *King Henry III and the Lord Edward*. Oxford: Clarendon Press, 1947.

———. *The Loss of Normandy*. Manchester: Manchester University Press, 1913.

Rad, Gerhard von. 'Der Anfang der Geschichtsschreibung im alten Testament'. *Archiv für Kulturgeschichte* 32 (1944):1-41.

———. *Der heilige Krieg im alten Israel*. Göttingen: Vandenhoeck & Ruprecht, 1958.

Ranke, Leopold von. *Geschichte und Politik.* Edited by Hans Hofmann. Leipzig: A. Kröner, 1940.

Renfrew, Colin. *The Emergence of Civilisation: The Cyclades and the Aegean in the Third Millennium B.C.* London: Methuen, 1972.

———, ed. *The Explanation of Culture Change: Models in Prehistory. Proceedings.* Research Seminar in Archaeology and Related Subjects, University of Sheffield, 1971. London: Duckworth, 1973.

———. 'Models in Prehistory'. *Antiquity* 42 (1968):132–34.

Reuter, Hermann R. *Geschichte Alexanders III und der Kirche seiner Zeit.* 3 vols. Berlin and Leipzig: Müller & Teubner, 1845–64.

Revel, Jean-François. *On Proust.* Translated by Martin Turnell. London: Hamilton, 1972.

Rickert, Heinrich. *Die Grenzen der naturwissenschaftlichen Begriffsbildung.* 5th ed. Tübingen: Mohr, 1929.

———. *Die Probleme der Geschichtsphilosophie.* Heidelberg: C. Winter, 1924.

Ricoeur, Paul. *History and Truth.* Translated and with an introduction by Charles A. Kelbley. Evanston: Northwestern University Press, 1965.

Riesman, David et al. *The Lonely Crowd: A Study of the Changing American Character.* New Haven: Yale University Press, 1950. (Abridged ed. 1961.)

Robin, Regine. *La Société française en 1789: Semur-en-Auxois.* Paris: Plon, 1970.

Rothaker, Erich. *Logik und Systematik der Geisteswissenschaften.* New ed. Darmstadt: Wissenschaftliche Buchgemeinschaft, 1965.

Rowse, Alfred Leslie. *The England of Elizabeth.* London: Macmillan, 1951.

Rudé, George. 'The Origins of the French Revolution'. *Past and Present* 8 (1955):28–40.

Runciman, Steven. *A History of the Crusades.* Cambridge: Cambridge University Press, 1951–54.

———. *The Sicilian Vespers.* Cambridge: Cambridge University Press, 1958.

Rüsen, Jörn. *Begriffene Geschichte: Genesis und Begründung der Geschichtstheorie J. G. Droysens.* Paderborn: Schöningh, 1969.

———, ed. *Historische Objektivität.* Göttingen: Vandenhoeck & Ruprecht, 1975.

Salmon, Pierre. *Histoire et critique.* 2nd ed., Brussels: Editions de l'Université de Bruxelles, 1976.

Sartre, Jean-Paul. *Critique de la raison dialectique.* Paris: Gallimard, 1960.

———. *Les Mains sales.* Paris: Gallimard, 1948.

———. *Nausea.* Translated by Robert Baldick. Harmondsworth: Penguin, 1965.

Schachermeyr, Fritz. *Alexander der Grosse: Ingenium und Macht.* Vienna: A. Pustet, 1949.

Schelsky, Helmut. *Einsamkeit und Freiheit: Idee und Gestalt der Deutschen Universität und ihrer Reformen.* Reinbek bei Hamburg: Rowohlt, 1963.

———. *Ortsbestimmung der deutschen Soziologie.* Cologne: E. Diederich, 1959.

Schieder, Theodor. *Geschichte als Wissenschaft.* Munich and Vienna: Oldenbourg, 1965.

———. 'Unterschiede zwischen historischer und sozialwissenschaftlicher Methode'. In *Festschrift für Hermann Heimpel* 1. Göttingen: Vandenhoek & Ruprecht, 1971.

Schnädelbach, Herbert. *Geschichtsphilosophie nach Hegel: Die Probleme des Historismus.* Freiburg: Alber, 1974.

Schramm, Percy Ernst. *Hitler: The Man and the Military Leader.* Translated, edited, and with an introduction by Donald S. Detwiler. London: Allen Lane, 1972.

Schröder, F. R. 'Mythos und Heldensage'. *Germanisch-Romanische Monats-schrift* 36 (1955):1-29.

Schweitzer, Albert. *The Quest of the Historical Jesus: A Critical Study of Its Progress from Reimarus to Wrede.* Translated by W. Montgomery. London: A. & C. Black, 1910.

Scriven, Michael. 'Truisms as Grounds for Historical Explanations'. In *Theories of History.* Edited by Patrick Gardiner. Glencoe: Free Press, 1959.

Sewell, William Hamilton. 'Marc Bloch and the Logic of Comparative History'. *History and Theory* 6 (1967):208-18.

Shattuck, Roger. *Proust.* London: Fontana, 1974.

Shennan, Joseph Hugh. *The Parlement of Paris.* London: Eyre & Spottiswoode, 1968.

Shoemaker, Sydney. 'Time Without Change'. *Journal of Philosophy* 66 (1969): 363-81.

Shotwell, James Thomson. *The Story of Ancient History.* New York: Columbia University Press, 1961.

Siegel, Martin. 'Henri Berr's *Revue de synthèse*'. *History and Theory* 9 (1970):322-34.

Simon, Ernst. *Ranke und Hegel. Historische Zeitschrift* 15. Munich: Oldenbourg, 1928.

Skagestad, Peter. *Making Sense of History: The Philosophies of Popper and Collingwood.* Oslo: Universitetsforlaget, 1975.

Skinner, Quentin. 'The Limits of Historical Explanation'. *Philosophy* 41 (1966):199-215.

Smith, Richard Edwin. *The Failure of the Roman Republic.* Cambridge: Cambridge University Press, 1955.

Snell, Bruno. *The Discovery of the Mind: The Greek Origins of European Thought.* Translated by T. G. Rosenmeyer. New York: Harper & Row, 1960.

Snow, Charles Percy. *The Masters.* London: Macmillan, 1952.

Snyder, P. L., ed. See: Becker, Carl. *Detachment and the Writing of History.*

Soboul, Albert. *The Parisian Sans-Culottes and the French Revolution, 1793-1794.* Oxford: Clarendon Press, 1964.

——. *Précis d'histoire de la révolution française.* Paris: Editions Sociales, 1962.

Southern, Richard William. 'Aspects of the European Tradition of Historical Writing'. *Transactions of the Royal Historical Society* 20 (1970): 173-96; 21 (1971):159-79; 22 (1972):159-80.

——. *The Shape and Substance of Academic History.* An Inaugural Lecture delivered before Oxford University. Oxford: Clarendon Press, 1961.

——. *Western Society and the Church in the Middle Ages.* Harmondsworth: Penguin, 1970.

Spaemann, Robert. *Der Ursprung der Soziologie aus dem Geist der Restauration: Studien über L. G. A. de Bonald.* Munich: Kösel Verlag, 1959.

Speiser, Ephraim Avigdor. 'Ancient Mesopotamia'. In *The Idea of History in the Ancient Near East.* Edited by Robert Claude Dentan. New Haven: Yale University Press, 1955.

Spengler, Oswald. *Der Untergang des Abendlandes.* Munich: Oskar Beck, 1922-23.

Starr, Chester G. *The Awakening of the Greek Historical Spirit.* New York: Oxford University Press, 1968.

Steel, Anthony Bedford. *Richard II.* Cambridge: Cambridge University Press, 1963.

Steiner, George. *After Babel: Aspects of Language and Translation.* London: Oxford University Press, 1975.

Stern, Joseph Peter. 'Karl Kraus'. *Encounter* 263 (1974):37–48.

———. *On Realism.* London: Routledge & Kegan Paul, 1973.

Strasburger, Hermann. 'Die Wesensbestimmung der Geschichte durch die antike Geschichtsschreibung'. *Sitzungsberichte der wissenschaftlichen Gesellschaft an der Johann Wolfgang Goethe-Universität,* Frankfurt/Main 5. Wiesbaden: Steiner (1966): 9–58.

Stretton, Hugh. *The Political Sciences: General Principles of Selection in Social Science and History.* London: Routledge & Kegan Paul, 1969.

Stroheker, Karl Friedrich. 'Studien zu den historisch-geographischen Grundlagen der Nibelungendichtung'. *Deutsche Vierteljahrsschrift für Literaturwissenschaft und Geistesgeschichte* 32 (1958):216–40.

Stromberg, Roland Nelson. *Arnold J. Toynbee: Historian for an Age in Crisis.* Carbondale: Southern Illinois University Press, 1972.

Suppes, Patrick Colonel. *A Probabilistic Theory of Causality.* Amsterdam: North-Holland, 1970.

Syme, Ronald. *The Roman Revolution.* Oxford: Clarendon Press, 1939.

Tarn, William Woodthorpe. *Alexander the Great.* Cambridge: Cambridge University Press, 1948.

———. 'Alexander the Great and the Unity of Mankind'. In *Alexander the Great: The Main Problems.* Edited by Guy Thompson Griffith. Cambridge: Heffer, 1966.

Tawney, Richard Henry. *Religion and the Rise of Capitalism.* London: John Murray, 1926.

Taylor, Alan John Percivale. *The Origins of the Second World War.* London: Hamilton, 1961.

Taylor, Charles. *Hegel.* Cambridge: Cambridge University Press, 1975.

———. 'The Opening Arguments of the *Phenomenology*'. In *Hegel: A Collection of Critical Essays.* Compiled by Alasdair Chalmers MacIntyre. Garden City, N.Y.: Doubleday, 1972.

Taylor, John. 'Revolutions in the Heavens'. *Encounter* 244 (1974):82–86.

Teggart, Frederick John. *Theory and Process of History.* Berkeley: University of California Press, 1941.

Thirsk, Joan. 'The Family'. *Past and Present* 27 (1964):116–22.

Thomas, Keith Vivian. 'The Relevance of Social Anthropology to the Historical Study of English Witchcraft'. In *Witchcraft Confessions and Accusations.* Edited by Mary Douglas. Association of Social Anthropologists of the Commonwealth Monograph, 9. London: Tavistock, 1970.

———. *Religion and the Decline of Magic.* London: Weidenfeld & Nicolson, 1971.

Thompson, James Westfall. *A History of Historical Writing.* New York: Macmillan, 1943.

Thomson, David. Review of *Introduction to the Study of History* by Langlois and Seignobos (new ed.). *History and Theory* (1967): 236–41.

Thomson, George Derwent. *Aeschylus and Athens.* London: Lawrence & Wishart, 1941.

Tiedemann, Rolf. *Studien zur Philosophie Walter Benjamins.* Frankfurt: Europäische Verlagsanstalt, 1965.

Tocqueville, Alexis Charles de. *De la Démocratie en Amérique.* Edited by André Gain. Paris: Librairie de Médicis, 1951.

Toliver, Harold E. *Animate Illusions; Explorations of Narrative Structure.* Lincoln: University of Nebraska Press, 1974.

Tönnies, Ferdinand. *On Social Ideas and Ideologies.* Edited, translated and annotated by E. G. Jacoby. New York: Harper & Row, 1974.

Toulmin, Stephen, and Goodfield, June. *The Discovery of Time.* Harmondsworth, Penguin Books, 1967.

Toynbee, Arnold Joseph. *A Study of History.* Abridged by D. C. Somervell. London: Oxford University Press, 1946-57.

Treharne, Reginald Francis. *The Glastonbury Legends: Joseph of Arimathea, The Holy Grail and King Arthur.* London: Sphere Books, 1971.

Trevor-Roper, Hugh Redwald. *Archbishop Laud, 1573-1645.* 2nd ed. London: Macmillan, 1940.

———. 'The Past and the Present: History and Sociology'. *Past and Present* 24 (1969):3-17.

———. 'The Toynbee Millennium'. *Encounter* 45 (1957):14-28.

Trilling, Lionel. *Sincerity and Authenticity.* London: Oxford University Press, 1972.

Troeltsch, Ernst. 'Der Historismus und seine Probleme'. In his *Gesammelte Schriften.* Vol. 3. Tübingen: Mohr, 1922.

———. *Der Historismus und seine Überwindung.* Berlin, Charlottenburg: Pan-Verlag R. Heise, 1924.

Tucker, Robert Charles. *Philosophy and Myth in Karl Marx.* 2nd ed. Cambridge: Cambridge University Press, 1972.

Unger, Rudolf. 'The Problem of Historical Objectivity: A Sketch of Its Development to the Time of Hegel'. *History and Theory* 11 (1971): 60-86.

Urban, George R., and Toynbee, Arnold Joseph. *Toynbee on Toynbee: A Conversation Between Arnold J. Toynbee and G. R. Urban.* New York: Oxford University Press, 1974.

Védrine, Hélène. *Les Philosophies de l'histoire.* Paris: Payot, 1975.

Vico, Giovanni Battista. *The New Science of Giambattista Vico.* Rev. translation of the 3rd ed. (1744) by Thomas Goddard Bergin and Max Harold Fisch. Ithaca: Cornell University Press, 1968.

Vidal-Naquet, Pierre. 'Temps des dieux et temps des hommes'. *Révue de l'histoire des réligions* 157 (1960):55-80.

Vinaver, Eugène. *The Rise of Romance.* New York and Oxford: Oxford University Press, 1971.

Vovelle, Michel. *Piété baroque et déchristianisation en Provence au XVIIIe siècle.* Paris: Plon, 1973.

Vries, Jan de. 'Das Motiv des Vater-Sohn-Kampfes im Hildebrandslied'. *Germanisch-Romanische Monatsschrift* 34 (1954):257-78.

———. *Heldenlied und Heldensage.* Bern: Francke, 1961.

Wachler, Johann Friedrich Ludwig. *Geschichte der historischen Forschung und Kunst.* Göttingen: J.F. Röwer, 1812.

Wagner, Fritz. 'Begegnungen von Geschichte und Soziologie bei der Deutung der Gegenwart'. *Historische Zeitschrift* 192 (1961):607-24.

———. *Moderne Geschichtsschreibung.* Berlin: Duncker & Humblot, 1960.

Waismann, Friedrich. *How I See Philosophy.* Edited by R. Harré. London: Macmillan, 1968.

Walbank, Frank William. 'History and Tragedy'. *Historia* 9 (1960):216-34.

Wallace-Hadrill, David Sutherland. *Eusebius of Caesarea.* London: Mowbray, 1960.

Walser, Gerold. 'Zur neueren Forschung über Alexander den Grossen'. *Schweizer Beiträge zur allgemeinen Geschichte* 14 (1956):346–79.

Walsh, William Henry. *An Introduction to the Philosophy of History.* London: Hutchinson, 1951.

Weber, Alfred. *Farewell to European History.* Translated by R. F. C. Hull. London: Kegan Paul, 1947.

Weber, Gottfried. *Das Nibelungenlied.* Stuttgart: J.B. Metzler, 1968.

Weber, Marianne. *Max Weber: Ein Lebensbild.* Tübingen: Mohr, 1926.

Weber, Max. *The Methodology of the Social Sciences.* Translated and edited by Edward A. Shils and Henry A. Finch. Glencoe: Free Press, 1949.

——. *The Protestant Ethic and the Spirit of Capitalism.* Translated by Talcott Parsons. London: Allen & Unwin, 1930.

Wedgwood, Cicely Veronica. *The Thirty Years War.* London: Jonathan Cape, 1938.

——. 'Tragic Wallenstein'. *Encounter* 278, 1976: 65–70.

Wehler, Hans Ulrich. *Geschichte als historische Sozialwissenschaft.* Frankfurt: Suhrkamp, 1973.

Weil, Eric. *Hegel et l'état.* Paris: Vrin, 1950.

Weingartner, R. H. 'The Quarrel about Historical Explanation'. *Journal of Philosophy* 58 (1961):29–45.

Weisinger, Herbert. *Tragedy and the Paradox of the Fortunate Fall.* London: Routledge & Kegan Paul, 1953.

West, Francis James. *Biography as History.* The Annual Lecture delivered to The Australian Academy of the Humanities at its fourth Annual General Meeting at Canberra on 15 May 1973. Sydney: Sydney University Press, 1973.

White, Hayden Victor. 'The Burden of History'. *History and Theory* 5 (1966):111–34.

——. 'Foucault Decoded'. *History and Theory* 12 (1973):23–54.

——. *Metahistory.* Baltimore: Johns Hopkins University Press, 1973.

White, Morton Gabriel. *Foundations of Historical Knowledge.* New York: Harper & Row, 1965.

White, Victor. *God and the Unconscious.* London: Harvill Press, 1952.

Whitehead, Alfred North. *Process and Reality: An Essay in Cosmology.* Cambridge: Cambridge University Press, 1929.

Whitfield, John Humphreys. *Petrarch and the Renaissance.* Oxford: Blackwell, 1943.

Whitrow, Gerald James. *What is Time?* London: Thames & Hudson, 1972.

Whyte, William Hollingsworth. *The Organization Man.* New York: Simon & Schuster, 1956.

Wilcken, Ulrich. *Alexander the Great.* Translated by G. C. Richards, with Introduction and notes by Eugene N. Borza. New York: W. W. Norton, 1967.

Wiles, Peter. See: Dumoulin, Jerome, and Moisi, Dominique, eds. *The Historian Between the Ethnologist and the Futurologist.*

Williams, Eric Eustace. *Capitalism and Slavery.* Chapel Hill: University of North Carolina Press, 1944.

Willmott, Peter. 'A Code for Research?' *Times Literary Supplement* 3449 (1968):341–42.

Winch, Peter. *The Idea of a Social Science, and its Relation to Philosophy.* London: Routledge & Kegan Paul, 1958.

Wind, Edgar. *Das Experiment und die Metaphysik.* Tübingen: Mohr, 1934.

——. 'Some Points of Contact between History and Science'. In *Philosophy and History: Essays Presented to Ernest Cassirer.* Edited by Raymond Klibansky and H. J. Paton. Oxford: Clarendon Press, 1936.

Wisdom, J. O. 'General Explanation in History'. *History and Theory* 15 (1976):257-66.

Wittgenstein, Ludwig. *Philosophical Investigations.* Translated by G. E. M. Anscombe. 2nd ed. Oxford: Blackwell, 1958.

Wolff, Hans Walter. *The Old Testament: A Guide to Its Writings.* Translated by Keith R. Crim. Philadelphia: Fortress Press, 1973.

Wolman, Benjamin B., ed. *The Psychoanalytic Interpretation of History.* New York: Basic Books, 1971.

Woolley, Charles Leonard. *Abraham: Recent Discoveries and Hebrew Origins.* London: Faber, 1936.

——. *The Sumerians.* New York: W. W. Norton, 1965.

Wright, Georg Henrik von. *Causality and Determinism.* Woodridge Lectures, 10. New York: Columbia University Press, 1974.

Wüstenmeyer, Manfred. 'Die *Annales:* Grundsätze und Methoden ihrer neuen Geschichtswissenschaft'. *Vierteljahresschrift für Sozial- und Wirtschafts-geschichte* 54 (1967):1-45.

INDEX